New Light on Alcoholism

This picture presented to Dr. Shoemaker by A.A. co-founder, Bill Wilson

Dear Sam –
With this, goes the affection
of our entire fellowship.
Ever Yours
Bill Wilson

Xmas
Fifty-seven.

A note to the clergy

"This carefully researched book will be valuable for clergy who are interested in the neglected religious roots of Alcoholics Anonymous. Sam Shoemaker, Frank Buchman and the Oxford Group movement are clearly part of the heritage of Alcoholics Anonymous, as this book shows. Ministers, priests and rabbis will find much to interest them here."

The Reverend Dr. Richard L. McCandless
Rector, St. Paul's Church, Akron, Ohio

New Light on Alcoholism

The A.A. Legacy from Sam Shoemaker

Dick B.

Good Book Publishing Company

Corte Madera, California

By the same author

Dr. Bob's Library
Anne Smith's Spiritual Workbook
The Oxford Group & Alcoholics Anonymous
The Akron Genesis of Alcoholics Anonymous
The Books Early AAs Read for Spiritual Growth

Good Book Publishing Company, Box 276, Corte Madera, CA 94976-0276

Printed in the United States of America

Cover Design: Richard Rose, Sun Lithographic Arts

We gratefully acknowledge permission granted by Alcoholics Anonymous World Services, Inc., to quote from Conference Approved publications with source attributions. The publication of this volume does not imply affiliation with nor approval or endorsement from Alcoholics Anonymous World Services, Inc.

Publisher's Cataloging in Publication
(Prepared by Quality Books Inc)

B., Dick.
New light on alcoholism: the A.A. legacy from Sam Shoemaker /Dick B.
p. cm.
Includes bibliographical references and index.
ISBN: 1-881212-06-8.
1. Alcoholics Anonymous--History. 2. Alcoholics Anonymous--Religious aspects. 3. Shoemaker, Samuel M. (Samuel Moor), 1893-1963. 4. Alcoholism--Treatment. 5. Alcoholism--Religious aspects. I. Title.

HV5278.B03 1994 362.29'286
QBI93-22641
Library of Congress Catalog Card Number: 93-77559

"But without faith *it is* impossible to please *him* [God]: for he that cometh to God must believe that he is, and *that* he is a rewarder of them that diligently seek him."

Hebrews 11:6

"So then faith *cometh* by hearing, and hearing by the word of God."

Romans 10:17

Contents

List of Appendices

Foreword by Nickie Shoemaker Haggart

When I was growing up, I often heard my Dad, Sam Shoemaker, say: "God has a plan. You have a part. Find it. Follow it." This book about Dad and A.A. brings home to me again how the part each of us has in God's plan fits so remarkably well with the parts that others have. Especially if we try to "stay tuned" to what God's plan is, and how our part fits in.

Who would have thought that a lonely little boy from a "grand old Maryland family," with charm and lineage galore but very little compassion (his parents didn't speak to each other much of the time), would grow up to be the person whom Jim Newton told me the other evening was "the greatest life-changer I have ever known"? And that Dick B. would emerge from his "cups" with such a deep conviction about the spiritual roots of A.A.? And that he would research those roots with such tenacity and understanding that now he can give this book to the Recovery Community with the hope and prayer that they will never forget their roots, and will "pass them on."

As for me, my part of the plan started long ago when I was about four years old. I was just big enough to answer the front door to our apartment at Calvary House and let my Dad know that there was a "drunker" there who wanted to talk to him. Our household was host to all who came there, in whatever "cups" they came! Dad never turned them away, and often he invited them in for supper. Other times, he asked them to go down the street to the Salvation Army to sleep it off, and he'd see them the next morning.

I vividly remember Bill Wilson coming in and out of our home—he and so many others who have healed, and learned to "pass it on." We cannot "pass it on," though, if we don't know what "it" is. And that's where Dick's book comes in. Without the spiritual connection, our healing is incomplete. Dick wants us to remember what all of it was about, so we won't lose part of the treasure.

You each have a part of the plan. All of us do. This book may help you find your part, or remember it if you have forgotten it. Or support you, if you are already part of the myriad wonderful and struggling souls who are sharing their lives with each other rather than trying to drink or "use" their despair away.

I asked my Dad not too long before he died who were his favorite people to work with. He answered without any hesitation, "The AA's. They are just wonderful. They are so appreciative. And they are such FUN!"

I was, and am, blessed to know so many of you, from Bill W. on to the present day, when I know you in my personal life and in my office as a professional person. Our family is grateful to Dick B. for all his loving labor to tell this story.

God bless you all.

NICKIE SHOEMAKER HAGGART, LCSW

Fort Myers, Florida
October, 1993

Foreword by Julia Harris

My first sight of Sam Shoemaker was as a teenager in the early 1920's, at a conference for school girls at Northfield, Mass. He was a very handsome young man, with blond, curly hair and exuding vitality and a radiant form of Christianity. All the girls sighed over him.

My next contact was in the early 1930's. My young mother, a heartbroken widow, had found an experience of God's love in a hospital bed and soon after joined the Oxford Group. She was so changed, I wanted what she had.

I went to live in Calvary Church's Parish House to help with the Book Room and live in fellowship with other Christians. It was an exciting time with so many of the spiritual greats as well as the hurt and needy who passed through the Parish House doors. Bill Wilson was one of these.

Sam Shoemaker married my husband, Irving Harris, and myself. He was godfather for our son and our children attended the same school. We helped with the outreach of Sam's ministry, and we always counted it a privilege to have known him.

Norman Vincent Peale described him like this: "No man has ever excelled Sam Shoemaker in sheer spiritual depth and persuasive power," and "Sam was perhaps the most gifted genius in intimate person-to-person evangelism in our time."

Sam's faith was contagious and absolute. You knew you could do anything if you let God guide your life. My husband used to say, "Sam was a rare combination of intellect, personality, commitment, guided insight and efficient genius for cutting through irrelevancies. He was one of the giants."

Dick B. has done a monumental job in researching and piecing together the many strains that make up the spiritual fabric of A.A.'s Steps and Traditions. It is good to go back to our roots. It's like using a plumb line to see that we are building a straight wall for the future.

JULIA HARRIS

Granville, Ohio
September 27, 1993

[Mrs. Julia Harris is the widow of one of Shoemaker's closest associates for many years. Her husband, Reverend W. Irving Harris, was Assistant Minister at Shoemaker's Calvary Episcopal Church in New York; was Editor of the parish newsletter, *The Calvary Evangel*; and was, for a time, in charge of the Calvary House office. He authored *The Breeze of the Spirit*. Irving and Julia Harris were close friends of both Sam Shoemaker and Bill Wilson. Wilson credited them both as well-springs of A.A. ideas. Mrs. Harris was in charge of the Oxford Group bookroom at Calvary House—where literature was sent all over America.]

Preface

From the beginning of his research into the Biblical/Christian roots of Alcoholics Anonymous, the author had been perplexed as to the role of Reverend Sam Shoemaker of Calvary Episcopal Church in New York. Bill Wilson said A.A. got most of its ideas from Shoemaker. Dr. Bob Smith said A.A.'s basic ideas came from the study of the Bible. There were many Oxford Group origins of A.A. that did not directly involve Sam Shoemaker. Further, there were some minor "new thought" sources of A.A. ideas, such as Emmet Fox, that could not even be called Christian. What, then, did Bill Wilson mean when he gave such far-reaching credit to Shoemaker as his source of inspiration?

The difficulty was that Wilson never said how he learned the ideas from Shoemaker or what the specific ideas were. By contrast, the author has unearthed ample evidence as to what AAs studied in, and learned from, the Bible; what they were being taught by Dr. Bob, Anne Smith, Henrietta Seiberling, and T. Henry and Clarace Williams; what they were reading from Oxford Group and other Christian literature; and where and when they used these materials.

But the puzzle as to Shoemaker remained. Remained, that is, until some new and exciting evidence was discovered. The first piece came from Bill's home at Stepping Stones, where the author discovered a very early letter from Shoemaker to Wilson. Next, Shoemaker's close friend, Julia Harris, found a memo her husband, Irving, wrote as to where and when Shoemaker and Wilson met and what they discussed. Next, long-time Oxford

Group activists Jim and Ellie Newton told the author of the Oxford Group businessman's team which was led by Shoemaker and to which Wilson and other Oxford Group friends belonged. Then, a good many early members of this team and of the Calvary Church circle began filling in blanks for the author. Finally, Shoemaker's daughters, Sally and Nickie, made available to the author Shoemaker's journals for the period from 1934 through early 1936; and the true picture emerged.

Shoemaker and Wilson *were* in close touch from the earliest days of Bill Wilson's sobriety through the publication of the A.A. Big Book in 1939. Then, with the author's review of all of Shoemaker's relevant books, articles, and addresses, the very close parallels between Shoemaker's writings and language, and that used in A.A.'s Big Book and Twelve Steps, made sense. There remains the question as to just how and where Bill Wilson extracted the Shoemaker language. And the author has not yet found the answer. But this book will, we hope, enable substantial understanding of what Shoemaker wrote, taught, and said that was relevant to A.A. ideas; how the ideas reached A.A.; and how understanding Shoemaker can help the reader understand A.A. and its early success.

Acknowledgements

The number of friends, scholars, historians, collectors, archivists, and AAs who have helped me pull together my six books on the spiritual roots of Alcoholics Anonymous has become quite large. And I will repeat the names and add to them here because all played a large part in this particular work.

Before I begin, however, there are four sets of people who deserve special attention. The first is my son, Ken, who has become more than editor, computer consultant, and patient assistant; he has become a collaborator in the work. He has traveled widely and researched with me, and has met many of those who have helped. The second group is the daughters of Dr. Shoemaker. Sally Shoemaker Robinson began supplying me with material early on. And then her sister, Nickie Shoemaker Haggart, helped me pour through the Shoemaker journals that made the Wilson-Shoemaker relationship come alive. The third is Mrs. W. Irving (Julia) Harris. She has been at this from my first book. She supplied memos, names, addresses, recollections, love, and support incredible for her age. She loved Shoemaker and Wilson, and she has been a love to me. Then there is the fourth group: Jim and Ellie Newton. Stalwart friends and supporters of Dr. Frank N. D. Buchman, Dr. Samuel M. Shoemaker, Calvary Church, and Moral Re-Armament, these two people have helped me in every way possible; including, of course, with their intimate and first-hand recollections of the founding people of A.A.

Then come the survivors of A.A. founders: Sue Smith Windows; Robert and Betty Smith; Dorothy Williams Culver; John

F. Seiberling, Dorothy Seiberling, and Mary Seiberling Huhn; and Nell Wing.

Then the A.A. archivists, authors, and historians: Ray G., Paul L., Gail L., Mel B., Bill P., Charlie B., Mary D., Mitch K., Dennis C., Bruce W., Joe McQ., Charlie P., Earl H., Dr. Ernest Kurtz, Joe S., Ray R., and Frank M.

The following have been of special help on this Shoemaker title: Dr. Paul Wood President of the National Council on Alcoholism and Drug Dependence; The Reverend Dr. Thomas F. Pike, Rector, and his staff at The Parish of Calvary/St. George's in the City of New York; The Reverend Stephen Garmey, Vicar of Calvary Episcopal Church in New York City; The Reverend Dr. Richard L. McCandless, Rector at St. Paul's Episcopal Church in Akron; The Reverend Dr. Norman Vincent Peale at the Peale Center for Christian Living in New York; Sarah F. Mullady consultant at the Center on Addiction and Substance Abuse at Columbia University; and David Sack at the Department of Religion, Princeton University.

From the U.S. and abroad, Oxford Group-M.R.A.-Shoemaker associates have sent me material and suggestions. They include Garth Lean, Michael Hutchinson, Kenneth Belden, George Vondermuhll, Jr., Parks Shipley, Charles Haines, Reverend Harry J. Almond, Reverend Howard Blake, and Reverend T. Willard Hunter.

Research would have been impossible without the cooperation of Stepping Stones Archives, the archives at Dr. Bob's Home, the Founders Day archives, Hartford Seminary, Golden Gate Baptist Seminary, San Francisco Theological Seminary, Graduate Theological Union, Akron University Libraries, Kahului Public Library, Makawao Public Library, Kihei Public Library, Wailuku Public Library, and the Seeley G. Mudd Manuscript Library, Princeton University.

Thanks also to my A.A. sponsor, Henry B., for his support and encouragement, and to my A.A. sponsees and Bible fellowship friends who have patiently endured and encouraged. My daughter-in-law, Cindy, has also been of special help on this book.

Introduction

Would you like to know why, in the 1930's, the early members of Alcoholics Anonymous had a fifty percent (50%) success rate in their work with "medically incurable" alcoholics.[1] Why still another twenty-five percent (25%) sobered up after some relapses?[2] Did you know that the picture is far different today? That one-third of all those being "poured" into A.A. by courts, recovery centers, churches, physicians, therapists, interventions, and other sources are out of the door within their first ninety days of A.A. participation?[3] The foregoing figures come from Alcoholics Anonymous itself. And the author—an active, recovered member of A.A., who has sponsored more than fifty men in their recovery—has studied A.A.'s early history and has seen the

---

[1] A.A.'s basic text, *Alcoholics Anonymous*, 3rd ed. (New York: Alcoholics Anonymous World Services, Inc., 1976), frequently points out that in the 1930's, the medical profession commonly pronounced the "real" alcoholic "incurable"—destined sooner or later to die of acute alcoholism or be institutionalized with wet brain. See pages 7, 11, 27, 30, 307-08. Unless otherwise noted, when we speak of the "basic text" of *Alcoholics Anonymous*, we will be referring only to the first 164 pages of that book. Also, throughout the remainder of our book, we shall refer to *Alcoholics Anonymous* as the "Big Book," the affectionate name bestowed upon it by AAs.

[2] The 50% and 25% statistics are from page xx of the third edition of *Alcoholics Anonymous*. In the words of that text, the figures applied to those alcoholics who "really tried" to recover.

[3] These figures were presented by A.A.'s current archivist at a large A.A. meeting in Marin County, California, in the spring of 1991, which was attended by the author, and at which the author was also a speaker.

present-day success factor firsthand at hundreds and hundreds of meetings he has attended.

Would you like to know the reason for the difference in today's picture—a possible secret to A.A.'s early success?

We don't claim this account of the A.A. legacy from Reverend Sam Shoemaker provides all the answers. There are many factors in early A.A. and in present-day A.A. that can account for the current, plummeting *rate* of success. But we do know there was a vast difference in emphasis in the formative years of A.A.'s development. We do know that much of that emphasis came from the teachings of Reverend Samuel Moor Shoemaker, Jr., rector of Calvary Episcopal Church in New York City in the 1930's[4]. And this is the story of Shoemaker's contribution to Alcoholics Anonymous.

We believe this account can shed new light on the dark world of alcoholism. A world involving seemingly hopeless conditions of mind and body from which recovery is possible, and from which the author, and many men he has sponsored, *have recovered*. This dark world also includes people addicted to substances other than alcohol. Lest some recoil at our use of the word "addiction" when speaking of the roots of A.A., we point out from personal observation that the vast majority of people entering A.A. today are hardly just alcoholics. Their stories are replete with involvement in marijuana, cocaine, LSD, pills, prescription drugs, and a host of other mind- or mood-altering substances. Sam Shoemaker had a large share in the recovery fabric that was fashioned by A.A. co-founders, Bill W. and Dr. Bob, between 1935 and 1939, and which later was adopted and adapted by other substance abuse programs.

And we begin with some remarks by A.A. co-founder, Bill W.

Alcoholics Anonymous co-founder, Bill Wilson, said many times and in many ways that almost all of A.A.'s spiritual principles came from the teachings of Sam Shoemaker. For example, in his

---

[4] Calvary Episcopal Church is located at the corner of Park Avenue South and 21st Street, New York City.

history of A.A., Bill recounted, "There were men like clergyman Sam Shoemaker, whose early teachings did so much to inspire Dr. Bob [A.A.'s other co-founder] and me."[5] Later, in the same book, he added, "It was from him that Dr. Bob and I in the beginning had absorbed most of the principles that were afterward embodied in the Twelve Steps of Alcoholics Anonymous, steps that express the heart of A.A.'s way of life."[6]

Bill also wrote:

> Every river has a wellspring at its source. AA is like that too. In the beginning, there was a spring which poured out of a clergyman, Dr. Samuel Shoemaker. 'Way back in 1934 he began to teach us the principles and attitudes that afterward came to full flower in AA's Twelve Steps for recovery.[7]

In 1963, he wrote Shoemaker:

> The Twelve Steps of A.A. simply represented an attempt to state in more detail, breadth, and depth, what we had been taught—primarily by you. Without this, there could have been nothing—nothing at all. . . . Though I wish the "co-founder" tag had never been hitched to any of us, I have no hesitancy in adding your name to the list![8]

In 1964, Bill wrote "In Memory of Dr. Sam," stating:

> Our ideas of self-examination, acknowledgement of character defects, restitution for harm done and working with others came straight from Sam. Therefore he gave to us the concrete knowledge

---

[5] *Alcoholics Anonymous Comes of Age: A Brief History of A.A.* (New York: Alcoholics Anonymous World Services, 1957), p. 2.

[6] *A.A. Comes of Age*, pp. 38-39. See also pp. 253, 261.

[7] *The Language of the Heart: Bill W.'s Grapevine Writings* (New York: The AA Grapevine, Inc., 1988), p. 177.

[8] From a letter from William G. Wilson to S. M. Shoemaker, dated April 23, 1963, a copy of which was supplied to the author by Shoemaker's daughter, Sally Shoemaker Robinson.

> of what we could do about our illness; he passed to us the spiritual keys by which so many of us have since been liberated.[9]

And as our book proceeds, the reader will see other, even more comprehensive statements.[10]

Yet with all these laudatory remarks and with Bill's having dubbed Shoemaker a "co-founder" of A.A., there is nothing about Shoemaker in A.A.'s basic text, *Alcoholics Anonymous*.[11] The absence of any reference to Shoemaker in the Big Book seems even more strange when one notes that others, whom Bill also called co-founders, are mentioned in it by name.[12] This, despite the fact that Bill always credited Shoemaker with a far greater contribution to A.A. than that he ascribed to these other co-founders.

Why the omission of any reference to Shoemaker?

Bill described in detail how the development of the A.A. recovery path began with Rowland Hazard's visit to Dr. Carl Jung in Switzerland. He continued with a description of Hazard's introduction of Bill's "sponsor," Ebby Thatcher, to the Oxford

---

[9] From a copy of an A.A. *Grapevine* article, January, 1964 issue, supplied to the author by Sally Shoemaker Robinson.

[10] One of the most touching and pervasive was that related to the author by Shoemaker's younger daughter, "Nickie" Haggart, in a phone conversation from her home in Florida on August 4, 1993. Nickie Haggart said she well remembered Bill Wilson's conversation with her in the driveway of Shoemaker's Burnside home at the time of her father's funeral. Bill said to Nickie: "Don't let anyone ever tell you that I founded A.A. If it wasn't for Sam Shoemaker, A.A. would have never been born."

[11] See the Big Book's basic text.

[12] Thus, the name of William D. Silkworth, M.D., appears in the Big Book in Silkworth's "Doctor's Opinion," just preceding the basic text. In *A.A. Comes of Age*, at page 13, Bill called Silkworth "very much a founder of A.A." On page 28 of the Big Book, Bill named and wrote about Professor William James, the well-known Harvard psychologist. Bill specifically mentioned the title of James's book, *The Varieties of Religious Experience*. And he later said James had been "a founder of Alcoholics Anonymous." See *Pass It On* (New York: Alcoholics Anonymous World Services, Inc., 1984), p. 28.

Group (in which Shoemaker was a major leader).[13] Then he gave details concerning Ebby's carrying of the Oxford Group message to him (Bill). Finally, he chronicled very specifically his successful meetings in 1935 with A.A.'s other acknowledged co-founder, Dr. Bob. Bill heaped praises on Shoemaker, but he never gave any details at all concerning his relationship with Shoemaker from the time of Bill's conversion at Shoemaker's Calvary Mission in 1934 to the date the Big Book was published in the spring of 1939.

Why the lack of details as to their interactions?

At A.A.'s Twentieth Anniversary Convention in St. Louis in 1955, Bill finally publicly recognized Shoemaker's substantial contribution to A.A. And yet, to this day, the author is unaware of a single, specific description of the Shoemaker words, phrases, and Christian ideas that found their way into A.A.—including the means by which they were transmitted to Bill. In fact, no such material can be found even in four recent, thorough examinations of A.A.'s history and roots.[14]

Again, why?

One explanation might be the persisting effort by some AAs, including Bill Wilson, to distance A.A. from the Oxford Group

---

[13] In *The Language of the Heart*, one of Bill's accounts appears at page 368. Bill summarizes how Rowland Hazard, Shep Cornell, and Cebra Graves had achieved their sobriety in the Oxford Groups; had Ebby paroled into their custody; and then "brought Ebby to New York where he fell under the benign influence of AA's great friend-to-be, Dr. Sam Shoemaker, the rector of Calvary Episcopal Church." For other specifics concerning the Jung-Hazard-Oxford Group-Ebby Thatcher story, see *The Language of the Heart*, pp. 276-281, 195-197; *A.A. Comes of Age*, pp. 58-59, 262; *Pass It On*, pp. 111-116; and the Big Book, pp. 8-15, 26-28. And note the absence of any specifics as to Shoemaker.

[14] See Mel B., *New Wine: The Spiritual Roots of the Twelve Step Miracle* (Minnesota: Hazelden, 1991); Ernest Kurtz, *Not-God: A History of Alcoholics Anonymous*, Expanded ed. (Minnesota: Hazelden, 1991); Charles Taylor Knippel, *Samuel M. Shoemaker's Theological Influence on William G. Wilson's Twelve Step Spiritual Program of Recovery*. Ph. D. dissertation, St. Louis University, 1987; and Robert Thomsen, *Bill W.* (New York: Harper & Row, 1975).

and from its founder, Dr. Frank N. D. Buchman.[15] And Shoemaker was, for many years, a significant figure in the Oxford Group and a principal American associate of Buchman's.[16] Another explanation for the Shoemaker blackout might be Shoemaker's important stature in the world of religion and Bill's fear that an explicit link with Shoemaker—the distinguished Episcopal clergyman who was cited as one of the ten greatest preachers in America and also as "Pittsburgh's Man of the Year in Religion"—would jeopardize a view widely held in later A.A. that A.A.'s program is "spiritual" and not "religious." But neither of these possibilities justifies the historical vacuum the author has found. And certainly not at this late date in history when Wilson himself long ago virtually beatified Shoemaker and then even expressed regret that he had never thanked Buchman during Buchman's lifetime for what A.A. owed to him.[17]

A thorough examination of Shoemaker's books and pamphlets, articles written for A.A., and speeches made to A.A., shows that Shoemaker ideas—whether they were his own or were simply a restatement of Oxford Group ideas—permeate the first 164 pages of the Big Book. As a result, there is great value to members of A.A., to substance abuse professionals, and to clergy, and to all others seeking to understand A.A., in knowing the specifics about Shoemaker's contributions to A.A. ideas. By specifics, we do not

[15] For a detailed discussion of Wilson's position and the conscious effort to avoid mention of the Oxford Group and its successor, Moral Re-Armament, see *Pass It On*, pp. 171-174; Mel B., *New Wine*, pp. 28-31.

[16] See Dick B., *The Oxford Group & Alcoholics Anonymous* (Seattle: Glen Abbey Books, 1992), pp. 76-80.

[17] See the discussion in *Pass It On* at pages 382-383 and 386-387. *Pass It On* tells of Bill Wilson's correspondence with Dr. Carl Jung in which he said Jung's conversation with Rowland Hazard was the first link in the chain of events that led to the founding of Alcoholics Anonymous. This official A.A. history then states: "The fact that Bill never made a similar personal acknowledgement of A.A.'s debt to Frank Buchman, who also died in 1961, remains a sore point with some, a matter of bewilderment to some others. Bill himself seriously regretted the omission. A month after Buchman's death, Bill wrote to a friend: 'Now that Frank Buchman is gone and I realize more than ever what we owe him, I wish I had sought him out in recent years to tell him of our appreciation.'"

mean the general principles of "self-examination, confession of character defects, restitution, and working with others" which Bill belatedly mentioned.[18] We mean the seemingly endless array of Shoemaker words, phrases, concepts, and theological ideas which can be traced to A.A. from Shoemaker.[19] To understand A.A. ideas, as articulated in Bill Wilson's Big Book and Twelve Steps, some may need a dictionary—as AAs are often told by their sponsors. But the author believes there is also an indispensable requirement that the student of A.A. must know about Shoemaker's books, concepts, phrases, and words if that student is to know the intended meaning of A.A.'s recovery ideas. After all, Bill Wilson, A.A.'s co-founder, said they came from Shoemaker!

Bill was fond of saying A.A.'s tools for recovery were borrowed mainly from medicine and religion.[20] At A.A.'s Twentieth Anniversary, he remarked: "A.A. can be likened to a temple supported by three pillars: one is religion, another is medicine, and the third is our own experience as people who have suffered from alcoholism."[21] He also said, "Most of A.A.'s spiritual principles had come to us through clergymen."[22]

In earlier years, A.A. seemed to want to hear specifics about its medical and religious sources. On the medical side, A.A.'s medical "mentor," Dr. William D. Silkworth, was invited to submit the "Doctor's Opinion" which was lodged at the beginning of the Big Book.[23] A report by Dr. Silkworth was also part of the

---

[18] See *A.A. Comes of Age*, pp. 39-40; see also the Big Book, p. xvi.

[19] Note how A.A.'s *Pass It On*—without being specific—speaks of the Oxford Group and its principles "from which Bill borrowed freely" (p. 169) and states that the basic material for the Big Book's "How It Works" chapter was "heavy with Oxford Group principles" (pp. 196-197).

[20] See, for example, *A.A. Comes of Age*, pp. 51, 235; and Nell Wing, *Grateful To Have Been There: My 42 years with Bill and Lois, and the Evolution of Alcoholics Anonymous* (Illinois: Parkside Publishing Corporation, 1992), p. 25.

[21] *A.A. Comes of Age*, p. 236.

[22] *A.A. Comes of Age*, p. 44.

[23] Big Book, pp. xxiii-xxx.

appendices in A.A.'s first "Conference Approved" history book.[24] A.A.'s Big Book included in one appendix the views of Dr. Foster Kennedy, neurologist; Dr. Harry M. Tiebout, psychiatrist; Dr. G. Kirby Collier, psychiatrist; Dr. W. W. Bauer for the American Medical Association; and Dr. John F. Stouffer, another psychiatrist.[25] The views of Doctors Tiebout and Kennedy were also incorporated in *Alcoholics Anonymous Comes of Age*.[26] On the religious side, a Big Book appendix included the views of Edward J. Dowling, S.J., who became Bill Wilson's "spiritual sponsor."[27] Another Big Book appendix presented the thoughts of Harry Emerson Fosdick, a famous Protestant pastor.[28] Later, several quotations from Dr. Fosdick's writings were included in *Alcoholics Anonymous Comes of Age*.[29] Among other things, Fosdick wrote, "these testimonies [in another A.A. publication, the *AA Grapevine*] bear witness to religion's reality, for Alcoholics Anonymous is deeply religious."[30]

Yet it was not until A.A.'s Twentieth Anniversary Convention in St. Louis that AAs heard from Shoemaker in any significant way when he and Father Ed Dowling were invited to speak.[31] Shoemaker did contribute a few articles to the *AA Grapevine* in later years; and he delivered a few speeches to A.A., which we shall review at another point in our book. In these articles and speeches, Shoemaker shared his ideas with his A.A. friends, but only in a very limited way. And to date, there has been no A.A. history which tells the Shoemaker-A.A. story: the facts about Shoemaker's A.A. contributions and the details as to how his

---

[24] *A.A. Comes of Age*, pp. 302-308.

[25] Big Book, pp. 571-572.

[26] *A.A. Comes of Age*, pp. 309-321.

[27] Big Book, p. 574; and see Nell Wing, *Grateful To Have Been There*, p. 65, for the statement that Father Dowling was Bill's "spiritual sponsor."

[28] Big Book, p. 574.

[29] *A.A. Comes of Age*, pp. 322-324.

[30] *A.A. Comes of Age*, p. 314.

[31] *A.A. Comes of Age*, pp. 253-271.

(Oxford Group and other) ideas found their way into A.A. Sadly, perhaps, A.A. itself has just tabled its "history book project" for two more years.[32] And the author was informed on May 20, 1993, by a member of A.A.'s General Service Staff, that even this project involves only "a history of A.A. from 1955 to the present."[33]

Learning the Details about the Shoemaker Teachings One Finds in A.A.

We believe we have made two major points about Shoemaker and A.A.

First, if Bill's comprehensive statements that A.A.'s ideas came from Shoemaker are true, then there simply must be a large body of material about A.A.'s early history and spiritual roots that needs to be studied. Bill Wilson attributed almost every significant A.A. spiritual idea to the teachings of Sam Shoemaker. And Bill was finally prompted to say:

> Where did the early AAs find the material for the remaining ten Steps? Where did we learn about moral inventory, amends for harm done, turning wills and lives over to God? Where did we learn about meditation and prayer *and all the rest of it*? The spiritual substance of our remaining ten Steps came straight from Dr. Bob's and my own earlier association with the Oxford Groups, as they were then led in America by that Episcopal rector, Dr. Samuel Shoemaker [emphasis ours].[34]

---

[32] See *AA Grapevine*, August 1993, p. 44.

[33] Letter to the author from the General Service office of Alcoholics Anonymous, May 20, 1993, from John G.

[34] *The Language of the Heart*, p. 198.

Second, if Bill's statement is true, wouldn't one expect there to be a record somewhere of the when, where, what, why, and how of the process of Bill and Dr. Bob's receiving the material from Shoemaker? This author had expected to find such details when he approached A.A. Archives in New York for information about Shoemaker; but there were few details in evidence. Neither did he find any information on Bill and Dr. Bob's early interactions with Shoemaker in A.A. "Conference Approved" literature, or in the writings and discussions of other A.A. "founders," including Bill's wife, Lois; Dr. Bob's wife, Anne; Henrietta Seiberling; or T. Henry and Clarace Williams.[35] And in none of his few public addresses did A.A. co-founder, Dr. Bob, comment on Shoemaker's important A.A. role.[36]

Our major reason for writing this book, then, is to discover precisely what principles and ideas Bill and Dr. Bob did learn from Shoemaker.[37]

---

[35] See *Lois Remembers: Memoirs of the co-founder of Al-Anon and wife of the co-founder of Alcoholics Anonymous* (New York: Al-Anon Family Group Headquarters, Inc., 1987); Dick B., *Anne Smith's Spiritual Workbook* (Seattle: Glen Abbey Books, 1993); and Dick B., *The Akron Genesis of Alcoholics Anonymous* (Seattle: Glen Abbey Books, 1993), pp. 65-105.

[36] See, for example, the last major address of Dr. Bob to Alcoholics Anonymous in 1948, transcribed in toto in *The Co-Founders of Alcoholics Anonymous: Biographical Sketches. Their Last Major Talks* (New York: Alcoholics Anonymous World Services, 1972, 1975).

[37] In the light of Dr. Bob's total emphasis on the Bible as A.A.'s source and the fact that he made no mention of Shoemaker, the author was intrigued by the remarks made to him in separate telephone conversations with Dr. Bob's children on October 17, 1993. Dr. Bob's daughter, Sue Smith Windows, and son, Bob Smith, both said they had no recollection that Dr. Bob knew Shoemaker. Sue Windows said she was totally unfamiliar with Shoemaker's books. Bob Smith said Dr. Bob often said he was "allergic to sky pilots" (Dr. Bob's term for ministers). "Smitty" added his father seemed interested in the "message," rather than the "messenger." Facts which tend to explain Dr. Bob's focus on the Bible and spiritual literature.

Solving the Puzzle as to How Shoemaker Ideas Reached A.A.

A second reason for this book recently appeared on the horizon. In our book, *The Oxford Group & Alcoholics Anonymous*, we discussed a problem we called "The Shoemaker Puzzle."[38] We used the word "puzzle" because many evidentiary pieces were missing from the picture Bill painted of Shoemaker's A.A. role. On the one hand, Bill said Shoemaker taught him (Bill) most of the religious ideas he utilized. On the other hand, there seemed to be much evidence that such could not have been the case. For example, Bill did not belong to Shoemaker's Calvary Church or to any church.[39] Shoemaker was not personally involved in many of the Oxford Group meetings Bill and Lois attended between December, 1934, and August, 1937, the time during which they "belonged" to the Oxford Group.[40] Further, within a year of his initial involvement with the Oxford Group, Bill was receiving a "slightly chilly" reception because he was working primarily with alcoholics and holding special meetings away from church influence.[41] Bill's wife, Lois, remarked: "[The] Oxford Group kind of kicked us out."[42] And Shoemaker himself later wrote Bill that, in the early years, the Calvary Church people had felt Bill had been off on his own spur, had been out of the mainstream of the Oxford Group work, and had received little encouragement from the people of Shoemaker's church.[43] Finally, Dr. Charles Taylor Knippel, a painstaking researcher, concluded—after an exhaustive search—that there had been little personal contact between Bill and Shoemaker in the critical years between 1934 and

---

[38] Dick B., *The Oxford Group & Alcoholics Anonymous*, pp. 92-109.

[39] Nell Wing, *Grateful To Have Been There*, p. 48.

[40] *Lois Remembers*, pp. 93-94.

[41] *Lois Remembers*, p. 103; and *Pass It On*, p. 169.

[42] *Pass It On*, p. 174.

[43] Nell Wing, *Grateful To Have Been There*, pp. 68-69.

1939 (the latter being the year the Big Book was published), and that there was no evidence—either in the Archives of Alcoholics Anonymous or of the Episcopal Church—of correspondence between the two prior to 1943.[44]

At one point, therefore, we concluded that Bill may have grossly overstated his relationship with Shoemaker in those early A.A. years; also that he may have misstated the facts about what Shoemaker taught him. But, as the author continued his research, new information surfaced which pointed ever more clearly to Shoemaker's influence on Bill. There is today a good deal of evidence of Shoemaker's personal relationship with Bill in A.A.'s early days. And that evidence is corroborated by the striking presence of so many Shoemaker words and ideas in the A.A. literature Bill wrote. What, then, were the facts about Bill's conversations, correspondence, studies, and meetings, with Shoemaker in the formative years? The quest for that answer goes on, but the present book seemed an important place to supply some of the puzzle's missing pieces.

Using Shoemaker's Ideas as Tools for Spiritual Growth

A third reason for this book relates to Bill Wilson's implied invitation to AAs to search beyond A.A. for spiritual growth and truth. And Dr. Bob spent a lifetime doing just that. Many times, Bill spoke of A.A. as a "spiritual kindergarten." For example, in *As Bill Sees It*, he wrote:

> We are only operating a spiritual kindergarten in which people are enabled to get over drinking and find the grace to go on living to

---

[44] See Knippel, *Samuel M. Shoemaker's Theological Influence on William G. Wilson's Twelve Step Spiritual Program of Recovery*, pp. 64 and 98.

> better effect. Each man's theology has to be his own quest, his own affair.[45]

In *DR. BOB and the Good Oldtimers*, Bill's remarks about Dr. Bob's continued spiritual quest and growth include the following:

> He [Dr. Bob] prayed, not only for his own understanding, but for different groups of people who requested him to pray for them. . . . I was always glad to think I was included in those prayers. . . . And I sort of depended on him to get me into heaven. Bob was far ahead of me in that sort of activity. I was always rushing around talking and organizing and "teaching kindergarten." I never grew up myself.[46]

A.A. historian and scholar, Dr. Ernest Kurtz, confirmed the frequency with which Bill characterized A.A. as a kindergarten of the spirit. Kurtz wrote:

> Bill made the point consistently, in many private letters as well as in his published writings, that even as "spiritual," A.A. was but a "kindergarten of the spirit."[47]

Kurtz specifically documented a number of Bill's "spiritual kindergarten" statements.[48]

Furthermore, in a tribute Bill wrote concerning A.A.'s debt to the clergy, Bill applauded the contributions of Reverend Samuel Shoemaker; of A.A. Trustee Willard S. Richardson (a clergyman);

---

[45] *As Bill Sees It: The A.A. Way of Life...selected writings of A.A.'s Co-Founder* (New York, Alcoholics Anonymous World Services, Inc., 1967), p. 95.

[46] *DR. BOB And The Good Oldtimers* (New York: Alcoholics Anonymous World Services, Inc., 1980), p. 315.

[47] Ernest Kurtz, *Shame and Guilt. Characteristics of the Dependency Cycle* (Minnesota: Hazelden, 1981), p. 12.

[48] See Kurtz, *Shame and Guilt*, at page 54, where he says: "Letters in which Bill Wilson used this phrase [kindergarten of the spirit] or 'spiritual kindergarten' include to Caryl Chessman, 3 May 1954; to Dr. Tom P., 4 April, 1955; to Walter B., 1 July 1958; to Father K., 18 July 1958; to Betty L., 8 December, 1967."

of the famous preacher, Dr. Harry Emerson Fosdick; and of "hundreds, and probably . . . thousands" of other men of the cloth. And then he added something AAs could well keep in mind today. Bill said:

> Some AAs say, "I don't need religion, because AA is my religion." As a matter of fact, I used to take this tack myself. After enjoying this simple and comfortable view for some years I finally awoke to the probability that there might be sources of spiritual teaching, wisdom, and assurance outside of AA. I recalled that preacher Sam [Shoemaker] probably had a lot to do with the vital spiritual experience that was my first gift of faith. He had also taught me principles by which I could survive and carry on. AA had provided me with the spiritual home and climate wherein I was welcome and could do useful work. This was very fine, all to the good. Yet I finally discovered that I needed more than this. Quite rightly, AA didn't try to answer all my questions, however important they seemed to me. Like any other adolescent, I had begun to ask myself: "Who am I?" "Where did I come from?" "What is my purpose here?" "What is the real meaning of life?" "When the undertaker gets through with me, am I still alive, or not?" "Where, if any place, do I go from here?" Neither science nor philosophy seemed able to supply me convincing answers. . . . Though still rather gun-shy about clergymen and their theology I finally went back to them—the place where AA came from. If they had been able to teach me the principles on which I could recover, then perhaps they might now be able to tell me more about growth in understanding, and in belief.[49]

This was humble language from Bill. It further documented his view that A.A. *was* just a kindergarten, in terms of spiritual teaching and development; that A.A. had learned much from clergymen such as Shoemaker; and that individual AAs could attain significant spiritual growth by returning for answers to their spiritual roots—"the place where AA came from." And Bill

---

[49] *The Language of the Heart*, pp. 178-179.

included in the Big Book a similar, strong suggestion: "Be quick to see where religious people are right. Make use of what they offer."[50] At the Twentieth Anniversary Convention, he added:

> Let us constantly remind ourselves that the experts in religion are the clergymen; that the practice of medicine is for physicians; and that we, the recovered alcoholics, are their assistants.[51]

Such remarks by Bill invited a book which would tell people what A.A.'s "religious expert," Sam Shoemaker, was teaching Bill and other early AAs, and which would enable AAs to move out of kindergarten and on to spiritual growth—commencing with the foundation Shoemaker laid.

Reconciling Dr. Bob's Bible Remarks with Bill's Shoemaker Comments

There are other reasons for this book. A fourth involves an important remark by Dr. Bob. He said quite plainly that the early AAs got their basic ideas from their study of the Bible.[52] However, as we saw earlier, Bill said A.A.'s basic ideas came from the Oxford Group and Shoemaker. The contrast between these two statements assumes even more significance when one considers that Dr. Bob probably had no significant personal contact with Sam Shoemaker. Did these statements present a conflict in the evidence as to the origin of A.A. ideas? Or, was there a conflict

[50] Big Book, p. 87.

[51] *A.A. Comes of Age*, p. 232.

[52] See *DR. BOB and the Good Oldtimers*, pp. 96-97. Dr. Bob's remarks came from his last major talk at Detroit, Michigan, in December, 1948. He said, among other things, "I didn't write the Twelve Steps. I had nothing to do with the writing of them. . . . We already had the basic ideas, though not in terse and tangible form. We got them, as I said, as a result of our study of the Good Book." *Co-Founders*, p. 14.

in the views of A.A.'s two co-founders? We felt there should be a book which examined what Dr. Bob might have learned from the Bible *via* Shoemaker, and which would, as well, show what Shoemaker might have taught Bill Wilson *from* the Bible.

Soaking up the Beauty of Shoemaker's Writing

Another major reason for looking at Shoemaker and A.A. simply relates to the force of Shoemaker's writings. As the author examined Shoemaker's books, he was struck by their depth, importance, and beauty. Bill Wilson seems to have been similarly impressed, if not by the writings themselves, then at least by what he learned from exposure to their contents. So too Dr. Bob, Anne Smith, and Henrietta Seiberling; for all of them read the Shoemaker books of the 1920's and 1930's.[53] The author personally found several Shoemaker books in the possession of Dr. Bob's family; and he found them highly recommended in the spiritual workbook of Dr. Bob's wife, Anne.[54] Thus, if these early "founders of A.A." felt Shoemaker was important, and if the works themselves were clearly relevant, there was ample justification for a book that would illuminate AAs and others interested in Twelve Step programs as to the nature and value of Shoemaker's spiritual writings.

---

[53] Dick B., *The Books Early AAs Read For Spiritual Growth* (Seattle: Glen Abbey Books, 1993), pp. 10-11, 16-17, 19, 20, 22, 24-25; and Dick B., *The Akron Genesis of Alcoholics Anonymous*, pp. 84-90, 110-112, 128-133, 335-336, 343-348.

[54] See Dick B., *Anne Smith's Spiritual Workbook*, pp. 12-17.

Helping to Bring into Focus A.A.'s Real Relationship with Religion

There is a sixth reason for our study. In his very first book, *Realizing Religion*, Shoemaker said that the modern mind suffers from a great deal of spiritual misery. He said that everyone has his "own religion," and nearly everyone made it himself, or thinks he did.[55] It was Shoemaker's contention that only a conversion experience could help, through enabling people to have a vital religious experience which would fulfil their need to find God. And we believe our reader will not get far into either the Shoemaker writings or those in early A.A. without seeing that finding God through such a religious experience was paramount in Big Book thinking.[56] The answer did not lie in self-made religion, for that was the very type Sam Shoemaker said was the cause of spiritual misery. It is common for many AAs today to shun reference to "religion" in favor of reference to "spirituality." This seems to have become, in the minds of some, a reason for ignoring literally hundreds of religious writings that were read by early AAs.[57] The shelving of religious origins and language was not, however, the emphasis in the early days. As Frank Amos (who became one of A.A.'s first trustees) stated, when he was reporting to John D. Rockefeller on the nature and successes of early A.A.:

> It is important, but not vital, that he [the alcoholic involved in AA] meet frequently with other reformed alcoholics and form both a

---

[55] Samuel M. Shoemaker, *Realizing Religion* (New York: Association Press, 1923), pp. 2-4.

[56] See Big Book, p. 59: "Without help it is too much for us. But there is One who has all power—that One is God. May you find Him now!" And see Bill's statement to Dr. Carl Jung that Jung's prescription for Rowland Hazard of a spiritual or religious experience—in short, a genuine conversion, had proved to be the foundation of such success as Alcoholics Anonymous had since achieved. *Pass It On*, pp. 382-383.

[57] See Dick B., *The Books Early AAs Read For Spiritual Growth*.

> social and a religious comradeship. . . . Important, but not vital, that he attend some religious service at least once weekly.[58]

In its Foreword to the Second Edition of the Big Book, A.A. stated:

> Alcoholics Anonymous is not a religious organization. . . . though we cooperate widely with men of medicine as well as with men of religion (p. xx).

In its current edition, the Third Edition, the Big Book states:

> We think it no concern of ours what religious bodies our members identify themselves with as individuals. This should be an entirely personal affair which each one decides for himself in the light of past associations, or his present choice. Not all of us join religious bodies, but *most of us favor such membership* (p. 28) [emphasis ours].

The author himself would not have lasted long past his initial, shaky, confused withdrawal period had he felt he was being asked in A.A. to subscribe to the doctrines of some particular sect, denomination, or religion. But to study any textbook—and the Big Book specifically calls itself a basic text—one should understand the intended meaning of the words used by the author. Bill Wilson was borrowing religious ideas from a religious leader when he took words, phrases, and ideas from Shoemaker. Therefore, a study of Shoemaker's religious ideas will help insure that a Big Book reader is not blinded to an intended meaning because of some nameless fear that he might possibly be accepting some particular religious view not of his own choosing. The author has never been a communicant in Reverend Shoemaker's denomination—the Protestant Episcopal Church. But that fact has not deterred him from looking at Episcopalian views, or from

---

[58] *DR. BOB and the Good Oldtimers*, p. 131.

attempting to understand them in order to understand Shoemaker, or from appreciating the beauty in them. A.A. borrowed much from Shoemaker; and every student of A.A. ought to know just what A.A. borrowed, whether or not that student agrees with the ideas borrowed.

Bill stated convincingly that A.A. borrowed its main ideas from religion. He made a strong case for linking A.A.'s religious origins largely to Shoemaker's teachings. And Shoemaker added the ingredient that self-made religion results in self-inflicted spiritual misery. We believe that just as the Big Book has become the standard of truth in A.A. for a program which insures recovery from alcoholism; so A.A.'s roots in religion—specifically, in the Bible, Christianity, and the Oxford Group-Shoemaker teachings—should become the standard for truth for knowing how and why early AAs achieved recovery by the grace of God. That is A.A.'s real relationship with religion; and Shoemaker was a big part of it.

Feeling Comfortable with God and One's Religious Faith in Today's A.A.

There is a final reason for this book. A reason personal to the author. One which has grown out of his experience in sponsoring more than fifty men in their recovery program, in helping them study the Big Book, and in coaching them through the Twelve Steps of A.A.

The author is a recovered alcoholic and a member of the Fellowship of Alcoholics Anonymous. He is also a Christian and a student of the Bible, however much or little he may have practiced the principles of Christianity and the Bible. And there are a great many Christians who belong to the A.A. fellowship or who might very much benefit from what A.A. has to offer. The author was certainly one of these. But, in his early days of sobriety, he encountered formidable barriers to his pursuit of Bible study and Christian worship. And he was not alone. The cause of the barriers, we believe, was the lack of accurate and positive information about the spiritual roots of A.A. as they came from the Bible, Christianity, the Oxford Group, and Sam Shoemaker. Also lacking was a forceful conviction, on the part of those with whom the author associated, that the recovery program as practiced by Dr. Bob and the Akron AAs, and as taught by Reverend Sam Shoemaker in New York, was relevant to present-day recovery in A.A.

Today, after considerable research, the author has learned much about A.A.'s Christian origins. For example, the original name of the Oxford Group, of which A.A. was an integral part at its beginnings, was "A First Century Christian Fellowship."[59] A.A.'s *Pass It On* says of this "First Century Christian Fellowship" that, "in the late 1930's, Dr. Bob, co-founder of A.A., and the other Akron, Ohio, members continued to refer to it [the Oxford Group] in that way [i.e., as 'A First Century Christian Fellowship']."[60] And Dr. Bob often referred to A.A.'s own early Akron meetings as "a Christian fellowship."[61] Albert Scott, Chairman of the Trustees for New York's Riverside Church, and one of John D. Rockefeller's assistants who originally met with Bill Wilson, made a similar observation as he reviewed a report of early A.A. that was submitted to Rockefeller by Frank Amos. Scott noted, "Why this is first-century Christianity."[62]

---

[59] See Samuel Shoemaker, *Twice-Born Ministers* (New York: Fleming H. Revell, 1929), pp. 23, 90, 95, 101, 122, 147, 148; and Dick B., *The Akron Genesis of Alcoholics Anonymous*, pp. 219-220.

[60] *Pass It On*, p. 130.

[61] See *DR. BOB and the Good Oldtimers*, pp. 118-119. Dr. Bob's daughter, Sue Smith Windows, informed the author in a personal interview at Akron, Ohio, in June of 1991, that Dr. Bob described every King School Group meeting (of A.A.) as a "Christian Fellowship." Also, early Akron AA, Bob E., wrote a note to Lois Wilson, Bill Wilson's wife, on a "Four Absolutes" pamphlet of which the author has a copy. In the note, Bob E. told Lois that Dr. Bob referred to A.A. as a "Christian Fellowship." See also Dick B., *The Akron Genesis of Alcoholics Anonymous*, pp. 218-220, for a similar statement by Bob E. to Nell Wing, Bill Wilson's secretary.

[62] *A.A. Comes of Age*, p. 148.

Dr. Bob and his wife, Anne Smith, were Christians and belonged to Christian churches in A.A.'s formative and later years. In June of 1993, the author personally researched the Parish Register at St. Paul's Episcopal Church in Akron. In company with St. Paul's current rector, The Reverend Dr. Richard L. McCandless, the author found the record of Dr. Bob's becoming a communicant at St. Paul's. He confirmed that St. Paul's former rector, Dr. Walter Tunks, had delivered Dr. Bob's funeral oration and presided over the burial services of both Dr. Bob and Anne. The author also verified with Madge Beatty, Keeper of the Church Register and membership records at Westminster United Presbyterian Church in Akron, Ohio, that Dr. Bob and his wife, Anne, were charter members of that church from June 3, 1936, to April 3, 1942. The Register at the Presbyterian church shows that both joined the church in 1936 by letter of transfer. Thus, in the eyes of that church, Dr. Bob and Anne were both Christians prior to their joining Westminster Church. As to Bill Wilson, the author has discovered more and more convincing evidence which establishes that Bill Wilson made a decision for Christ at Calvary Mission in New York in November of 1934, prior to his entry into Towns Hospital, and thereafter believed and wrote that he had been "born again."[63]

None of this information would be relevant if one were attempting to establish that A.A. is or wants to be a Christian Fellowship today. The Foreword to the Big Book's Second Edition specifically states: "By personal religious affiliation, we include Catholics, Protestants, Jews, Hindus, and a sprinkling of Moslems and Buddhists."[64] Certainly, too, there are a good many atheists and agnostics in A.A. Wilson wrote in the Big Book, "But cheer up, something like half of us thought we were atheists or agnostics. Our experience shows that you need not be discouraged."[65] A.A.'s Third Tradition states, "The only

---

[63] See Dick B., *The Akron Genesis of Alcoholics Anonymous*, pp. 328-331.

[64] Big Book, p. xx.

[65] Big Book, p. 44.

requirement for A.A. membership is a desire to stop drinking."[66] And its preamble—read at almost every meeting of A.A.—states, "A.A. is not allied with any sect, denomination, politics, organization or institution."[67]

But, oddly enough, there is often discomfort today for a new, shaky, frightened, and confused newcomer of the Christian faith as he enters the rooms of Alcoholics Anonymous. He seldom hears about Dr. Bob. He rarely hears that A.A. was born in Akron. And he would probably be immensely surprised to hear a speaker say that almost every spiritual idea in Alcoholics Anonymous came—as its Co-founder, Bill Wilson, stated—from the teachings of Sam Shoemaker.

Instead, the confused new member begins, almost at once, to hear, as the author so often does in today's A.A. meetings, that A.A. is a "spiritual rather than a religious program." He or she is exposed to dogmatic statements that some particular member's "god of his understanding" is a "Higher Power," a "Power greater than ourselves," "Good Orderly Direction," a "Group Of Drunks," "Good," the "Group itself," "It," a doorknob, a tree, a stone, a table, the Big Dipper, Santa Claus, and even "Ralph."[68] The author has heard all these appellations—many times! So have others who regularly attend A.A. meetings; and so did Bill Wilson.[69] But these are not concepts that had any accepted usage

---

[66] Big Book, p. 564.

[67] From the A.A.preamble—quoted in every issue of A.A.'s *Grapevine*.

[68] Examples can be found in *Daily Reflections* (New York: Alcoholics Anonymous World Services, Inc., 1990) at pp. 79, 175, 334.

[69] See Barnaby Conrad, *Time Is All We Have* (New York: Dell Publishing, 1986), p. 21; Nan Robertson, *Getting Better: Inside Alcoholics Anonymous* (New York: Fawcett Crest, 1988), pp. 124, 129; Jan R. Wilson and Judith A. Wilson, *Addictionary: A Primer of Recovery Terms and Concepts From Abstinence to Withdrawal* (New York: Simon & Schuster, 1992), pp. 181-183; Dick B. *The Oxford Group & Alcoholics Anonymous*, p. 257; *Anne Smith's Spiritual Workbook*, p. 22; *Twelve Steps And Twelve Traditions* (New York: Alcoholics Anonymous World Services, Inc., 1953), p. 27; *A.A. Comes of Age*, p. 81; *Daily Reflections* (New York: Alcoholics Anonymous World Services, 1990), pp. 79 ("Good Orderly Direction"), 175 ("a table, a tree, then my A.A. group"), 334 (continued...)

prior to, or at the time of, the writing of the Big Book by Bill Wilson. At best, two of the expressions—"power greater than ourselves" and "God as we understood Him"—were simply the outcome of a "compromise" which Bill Wilson's secretary, Ruth Hock, felt never "had much of a negative reaction anywhere."[70]

Bill said about his *initial* writing of the Big Book:

> I had consistently used the word "God," and in one place the expression "on our knees" was used. . . . Who first suggested the actual compromise words I do not know, but they are words well known throughout the length and breadth of A.A. today: In Step Two we decided to describe God as a "Power greater than ourselves." In Steps Three and Eleven we inserted the words "God *as we understood Him.*" . . . Such were the final concessions to those of little or no faith. . . . God was certainly there in our Steps, but He was now expressed in terms that anybody—anybody at all—could accept and try.[71]

As we will show in this book, Bill could have said that the idea of "God as we understood Him" came from the long-utilized Oxford Group-Shoemaker suggestion of an experiment of faith. The Oxford Group idea then in vogue for learning about God was to "surrender as much of yourself as you know to as much of God as you understand." But Bill chose simply to say that there had been a "compromise" (with resultant, and probably misguided, extrapolations involving trees, door knobs, Santa Claus, and good orderly direction); and the compromise may have made A.A. more approachable, acceptable, and comfortable for many of little or no

---

[69] (...continued)
("Him, or Her, or It"); and the Big Book, p. 248. Note that A.A.'s Conference-Approved pamphlet "Members of the Clergy Ask about Alcoholics Anonymous," (New York: Alcoholics Anonymous World Services, 1961—revised 1992), states at page 13: "Some [members] choose the A.A. group as their 'Higher Power'; some look to God—*as they understand Him*; and others rely upon entirely different concepts."

[70] *Pass It On*, p. 199.

[71] *A.A. Comes of Age*, pp. 166-167.

faith. But the "compromise" can be a problem for the Christian. And how easily, perhaps, could that problem have been resolved had all AAs been made familiar with the fact that in Sam Shoemaker's groups it was very common in the conversion process for a parishioner to "surrender as much of himself as he could to as much of Christ as he understood," or "to as much of God as he understood, removing first the hinderance of self-will."[72] In other words, a little bit of Shoemaker history could have made a world of difference to the Christian who knew Bill Wilson was talking about God and not about a doorknob or a tree.

The author has been at many a meeting where an A.A. gingerly mentioned God, or Jesus Christ, or the Bible, only to be reproached by another A.A. for "scaring away the newcomer," perhaps with the added admonition that "A.A. is a spiritual program, and not a religious program." Even more, many a Christian *newcomer* who has mentioned his Christian beliefs has been trounced by another member with more sobriety who speaks disapprovingly of any mention of a religious conviction.

Ill-conceived remarks which discourage religious beliefs by an individual AA not only flout A.A. Traditions; they display ignorance about A.A.'s roots in religion, the Bible, and Christianity. And they can do much to drive Christians away from A.A. More importantly—back to a drink! They can discourage spiritual growth. They tend to deify the questionable idea that a "power greater than ourselves" was intended to, or can appropriately, be identified with an A.A. group, a tree, or Santa Claus. And such results have deservedly caught the attention and

[72] Samuel M. Shoemaker, Jr., *Children of the Second Birth* (New York: Fleming H. Revell, 1927), pp. 25 and 47; Samuel M. Shoemaker, Jr., *How to Become a Christian* (New York: Harper & Bros., 1953), p. 72. Both Anne Smith, as well as Oxford Group adherents in New York and elsewhere, were quite familiar with this "God as we understood Him" concept. See Dick B., *Anne Smith's Spiritual Workbook*, p. 28; Stephen Foot, *Life Began Yesterday* (New York: Harper & Bros., 1935), p. 72; and James D. Newton, *Uncommon Friends* (New York: Harcourt Brace Jovanovich, 1987), p. 154.

criticism of knowledgeable Christian writers, including Dr. Bob's wife, Anne.[73]

An important reason, therefore, for the author's writing of this book has been his hope that it will enable those who come into A.A. as Christians, or those who might want to return to any church, including a Christian church, or those who want to study the Bible—as Dr. Bob and most early AAs did—, to feel just as comfortable in A.A. rooms as those who talk about a "god" in agnostic, atheistic, or other non-Christian terms. The author has never heard anyone who has characterized his or her "god" as a "higher power," a "group," or even "Ralph," criticized or ridiculed at an A.A. meeting. And, consistent with the Big Book, A.A. Traditions, and A.A.'s history, no Christian believer should ever be condemned at an A.A. meeting for believing in the God of the Bible and of Christianity.

Today, the author feels both comfortable and grateful in A.A. And why? Because he has spent a number of years researching the contents of A.A.'s Big Book, Twelve Steps, and Twelve Traditions. Also, because he has learned much about A.A.'s Biblical roots. And finally, because he is gaining an ever-growing familiarity with, and admiration for, the principles of the Bible and Christianity that Shoemaker passed on to Bill Wilson, and possibly to a good many others involved in A.A.'s earliest, founding days.

The author has passed this information on to the men he has sponsored; and many have returned to Protestant and Roman Catholic churches, and to Bible fellowships of their own choosing. Like the author, they feel comfortable, we think, because they have been coached in A.A.'s history and believe that A.A.'s "God as we understand Him" can most assuredly include "God as they understand Him"—the God of the Bible and of Christianity—with whom they choose to identify and whom they choose to worship.

---

[73] See William L. Playfair, M.D., *The Useful Lie* (Illinois: Crossway Books, 1991); and Dick B., *Anne Smith's Spiritual Workbook*, p. 22, where Dr. Bob's wife, Anne, in the spiritual workbook she read to AAs, criticized an attitude of unwillingness to use the word "Christ." She said that using the word "Group" instead of "Christ" could be characterized as a "Funk Hole."

And we hope our book will raise the comfort level of any religiously-inclined A.A. member or newcomer who learns more about A.A.'s first spiritual teacher, Reverend Samuel Shoemaker, Jr. For Shoemaker was known as a "Bible Christian." He urged Bible study and church attendance as part of the vital spiritual experiences he helped bring about. Oxford Group meetings—of which Shoemaker was a leader, and in which others in early A.A., in both Akron and New York, were actively involved—opened with prayer and Bible study, frequently involved the study of Christian literature, and closed—as do most A.A. meetings even today—with the Lord's Prayer from Matthew 6:9-13 in the Bible.

There are several things this book is not. It is not a biography of Sam Shoemaker. It is not a review of *all* of Shoemaker's religious views or religious writings. It does not contain a lengthy account of Shoemaker's part and leadership role in the Oxford Group or his later separation from that group. It is not a manual on what A.A. might have subscribed to, or agreed or disagreed with, in Oxford Group or Shoemaker ideas. And it does not stem from a conviction that A.A.: (1) should never have left the Oxford Group, or (2) should rejoin the Oxford Group (now, "Moral Re-Armament").

In the first part of our book, we will discuss what a number of people—including A.A. co-founder, Bill Wilson—had to say about Sam Shoemaker. We'll take a brief glimpse at his life, both religious and secular. And we will deal at some length with the interrelationship of Shoemaker, the Oxford Group, and A.A. We will also show, we believe, that A.A.'s spiritual ideas—even those from the Oxford Group—cannot be presumed to have come from Shoemaker alone.

In our second part, we will cover in much detail what Shoemaker wrote and said in his twenty-eight major books, his articles and pamphlets, and his speeches and sermons, that had a bearing on A.A. ideas.

In our next part, we'll tell as much of the story as we have discovered about just what Shoemaker's personal involvement was with Bill Wilson in A.A.'s formative years. This will include

Shoemaker's indirect influences on Bill through Oxford Group houseparties, the Oxford Group businessmen's team, Shoemaker's clergy and lay associates who worked with Bill, and the Oxford Group meetings themselves which Shoemaker led and which Bill and his wife, Lois, attended. There will also be a section on how Shoemaker probably made his influence felt through Dr. Bob, Anne Smith, Henrietta Seiberling, and T. Henry and Clarace Williams in Akron. And also through his emphasis on the Bible.

In our final part, we will call particular attention to the striking resemblance that a host of Shoemaker words and phrases bear to words and phrases in A.A. literature, particularly the Big Book. Then we will set out those Shoemaker ideas which seem to have been adopted—however they were modified—by A.A. And we will cover what Shoemaker said directly to and about A.A.

We will endeavor to show how this book can be of use to AAs and to the public at large in helping them to understand and utilize Twelve Step recovery programs.

In a nutshell, the reader can buy the idea that neither the Bible, Christianity, the Oxford Group, nor Shoemaker has any real relevance in today's picture of the A.A. program; or the reader can join the author in the quest to discover and communicate as many of the details as possible about A.A.'s spiritual roots. This, so that a fuller understanding of the miracle of A.A.'s early success can help all who suffer from the disease of alcoholism. Alcoholism—a malady which each year cuts short more than 100,000 American lives, which drains $144 billion from the American economy yearly, and to which 75 million Americans—almost half of America's adult population—have been exposed in the family.[74] We believe A.A. *is* a spiritual program. And we believe, with its co-founders, Bill Wilson and Dr. Bob Smith, that its spiritual principles and recovery power came from God. With that before us, we see great importance in this quest for

[74] See statistics quoted from a letter from Harold Hood, Chairman of the Board, National Council on Alcoholism and Drug Dependence, in the NCADD 1992 Annual Report.

the truth about Reverend Samuel Shoemaker, Jr.'s recovery ideas—ideas which Shoemaker took from the Bible and the success story of first century Christianity.

Part 1

Sam

1

What They Said about Sam

There have been many comments about The Reverend Canon Samuel Moor Shoemaker, Jr., D.D., S.T.D.[1]

Reverend Billy Graham said, "I doubt that any man in our generation has made a greater impact for God on the Christian world than did Sam Shoemaker."[2] Shoemaker's good friend, Dr. Norman Vincent Peale, said, "The secret of Sam Shoemaker lay in the fact that he was an all-out Christian who had given all that he was to the Lord Jesus Christ. The happiness that bubbled forth from him grew out of commitment in depth. That is the basic answer to this man's great life—spiritual depth."[3] Dr. Theodore D. Stevenson of the United Presbyterian Church said, "He influenced my life by his witness and superb ability to interpret

---

[1] For biographical material on Shoemaker, see Helen Smith Shoemaker, *I Stand By The Door: The Life of Sam Shoemaker* (Waco, Texas: Word Books, 1967); Irving Harris, *The Breeze of the Spirit: Sam Shoemaker and the Story of Faith-at-Work*. (New York: The Seabury Press, 1978); *Faith at Work*, a symposium edited by Samuel Moor Shoemaker (Hawthorn Books, 1958), pp. 80-84; John Potter Cuyler, Jr., *Calvary Church in Action* (New York: Fleming H. Revell, 1934); A. J. Russell, *For Sinners Only* (London: Hodder and Stoughton, 1932), pp. 205-18; Harold Begbie, *Life Changers* (London: Mills & Boon, 1932), pp. 147-59; Samuel M. Shoemaker, *Calvary Church Yesterday And Today* (New York: Fleming H. Revell, 1936); Garth Lean, *On The Tail of a Comet* (Colorado Springs: Helmers & Howard, 1988); *Centennial History: Calvary Episcopal Church, 1855-1955* (Pittsburgh: Calvary Episcopal Church, 1955), pp. 81-85; and "Crusaders of Reform," *Princeton Alumni Weekly* (June 2, 1993).

[2] Helen Shoemaker, *I Stand By The Door*, p. 220.

[3] From *Faith At Work Magazine*, Jan-Feb, 1964.

God's word and will to me."[4] The Reverend W. Irving Harris, one of Shoemaker's closest associates at Calvary Church and a long-time friend, said:

> To understand Sam Shoemaker's power in the pulpit one must first realize his great talent as a writer. . . . What did he talk about? The Person of Jesus Christ formed the subject of perhaps every fourth or fifth sermon. . . . He constantly underlined the supernatural aspects of Christianity and strongly advocated that people dedicate their natural gifts to their Creator. . . . The Scriptures formed the basis of Sam Shoemaker's preaching. He was a "Bible Christian." Shoemaker sought to present a Christian message vital enough to challenge both materialism and immorality. . . . As Calvary's program developed, two interesting points became ever more apparent: (1) Here was a place to learn the how of faith, both in sermons and in groups—How to find God. How to pray. How to read the Bible. How to pass faith on. And (2) much of the *how* flowed straight from the fellowship itself and a quality of life which is centered, not in individual hopes or even in personal vocations, but in that super-natural Other.[5]

And, lest any think the comments were always laudatory, Shoemaker's widow and biographer said, "He has been evaluated, criticized, scandalized, and eulogized variously."[6]

Our account concerns Shoemaker and Alcoholics Anonymous. And what have those associated with A.A. had to say?

First, Shoemaker's widow recorded receiving the following in two letters from AAs written to her at the time of Shoemaker's death—the first, from an attorney in Washington, and the second, from a noted actor:

> This . . . is a letter of appreciation for Sam and for God's Grace that sent him amongst us, the agnostics, the spiritually crippled, the

---

[4] Shoemaker, *I Stand By The Door*, p. 219.

[5] Harris, *The Breeze of the Spirit*, pp. 15, 17-18, 25.

[6] Shoemaker, *I Stand By The Door*, p. 113.

> sinners, the drunks, those that travail and are heavy laden, to refresh us, to give us courage and peace, and above all, as Sam used to put it, to give us an introduction to God.
>
> Of course, as you must know, his name repeatedly bounces up in AA meetings and among AAs in conversation everywhere. I feel certain in my heart that his spirit, as his Master's, will live on and on in an ever-widening circle among those who seek His way.[7]

But what did A.A.'s *founders* say? Interestingly, with the exception of Bill Wilson, they said very little.

Dr. Robert Holbrook Smith (A.A.'s co-founder, "Dr. Bob") seems to have had virtually no contact with Sam Shoemaker at all. At least the author has found no record of any.[8] Thus A.A.'s Conference Approved biography of Dr. Bob contains no reference to Shoemaker in its index.[9] The accounts of Dr. Bob's children are similarly devoid of Shoemaker references.[10] However, Dr. Bob very definitely did own, read, and circulate among early AAs most of the important Shoemaker books of the 1920's and 1930's.[11]

In the spiritual workbook which she assembled and read to AAs in the Smith home in Akron at the time of A.A.'s birth and development, Dr. Bob's wife, Anne Ripley Smith (called by many the "Mother of A.A."), gives no indication she had ever met or heard Shoemaker. But she did recommend several of his important

---

[7] Shoemaker, *I Stand By The Door*, p. 193.

[8] However, see Appendix 10, where the author records newly found evidence that both Victor Kitchen and Reverend John Cuyler of Calvary Church spoke of an Oxford Group team, including Shoemaker and others from the church, who went to the Midwest in 1934 when Dr. Bob was active in the Oxford Group. These Calvary Church people met one-on-one with Oxford Group adherents in Akron; and Dr. Bob may have been one of those with whom he met or spoke.

[9] *DR. BOB and the Good Oldtimers* (New York: Alcoholics Anonymous World Services, 1980).

[10] See Bob Smith and Sue Smith Windows, *Children of the Healer The Story of Dr. Bob's Kids* (Illinois: Parkside Publishing, 1992).

[11] See Dick B., *Dr. Bob's Library: An AA-Good Book Connection* (WV: The Bishop of Books, 1992), pp. 2, 6, 23-25, 48-52, 81-90.

books.[12] The same appears to have been true for Henrietta Buckler Seiberling, who was very instrumental in the founding of A.A. in Akron. Henrietta had probably read all Shoemaker's books.[13] But in the interviews and correspondence the author had with Henrietta's children, there was no indication Henrietta was acquainted with Shoemaker on a personal basis.

Recent investigation by the author has uncovered the fact that T. Henry Williams, the Akron Oxford Group member in whose home early AAs held their meetings during the founding days, actually attended meetings of an Oxford Group businessmen's team in New York, where Shoemaker was frequently involved.[14] And Shoemaker's books were apparently available for distribution in Akron at meetings held in the Williams home.[15] But we have discovered no statements either by T. Henry or his wife, Clarace, as to what they thought about, or read from, Sam Shoemaker.

The person who sang Sam Shoemaker's praises as far as A.A. was concerned was A.A.'s other co-founder, William Griffith Wilson (known as "Bill W.").

Some of Wilson's most significant remarks about Shoemaker were made in his history of early A.A. Bill said, speaking of Shoemaker's attendance at A.A.'s St. Louis Convention in 1955:

> Sam's appearance before us was further evidence that many a channel had been used by Providence to create Alcoholics Anonymous. And none had been more vitally needed than the one opened through Sam Shoemaker and his Oxford Group associates of a generation before. The basic principles which the Oxford Groupers had taught were ancient and universal ones, the common property of mankind. . . . But the important thing is this: the early A.A. got its ideas of self-examination, acknowledgment of character

[12] See Dick B., *Anne Smith's Spiritual Workbook: An AA-Good Book Connection* (Seattle: Glen Abbey Books, 1993), pp. 13-14.

[13] See Dick B., *The Akron Genesis of Alcoholics Anonymous: An AA-Good Book Connection* (Seattle: Glen Abbey Books, 1993), pp. 85-86.

[14] Dick B., *The Akron Genesis*, p. 76.

[15] Dick B., *The Akron Genesis*, p. 76.

> defects, restitution for harm done, and working with others straight from the Oxford Groups and directly from Sam Shoemaker, their former leader in America, and from nowhere else. He will always be found in our annals as the one whose inspired example and teaching did most to show us how to create the spiritual climate in which we alcoholics may survive and then proceed to grow. A.A. owes a debt of timeless gratitude for all that God sent us through Sam and his friends in the days of A.A.'s infancy.[16]

As we showed in our Introduction, Wilson spoke of Shoemaker in these glowing terms many, many times.[17] And we might put the cap on all these remarks by quoting the following by Helen Smith Shoemaker about her husband, Sam Shoemaker, and A.A.:

> The insights Sam gained through his obedience in bringing into being Calvary Mission, as well as his experience in working with the Oxford Group, later inspired Bill [Wilson] to write the famous Twelve Steps of Alcoholics Anonymous.[18]

There are, however, other issues as to just how many of the A.A. ideas came from Shoemaker, rather than from the Bible, the Oxford Group itself, and other Christian writings. To give some initial flavor to our study, we quote the following from the last major address by A.A. co-founder, Dr. Bob:

> When we started in on Bill D. [A.A. Number Three], we had no Twelve Steps, either; we had no Traditions. But we were convinced that the answer to our problems was in the Good Book. To some of us older ones, the parts that we found absolutely essential were the

---

[16] *Alcoholics Anonymous Comes of Age* (New York: Alcoholics Anonymous World Services, Inc., 1957), pp. 38-40.

[17] And see Robert Thomsen, *Bill W.* (New York: Harper & Row, 1977), pp. 261-62; Nell Wing, *Grateful To Have Been There*, p. 25; *Pass It On*, pp. 127-29, 174, 199; *Alcoholics Anonymous Comes of Age*, pp. 2, 38-40, 253, 261; and *The Language of the Heart*, pp. 177-78, 279, 298, 368, 379-80.

[18] Shoemaker, *I Stand By The Door*, p. 192.

> Sermon on the Mount, the thirteenth chapter of First Corinthians, and the Book of James. . . .[19]
>
> I didn't write the Twelve Steps. I had nothing to do with the writing of them. But I think I probably had something to do with them indirectly. After my June 10th episode, Bill came to live at our house and stayed for about three months. There was hardly a night that we didn't sit up until two or three o'clock talking. It would be hard for me to conceive that, during these nightly discussions around our kitchen table, nothing was said that influenced the writing of the Twelve Steps. We already had the basic ideas, though not in terse and tangible form. We got them, as I said, as a result of our study of the Good Book.[20]

Then there was Bill's own statement made to T. Henry and Clarace Williams when he interviewed them on December 12, 1954:

> I learned a great deal from you people, from the Smiths themselves, and from Henrietta [Seiberling]. I hadn't looked in the Bible, up to this time at all. You see, I had the [conversion] experience first and then this rushing around to help drunks and nothing happened.[21]

Consider also the following versions A.A.'s two founders (Bill W. and Dr. Bob) provided as to their initial meeting on Mother's Day, 1935, at Henrietta Seiberling's home. Both of the men make it clear that Dr. Bob—who at that time had probably not met Shoemaker—had already learned the spiritual solution from the Bible, the Christian literature he was studying, and from the Oxford Group meetings he was attending.

---

[19] See analysis in Dick B., *The Akron Genesis of Alcoholics Anonymous*, pp. 270-313, discussing traces of these three segments of the Bible in the A.A. Big Book, Twelve Steps, and language.

[20] *The Co-Founders of Alcoholics Anonymous. Biographical sketches. Their last major talks* (New York: Alcoholics Anonymous World Services, Inc., 1972, 1975), pp. 9-10.

[21] See Dick B., *The Akron Genesis*, p. 64, 132, 136.

Thus Bill said of Dr. Bob:

> Always better versed in spiritual matters than I, he had paid little attention to that aspect of my story. Even though he could not make them work, he already knew what the spiritual answers were.[22]

And Dr. Bob said of himself and Bill:

> We had both been associated with the Oxford Group, Bill in New York, for five months, and I in Akron, for two and a half years. Bill had acquired their idea of service. I had not, but I had done an immense amount of reading they had recommended. I had refreshed my memory of the Good Book, and I had had excellent training in that as a youngster.[23]

In his scholarly history of A.A., Dr. Ernest Kurtz made the following observation about the impact that Dr. Bob's spiritual background had upon Bill from the very beginning—especially during the first three weeks of Bob's and Bill's acquaintance. Kurtz said:

> So began three weeks of intensive Oxford Group living [during which Shoemaker was in no way involved since the events occurred in Akron]. Bill Wilson found himself in awe of Dr. Bob's "spiritual knowledge" and cherished the guidance of Anne Smith as each morning her pleasant voice read and interpreted the Christian Scriptures and Oxford Group devotional books.[24]

Several writers on A.A.'s spiritual roots have noted that Bill Wilson's public writings possibly focused too much on Sam

---

[22] *Alcoholics Anonymous Comes of Age*, p. 69.

[23] *Co-Founders*, p. 7.

[24] Ernest Kurtz, *Not-God. A History of Alcoholics Anonymous*. Expanded ed. (Minnesota: Hazelden, 1991), p. 32. For evidence that Anne's reading extended beyond Oxford Group literature and covered a great many other Christian writings, see Dick B., *The Akron Genesis*, p. 110-112, 211-215.

Shoemaker as the principal source of A.A. ideas and virtually ignored other important spiritual sources, including the Bible, the Oxford Group itself, other Christian literature, and even "new thought" sources such as Emmet Fox, upon which Bill drew.[25]

But the fact remains that Wilson gave enormous credit to Sam Shoemaker. And a study of the Wilson-Shoemaker relationship and of the language found in A.A. literature supports Bill's thesis that it was Shoemaker's ideas, however they may have reached Bill Wilson, which strongly influenced the actual language Wilson used in the A.A. materials he wrote.

[25] See *DR. BOB and the Good Oldtimers*, pp. 96-97, 150-155, 220, 228; *Pass It On* (New York: Alcoholics Anonymous World Services, 1984), pp. 114-116, 127-132, 167-174, 386-387; Mel B., *New Wine. The Spiritual Roots of the Twelve Step Miracle* (Minnesota: Hazelden, 1992), pp. 27-45; Bill Pittman, *AA The Way It Began* (Seattle: Glen Abbey Books, 1988), pp. 186-187; Dick B., *The Oxford Group & Alcoholics Anonymous* (Seattle: Glen Abbey Books, 1992), pp. 73-84, 92-109.

2

A Look at Sam's Life

Samuel Moor Shoemaker, Jr., was born in Baltimore, Maryland, on December 27, 1893. When he was two, his family moved to a 467-acre country estate called Burnside, about ten miles north of Baltimore. Originally, many of the Shoemakers were Mennonites from Europe who later were converted to the Quaker faith. Shoemaker himself had a strong interest in Quakers and was a long-time member of the Wider Quaker Fellowship. But the Shoemaker family were Episcopalians from the early 1800's.

In the fall of 1908, Sam was enrolled at St. George's, an Episcopal boys school in Newport, Rhode Island, and graduated in 1912. From there he went to Princeton University, where he became involved in the campus Christian organization, called the Philadelphian Society. As an undergraduate, Shoemaker served as president of the Society. The General Secretary was Thomas St. Clair Evans, who described the work of the Society as follows:

> Princeton's entire religious work is based on a strong faith in God and His Son, Jesus Christ, as revealed in His Word, the Bible.[1]

The Society served as the campus YMCA and helped give birth to the World Christian Student Federation. And, after a stint as Assistant Secretary of the Society, and also as a YMCA secretary in Peking (of which we shall speak in a moment), Shoemaker was

---

[1] Report of the General Secretary, April 13, 1916, Philadelphian Society Princeton.

called to replace St. Clair Evans as General Secretary. In a report after his first year, 1919-1920, Shoemaker described the different things with which the Society was involved, and which included courses in Bible study, Missions, and Social Problems. The students who asked for Shoemaker were seeking "a more aggressive personal evangelistic program;" and Shoemaker reported that in 1919-1920, such aggressive personal evangelism became "*the* programme."

Shoemaker received an A.B. degree from Princeton in 1916. Many years later, in 1948, he was granted a Doctorate of Divinity from the Virginia Theological Seminary and a Doctorate of Sacred Theology from the Berkeley Divinity School.

In 1916, during World War I, Shoemaker answered calls to serve the Y.M.C.A. in the camps of troops training in Texas, and later in camps at Kent, England. Dr. Sherwood Eddy persuaded Shoemaker to go to China with him to work for the Princeton-in-Peking project, and Princeton alumni staffed the center there. Shoemaker arrived in Peking on October 29, 1917. And he spent two years in China teaching English, Bible, and a business course.

Shoemaker had previously met the Oxford Group's founder, a Lutheran Minister, Frank N. D. Buchman; and Buchman came to China in 1918 on a personal-work campaign. Buchman arrived, urging the application of the Four Absolutes—Honesty, Purity, Unselfishness, and Love—which Dr. Robert E. Speer considered to be the essence of Jesus Christ's ethical teachings. Shoemaker tried to apply these to himself, finding himself wanting. He felt he had never been absolutely honest about himself with another human being. He believed he had not lived up to the standard of Absolute Purity, in that he had never found an all-consuming and high faith and purpose; that he had not been absolutely unselfish; and that he had fallen short of Absolute Love in his relationship with his father.

Shoemaker frequently quoted a passage from Professor William James's book, *The Varieties of Religious Experience*; and the James language actually wound up in the phraseology of A.A. It concerned the "turning point" in one's life. James wrote, "The crisis of self-surrender has always been and must always be regarded as the vital turning point of the religious life."[2] On January 19, 1918, Shoemaker went through such a crisis after he had asked Buchman what was the matter in his life. Buchman had opined that it might be sin which was excluding Shoemaker from vital consciousness of God and which was making him spiritually impotent. Buchman tendered to Shoemaker Dr. Speer's "four absolutes."[3]

Shoemaker then knew he had to surrender. And, as he often put it in his journals, he made his "great decision to surrender all to God."[4] He walked to his room and (as he later recounted) thought:

> My sins rose up before me straight as tombstones. If I took this plunge it meant a clearing up all along the line. It meant confession. It meant a break with all that had gone before—a new life. . . . Was I willing to do this thing, or was I not willing? . . . Without a scrap of emotion, but with what I can only call a great heave of my will, I knelt down to make my submission, to give myself, without reservation, to God. . . . I was sensible only of calm, of a feeling that something needful and right had been done. I felt very little at the time. I simply realized that I had jumped a fence at which I had

---

[2] William James, *The Varieties of Religious Experience* (New York: First Vintage Books/The Library of America Edition, 1990), p. 196. For the frequency of Shoemaker's quotation of this passage from William James, see Samuel M. Shoemaker, *Realizing Religion* (New York: Association Press, 1923), p. 30; *A Young Man's View of the Ministry* (New York: Association Press, 1923), p. 55; *Children of the Second Birth* (New York: Fleming H. Revell, 1927), p. 16; *Religion That Works* (New York: Fleming H. Revell, 1928), p. 48; *The Church Can Save The World* (New York: Harper & Brothers, 1938), p. 113; *God's Control* (New York: Fleming H. Revell, 1939), p. 138. And compare *Alcoholics Anonymous*. Third ed. (New York: Alcoholics Anonymous World Services, 1976), p. 59: "We stood at the turning point. We asked His protection and care with complete abandon."

[3] *Faith at Work*, p. 81.

[4] In examining Shoemaker's journals, which extended over many years, the author noted that Shoemaker invariably made an entry on January 19 of each year and mentioned this decision. The language quoted in the text above is from Shoemaker's journal entry for January 19, 1933.

> long balked. There was no breaking in of light upon me, nor anything unusual. After the prayer, which tore away a wall of my own erection—the wall of unwillingness to face God's Will fully—I prayed again, but without ecstasy. I rose from that prayer hoping that I might be used to help others, and feeling I had done what was required of me. . . . As I lay in bed there came to me a distinct Voice, and that Voice said, "There is no work of Mine to do for him who is not wholly Mine." They were no words of mine. . . . And they revealed to me what I believe to be the central truth of religion.[5]

For Shoemaker, the best test of whether he had made a start in overcoming his sins was whether God could use him in the life of someone else. Therefore, in China, he immediately launched out from this experience by leading a young Chinese business friend to a decision which enabled the man to find Christ. And in his Peking days, Sam's greatest excitement was passing on to the young people around him his own new-found spiritual experience.[6]

Shoemaker returned to America and, in 1920, was ordained a deacon in the Protestant Episcopal Church—with Frank Buchman present. He attended General Theological Seminary in Chelsea Square in New York City. He was ordained a priest in 1921 and began serving as assistant minister in Grace Church, in New York. It was also in 1921, that his first book (the first of some twenty-eight), *Realizing Religion*, was copyrighted by the International Committee of Young Men's Christian Association. About 1924, he began traveling with Dr. Frank Buchman, the founder of the Oxford Group. Buchman, Shoemaker, and some others went on an extended tour through the Mideast and India—working largely in universities and mission centers. And, in 1925, Shoemaker accepted a call to be rector of Calvary Protestant Episcopal Church

---

[5] Harold Begbie, *Life Changers* (New York: G. P. Putnam's Sons, 1927), p. 154. See also, A. J. Russell, *For Sinners Only* (London: Hodder & Stoughton, 1932), p. 210.

[6] Helen Smith Shoemaker, *I Stand By The Door* (New York: Harper and Row, 1967), p. 26.

in New York City. He remained at that post for the next twenty-six years.

Shoemaker had his ups and downs as a clergyman. He could have had the deanship of a Manhattan convocation but nominated another for the post; and that person was elected. Three times he was hoping for high office in his church. He had aspired to be dean of Washington Cathedral, dean of St. John the Divine, and Suffragan Bishop of New York. In each case, he was defeated. The Right Reverend Karl Morgan Block, Bishop of California, had proposed to Sam the deanship of San Francisco Cathedral; but Shoemaker declined. Shoemaker had many successes in radio preaching and in college work on the east coast. In 1952, he accepted the rectorship of Calvary Episcopal Church in Pittsburgh; and he retired from that post in January of 1962. He was very much involved in the "Pittsburgh Experiment"—a plan to encourage people to bring Christianity into their normal daily meetings with each other. Its primary emphasis was on the conduct of business relationships.

In a later chapter, we will be reviewing Shoemaker's writings for their relationship to A.A. ideas; and we will be covering, in one way or another, literally hundreds of Bible verses which Shoemaker used in articulating his ideas. But there are several verses which standout in any viewing of Shoemaker's work.

The first is John 7:17:

> If any man will do his will, he shall know of the doctrine, whether it be of God, or *whether* I speak of myself.

A. J. Russell, who wrote the popular Oxford Group book, *For Sinners Only*, said this was Sam Shoemaker's favorite Biblical quotation.[7] And Shoemaker certainly quoted it with much

[7] Russell, *For Sinners Only*, p 211.

frequency.[8] In doing so, Shoemaker took his cue from Henry Drummond and Henry Wright, both of whom were much influenced by this verse, and both of whose ideas became incorporated in Oxford Group thinking. Shoemaker quoted the verse to establish that "willingness" is an essential for obtaining spiritual knowledge. He also cited the verse as authority for the concept that obedience to God's known will (as set forth in the Bible) is the organ of knowing His particular will (as given by revelation).

Secondly, Shoemaker frequently quoted Jesus Christ's words in Luke 22:42: "nevertheless not my will, but thine, be done."[9] This concept ("Thy will be done"), which is also a specific part of the Lord's Prayer, appears several times in the book *Alcoholics Anonymous*.[10]

Thirdly, there are two verses often quoted by Shoemaker in connection with the necessity for waiting on God for guidance, rather than directing God as to what He should do. The first is 1 Samuel 3:9: "Speak, Lord; for thy servant heareth."[11] The second is Acts 9:6: "Lord, what wilt thou have me to do?"[12]

---

[8] Shoemaker, *A Young Man's View of the Ministry*, p. 41; *Religion That Works*, pp. 45-46, 58, 86; *The Church Can Save The World*, p. 110; *How To Find God* (Reprint from *Faith At Work Magazine*, n.d.), pp. 5-6, 15; *Extraordinary Living for Ordinary Men* (Michigan: Zondervan, 1965), p. 43; *And Thy Neighbor* (Waco, Texas: Word Books, 1967), p. 111.

[9] Shoemaker, *A Young Man's View of the Ministry*, pp. 70, 182; *Children of the Second Birth*, p. 58, 175-187; *If I Be Lifted Up* (New York: Fleming H. Revell, 1931), p. 93; *How To Find God*, pp. 10-11; *Extraordinary Living For Ordinary Men*, pp. 43, 130.

[10] *Alcoholics Anonymous*. 3rd Ed. (New York: Alcoholics Anonymous World Services, 1976), pp. 67, 85, 88.

[11] Shoemaker, *Children of the Second Birth*, p. 16; *The Church Can Save The World*, p. 30; *God's Control*, pp. 115-16, 121; *National Awakening* (New York: Harper & Brothers, 1936), pp. 78, 83, 86, 88.

[12] Shoemaker, *A Young Man's View of the Ministry*, pp. 80, 86; *Religion That Works*, p. 85. Compare a similar account by the Apostle Paul in Acts 22:10: "What shall I do, Lord?" and see Shoemaker, *Confident Faith (New York: Fleming H. Revell, 1932)*, pp. 107, 110, 115; *How To Find God*, p. 10; *Extraordinary Living For Ordinary Men*, pp.
(continued...)

Finally, Shoemaker delivered a sermon which he titled, "What If I Had But One Sermon To Preach?"[13] And the theme verse was John 17:3:

> And this is life eternal, that they might know thee the only true God, and Jesus Christ, whom thou hast sent.[14]

At a later point in his life, Shoemaker was to use this John 17:3 verse to show how a person can get an anchor on faith by *beginning* with as much faith and understanding of God and Christ as one has and then obeying, following, and believing. Here was a fundamental in Shoemaker's "experiment of faith." In 1956, Shoemaker wrote:

> We do not start by trying to believe in immortality, we start with believing truly in God and Jesus Christ. This verse [John 17:3] seems to say to us, Begin with as much faith in God, in Christ, as you can. Give yourself to as much of the truth as you see in Christ. Obey Him and follow Him and believe in Him. And as the relationship between Him and you develops and deepens, there begins to be born within you a new life that is of God, a life that is incommensurate with death. The more you come to know and trust and love God, the less likely does it seem that in the end He will allow that to be destroyed which He has taken such care to create and to redeem. follow the faith that can be real to you here and now, and you will come to assurance later concerning the life beyond.[15]

We turn now to specifics which had great impact on the development of Alcoholics Anonymous.

---

[12] (...continued)
40-48. Dr. Bob's wife, Anne, used this concept at page 61 of the spiritual workbook she read to early AAs in the Smith home. See Dick B., *Anne Smith's Spiritual Workbook* (Seattle: Glen Abbey Books, 1993), pp. 61-63.

[13] Shoemaker, *Religion That Works*, pp. 9-20.

[14] See also Shoemaker, *Confident Faith*, p. 90.

[15] Samuel M. Shoemaker, "In Memoriam" (Princeton: The Graduate Council, June 10, 1966), pp. 2-3.

First, for at least twenty years—from 1918 to 1938—Shoemaker was a close friend and associate of Dr. Frank N. D. Buchman. In 1921, Buchman had a sense of specific mission to remake the world. By autumn of 1922, Buchman and a few friends had formed what they called "A First Century Christian Fellowship."[16] This name was very much in use throughout the 1920's, and continued to be used until the mid-1930's, particularly in America. At one point, Buchman's followers were called "The Groups;" and then, in 1928, a newspaper article described several members as the "Oxford Group." Although the groups themselves were in no way officially connected with Oxford University, the name "Oxford Group" appealed to Buchman; and it stuck. The "Oxford Group" often called itself "A First Century Christian Fellowship;" and Shoemaker, his associates, and early AAs often referred to themselves in that way.[17] But the name "Oxford Group" was very much in use by the time Dr. Bob became associated with the fellowship in early 1933 and when Bill became connected with it in late 1934. The Oxford Group became the legal name of the entity in England. However, in 1938, the concept of "Moral Re-Armament" came to Frank Buchman's mind. Group people often called themselves "Moral Re-Armament" from 1938 on; and the American contingent adopted "Moral Re-Armament, Inc." as the legal name for their corporation several years later. The Oxford Group and Moral Re-Armament are very much alive in the United States, Great Britain, Switzerland, Australia, and

---

[16] For a discussion of Oxford Group history, see Dick B., *The Oxford Group & Alcoholics Anonymous* (Seattle: Glen Abbey Books, 1992), pp. 11-15, 61-67.

[17] See Walter Houston Clark, *The Oxford Group Its History and Significance* (New York: Bookman Associates, 1951), p. 35; James D. Newton, *Uncommon Friends* (New York: Harcourt Brace Jovanovich, 1987), p. 187; Begbie, *Life Changers*, p. 122; Samuel M. Shoemaker, *Twice-Born Ministers* (New York: Fleming H. Revell, 1929), pp. 23, 90, 95, 100, 122, 147, 148; *Calvary Church Yesterday And Today* (New York: Fleming H. Revell, 1936), p. 270; Olive M. Jones, *Inspired Children* (New York: Harper & Brothers, 1933), p. ix; John Potter Cuyler, *Calvary Church in Action* (New York: Fleming H. Revell, 1934), p. 11; Irving Harris, *The Breeze of the Spirit* (New York: The Seabury Press, 1978), pp. 47, 58, 64; and Dick B., *Dr. Bob's Library*, p. 18.

many other parts of the world at the date of this writing. We shall have much more to say of the Oxford Group ideas at a later point.

Shoemaker was tremendously involved with the "Oxford Group" from its beginning. His books frequently referred to the Group's original name, "A First Century Christian Fellowship." Calvary Church, through its Calvary Rescue Mission (opened February 1, 1926), became a vehicle for carrying the Oxford Group message to thousands of alcoholics, including Bill Wilson's "sponsor," Ebby Thatcher, and Bill Wilson himself.[18]

Like a number of other non-alcoholics who played a role in A.A.'s founding, Sam Shoemaker had an interest in helping, and a compassion for, those who suffered from alcoholism. And it commenced long before Bill Wilson got sober or A.A. began. Shoemaker's daughter, Sally, informed the author that Shoemaker's concern may have arisen out of the Shoemaker family's own alcoholic, "Uncle Ned," who suffered from disastrous bouts with alcohol.[19] Shortly after beginning his ministry at Calvary Church in 1925, Shoemaker took an interest in the Calvary Rescue Mission where thousands of alcoholics received help.[20] Shoemaker helped Russell Firestone, the son of rubber magnate, Harvey Firestone, Sr., to sobriety through a Christian conversion experience in 1931.[21] Bill Wilson wrote Dr. Carl Jung that, at the time Rowland Hazard had begun working with the Oxford Group (between 1932 and 1934) and apparently with Shoemaker, "the Oxford Groups had already sobered a

---

[18] The Calvary Rescue Mission has been torn down, but was located at 346 East 23rd Street on the south side of the street between 1st and 2nd Avenues, New York City.

[19] Related to the author in a telephone conversation with Sally Shoemaker Robinson in July, 1993, at her home in Maryland.

[20] See Samuel M. Shoemaker, *Calvary Church Yesterday and Today*, pp. 247-50; *Children of the Second Birth*, pp. 14-16, 121-25, 127-28; Cuyler, *Calvary Church in Action*, pp. 61-70; and *Pass It On* (New York: Alcoholics Anonymous World Services, 1984), pp. 116-17.

[21] See Newton, *Uncommon Friends*, pp. 26-92; and Dick B., *The Akron Genesis of Alcoholics Anonymous* (Seattle: Glen Abbey Books, 1992), pp. 17-36.

number of alcoholics."[22] According to Bill, Shoemaker had even "housed a batch of drunks in an apartment near his church."[23] Shoemaker's younger daughter, Nickie Haggart, vividly recalls the frequency with which drunks appeared at the door of Shoemaker's quarters at Calvary House and were, by Shoemaker, fed and often sent to the Rescue Mission to "dry out" with the invitation that they later return and have a talk with Shoemaker.[24] And it was Shoemaker who worked with Charles Clapp, Jr., to help him recover from alcoholism. Clapp's recovery occurred about the same general time Bill first met Shoemaker.[25] So history records that Shoemaker's great interest in helping alcoholics to recovery through Christian conversion experiences was not limited to his association either with Bill Wilson or with A.A.

Shoemaker's Calvary House (opened in the autumn of 1928) became the place where Oxford Group founder Dr. Frank Buchman lived when he was in America. It was the site of many Oxford Group meetings and a major center of group work in America. In fact, it was virtually the American Headquarters for the Oxford Group. It housed the Oxford Group bookstore and staff offices and was the source of its major American outreach publication—*The Calvary Evangel*. Shoemaker himself was a principal American associate of Buchman's. He wrote the greatest number of Oxford Group books, participated widely in Oxford Group team activities around the world, and was one of the leaders at many Oxford Group houseparties, particularly those on the East Coast of the United States.

However, the greatest rift in Shoemaker's life came with the termination of his association with Frank Buchman and Moral Re-

---

[22] *The Language of the Heart* (New York: The A.A. Grapevine, Inc., 1988), pp. 277-78.

[23] *Alcoholics Anonymous Comes of Age* (New York: Alcoholics Anonymous World Services, 1979), p. 64.

[24] Interview of Nickie Haggart by the author at the Haggart home in Florida on September 22, 1993. (Calvary House is adjacent to, and east of, the church at 61 Gramercy Park North, New York City.)

[25] See Charles Clapp, Jr., *The Big Bender* (New York: Harper & Row, 1938).

Armament. In 1941, Sam announced to the American and British press that he had decided to end his association with Buchman.[26] Shoemaker asked Buchman to remove all personal and Oxford Group material and personnel from Calvary House, the large parish house attached to Calvary Church, which had, for fifteen years, been the home of, and office for, Buchman's work in America. The breach has never been fully explained or discussed, but it caused great distress among the followers of Buchman and of Shoemaker, and within Shoemaker's own family. In his press announcement, Shoemaker said he had misgivings about certain policies and points of view that had accompanied the development of Moral Re-Armament. In a telephone interview with the author in July of 1993, Shoemaker's daughter, Sally Shoemaker Robinson, said her father had told her that the principal reason for his break with Buchman was that Buchman had asked Sam to give up his post as rector of Calvary Church and assume a leadership position in the Oxford Group. Shoemaker told his daughter, Sally, that he had taken his vows and could not do this. In any event, Buchman apparently chose not to make a public response to the Calvary Church eviction and breach. Buchman went his way with Moral Re-Armament's world outreach while Shoemaker thereafter focused on personal work within the churches.[27]

Sam Shoemaker married Helen Smith Shoemaker, daughter of United States Senator and Mrs. H. Alexander Smith, in Princeton, New Jersey, on April 26, 1930. The pair had two children, Sally Falls Shoemaker (born December 11, 1931), and Helen Dominick

---

[26] See "Church Ejects Buchman Group," *New York Times*, November 8, 1941, p. 21.

[27] See Dick B., *The Oxford Group & Alcoholics Anonymous*, pp. 70-71; Garth Lean, *On The Tail of a Comet* (Colorado Springs: Helmers and Howard, 1988), p. 304; and Helen Shoemaker, *I Stand By The Door*, pp. 90-94. For extensive information about Sam Shoemaker's involvement with Faith At Work, see Karl A. Olsson, M.D., "The History of Faith At Work," (a five-part series of articles in *Faith At Work News*, 1982-1983; and "Sam Shoemaker and Faith at Work," a pamphlet on file at Faith At Work, Inc., 150 S. Washington St., Suite 204, Falls Church, VA 22046.

Shoemaker (born May 16, 1942).[28] Shoemaker died on the eve of All Saints' Day, October 31, 1963; and his wife, Helen, died on January 29, 1993.

---

[28] Shoemaker's older daughter, Sally Shoemaker Robinson, presently lives in Maryland. She is Canon to the Ordinary and Director of Episcopal Social Ministries for the Episcopal Archdiocese of Maryland. His younger daughter, Helen ("Nickie") Shoemaker Haggart, MSW, LCSW, is a clinical social worker and psychotherapist in private practice. She lives in Florida.

3

Sam and the A.A.-Oxford Group Link

The Oxford Group Origins of A.A.

You cannot speak of Sam Shoemaker and A.A. without speaking about the Oxford Group and A.A. For A.A., at its birth, was an integral part of the Oxford Group, and Shoemaker's ministry was similarly linked to the Oxford Group during A.A.'s formative years.

Alcoholics Anonymous has two distinctly different points of commencement in the Oxford Group. Each was linked with Sam Shoemaker, but each appears to have originated independently of Shoemaker and to have arisen from the Oxford Group itself.

The first point of origin had to do with the "Akron genesis" of Alcoholics Anonymous and is exemplified by A.A.'s original Akron, Ohio, nickname: "The alcoholic squad of the Oxford Group."[1] The second point of origin is a bit more complex and really is marked by the events during which Bill Wilson's old friend and "sponsor," Ebby Thatcher, carried the Oxford Group message to Bill when Bill was "in his cups" at the Wilson home in Brooklyn, New York.[2]

---

[1] *Dr. Bob and the Good Oldtimers* (New York: Alcoholics Anonymous World Services, Inc., 1980), pp. 137, 128, 156, 100.

[2] *Alcoholics Anonymous Comes of Age* (New York: Alcoholics Anonymous World Services, Inc., 1957), pp. 58-59; and *Pass It On* (New York: Alcoholics Anonymous World Services, Inc., 1984), pp. 111-116.

Our book will be very much concerned with A.A.'s "New York genesis" and how the events in New York produced Shoemaker's strong influence on A.A. But first, we believe a quick review is in order—a summary of the sequence of events at Akron which actually gave birth to A.A. in Akron, Ohio.[3]

In 1928, James D. Newton, a young and ardent Oxford Group adherent, came to Akron, at the behest of Harvey Firestone, Sr., to join Firestone Tire and Rubber Company. In Akron, Jim befriended Harvey's alcoholic son, Russell ("Bud"); and, in September of 1931, with the help of Sam Shoemaker, he managed to get Bud to a Conference of Episcopal Bishops in Denver, where a number of Oxford Group people were present. Sam Shoemaker—an Episcopal priest and an Oxford Group leader—was attending the conference. Shoemaker accompanied Jim and Bud on the train both to and from the Denver conference. During the train-ride back from Denver, on October 1, 1931, Shoemaker led Bud to a Christian conversion experience which relieved Bud of his alcoholism for a time. Shoemaker himself recorded the specifics about the Firestone conversion at great length in his journal.[4] There ends, so far as the author has learned, the only significant personal link between Shoemaker and early Akron A.A.

For once Bud had recovered and become active in the Oxford Group, Harvey Firestone, Sr., Bud Firestone, and Jim Newton persuaded Oxford Group Founder, Dr. Frank Buchman, to come to Akron in January of 1933 with an Oxford Group "team." Buchman and his team witnessed at public meetings and in church

[3] For a study of the Akron story, see Dick B., *The Akron Genesis of Alcoholics Anonymous* (Seattle: Glen Abbey Books, 1992).

[4] The author personally inspected the Shoemaker journal entries for the period September 18 through October 6, 1931. The author was permitted to do this at the home of Shoemaker's younger daughter in Florida during the author's visit there in September of 1993. The journal entries are filled with details about Shoemaker's interaction with Bud, Bud's wife Dorothy, and Harvey Firestone, Sr. During this same visit to Florida, the author compared the Shoemaker journal entries with those in Jim Newton's diary for the same period. The entries in Shoemaker's journal and in Newton's diary were very much in accord. The comparison took place at the home of Mr. and Mrs. James Newton in Fort Myers Beach, Florida, with Nickie Shoemaker Haggart also present.

pulpits to the life-changing deliverance of Bud Firestone and of many other Oxford Group people. Shoemaker was *not* among those present. But the meetings, the pulpits, and the newspapers were filled with Oxford Group language, ideas, and practices. Henrietta Seiberling, Anne Smith (Dr. Bob's wife), Clarace Williams, and Delphine Weber (all Akron citizens), attended the 1933 Oxford Group testimonials and soon got Dr. Bob interested in the Oxford Group. Dr. Bob's intense interest in, and enthusiasm for, the Oxford Group continued for at least the next six years.

Two-and-a-half years after the 1933 Oxford Group events in Akron, Bill Wilson met Dr. Bob at Henrietta Seiberling's home in Akron on Mother's Day, 1935. But by that time, Dr. Bob had already thoroughly immersed himself in Bible study; in Oxford Group, Christian, and other religious literature; in Oxford Group meetings; and in Oxford Group friendships. As far as the author's research to date has revealed, Sam Shoemaker never personally had any part in the Akron-Oxford Group beginnings except for the fact that several Shoemaker books, along with other Oxford Group and Christian literature, were widely read by all the Akron founders (Dr. Bob, Anne, Henrietta, T. Henry and Clarace Williams) and by other early members of "the alcoholic squad of the Oxford Group."[5] In any event, Dr. Bob was not getting sober with this vigorous program, though he was very much involved in it.

The picture on the East Coast was entirely different.

In 1931, a New Englander named Rowland Hazard had treated with the noted psychiatrist Dr. Carl Jung in Switzerland in an attempt to solve his alcohol problem.[6] Finally, after extensive and unsuccessful therapy, Rowland was told by Jung that there was no

---

[5] But see Appendix 10, which indicates Shoemaker may have been in Akron personally in 1934 and may have met with members of the "alcoholic squad" and others such as Anne Smith, Henrietta Seiberling, T. Henry Williams, and Clarace Williams.

[6] As to the time of Rowland's treatments with Dr. Jung, see Mel B., *New Wine* (Minnesota: Hazelden, 1991), pp. 16-17.

hope except through a conversion experience.[7] Jung recommended that Rowland align himself with a religious group and seek a religious conversion experience—a union with God (as Jung later explained). Rowland returned to the United States, became associated with the Oxford Group, had such an experience, and maintained sobriety for the rest of his life. At the point of this writing, little has been written as to how Rowland first "joined" the Oxford Group or who his early associates were. But Rowland soon became thoroughly versed in Oxford Group principles. He definitely became associated with Sam Shoemaker. And he also became a member of the vestry of Shoemaker's Calvary Episcopal Church in New York. In fact, in Calvary Church today, there are two stained glass windows to the south of the center street doors. They were given in memory of Rowland Hazard. Shoemaker spoke of these in one of his addresses to AAs; and the author has personally inspected the windows and then read the explanation about them in a Calvary Church publication.[8]

In any event, Rowland Hazard, F. Shepard ("Shep") Cornell, and Cebra Graves—all Oxford Group people—soon rescued Bill's old friend, Ebby Thatcher, from institutionalization for alcoholism. The three Oxford Group members all had endeavored to help alcoholics. Cebra was the son of the judge who released Ebby to the three men. Like Rowland, Shep was very much involved in Oxford Group activities and Oxford Group houseparties, and was thoroughly conversant with the Oxford Group life-changing program. Shep also was associated with Shoemaker; and he too became a member of the vestry of Shoemaker's Calvary church. Rowland, Shep, and Cebra led Ebby Thatcher to a conversion

---

[7] *Pass It On* contains the correspondence between Bill Wilson and Dr. Carl Jung in which Jung gave Wilson his recollection of the Rowland Hazard events. He told Wilson that Rowland's "craving for alcohol was the equivalent on a low level of the spiritual thirst of our being for wholeness, expressed in medieval language: the union with God." Jung quoted to Wilson the following from Psalm 42:1: "As the hart panteth after the water brooks, so panteth my soul after thee, O God" (See pp. 384-85).

[8] See Stephen S. Garmey, *Calvary Church New York City: A Guide To The Church* (New York: The Parish of Calvary-St. George's, n.d.), pp. 4-7.

experience through Oxford Group surrender "steps." And Ebby, in turn, carried the message to Bill Wilson that God had done for him (Ebby) what Ebby had been unable to do for himself: God had relieved Ebby of his alcoholism.[9]

Ultimately, Ebby took Bill Wilson to Shoemaker's Calvary Rescue Mission in New York located at 346 East 23rd Street on the south side of the street between 1st and 2nd Avenues. And Bill made a decision for Christ there at one of the rescue mission meetings. After several days of continued drinking, Bill made his way to Towns Hospital in New York where he had previously been three times hospitalized for alcoholism. Bill told Dr. William D. Silkworth, the Towns medical director, that he had "found something," and checked in for hospitalization this one, last time. As Bill's story at Towns is told in A.A.'s "Big Book" (*Alcoholics Anonymous*), and in many other Wilson accounts, Bill "humbly offered [himself] to God," went through the equivalent of some Oxford Group surrender steps he had learned from Ebby, and then had a conversion experience. In two different accounts of this religious experience, Bill himself said explicitly that he had been "born again."[10] These precise "born again" words have seldom, if ever, been mentioned. But they were common in Shoemaker's

---

[9] Ebby's recovery from alcoholism was far from immediate. He began drinking shortly after he had "converted" Bill. And his subsequent years were beset with frequent drinking bouts and institutionalization. He finally got sober in Texas many years later.

[10] During a research trip to the archives at Bill's home at Stepping Stones in Bedford Hills, New York, the author—in August of 1992—inspected, and was permitted to copy, a manuscript of Bill's dictation to Ed. B. on September 1, 1954, at the Hotel Bedford (Bedford Hills, New York). The manuscript is titled "*W. G. Wilson Recollections*." After transcribing Bill's description of his conversion experience, the manuscript quotes him on page 130, as saying: "For sure, I'd been born again." Another transcript of the September 1, 1954, dictations—also located at Stepping Stones Archives and inspected and copied by the author, with the permission of the archivist, contains the identical "born again" words at page 103. The phrase "born again" was not included either in the account in *Pass It On* at page 121, nor in the version of Bill's Story that was published in the Big Book. See also Dick B., *The Akron Genesis of Alcoholics Anonymous*, p. 330.

books, sermons, and teachings from John 3:3-7.[11] In any event, Bill's conversion experience came to be called, by Bill and by several others, Bill's "hot flash" experience, after which he never drank again.

Bill was discharged from Towns Hospital on December 18, 1934, and he immediately plunged into Oxford Group activities which centered around Sam Shoemaker's Calvary Rescue Mission and also Calvary House—a parish building which Shoemaker's church had erected next door to Calvary Church at 61 Gramercy Park North, and which housed Oxford Group meetings and personnel.[12] For the next two-and-a-half years, Bill was very much involved in Oxford Group meetings, in Oxford Group houseparties, and with Oxford Group people. During that period (mid-December of 1934 to mid-August of 1937), Shoemaker's influence on Bill—however it occurred—was at its peak as far as any absorption by Bill of Shoemaker ideas which would later be incorporated into the Big Book and Twelve Steps is concerned. Just following his release from Towns in December, 1934, and for the next five months, Bill tried feverishly, but without success, to convert other drunks and help them recover. Then, after receiving from Dr. Silkworth the suggestion that he approach alcoholics first with the deadly medical facts about their problem, Bill landed in Akron and met Dr. Bob. Apparently he followed Dr. Silkworth's suggestion with Dr. Bob. *Pass It On* reported:

---

[11] In John 3:3, the Bible states: "Jesus answered and said unto him, 'Verily, verily, I say unto thee, Except a man be born again, he cannot see the kingdom of God." In John 3:5, Jesus said, "Verily, verily, I say unto thee, Except a man be born of water and *of* the Spirit, he cannot enter into the kingdom of God." In John 3:7, Jesus said, "Marvel not that I said unto thee, Ye must be born again." For one of many examples of Shoemaker's teaching on this subject, see his book, *National Awakening* (New York: Harper & Brothers, 1936), pp. 55-66, which contains a sermon preached in St. Paul's Church, Stockbridge, Mass., June 7, 1936. See also Samuel Shoemaker, *Children of the Second Birth* (New York: Fleming H. Revell, 1927), pp. 25, 47; and *Twice-Born Ministers* (New York: Fleming H. Revell, 1929), pp. 10, 56.

[12] A photostat of Bill's record of admission to the Charles B. Towns Hospital on December 11, 1934 and of his release on December 18, 1934, appears in *Pass It On* at page 104.

> [Bill] "went very slowly on the 'fireworks' of religious experience." First, he talked about his own case until Bob "got a good identification with me." Then, as Dr. William D. Silkworth had urged, Bill hammered home the physical aspects of the disease, "the verdict of inevitable annihilation." . . .
>
> Dr. Bob noted that Bill "was a man . . . who had been cured by the very means I had been trying to employ, that is to say, the spiritual approach. He gave me information about the subject of alcoholism which was undoubtedly helpful. Of far more importance was the fact that he was the first living human with whom I had ever talked who knew what he was talking about in regard to alcoholism from actual experience. In other words, he talked my language" (p. 68).

There the two streams of Oxford Group beginnings converged, and the birth of A.A. occurred a short time later at Dr. Bob's Akron home at 855 Ardmore Avenue on June 10, 1935—the date on which Dr. Bob had his last drink.

The foregoing brief summary is discussed and documented by the author in much detail in his books, *The Oxford Group & Alcoholics Anonymous* and *The Akron Genesis of Alcoholics Anonymous*.[13] Accounts can also be found in A.A.'s Conference Approved *Alcoholics Anonymous Comes of Age*, *DR. BOB and the Good Oldtimers*, *Pass It On*, and *The Language of the Heart*, as well as the Big Book.[14] The history is also covered in two excellent works by Dr. Ernest Kurtz and Mel B.[15]

The important point to be made here is that the evidence thus far unearthed by this author does not support the idea that the spiritual

---

[13] See Dick B., *The Oxford Group & Alcoholics Anonymous* (Seattle: Glen Abbey Books, 1992), pp. 69-71, 89-109; and *The Akron Genesis of Alcoholics Anonymous*, pp. 1-4, 139-166, 181-182, 200, 326-333.

[14] *A. A. Comes of Age*, pp. 58-75; *DR. BOB and the Good Oldtimers*, pp. 60-75; *Pass It On*, pp. 109-145; *The Language of the Heart* (New York: The A.A. Grapevine, Inc., 1988), pp. 195-200, 244-247, 276-286, 355-360, 367-368; and Big Book, pp. xv-xvi, 8-15, 26-28.

[15] Ernest Kurtz, *Not-God: A History of Alcoholics Anonymous*. Expanded ed. (Minnesota: Hazelden, 1991), pp. 7-36; and Mel B., *New Wine*, pp. 9-26, 67-73, 77-88.

program of the fellowship of Alcoholics Anonymous originated with Reverend Sam Shoemaker. Instead, the evidence probably indicates that it originated with the Oxford Group.[16] And, in this study of Shoemaker and those of his ideas which influenced A.A., we will first discuss the Shoemaker contributions in terms of Oxford Group principles Shoemaker supported, articulated, taught, and probably partially authored. Frank Buchman's close associate and biographer, Garth Lean, who was also a resident at Calvary House for a time and was a good friend of Sam Shoemaker's, observed to the author that almost every Shoemaker idea that can be found in A.A. can also be found in contemporaneous Oxford Group literature that was not written by Shoemaker. However, as he researched for this book—and particularly as he interviewed Shoemaker's daughters, Sally Shoemaker Robinson and Helen Shoemaker Haggart—the author began to see more and more evidence of Bill's close contact with Shoemaker from the beginnings of his sobriety and therefore that Bill must himself have been very much influenced in his Oxford Group thinking by Shoemaker's teaching. And this, of course, is what Bill said.

Nonetheless, the Oxford Group ideas in A.A. were those taught not only by Shoemaker, but also by many other Oxford Group writers. And this author, at least, cannot be sure the ideas reached A.A. only through Shoemaker. In fact, Bill Wilson seemed careful, in his statements about A.A.'s roots, to mention *both* the Oxford Group and Shoemaker whenever he specified the principles themselves. We will therefore review, at this point, those basic

---

[16] As discussed in the next footnote, some of A.A.'s basic *ideas* appear to have come neither from Shoemaker nor from the Oxford Group but rather from the Bible itself, from such Bible devotionals as *The Upper Room*, and from a number of non-Oxford Group writers such as James Allen, Oswald Chambers, Glenn Clark, Henry Drummond, Emmet Fox, E. Stanley Jones, and Toyohiko Kagawa, to name only a few. However, many of the Oxford Group people, particularly those associated with early A.A. in Akron, regularly read many titles by these non-Oxford Group authors. For a discussion of the uncertainty as to where and how Rowland Hazard first became aligned with the Oxford Group—very possibly in Switzerland—see Mel B., *New Wine*, p. 19.

Oxford Group principles which we found by research and analysis to have influenced A.A.[17]

In this respect our approach differs substantially from that of Dr. Charles Taylor Knippel, who did a thorough and scholarly review of what Knippel considered to be the theological influence of Sam Shoemaker on Bill Wilson's Twelve Step program of recovery.[18] Knippel rightly concludes, we believe, that Shoemaker's theology influenced Bill Wilson. His research centered largely around Shoemaker documents he discovered at the Episcopal Church Archives in Texas. He points to the fact that previous A.A. historians, such as Dr. Ernest Kurtz, William Pittman, and John Woolverton, as well as the authors of *Pass It On*, made few references to Sam Shoemaker. And Knippel attributes the dearth of extrinsic evidence about the Shoemaker-Wilson relationship to the fact that prior historians simply lacked access to Shoemaker papers that were later made available to Knippel. The problems arising out of Dr. Knippel's approach are two: (1) he did not examine and analyze the Oxford Group influences—other than those from Shoemaker—on Wilson or on the other founders of A.A. in Akron; and (2) he himself said he really had found little evidence concerning Shoemaker and Wilson in the period of the 1930's—other than the statements that Wilson and Shoemaker themselves had made. His conclusions, therefore, are not grounded on a treatment of other Oxford Group—A.A. roots; and they do not rest on adequate extrinsic evidence of what Shoemaker and A.A. did together in A.A.'s formative period.

This author believes that the intrinsic evidence in A.A. writings shows a remarkable resemblance to Shoemaker writings—those that Knippel saw and those available in Shoemaker's published books. But it also shows a remarkable resemblance to language found in

---

[17] For our discussion and presentation of these principles, see Dick B., *The Oxford Group & Alcoholics Anonymous*; *The Akron Genesis of Alcoholics Anonymous*; and *Anne Smith's Spiritual Workbook* (Seattle: Glen Abbey Books, 1993).

[18] See Charles Taylor Knippel, *Samuel M. Shoemaker's Theological Influence on William G. Wilson's Twelve Step Spiritual Program of Recovery (Alcoholics Anonymous)*. Dissertation. St. Louis University, 1987.

Oxford Group literature written by others—people whose writings were known to have been read by, and to have influenced, Dr. Bob, Anne Smith, Henrietta Seiberling, T. Henry and Clarace Williams, and even—in two or three cases—Bill and Lois Wilson. Further, many strong influences on A.A. ideas can, in the words of Dr. Bob, be found in, and traced to, the Bible. Also, to non-Oxford Group Christian writers, to the non-Oxford Group Bible devotionals used in early A.A., and even to "new thought" writers such as Emmet Fox—who appears to have had no connection either with the Oxford Group or with Shoemaker. In short, the jury is still out on precisely where Bill Wilson got his ideas. And it is the author's purpose to pin-point as accurately as possible, in the various titles he has written and will write, the precise places in the Bible, the Bible devotionals, non-Shoemaker Oxford Group literature, Shoemaker literature, other Christian literature, and other religious sources where A.A. ideas can be found. Other writers are doing and have done similar research and writing; and much more remains to be done.[19]

The Twenty-Eight Oxford Group Ideas That Influenced A.A.

In writing *The Oxford Group & Alcoholics Anonymous* and *Anne Smith's Spiritual Workbook*, the author reviewed an immense amount of Oxford Group literature and corresponded with, and interviewed, many Oxford Group writers and activists.[20] As a

[19] See, for example, Mel B., *New Wine*; and Bill Pittman, *AA The Way It Began* (Seattle: Glen Abbey Books, 1988).

[20] Among these were: (1) Garth Lean, of Oxford, whose book, *On The Tail of a Comet*, is the principal biography of Oxford Group Founder, Dr. Frank N. D. Buchman. Lean wrote a large number of other Oxford Group books. (2) Kenneth. D. Belden, of London, Oxford Group activist from the 1930's to date, who edited and designed successive editions of *Remaking The World* (the collected speeches of Dr. Frank N. D.

(continued...)

result, he identified in the Oxford Group some twenty-eight concepts which can be found in A.A. These have been grouped, in the manner set forth below, for easier understanding.

Quite remarkably, almost every concept can be found in the spiritual workbook which Dr. Bob's wife, Anne, compiled, wrote, and read to early AAs and their families in the Smith home *before* either the Big Book or the Twelve Steps were written. This point is extremely important in examining A.A.'s Big Book, whose writing did not begin until well after Anne Smith had compiled and written most of her spiritual workbook. The fact is that Anne Smith, though she had read several Shoemaker books and several other Oxford Group books, had probably never met Sam Shoemaker at the time she was writing down and passing on the Oxford Group ideas she discussed in her spiritual workbook. Though the author has as yet found no eye-witness who can verify that Anne read her workbook material to Bill Wilson, there is eye-witness recollection that Anne read the material to early AAs in her home and also clear evidence that Bill Wilson was living in the Smith home for three months in the summer of 1935 when Anne was reading to Bill from Scripture and Christian literature.

---

[20] (...continued)
Buchman) and also authored a number of Oxford Group books. (3) Michael B. Hutchinson, of Oxford, long an Oxford Group activist and associate of Garth Lean. (4) George Vondermuhll, Jr., of Connecticut, corporate secretary of Moral Re-Armament, Inc. for many years, and an Oxford Group activist. (5) Eleanor Napier Forde Newton, of Florida, close friend of both Dr. Frank N. D. Buchman and Dr. Samuel Shoemaker, Jr.—connected with the Oxford Group from the 1920's to date—and the author of one of the first and most important Oxford Group pamphlets, *The Guidance of God*, published in 1930. (6) James Draper Newton, of Florida, close friend of both Buchman and Shoemaker, also connected with the Oxford Group from the 1920's, and author of a recent book—*Uncommon Friends*—about several of his famous friends, including Oxford Group people. (7) Mrs. W. Irving Harris, presently of Ohio, widow of Reverend W. Irving Harris, and who was a friend of Shoemaker and of Bill Wilson, and lived at and was in charge of the Oxford Group bookstore at Shoemaker's Calvary House in New York. (8) Reverend T. Willard Hunter, of Claremont, California, author, columnist, friend of Buchman and Shoemaker, and currently a frequent writer and speaker on the Oxford Group and Alcoholics Anonymous. The writings of these people are described in the bibliography at the end of our book.

Because of this fact, and the fact that much of Anne's language closely resembles that used by Bill in his writing, the author has concluded that many of Anne's ideas directly inspired Bill's language in the Big Book and Twelve Steps. The conclusion is buttressed by the evidence that Bill Wilson actually asked Dr. Bob's wife, Anne, to write the Big Book chapter which came to be called "To Wives."[21]

The facts about the Wives chapter are these: (1) Bill suggested that Anne have a chapter in the Big Book to herself. He stated, "Anne should do the one portraying the wife."[22] (2) Anne apparently declined and, as speculated in A.A.'s conference approved history, "Her modesty—her inclination toward staying in the background—may have been the reason that she did not write it."[23] (3) Bill did not ask his wife, Lois, to write the chapter.[24] (4) Lois actually suggested that she (Lois) write the chapter; and Bill said, "Oh, no. It should be in the same style as the book."[25] (5) Ultimately, Bill Wilson wrote that chapter, and Lois was both mad and hurt.[26] Whatever significance the "Wives" chapter incident may have, the observations of a number of other writers, including early A.A. member, John R., tend to support the author's thesis that Anne's words and phrases had substantial impact and influence on Big Book language.[27]

---

[21] Big Book, pp. 104-121.

[22] *DR. BOB and the Good Oldtimers*, p. 152.

[23] *DR. BOB and the Good Oldtimers*, p. 152.

[24] *DR. BOB and the Good Oldtimers*, p. 152.

[25] *DR. BOB and the Good Oldtimers*, p. 152.

[26] *Pass It On*, p. 200.

[27] See Bob Smith and Sue Smith Windows, *Children of the Healer: The Story of Dr. Bob's Kids* (Illinois: Parkside Publishing Corporation, 1992), pp. 28-29, 41, 2. Dr. Bob's daughter observes, at page 41: "There wasn't any program then. The restitution idea was one of the things he [Bill Wilson] got from the Oxford Group. Mom's notebook [Anne Smith's spiritual workbook] shows how much of A.A. came from there—restitution, surrendering, and so forth." See also Mary C. Darrah, *Sister Ignatia: Angel of Alcoholics Anonymous* (Chicago: Loyola University Press, 1992), pp. 115-116. Darrah states:

(continued...)

And now to the twenty-eight Oxford Group ideas that influenced A.A. Our footnotes in this chapter identify the places in Shoemaker's writings where each of these ideas can be found. And Appendix One sets out in its footnotes the specific places where these *same* principles can be found in the Bible itself, in non-Shoemaker Oxford Group books, in Anne Smith's Spiritual Workbook, in Shoemaker's writings, and—where it is the case—in A.A. literature.

The Twenty-Eight Oxford Group Ideas

In the beginning, God.

1. *God*—Biblical descriptions of Him as Creator, Maker, Father, Spirit, Love, Living God.[28]
2. *God has a plan*—His will for man—and provides definite, accurate information for the individual who wants the plan fulfilled.[29]

---

[27] (...continued)
"Many present day A.A. practices, slogans and ideas leap out of Anne Smith's Oxford Group journal" [which we prefer to call Anne Smith's Spiritual Workbook, because it contains far more than just 'Oxford Group' ideas]. See also Dick B., *The Akron Genesis of Alcoholics Anonymous*, pp. 109-110. There we quote John R., an A.A. oldtimer, who said verbally and in writing "Before one of those meetings [in Dr. Bob's home], Anne used to pull out a little book [her spiritual workbook] and quote from it. We would discuss it. Then we would see what Anne would suggest from it for our discussion." Furthermore, Bill Wilson many times referred to Anne's morning guidance sessions in which she would *read* to Bill and Dr. Bob. See, for example, *Pass It On*. p. 147.

[28] Samuel M. Shoemaker, *The Conversion of the Church* (New York: Fleming H. Revell, 1932), pp. 33, 49, 50, 51, 124; *National Awakening* (New York: Harper & Brothers, 1936), pp. 48, 55, 97, 107, 108; *Confident Faith* (New York: Fleming H. Revell, 1932), pp. 38, 54, 59, 74, 83, 96, 106, 107, 152, 183; *Realizing Religion* (New York: Association Press, 1921), p. 35; *Children of the Second Birth*, p. 42; and *Christ's Words From The Cross* (New York: Fleming H. Revell, 1933), p. 43.

[29] Shoemaker, *Children of the Second Birth*, p. 27; *Religion That Works* (New York: Fleming H. Revell, 1928), p. 19; and *National Awakening*, pp. 41, 83, 89-98.

3. *Man's chief end*—To do God's Will, thereby receiving the blessings God promises to those who align their lives with His Will.[30]
4. *Belief*—We must start with the belief that God IS.[31]

Sin—Estrangement from God—The Barrier of Self.

5. *Sin is a reality*—The selfishness and self-centeredness that blocks man from God and from others.[32]

Finding or Rediscovering God.

6. *Surrender*—The turning point which makes it possible for man to have a relationship with God by surrendering his will, ego, and sins to God.[33]
7. *Soul-Surgery*—The "art" or way which enables man through the steps of Confidence, Confession, Conviction, Conversion, and Conservation (the 5 C's) to have the sin or spiritual disease cured.[34]

---

[30] Shoemaker, *National Awakening*, pp. 42, 47; and *Christ's Words From The Cross*, p. 50.

[31] Shoemaker, *National Awakening*, pp. 40-41; *Children of the Second Birth*, p. 40; *Religion That Works*, p. 55; *Confident Faith*, p. 187; and *The Gospel According To You* (New York: Fleming H. Revell, 1934), p. 47.

[32] Shoemaker, *The Conversion of the Church*, p. 29; *If I Be Lifted Up* (New York: Fleming H. Revell, 1931), p. 131; *Twice-Born Ministers*, p. 30; *God's Control* (New York: Fleming H. Revell, 1939), p. 56; *How To Become a Christian* (New York: Fleming H. Revell, 1953), p. 56; and *They're On The Way* (New York: E.P. Dutton & Co., 1951), p. 154.

[33] Shoemaker, *Realizing Religion*. p. 30; *A Young Man's View of the Ministry* (New York: Association Press, 1923), p. 55; *Children of the Second Birth*, p. 16; *The Conversion of the Church*, p. 78; *The Church Can Save The World* (New York: Harper & Brothers, 1938), pp. 113-114; *God's Control*, p. 138; and *The Experiment of Faith* (New York: Harper & Brothers, 1957), p. 25.

[34] Shoemaker, *The Conversion of the Church*, p. 12; and *Realizing Religion*, pp. 79-80.

8. *Life-change*—The result in which man, through a spiritual experience, becomes God-centered instead of self-centered and focuses on helping others.[35]

The Path They Followed to Establish a Relationship with God.

9. *Decision*—The action by which man verbalizes his surrender and gives in to God, saying, essentially, "Thy will be done."[36]
10. *Self-examination*—A "moral" inventory in which man takes stock of his sins and their consequences.[37]
11. *Confession*—Sharing with God and another person the inventory results.[38]
12. *Conviction*—Readiness to change resulting from man's conviction that he has sinned and that Christ miraculously can cure.[39]
13. *Conversion*—The New Birth, Change, namely, that which occurs when man gives himself to God, is regenerated, has part of God's nature imparted to him, and finds the barrier of sin gone.[40]

---

[35] Shoemaker, *The Church Can Save The World*, pp. 93, 118, 124, 153; and *God's Control*, pp. 21-22.

[36] Shoemaker: *Children of the Second Birth*, pp. 58, 175-187 (where an entire chapter is devoted to the topic); *If I Be Lifted Up*, p. 93; *The Conversion of the Church*, pp. 39-40, 77; *National Awakening*, pp. 45, 46, 48, 51; *The Church Can Save The World*, p. 120; *Religion That Works*, pp. 46-47; and *How To Find God* (Reprint from *Faith at Work Magazine*, n.d.).

[37] Shoemaker, *The Conversion of the Church*, pp. 30-34; *Twice-Born Ministers* (New York: Fleming H. Revell, 1929), p. 182; *How To Become A Christian*, pp. 56-67; and *God's Control*, pp. 104-105.

[38] Shoemaker, *The Conversion of the Church*, pp. 26-39; *Realizing Religion*, pp. 80-81; and *The Church Can Save The World*, pp. 110-112.

[39] Shoemaker, *Realizing Religion*, pp. 21, 81-82; *The Church Can Save The World*, pp. 153, 93-94; and *National Awakening*, p. 5.

[40] Shoemaker, *Children of the Second Birth*, p. 32; *National Awakening*, pp. 55, 57-58; *How To Become A Christian*, pp. 65-82; and *How To Find God*, p. 7.

14. *Restitution*—Righting the wrongs and enabling man to cut the cord of sin that binds him to the past.[41]

Jesus Christ

15. *Jesus Christ*—The source of power as the Divine Redeemer and Way-Shower by whose transforming power man can be changed.[42]

Spiritual Growth—Continuance.

16. *Conservation*—Continuance as an idea, by which man maintains and grows in his life of grace.[43]
17. *Daily Surrender*—A process in which man engages in daily self-examination and surrender to get rid of newly accumulated sin and selfishness.[44]
18. *Guidance*—The walk by faith in which the Holy Spirit gives Divine Guidance to a life that is changed from sin to God.[45]

---

[41] Shoemaker, *The Conversion of the Church*, pp. 47-48; *Children of the Second Birth*, pp. 93-96; and *God's Control*, pp. 63-64.

[42] Shoemaker, *Religion That Works*, pp. 21-25; *With the Holy Spirit and With Fire* (New York: Harper & Brothers, 1960), pp. 29-33; *Christ and This Crisis* (New York: Fleming H. Revell, 1943), p. 35; and *They're On The Way*, p. 153 .

[43] Shoemaker, *Realizing Religion*, p. 80; *Religion That Works*, pp. 14-15; and *Children of the Second Birth*, p. 16.

[44] Shoemaker, *The Gospel According To You*, pp. 81-91; *The Church Can Save The World*, pp. 96-97; *The Conversion of the Church*, p. 79; and *Children of the Second Birth*, p. 157..

[45] Shoemaker, *With The Holy Spirit and With Fire*, pp. 30-31; *The Conversion of the Church*, pp. 49-50, 86; *Twice-Born Ministers*, pp. 184-185; and *National Awakening*, p. 86.

19. *The Four Absolutes*—Christ's standards, the standards of absolute honesty, purity, unselfishness, and love, by which man's life can be tested for harmony with God's will.[46]
20. *Quiet Time*—A period in which man can receive Divine Guidance and be sensitive to the sway of the Spirit.[47]
21. *Bible study*—Meditation which enables man daily to feed his soul on God's revelation of His Universal Will in the written Word.[48]
22. *Prayer*—Talking to God.[49]
23. *Listening to God for Leading Thoughts and Writing Down Guidance Received*—The means of receiving revelation of God's Particular or Private Will for a man.[50]
24. *Checking*—Testing thoughts to be sure they represent God's Guidance and not just self-deception.[51]

The Spiritual Experience or Awakening.

25. *Knowledge of God's will*—Attaining, with the Guidance of the Holy Spirit, a knowledge of God's Universal Will as

[46] Shoemaker, *Twice-Born Ministers*, p. 150; *The Church Can Save The World*, pp. 110, 119-120; *How To Become a Christian*, p. 57; *How You Can Help Other People* (New York: E. P. Dutton and Co., 1946), p. 59; and Helen Smith Shoemaker, *I Stand By The Door* (New York: Harper & Row, 1967), pp. 24-26.

[47] Shoemaker, *Realizing Religion*, pp. 65-66; *The Conversion of the Church*, p. 60; *The Church Can Save The World*, p. 126; and *Children of the Second Birth*, p. 97.

[48] Shoemaker, *Realizing Religion*, pp. 58-62; *The Conversion of the Church*, pp. 49, 60, 79; *Children of the Second Birth*, p. 97; and *Twice-Born Ministers*, p. 184.

[49] Shoemaker, *Realizing Religion*, pp. 63-65; *National Awakening*, p. 53; and *Children of the Second Birth*, p. 149.

[50] Shoemaker, *The Conversion of the Church*, pp. 60-66; *Children of the Second Birth*, p. 47; and *Religion That Works*, pp. 64-65.

[51] Shoemaker, *The Conversion of the Church*, pp. 51-57; and *Twice-Born Ministers*, p. 125.

revealed in the Bible, and receiving knowledge of His particular Will through obedience to His Universal Will.[52]

26. *God-consciousness*—The total change resulting from the experience of God when His will is known, lived, and witnessed.[53]

Fellowship with God and Believers, and Witness by Life and Word.

27. *Fellowship*—The Fellowship of the Holy Spirit in which believers maintain fellowship with God and mutually sacrifice to win others to the fellowship of the love of God revealed by Jesus Christ.[54]
28. *Witness by Life and Word*—Sharing with others by personal evangelism the fruits of the life changed and the proof of God's forgiveness and power.[55]

Other Statements of Oxford Group Ideas

We have just described, in our own words, the Oxford Group principles we believe influenced A.A. We have also shown that Shoemaker wrote extensively about each idea. But there are other statements of Oxford Group principles—statements much more

---

[52] Shoemaker, *The Conversion of the Church*, pp. 49-50; *Twice-Born Ministers*, pp. 184-185; *A Young Man's View of the Ministry*, pp. 78, 80; *Religion That Works*, pp. 36, 46, 58; *Christ And This Crisis*, p. 106; and *The Church Can Save The World*, p. 110.

[53] Shoemaker, *Twice-Born Ministers*, p. 123; *How To Become A Christian*, p. 52; and *By The Power of God* (New York: Harper and Brothers, 1954), pp. 134-56.

[54] Shoemaker, *Religion That Works*, pp. 66-76; *The Conversion of the Church*, pp. 87-104, 114-115; *The Gospel According To You*, p. 190; and Helen Smith Shoemaker, *I Stand By The Door*, pp. 109-110.

[55] Shoemaker, *One Boy's Influence* (New York: Association Press, 1925), p. 15; *They're On The Way*, p. 159; *How To Become A Christian*, p. 80; and *The Church Alive* (New York: E. P. Dutton, 1951), p. 139.

brief and summary in nature. They have been used in the Oxford Group and elsewhere to describe the Oxford Group program; and we set them out below to show that Shoemaker also subscribed to these ideas.

Reverend Sherwood Day's Seven Bible Principles

Reverend Sherwood Sunderland Day began playing an important role in the Oxford Group at least as early as 1917.[56] In that year, a small group of men gathered around Oxford Group Founder, Dr. Frank Buchman, in what he called "a companionship of fellowship and silence." These included John Mott, the son of the world YMCA leader, Dr. John R. Mott; Howard Walter, who later authored *Soul-Surgery*, a basic Oxford Group primer on the 5 C's; and Reverend Day, who was one of Dr. Frank Buchman's earliest traveling companions, and who later became a good friend of Reverend Sam Shoemaker's. Prior to the time in 1925 when Shoemaker was called to be rector of Calvary Episcopal Church in New York, Buchman, Day, and Shoemaker traveled abroad together.

Day put together an Oxford Group pamphlet, titled *The Principles of The Group*.[57] It was printed in Great Britain. Day stated at the beginning of his pamphlet:

> The principles of "The Oxford Group" are the principles of the Bible. The Oxford Group is not an organization, not a sect, not even a new method. The Group is a life—that life which is hid with Christ in God. . . .[58]

---

[56] In an interview with the author at her home in Florida in September, 1993, Shoemaker's daughter, Nickie Haggart, told the author that Sherwood Day was probably Shoemaker's closest friend.

[57] Sherwood Sunderland Day, *The Principles of the Group* (Oxford: University Press, n.d.).

[58] See Colossians 3:2,3: "Set your affection [thoughts] on things above, not on things on the earth. For ye are dead, and your life is hid with Christ in God."

> The principles of the "Group" are as old as the experiences recorded in the Bible, and should be to-day, as they were in the early Church, the normal and constant practice of Christians.

Day then set forth the following seven Biblical principles:

1. *God-Guidance*. He said: "By 'guidance' is meant communion—communion with our Father, the Living God. 'Listening to God,' 'two-way prayer,' 'thinking God's thoughts after Him,' are all phrases often used of the experience."[59]

2. *Fearless Dealing with Sin*. He said: "While the first great fact of history is Jesus Christ, the second is the presence of sin." He defined sin as "Anything that separates from God or from another person." He continued: "The Bible frankly faces the fact of sin and offers a cure. . . . Christ gave men courage honestly and fearlessly to face their sins, and then showed them the *way out*" [emphasis ours].[60]

3. *Sharing*. He said: "A sharing Christian is a propagating Christian," a sentence often used by Shoemaker.[61] Day explained: "Sharing, as the word is used by the Group, covers two distinct things, further described as confession and witness." He said the facts about sharing were, in the words of James 5:16, that one must "Confess your faults one to another." The other aspect of sharing is its necessity in helping others because it immediately

---

[59] Compare the language of A.A.'s Eleventh Step: "Sought through prayer and meditation to improve our conscious contact with God *as we understood Him*, praying only for the knowledge of His will for us and the power to carry that out." Both the Wilsons and the Smiths frequently spoke of seeking the guidance of God. See *Lois Remembers* (New York: Al-Anon Family Group Headquarters, 1979), p. 101; *Alcoholics Anonymous Comes of Age* (New York: Alcoholics Anonymous World Services, 1957), p. 48; *DR. BOB and the Good Oldtimers*, pp. 86-87, 115, 187.

[60] As to this language, compare A.A.'s Step Four: "Made a searching and fearless moral inventory of ourselves." Interestingly, AAs originally wanted to call their Big Book "The Way Out." See discussion of the various names that were considered and the majority vote for "The Way Out." *Pass It On*, pp. 202-203.

[61] See, for example, Shoemaker, *The Conversion of the Church*, p. 43.

establishes confidence. He said: "This we never do by 'preaching' but by sharing our own experiences."[62]

4. *The Necessity For Adequate Intelligent Expressional Activity*. He said: "There is no vital sustained experience of Jesus Christ where there is not expressional activity." He said: "The answer is a God-guided, released life with constant outgo into the lives of needy people. We really come to know God as we share Him with others."[63]

5. *Stewardship*. He said: "A surrendered life means a life in which every possession of whatever kind is held in trust to be administered under the guidance of the Holy Spirit."

6. *Team-Work*. He said: "Jesus Christ believed in teamwork. He gathered a small group about Him and set the example for all His followers in this respect. . . . Individuals were members of a living body whose Head was Jesus Christ. . . . Truth is presented more adequately through a group than through an individual."[64]

7. *Loyalty*. He said: "The person or group of persons embodying for us the highest challenge we know, the person or persons that have been used to reveal Jesus Christ to us, are persons and groups which demand our loyalty."

In his book, *The Breeze of the Spirit*, Reverend W. Irving Harris said Shoemaker had encouraged Reverend Day to outline the primary New Testament principles which he and Day had learned to accept together and which had come to form a part in his own (Shoemaker's) credo. Harris said that, in one of the 1926 issues of *The Calvary Evangel* (Shoemaker's parish publication), "Sherry"

---

[62] Compare A.A.'s concept of sharing experience as expressed in its Preamble and, as follows, in the Foreword to the Big Book's Third Edition: "Each day, somewhere in the world, recovery begins when one alcoholic talks with another alcoholic, sharing experience, strength, and hope" (p. xxii).

[63] Compare Big Book, p. 20: "Our very lives, as ex-problem drinkers, depend upon our constant thought of others and how we may help meet their needs."

[64] Compare Tradition Five of A.A.'s Twelve Traditions in The Long Form, at page 565 of the Big Book: "Each Alcoholics Anonymous group ought to be a spiritual entity *having but one primary purpose*—that of carrying its message to the alcoholic who still suffers."

(Day) had summed up the Shoemaker-Day convictions. In *The Breeze of the Spirit*, Harris set out "Sherry" Day's convictions as they had appeared in Shoemaker's *Calvary Evangel*. And these "convictions" are, in only slightly modified form, the principles set forth in Day's Oxford Group pamphlet which we reviewed above.[65] Reverend Harris gave Day's principles as an example of a typical sermon which people in Calvary pews began to hear when Shoemaker took over the post as their pastor at the beginning of his Calvary ministry.

"What is the Oxford Group?"

To avoid redundance, we will only outline here the principles of the Oxford Group that were stated in a little anonymous book, *What Is The Oxford Group?*. This book was widely read by Dr. Bob and circulated in early Akron A.A.[66] Interestingly, we have been unable to find, from today's Oxford Group people, just who wrote this book; but it seems generally agreed that it was written by a Roman Catholic, who was *not* a "member" of the Oxford Group.[67] These are the subjects in its table of contents:

---

[65] See Irving Harris, *The Breeze of the Spirit* (New York: The Seabury Press, 1978), pp. 18-21.

[66] The Layman with a Notebook, *What Is The Oxford Group?* (London: Oxford University Press, 1933); and see the discussion in Dick B., *Dr. Bob's Library* (WV: The Bishop of Books, 1992), p. 48.

[67] Correspondence with the author from Garth D. Lean and K. D. Belden.

1. *The Oxford Group*—a statement of the group's nature.[68]
2. *Sin.*[69]
3. *Sharing For Confession And Witness.*[70]
4. *Surrender.*[71]
5. *Restitution.*[72]
6. *Guidance.*[73]
7. *The Four Absolutes.*[74]
8. *The World.*[75]
9. *You.*[76]

---

[68] For descriptions of the nature of the Oxford Group as set forth in *What is The Oxford Group?* and in the popular Oxford Group book, *For Sinners Only*, see Dick B., *The Oxford Group & Alcoholics Anonymous*, pp. 15, 61-67. In the Foreword to his 1929 book, *Twice-Born Ministers*, Shoemaker wrote the following about the Oxford Group, which was then holding houseparties in the United States that announced that the group was "A First Century Christian Fellowship." Shoemaker wrote: "The First Century Christian Fellowship is now a movement of international proportions, and we at Calvary are a part of it. With the experiences of some of the men in this book I personally had nothing to do. They came about by means of other members of the Fellowship, some of them in other lands. I am glad to be able through this book to pay a little of my debt to the First Century Christian Fellowship, and to record again my wholehearted and unconditional identification with it" (p. 23).

[69] Compare Shoemaker, *Realizing Religion*, pp. 10-21.

[70] Compare Shoemaker, *Realizing Religion*, pp. 71-83.

[71] Compare Shoemaker, *Realizing Religion*, pp. 22-35.

[72] Compare Shoemaker, *The Conversion of the Church*, pp. 41-48.

[73] Compare Shoemaker, *Realizing Religion*, pp. 58-70.

[74] Compare Shoemaker, *Twice-Born Ministers*, p. 150; *The Church Can Save The World*, p. 110, 119-120; *How To Become A Christian*, p. 57; *How You Can Help Other People*, p. 59; and Helen Shoemaker, *I Stand By The Door*, pp. 24-26.

[75] See Shoemaker, *God's Control*, pp. 7-26, 33-41, 136-45.

[76] See Shoemaker, *The Church Can Save The World*, pp. 81-100.

"The Eight Points of the Oxford Group"

We mention the following book because it has apparently been considered to be an authoritative statement of Oxford Group ideas which influenced A.A. Thus, in his recent book, *Changed Lives*,[77] Dennis C. Morreim chose to study the roots of Alcoholics Anonymous from the perspective of Clarence I. Benson's book, *The Eight Points of the Oxford Group*.[78] We utilized Benson's book in our study of the Oxford Group. But we found no evidence that the book was used or quoted in the United States in the 1930's. It is not included in the Oxford Group Literature list published in the March, 1939, issue of *The Calvary Evangel*; and to assist the reader in seeing those Oxford Group books which *were* very much read in the 1930's in America, we have included the Oxford Group Literature List in Appendix Two.[79] Nor did we find mention of the book or its author in Garth Lean's exhaustive biography of Oxford Group Founder, Frank Buchman. Our opinion is that *The Eight Points* certainly conforms to, and provides an excellent exposition of, Oxford Group ideas; but, at this point in our research, we are not convinced it was a direct source of any Oxford Group language that can be traced into A.A.

Consequently, we list the "eight points" below and refer the reader to our own, more extensive discussion above of the Oxford Group's twenty-eight Biblical principles. Benson's "eight" points are: (1) *Surrender*, (2) *Sharing*, (3) *Restitution*, (4) *The Four Absolutes*, (5) *The Quiet Time*, (6) *Guidance*, (7) *Witness*, and (8) *Fellowship*. If the reader will study these eight points and compare them with the twenty-eight concepts we listed, he or she will see that the eight points do not "point up" such important Oxford

---

[77] Dennis C. Morreim, *Changed Lives: The Story of Alcoholics Anonymous* (Minneapolis: Augsburg, 1991).

[78] Clarence I. Benson, *The Eight Points of the Oxford Group* (London: Oxford University Press, 1936).

[79] See also Dick B., *The Oxford Group & Alcoholics Anonymous*, pp. 81-84.

Group-Shoemaker-A.A. related ideas as "God," "God's Plan," "Man's chief end," "Belief," "Life-change," "Decision," "Conviction," "Conservation," "God-consciousness," "Knowledge of God's will," and so on—all of these being important root ideas in the A.A. path to the relationship with God which is described in Big Book.[80]

Further, Shoemaker, in later years, talked much about a "spiritual awakening."[81] Dr. Frank Buchman had often spoken of the need for a moral and spiritual awakening.[82] Shoemaker titled one of his later books, *National Awakening*. And in 1952, he devoted an entire chapter of his book, *By The Power of God*, to the topic: "What Awakening Takes."[83] Shoemaker discussed this "spiritual awakening" at A.A.'s St. Louis Convention and said it involved four factors: "conversion, prayer, fellowship, and witness."[84] Benson's "eight points" do not highlight either the "spiritual awakening" or the "conversion" and "prayer" factors of such an awakening—factors which Shoemaker articulated for A.A. and which A.A. incorporated into its steps.[85] Hence they only present part of the A.A. picture.

---

[80] Big Book, pp. 29, 58-60.

[81] Thus Shoemaker wrote in *The Conversion of The Church*, at page 124: "Nothing less than a God-inspired awakening, a "rushing mighty wind" from heaven, bearing upon its wings the fire of grace from the throne of God, is sufficient for the need of the world and the Church of this hour." Compare the commencing line in A.A.'s Twelfth Step: "Having had a spiritual awakening as the result of these steps. . . ."

[82] Frank N. D. Buchman, *Remaking The World* (London: Blandford Press, 1961), pp. 19, 24, 35, 54.

[83] Shoemaker, *By The Power of God*, pp. 133-154.

[84] See *Alcoholics Anonymous Comes of Age*, p. 267; and compare Shoemaker, *Extraordinary Living For Ordinary Men*, pp. 126-134. For Shoemaker's very early discussion of "conversion" and "prayer," see *Realizing Religion*, pp. 22-35, 63-65.

[85] Thus *Pass It On* quotes Bill's statement to Dr. Carl Jung: "This concept [the spiritual awakening, or spiritual experience, or "genuine conversion"] proved to be the foundation of such success as Alcoholics Anonymous has since achieved. This made conversion experience . . . available on an almost wholesale basis" (pp. 382-383).

The A.A. Source: Oxford Group or Shoemaker?

This leads us to the remarkable set of writings which Sam Shoemaker began in 1921 and continued throughout his life. He wrote twenty-eight major books, countless pamphlets, and, for many years, regular monthly articles in *The Calvary Evangel* and later in its successor, *Faith At Work*. Half of Shoemaker's books were completed prior to the time A.A.'s recovery book, *Alcoholics Anonymous*, was published in 1939. By that time, Sam had become a major American leader in Frank Buchman's Oxford Group. He was the Oxford Group's most prolific writer of published books. He was probably the greatest source of the Oxford Group words and ideas that became incorporated in the first edition of the Big Book, published in 1939.

But did Bill Wilson's Oxford Group ideas come *only* from Shoemaker, as Bill sometimes seemed to suggest? Of the Oxford Group, Shoemaker, and A.A., *Pass It On*, A.A.'s "official" biography of Bill Wilson, states:

> While Bill was always generous in recognizing A.A.'s debt to the Oxford Group, he would always tie the Oxford Group connection to Dr. Shoemaker (p. 174).
>
> Fear of controversy loomed large in Bill's thinking; he had even consulted Father Dowling and others before giving credit to the Oxford Group in *Alcoholics Anonymous Comes of Age* (p. 387).
>
> Criticism and rejection notwithstanding, Lois and Bill did not become immediately disillusioned with the Oxford Group or with its principles, *from which Bill borrowed freely* (p. 169) [emphasis ours].
>
> Bill was about to write the famous fifth chapter, "How it Works." The basic material for the chapter was the word-of-mouth that Bill had been talking ever since his own recovery. *It was heavy with Oxford Group principles*, and had in addition some of the ideas

> Bill gleaned from William James and from Dr. Silkworth (pp. 196-197) [emphasis ours].
>
> Bill's first three steps were culled from his reading of James, the teachings of Sam Shoemaker, *and those of the Oxford Group* (p. 199) [emphasis ours].

We believe the foregoing quotes show that A.A.'s own "official" historians have not been thoroughly convinced that Bill's lavish praises of Shoemaker presented the Oxford Group-Shoemaker-A.A. relationship with complete accuracy.

At the time A.A.'s basic, spiritual recovery principles were being developed—between 1934 and 1939—Oxford Group language was in the air—in New York and in Akron. Early AAs were not confined, even in their Oxford Group activities and meetings, just to contacts with Shoemaker personally or with Shoemaker's writings and teachings. As we have just shown, Shoemaker wrote about all the Oxford Group ideas. But early AAs were also exposed to Oxford Group *writings* that were not those of Shoemaker. These included: *For Sinners Only*, *What is the Oxford Group?*, *Soul Surgery*, *He That Cometh*, *I Was A Pagan*, and *Life Began Yesterday*.[86]

Early AAs also *heard* many Oxford Group ideas from people other than Shoemaker. For example, in Akron, Dr. Bob, Anne Smith (his wife), Henrietta Seiberling, and T. Henry and Clarace Williams were all thoroughly versed in Oxford Group ideas and passed them on to early AAs. On the East Coast, as Lois Wilson's

---

[86] Geoffrey Francis Allen, *He That Cometh* (New York: The Macmillan Company, 1932); Stephen Foot, *Life Began Yesterday* (New York: Harper & Brothers, 1935); Victor Kitchen, *I Was A Pagan* (New York: Harper & Brothers, 1934); Arthur J. Russell, *For Sinners Only* (New York: Harper & Brothers, 1932); The Layman with a Notebook, *What Is The Oxford Group?* (New York: Oxford University Press, 1933); Howard A. Walter, *Soul-Surgery*, 6th ed. (Oxford at the University Press by John Johnson, 1940). For a discussion of these and other non-Shoemaker Oxford Group books that were read by early AAs, see Dick B., *The Books Early AAs Read For Spiritual Growth* (Seattle: Glen Abbey Books, 1993); *Dr. Bob's Library* (WV: The Bishop of Books, 1992); and *Anne Smith's Spiritual Workbook*.

Oxford Group Notes reveal, Bill and Lois attended the Oxford Group's First Century Christian Fellowship houseparties and met Oxford Group leaders from around the world—Jim Newton, Garth Lean, Irving Harris, Ray Purdy, Victor Kitchen, Philip Marshall Brown, Eleanor Forde, Cleveland Hicks, Loudon Hamilton, and Frank Buchman himself.[87] East Coast AAs certainly *saw* Oxford Group people other than Shoemaker, people such as Rowland Hazard, Shep Cornell, Charles Clapp, Jr., and Hanford Twitchell. It therefore seems fair to say that Sam Shoemaker has to be considered just one part of the Oxford Group-Shoemaker-A.A. picture. But we will see he was a major part, whether his influence was direct or indirect.

So now to Shoemaker and his teachings.

---

[87] See Dick B., *The Akron Genesis of Alcoholics Anonymous*, pp. 150-155.

Part 2

What Sam Said

4

The Shoemaker Writings Prior to A.A.'s Big Book

People familiar with the words and concepts in A.A.'s basic text, *Alcoholics Anonymous*, would quickly find themselves at home reading the titles which Sam Shoemaker wrote prior to the publication of the First Edition of the Big Book in the spring of 1939.[1] But Shoemaker's writings in this period covered a tremendous range of religious topics. Before we review the Shoemaker books, we want to focus the reader's attention on two points. First, on a group of Shoemaker ideas which A.A. very probably adopted as the core of what it called a set of spiritual tools for recovery. Second, on some vital Biblical ideas which took a back seat.

Spiritual Tools from Shoemaker

From the very beginning of his ministry, Shoemaker began articulating concepts which later could be recognized, whatever their source, as core tools in A.A.'s spiritual program of recovery.

---

[1] *Alcoholics Anonymous*, 3rd ed. (New York: Alcoholics Anonymous World Services, Inc., 1976). As noted earlier, we will normally use the name "(the) Big Book,"—the affectionate name given this text by AAs—throughout our book.

Shoemaker was speaking of: (1) spiritual misery; (2) the need for a vital religious experience as a solution to that misery; (3) people's need for a "vast power outside themselves;" (4) finding God; (5) the "turning point" in the path to God; (6) aligning one's life with the will of God; (7) a decision to surrender self and self-will to the will of God; (8) eradicating selfishness and self-seeking—the blocks to God; (9) self-examination, confession, and conviction of sin as part of the elimination process; (10) restitution as the means for setting things right with others and eliminating that aspect of sin from life; (11) the critical need for guidance from the Bible, prayer, and listening to God in order to learn God's will and live in harmony with it; (12) the God-consciousness which results from the whole conversion or surrender process; (13) the idea that one has to give the life-changing experience away to keep it; (14) the need to go "fishing for men," as Jesus put it; (15) the method of witnessing through the sharing of experience—giving "news not views;" (16) the importance of teamwork, loyalty, and fellowship in maintaining and growing in the life of grace; and (17) the importance of the group as the vehicle for sharing of experience.

Shoemaker said: "the most important work in all the ministry [is] . . . personal work with individuals."[2] To him, this meant helping others to have a conversion experience; that is, helping them to be born again of the spirit. And it meant bringing them to a breach, a breaking off, a turning, a change. It meant they could put a "period" to the past which they had rejected, and that they could enter with enthusiasm into the new life they had adopted.

---

[2] Samuel Shoemaker, Jr., *A Young Man's View of the Ministry* (New York: Association Press, 1923), p. 11.

God, Jesus Christ, the Holy Spirit, and the Bible

In reading Shoemaker's books, one cannot escape the primary emphasis Shoemaker places on God, Jesus Christ, the Holy Spirit, and the Bible. But these basics in Shoemaker's thinking took on a different hue in A.A. as Bill Wilson fashioned his Big Book here and there in a way he felt would make it palatable to atheists, agnostics, and non-Christians. Witness the following three comments.

Bill's wife, Lois, said:

> The pros and cons were mostly about the tone of the book [i.e., the Big Book]. Some wanted it slanted more toward the Christian religion; others less. Many alcoholics were agnostics or atheists. Then there were those of the Jewish faith and, around the world, of other religions. Shouldn't the book be written so it would appeal to them also? Finally it was agreed that the book should present a universal spiritual program, not a specific religious one, since all drunks were not Christian.[3]

Consider also the comments of the authors of *Pass It On* as they described the "battle" over the writing of the Big Book—a battle which took place in the New Jersey office of Bill's secretary, Ruth Hock. It involved atheists, Hank P. and Jim B., on the one hand, and Bill's good friend, John Henry Fitzhugh M., the son of an Episcopalian minister, on the other. Concerning the conflict, the authors of *Pass It On* said:

> Ruth Hock said that Bill appeared in the office one day with the steps practically complete. But when he showed the manuscript to local members, there were heated discussions and many other suggestions. Jimmy B. opposed the strong references to God, in both the steps and the rest of the early chapters. Hank wanted to

[3] *Lois Remembers. Memoirs of the co-founder of Al-Anon and wife of the co-founder of Alcoholics Anonymous* (New York: Al-Anon Family Group Headquarters, 1987), p. 113.

soft-pedal them; but Fitz insisted that the book should express Christian doctrines and use Biblical terms and expressions. Ruth remembered: "Fitz was for going all the way with 'God'; you [Bill] were in the middle; Hank was for very little; and I—trying to reflect the reaction of the nonalcoholic—was for very little. The result of this was the phrase 'God as we understood Him,' which I don't think ever had much of a negative reaction anywhere."[4]

A.A. historian, Dr. Ernest Kurtz, summarized his view of the end result as follows:

> The Oxford Group was a conscious attempt to return to primitive fundamental Christianity. The briefest statement of the fundamental Christian message runs: "Jesus saves." The fundamental first message of Alcoholics Anonymous, proclaimed by the very presence of a former compulsive drunk standing sober, ran: "Something saves." "Salvation" as the message remained. Yet A.A.'s total omission of "Jesus," its toning down of even "God" to a "Higher Power" which could be the group itself, and its changing of the *verbal* first message into hopeless helplessness rather than salvation: these ideas and practices, adopted to avoid any "religious" association, were profound changes.[5]

Our first question is whether the foregoing comments by Lois, by the authors of *Pass It On*, and by Dr. Ernest Kurtz, actually establish that some fundamental change occurred in early A.A. concerning its receptivity to the message about God, Christianity, and the Bible. Do these comments correctly describe the approach that Bill Wilson took in the Big Book?

Lois Wilson seemed to say that, by the time the Big Book was written, A.A. had moved from a Christian, religious program to a "universal spiritual" program. As we have pointed out, A.A.

---

[4] *Pass It On* (New York: Alcoholics Anonymous World Services, Inc., 1984), p. 199. See also *Alcoholics Anonymous Comes of Age* (New York: Alcoholics Anonymous World Services, Inc., 1957), p. 17.

[5] Ernest Kurtz, *Not-God: A History of Alcoholics Anonymous*. Expanded ed. (Minnesota: Hazelden, 1991), p. 50

members *today* do often say "A.A. is a spiritual program, but not a religious program." Yet one should consider, when looking at any of the foregoing three statements, that the Big Book uses the word "God" 132 times and pronouns describing "God" another eighty times, with additional Biblical descriptions of Him such as "Creator," "Maker," "Father of Light" [sic], "Spirit," and "Friend."[6] Bill was still using these expressions in his addresses at A.A. Conventions many years after the Big Book was written.[7] The Twelve Traditions speak of a "loving God."[8] As previously stated, a "Conference Approved" book included Reverend Fosdick's view that "Alcoholics Anonymous is deeply religious."[9] Anne Ripley Smith (Dr. Bob's wife), whom Bill Wilson called the "Mother of A.A.," spoke frequently of God, Jesus Christ, and the Bible; and made fun of the idea that a deity could be "the group." She called that idea a "funk hole."[10] And while some Christian writers characterize A.A. as distinctly non-Christian, some Rational Recovery writers characterize it as definitely Christian.[11]

---

[6] See, for example, Stewart C. *A Reference Guide To The Big Book* (Seattle: Recovery Press, Inc., 1986), pp. 115-116; Stephen E. Poe and Frances E. Poe. *A Concordance to Alcoholics Anonymous* (Nevada: Purple Salamander Press, 1990), pp. 325-28, 174, 274-75, 305-06, 719.

[7] See, for example, in *A. A. Comes of Age*: (1) pp. 9, 44 ("my Creator really did know me and love me. . . . We knew that ours was a fellowship of the Spirit and that the grace of God was there"), (2) p. 48 ("the conscience of Alcoholics Anonymous as moved by the guidance of God"), (3) p. 51 ("God's grace among us"), (4) p. 79, p. 87, p. 98 ("a loving God"), p. 105 ("There is God, our Father, who very simply says, 'I am waiting for you to do my will.'"), (5) p. 221, p. 224, p. 225 ("the Father of Lights, who presides over all men"), and (6) p. 234 ("We give thanks to our Heavenly Father").

[8] Big Book, p. 564.

[9] *Alcoholics Anonymous Comes of Age*, p. 324.

[10] Dick B., *Anne Smith's Spiritual Workbook* (Seattle: Glen Abbey Books, 1993), p. 21.

[11] For a view that A.A. is non-Christian, see William L. Playfair, M.D., *The Useful Lie* (Illinois: Crossway Books, 1991). For an opinion as to A.A.'s "religiosity," see Charles Bufe, *Alcoholics Anonymous: Cult or Cure?* (San Francisco: Sharp Press, 1991). For a view that A.A. has a confused mixture, see Tim Stafford, "The Hidden Gospel of the 12 Steps," *Christianity Today*, July 22, 1991.

Where does one go with all this in a study of Shoemaker and A.A.? The whole body of Shoemaker's teaching concerned God, Jesus Christ, the Holy Spirit, and the Bible. Bill said he and Dr. Bob were inspired and taught by Shoemaker. There certainly was no absence of mention of God, Jesus Christ, the Holy Spirit, or the Bible in early A.A.—particularly in Akron. And though some observers have suggested that A.A.'s Big Book made a change of course from the God of the Bible toward "universalism" or "humanism," and even idol worship, we question whether either Dr. Bob or Bill intended to be involved in such a religious course.[12]

Bill talked repeatedly in the Big Book about a relationship with God.[13] And a look at the dictionary is quite enlightening if one thinks there is much difference between the words "religious" and "spiritual" when one is talking about a relationship with God.[14] Bill himself did suggest "God as we understood Him" was a great contribution to A.A. made by two early atheist members.[15] Yet Bill never removed from the Big Book his frequent and clear use of the word "God" or the clear, Biblical concepts concerning God.

---

[12] For example, in all of our books, we have discussed at some length Dr. Bob's continuous and intense interest in the Bible, in Christian literature, and even—during most of his sobriety—in membership in Christian churches. Also, throughout his long-term sobriety, Bill Wilson maintained close contact, and personal friendship, with Reverend Sam Shoemaker; and for years—as we point out in this book—was involved with Father Ed Dowling, S.J., as his "spiritual sponsor"; with actual instruction for membership in the Roman Catholic Church; and with Father John Ford, S.J., as an actual editor of two of Bill's own major A.A. writings. See also Bill's comments about the clergy in *The Language of the Heart* (New York: The A.A. Grapevine, Inc., 1988), pp. 177-79.

[13] See Big Book, p. 29: "Each individual, in the personal stories, describes in his own language and from his own point of view the way he established his relationship with God." See also Big Book, p. 13 ("relationship with my Creator"), p. 28 ("children of a living Creator with whom we may form a relationship"), p. 100 ("It is dependent upon his relationship with God"), and p. 164 (speaking of "God": "See to it that your relationship with Him is right").

[14] *Merriam Webster's Collegiate Dictionary*, Tenth ed., p. 988 ("religious," usage 1), and p. 1134 ("spiritual," usage 5).

[15] *A.A. Comes of Age*, p. 17.

Bill simply "compromised" (as he put it) in two phrases—"God as we understand Him" and "Power greater than ourselves." When writing the Big Book, Bill did use a phrase "Higher Power," but he used it only twice—both times in the context of "God."[16] Moreover, the "Higher Power" expression used in the Oxford Group (of which A.A. was still a part in Akron) was used to describe the God of the Bible.[17] Finally, the idea that the "higher power" could be "the group" is something Bill added to A.A. verbiage quite some time after the Big Book was published and primarily when he wrote *The Twelve Steps and Twelve Traditions* which was published in 1953.

We believe that, as A.A. stood when the First Edition of the Big Book was published, the Biblical/Oxford Group/Shoemaker concepts about God were still very much present—though the specific words "Bible," "Jesus Christ," and "Holy Spirit" were not. We believe that the presence of the concepts about the God of the Bible enabled Bill to continue, throughout subsequent years, to emphasize the importance of Shoemaker's influence. Bill suggested that A.A. had made a "compromise" over "God." If it did, we believe, it made the compromise far more to enable atheists, agnostics, and people of non-Christian religious convictions to be

---

[16] See Big Book, page 43, where Bill uses the phrase (with capital letters) "Higher Power," having just written about divine help, and then—in the next chapter, states at page 45: "And it means, of course, that we are going to talk about God." On page 46, he speaks of "that Power, which is God." The other use of the phrase "Higher Power" is on page 100 of the Big Book where Bill states: "When we look back, we realize that the things which came to us when we put ourselves in God's hands were better than anything we could have planned. Follow the dictates of your Higher Power. . . ."

[17] See, for example, V. C. Kitchen, *I Was A Pagan* (New York: Harper & Brothers, 1934), p. 85; and James D. Newton, *Uncommon Friends* (New York: Harcourt Brace, 1987), pp. 85-88. In a personal interview with the author at the Peale Center For Christian Living in Pawling, New York, in August of 1992, Dr. Norman Vincent Peale spoke with the author about his conversations with Bill Wilson. Peale said he had never talked to anyone familiar with the expression "Higher Power," who did not believe that expression referred to God. See also Norman Vincent Peale, *The Power of Positive Thinking* (New York: Prentice-Hall, 1952), where Peale was writing about Alcoholics Anonymous and twice indicated that the expression "Higher Power" referred to God (pp. 268, 272).

comfortable at the *beginning* of their A.A. path when they heard religious expressions, than to promulgate some doctrinal idea that A.A. had abandoned the God of the Bible in the book it published in 1939. Both Ebby and the Big Book spoke of choosing one's own conception of God to "start," to "commence," or to "begin."[18] But both Ebby and the Big Book made explicit statements about a belief in God, the *Creator*.[19] As we will see from Shoemaker's writings, the idea of choosing one's own conception of God *for a beginning* was wholly in accord with Shoemaker's teachings about the "experiment of faith." One commences, taught Shoemaker, with the fact that God IS, and with a conception of God, however dim. Then he or she seeks Him and obeys Him. And then one "discovers" and "knows" Him. But the teachings did not disavow or compromise God!

Why all this discussion of God, Jesus Christ, the Holy Spirit, the Bible, and religion as we move to a discussion of Shoemaker? The reason is that Shoemaker very often spoke specifically about each of these in his books, other writings, sermons, speeches, and conversations. Bill Wilson frequently spoke of Shoemaker's great influence upon both Dr. Bob and himself. Hence, one can hardly study Shoemaker and omit Shoemaker's views and statements about God and the Bible. And we, therefore, certainly include Shoemaker's Biblical/Christian views in our discussion and analysis of those Shoemaker writings which were relevant to A.A.

And now to Shoemaker's writings that were published prior to the publication of the Big Book in 1939.

---

[18] Big Book, pp. 12, 46-47.

[19] Big Book, pp. 11, 13, 47, 49, 56.

Realizing Religion

Shoemaker's first book was *Realizing Religion*.[20] In it, he laid out the ingredients for attaining "a vital religious experience"—for finding God. These ingredients became major points in the spiritual message he propounded for the rest of his life. The ingredients were intended to lead to the very religious conversion experience that Dr. Carl Jung had told Rowland Hazard would be necessary for Rowland to overcome the disease of alcoholism.[21] Jung had encouraged Rowland to join a religious group.

Accordingly, Rowland aligned himself with the Oxford Group, attained the experience, and then carried the message of his "spiritual experience" to Bill Wilson's long-time friend and sponsor, Ebby Thatcher. Ebby, in turn, inspired Bill to seek such an experience. Bill sought it first through his decision for Christ at Shoemaker's Calvary Rescue Mission and then, just days later, during his final stay at Towns Hospital. In the latter case, Bill proclaimed he had undergone such a conversion. In his mind, he had validated the experience by examining Professor William James's *The Varieties of Religious Experience*.[22] Originally, Bill could not be sure whether it was Ebby or Rowland who had given him the James book to read. But it is not surprising that the book was given to Bill by an Oxford Group adherent from the Shoemaker circle (whether Ebby *or* Rowland) because of the frequency with which Sam mentioned this William James book and the crisis of self surrender which both Shoemaker and James held to be necessary for a conversion. Shoemaker had spoken of William James and conversion experiences not only in *Realizing Religion*—written in 1921—, but also in a good many later books published *before* Bill Wilson had his Towns Hospital religious experience.

---

[20] Samuel Shoemaker, *Realizing Religion* (New York: Association Press, 1923).

[21] Note, however, that Jung himself did not speak of alcoholism as a *disease*.

[22] *A.A. Comes of Age*, p. 64.

The Foreword to *Realizing Religion* explains that Shoemaker wished to record the series of thoughts which made possible a "vivid religious experience." Shoemaker said he found this very old group of ideas could help others to have spiritual needs met and who, he felt, could be helped if the few essentials were simply put. Shoemaker summarized the essentials as follows:

> A superb and conquering self-assurance, melting under a growing spiritual aspiration into conscious inadequacy, the increasing sense of sin and later the serpent putting up his head for one final attack, a deep hunger for rebirth, the actual discovery of Christ in conversion, and the search for means to keep this experience alive (p. viii).

Compare the language Bill Wilson used years later as he phrased the three aspects of A.A.'s Twelfth Step as those aspects appeared in the First Edition of the Big Book:

> [1] Having had a spiritual experience as the result of these steps, [2] we tried to carry this message to alcoholics, and [3] to practice these principles in all our affairs.

Let's see how Shoemaker articulated in his first book this very "old group of ideas" about how to have a vital spiritual experience.

His first chapter spelled out man's need. He said the modern world is restless and easily bored. It is intensely individualistic. Everyone has his "own religion," and nearly everyone made it or thinks he did. Shoemaker said this "paganism" is an elaborate device to get along without the Cross. Man's "problems" and "complex situations" stem from "*spiritual misery*, a maladjustment to the eternal things that throws out the whole focus of life." Shoemaker said the root of the malady is estrangement from God—estrangement from Him in people that were made to be His companions. Note that A.A.'s Big Book speaks of a "spiritual malady;" and it uses three different terms for it—a spiritual disease, a spiritual sickness, and a spiritual malady.[23]

In his first chapter, Shoemaker prescribed a solution for the spiritual malady which early A.A. seemed to accept. He said:

> What you want is simply a *vital religious experience.* You need to find God. You need Jesus Christ (p. 9) [emphasis ours].

Even the Big Book's Third Edition used similar language—sans mention of Jesus Christ. It quoted Jung as saying there could be no recovery in the mind of the chronic alcoholic without a "vital spiritual experience" (p. 27). Then the Big Book said to its reader: "There is One who has all power—that One is God. May you find Him now!" (p. 59).

Having described the need for man's escape from spiritual misery through a conversion experience and finding God, Shoemaker then dealt with the cause of the misery (sin) and the solution to the spiritual problem (conversion). In other writings, Shoemaker and the Oxford Group defined "sin" as "that which blocks man from God and from others." And A.A. adopted this "blockage" idea.[24] But Shoemaker's first book proposed a somewhat different sin idea which also found a place in A.A. Shoemaker said, "For most men the world is centered in self, which is misery" (p. 11). A.A.'s Big Book says:

> Our actor [the man who tries to run life on self-will] is self-centered—ego centric. . . . Selfishness—self-centeredness! That, we think, is the root of our troubles. . . . (pp. 61-62).

Borrowing from the ideas of Professor William James, Shoemaker wrote that in man's very nature, there is a rift, a cleavage, a division in which man's individual sins flow from a disordered self. He said they are a symptom of a deep-seated

---

[23] Big Book, p. 64.

[24] Big Book, pp. 71, 64, 66.

malady—the expression of a nature, a character, a will, which needs to be changed. Shoemaker utilized an oft-quoted expression of Frank Buchman's that sin has "binding power, blinding power, multiplying power, deadening power."[25] Shoemaker concluded with a quote from Romans 6:23: "The wages of sin is death." He said man needs to take a look at his inner self and tell himself frankly just how much plain, black, unmistakable sin he finds and how much that has to do with the restlessness and fretting and trifling disquietude in himself. He said man should ask how much he is the cause of the misery within and without. Note here that A.A.'s Big Book echoed this theme, stating: "After all, our problems are of our own making."[26]

Shoemaker then spoke of the necessity for changing. He stated that sin alone is capable only of evil, while the human mind, once it becomes awake to its own condition, is capable of something better. It can repent. And Shoemaker quoted this verse on repentance (p. 19):

> Repentance is to leave
> The sin we loved before,
> And show that we in earnest grieve
> By doing it no more.

This verse seems a poetic forerunner of A.A.'s Sixth Step idea: "Were entirely ready to have God remove all these defects of character." Shoemaker concluded his chapter on "sin" by stating:

> At the threshold of the spiritual life stands the dark and sinister figure of sin. . . . To realize the meaning of sin in feeling and in thought is not the mark of a sick soul, but rather the sign of return to spiritual health (p. 21).

---

[25] See Dick B., *The Akron Genesis of Alcoholics Anonymous* (Seattle: Glen Abbey Books, 1992), p. 151, where there is also a description of Lois Wilson's use of this phrase in her Oxford Group notes.

[26] Big Book, p. 103, 61-62.

The Big Book seemed to set this same stage by stating that alcoholics must be rid of selfishness, or it kills them (p. 62). It continued:

> Neither could we reduce our self-centeredness much by wishing or by trying on our own power. We had to have God's help (p. 62).

The Big Book described the Third Step in which the alcoholic must make a "decision" to turn to God. It then stated:

> Though our decision was a vital and crucial step, it could have little practical effect unless at once followed by a strenuous effort to face, and be rid of, the things in our selves which had been blocking us (p. 64).

What was Shoemaker's answer in this situation? "To be made over in the Spirit . . . a rebirth" (p. 21).

Shoemaker's next chapter defined the conversion which effects the rebirth. He quoted William James' definition of "conversion":

> The process, gradual or sudden, by which a self, hitherto divided and consciously wrong, inferior, and unhappy, becomes unified, consciously right, superior and happy.[27]

Shoemaker asked if we can have a conversion at will, and what we must do to have it. He answered that we must open ourselves to God, and be prepared to accept all it will mean to be a child of God. He said there must be a willingness to break finally with sin, to accept evils and wrongs as inevitable, and to embark upon the tremendous business of cleansing ourselves, through the grace of God, from top to bottom—best expressed, he said, in the old idea of self-surrender to God.

---

[27] William James, *The Varieties of Religious Experience* (New York: Vintage Books/The Library of America, 1990), p. 177.

How, said Shoemaker, is this done? This was his answer:

> Surrender of the whole self to God means the complete dedication, by deliberate act of the will, of one's entire personality to doing the will of God so far as one can discover it (p. 29).

Quoting William James on self-surrender as the turning point, he then said:

> You and God are reconciled the moment you surrender. You know it. The shackles fall away. Self recedes. God looms up. Self-will seems the blackest sin of all. . . . The peace that passes understanding steals over you. . . . Our part is to ask, to seek, to knock.[28] [God's] part is to answer, to come, to open (pp. 31-32).

Shoemaker further quoted William James:

> The real witness of the Spirit to the second birth is to be found only in the disposition of the genuine child of God, the permanently patient heart, the love of self eradicated (p. 35).

And let's look at these Big Book parallels:

> We stood at the turning point. We asked His protection and care with complete abandon. Here are the steps we took, which are suggested as a program of recovery. . . . [The Big Book then describes the twelve suggested steps and makes a statement about the first two—that alcoholics could not manage their own lives, that probably no human power could have relieved their alcoholism, and that God could and would if He were sought]. Being convinced [of these three ideas], *we were at Step Three*, which is that we decided to turn our will and our life over to God as we understood Him. Just what do we mean by that, and just what do we do? The first requirement is that we be convinced that any life run on self-will can hardly be a success. . . . The alcoholic is an extreme example

---

[28] For "the peace that passes understanding," see Philippians 4:6,7. For "ask . . . seek . . . knock," see the Sermon on the Mount, Matthew 7:7.

> of self-will run riot. . . . Above everything we alcoholics must be rid of this selfishness. . . . We had to have God's help. . . . First we had to quit playing God. Next we decided that hereafter in this drama of life, God was going to be our Director. . . . Established on such a footing we became less interested in ourselves. . . . As we felt new power flow in, as we enjoyed peace of mind, as we discovered we could face life successfully, as we became conscious of His presence, we began to lose our fear. . . . We were reborn. . . . Many of us have said to our Maker[,] . . . God I offer myself to Thee. . . . May I do Thy will always (pp. 59-63).

Shoemaker wrote two chapters on the importance of Jesus Christ and on what religion ought to do. Some might say Shoemaker's thinking in these chapters had no influence on A.A. And, most assuredly, the Big Book contains no reference to Christ as a regenerating power nor to any need for getting people into fellowship with Christ (the topics Shoemaker covered). But Shoemaker did dwell on several ideas that could have had an impact on A.A.

He spoke of the personal and spiritual contribution of Jesus to the life of the world; and Dr. Bob expressed his belief that Jesus Christ's "Sermon on the Mount" contained the underlying philosophy of A.A.[29] Shoemaker said that Jesus and sin cannot dwell in the same heart side by side, but that He (Jesus) must expel it and dwell there alone, His effect on sin simply being the effect of light on darkness. In A.A. meetings, one often hears the expression "the sunlight of the Spirit," which comes from the Big Book (page 66). This phrase is used in the context of getting rid of resentment because the harboring of such ill-feelings shuts one off from the sunlight. In Steps Six and Seven, the Big Book speaks of God's removing "all the things which we have admitted are objectionable," and of God's taking "them all—every one." It suggests a prayer to have that *Creator* "now remove from me every single defect of character" (page 76). Though the Big Book

[29] *DR. BOB and the Good Oldtimers* (New York: Alcoholics Anonymous World Services, 1980), p. 228.

calls only for "spiritual progress rather than spiritual perfection" (page 60), it also talks of God's removing "every single defect of character" (or *sin* as it was first called in A.A.).[30] And it speaks of the importance of letting in the "sunlight of the spirit."[31] We believe Shoemaker's talk of Jesus's expelling sin and bringing light to darkness might be an example of Shoemaker-Biblical thinking that had its effect on Bill's "sunlight-of-the-spirit" language.[32]

Shoemaker spoke of the forgiveness of God, which Christ makes real; and he spoke of a relationship with Christ, as a living companionship. He said that after conversion, religion may drive man to do something out of the ordinary as proof that something real has happened. He illustrated by stating one may be able to live in the thirteenth chapter of First Corinthians and possibly apply the Sermon on the Mount. These two portions of the Bible were considered by Dr. Bob and the early AAs to be "absolutely essential" in their recovery program.[33]

Let us assume that the foregoing Shoemaker ideas in *Realizing Religion* actually reached Bill and Dr. Bob. If they did, they might well have found expression in the Big Book's frequent mention of establishing a relationship with God, of living in conscious companionship with the Creator, of finding that the Creator has entered lives in a miraculous way, and of God's accomplishing things AAs could never do by themselves.[34]

In a subsequent chapter, Shoemaker moved on to ideas that he stressed in all his writings. Many of these ideas found their way

---

[30] See *Pass It On*, p. 197, where the original six steps, as listed by Bill, speak of "a moral inventory of our defects or sins."

[31] Big Book, p. 66.

[32] Compare 1 John 1:5-7: "This then is the message which we heard of Him, and declare unto you, that God is light, and in Him is no darkness at all. If we say that we have fellowship with Him, and walk in darkness, we lie, and do not the truth. But if we walk in the light as he is in the light, we have fellowship one with another, and the blood of Jesus Christ His Son cleanseth us from all sin."

[33] *DR. BOB and the Good Oldtimers*, p. 96.

[34] Big Book, pp. 13, 25, 28-29, 42, 45, 47, 51, 56, 62, 68, 70-72, 84, 88, 100, 116, 148, 162, 164.

into early A.A., and some remain today. In his chapter on the "Driving Power for the New Life," Shoemaker described three primary means God gives for sustaining the spiritual experience when the sharp lines of conversion seem to grow dim and we wonder whether it was real or not. The first is the Bible. The second is prayer. And the third is obedience to the "Voice" (listening for and receiving God's revelation). Shoemaker called for observing the "Morning Watch," when man is to come fresh to God with daily plans unmade, submitting first his spirit and then his duties to God for the shedding of His "white light" upon both. Shoemaker urged the importance of the Church where there is uniting not only for worship but also for work. As we've said, Dr. Bob frequently studied, taught from, and spoke of the Bible. And Bill certainly studied the Bible with Dr. Bob in the earliest Akron days. Though specific mention of the Bible has vanished from the text of the Big Book, there remain strong suggestions about the importance of prayer, of turning to God in the morning and throughout the day for guidance, about attending to worship when that is part of an AA's convictions, and about using "helpful books" which can be suggested by one's rabbi, minister, or priest.[35]

Shoemaker's last chapter deals with the importance of witnessing. He said, "There is no more delicate business in the world than relating human lives to God" (p. 77). And one is reminded of the Big Book's imprecation at the beginning of the Steps: "May you find Him now!" (p. 59). Shoemaker pointed out that God cannot bring the relationship about without the help of "us poor mortals" (p. 78). He said the life-changing process requires that the life-changer himself surrender to the Divine Life. This carried over to the Oxford Group-Shoemaker expression that you cannot share or give away an experience of God which you have not had. Anne Smith stressed the same idea in her spiritual workbook. And the Big Book seems to express the idea in two ways: (1) "Having *had* a spiritual awakening as the result of these

---

[35] Big Book, pp. 85-88.

steps, we tried to carry *this* message. . . ." (p. 60) [emphasis ours]; (2) "But obviously you cannot transmit something you haven't got" (p. 164).

In this earliest book, Shoemaker mentioned Frank Buchman's Oxford Group formula for perceiving the need of people and for utilizing the Redeemer's power to save: the "Five C's"—Confidence, Confession, Conviction, Conversion, and Conservation. These Oxford Group concepts are discussed in Appendix One. The important thing is that Shoemaker was expressing them in his first book. He pointed to the importance of sharing in "*confidence*" one's own shortcomings; of first confessing *himself;* then of drawing the *other* into "*confession*;" then of bringing the other to "*conviction*" of sin; and then to a growing assurance that Christ can meet the need—sharing one's own "*conversion*" and one's own fundamental beliefs. Then he stressed that private prayer, Bible study, and public uniting with the Church were part of "*Conservation*" (or *Continuance*, as it was also called).

He concluded: "There is no more empowering habit in the lives of those who seek to live the Christ-life than "fishing for men," as Jesus called it (p. 82).[36] Shoemaker then quoted, as to the personal demand of witnessing, 1 Thessalonians 2:8:

> So being affectionately desirous of you, we were willing to have imparted unto you, not the gospel of God only, but also our own souls, because ye were dear unto us (p. 83).

Note the Big Book parallels in its extensive Twelfth Step chapter, "Working With Others":

> Practical experience shows that nothing will so much insure immunity from drinking as intensive work with other alcoholics. . . . To be vital, faith must be accompanied by self sacrifice and

---

[36] Matthew 4:19: "And he [Jesus Christ] saith unto them, Follow me, and I will make you fishers of men."

> unselfish, constructive action. . . . Helping others is the foundation stone of your recovery. A kindly act once in a while isn't enough. You have to act the Good Samaritan every day, if need be (pp. 89, 93, 97).[37]

A Young Man's View of the Ministry

In the Foreword to his second book, *A Young Man's View of the Ministry*, Shoemaker said he had some things to say to the large number of men in doubt about where to invest their lives.[38] He endeavored to show them the needs and opportunities for service in the ministry. But he also spelled out ideas that were add to the treasure he passed on to A.A.

His first chapter was "The Work." He said the most important work in all the ministry is personal work with individuals. The work carried with it the conviction that unless a person is converted and born again, he cannot see the Kingdom.[39] Shoemaker repeated the William James definition of conversion that he (Shoemaker) had quoted in *Realizing Religion*. In fact, this definition is repeated so often in Shoemaker books, along with several other William James ideas, that one is not surprised to find that Bill referred to William James in the Big Book, said James was a strong influence, and actually called James (whom Bill had never met) a "founder" of A.A.[40] Shoemaker said there are hosts of people in the church who are still divided or consciously wrong, inferior or unhappy, and who do not believe that Christianity can

---

[37] See Luke 10:25-37 for the story of the "Good Samaritan."

[38] Samuel Shoemaker, Jr., *A Young Man's View of the Ministry* (New York: Association Press, 1923).

[39] John 3:3: "Jesus answered and said unto him [Nicodemus], 'Verily, verily, I say unto thee. Except a man be born again, he cannot see the kingdom of God.'"

[40] Big Book, p. 28; *The Language of the Heart* (New York: The AA Grapevine, Inc., 1988), pp. 197-198; and *Pass It On*, p. 124.

actually do for them what it claims it can do. He said, amongst others, the main root of their trouble is unsurrender to God. He said the deliberate, voluntary, man-ward side of conversion is the surrender of self to God, to which can then be added God's acceptance and the gift of the Holy Ghost.

Next, Shoemaker wrote of "The Message." He said this message came from beyond. It welled up out of the life of Jesus of Nazareth. He said Jesus gives to men two kinds of truth: eternal truth and growing truth. What Jesus revealed of the being and nature of God is forever true, and the truth about Christ's own Person remains forever unalterably true. But, said Shoemaker, Jesus gave a kind of expansive truth which goes on, forever getting larger and larger. Shoemaker said the ever-new ways in which God deals with the hearts of societies of successive generations of men, and the experiments of faith which bring new visions of God, are part of the truth into which the Spirit of Truth is leading us.[41]

He said Jesus's belief in God was the foundation of all other beliefs for Christ. He pointed out that Jesus refers to God continually, with utter confidence in God's goodness, His interest, and His love. He said this is a staggering thing—this belief in a God of Love as the Source of all life.[42] He urged going with Jesus in believing that God is after this sort and said men should recognize that in Christ is the fulfillment of all the hopes of men. He said joy is unending when one dwells upon the perfect and selfless Christ. He said those who talk about themselves become self-seeking, self-centered, and play safe, and begin to use men for their ends. Shoemaker urged rediscovery of the Holy Ghost. He said man should think for all he is worth and then give himself utterly to listening to the guidance and direction of the Holy Spirit. He repeated the idea he introduced in *Realizing Religion* that sin

---

[41] See John 16:13.

[42] Dr. Bob and his wife, Anne, frequently referred to God as a God of Love. See, for example, *DR. BOB and the Good Oldtimers*, pp. 110, 117. See also Bill's reference in both the long and short forms of A.A.'s Twelve Traditions to "a loving God as He may express Himself in our group conscience." Big Book, pp. 564-65.

is not mixing up the relationship between men only; it is the estrangement of lives from God. The Christian message, he said, is one of unconquerable joy and hope. It makes life dignified, valuable, and happy as nothing else can. And note the Big Book: "We are sure God wants us to be happy, joyous, and free."[43] Also, its vision for the new AA: that others "had seen the miracles, and one was to come to them. They had visioned the Great Reality—their loving and All Powerful Creator" (Big Book, p. 161).

In his chapter, "The Call," Shoemaker suggested six steps, which he attributed to Henry Drummond, and which, he said, will usually bring people into clear daylight. These steps were: (1) Prayer, based on a continual attitude of listening so that there is a surface upon which God can make a mark; (2) Thinking, which means we must have our thoughts, plus God's light which will illumine the mind; (3) Talking to wise people, but not necessarily regarding their view as final; (4) Looking out for one's own bias; (5) Using the Bible, and (6) Understanding that Guidance is not always conscious.

God's hand, said Shoemaker, is upon every life which makes Him welcome. And it was at this point that Shoemaker introduced what has been called his favorite Bible verse, John 7:17.[44] His thesis was that men must first give their wills wholly to God, and then they will know the truth. That solution came from his observation that there are people who are unselfish, useful, and do not lose their temper or their heads. They seemed, said Shoemaker, "propelled by a vast Power outside themselves" (p. 42).[45] He said he knew that he and others needed to get in touch

---

[43] Big Book, p. 133.

[44] See John 7:17, where Jesus Christ said: "If any man will do his will, he shall know of the doctrine, whether it be of God, or *whether* I speak of myself." As to a comment about the popularity of this verse with Shoemaker, See A. J. Russell, *For Sinners Only* (New York: Harper & Brothers, 1932), p. 211.

[45] Note that this expression "Power outside themselves" is one of several Shoemaker uses in referring to God, and it bears close resemblance to the "power greater than ourselves" idea found in A.A.'s Second Step.

with that Power. And he said he went into the ministry to keep people from missing the track by showing them The Way (Jesus Christ).[46]

In his chapters on "The Need" and "The Reward," Shoemaker spoke again of William James' statement that the need for absolute self-surrender to God is the "vital turning point of the religious life" (p. 55). Shoemaker talked of the amazement one will have at the amount of direction God will give when one listens, and at the way He will answer prayer if it has been brought into captivity to "Nevertheless, not my will, but thine, be done" (p.70).[47]

Shoemaker's concluding chapter was "An Appeal." He referred to concepts treated at length in the books of Oxford Group mentors, Henry Drummond and Henry B. Wright,[48] Shoemaker first talked of the "general will of God" (p. 78) [to be found in the Bible]. Then of the "particular will of God" (p. 78) [which God can, if He chooses, make available by revelation when man asks, as Paul did, "Lord, what wilt thou have me to do?"].[49] As to the latter (asking what he would have us do), we have got to wipe the slate clean, said Shoemaker, and then ask God to write His will upon that slate. This meant, he said, that doing the will of God requires emancipation from selfish consideration so far as that is possible.[50] And Shoemaker set out two verses which epitomized his thesis that the hope of the world lies in men who will do the will of God (p. 86). The first verse was: "He that doeth the will

---

[46] See John 14:6, where Jesus Christ said: "I am the way, the truth, and the life: no man cometh unto the Father, but by me."

[47] See Big Book, p. 85. For the Biblical reference, see Luke 22:42, with Jesus—kneeling in prayer—"Saying, Father, if thou be willing, remove this cup from me; nevertheless not my will, but thine, be done."

[48] Henry Drummond, *The Ideal Life* (New York: Hodder & Stoughton, 1897); and Henry B. Wright, *The Will of God and a Man's Lifework* (New York: The Young Men's Christian Association Press, 1909).

[49] See Acts 9:6.

[50] Compare page 64 of Shoemaker's book with the Big Book "clean slate" expression at page 98, where the Big Book speaks of dependence upon God and then says of getting well, "The only condition is that he (the A.A. newcomer) trust in God and clean house."

of God abideth forever."[51] The second was a portion from Acts 9:6, "Lord, what wilt thou have me to do?"[52]

Children of the Second Birth

The subtitle of Shoemaker's third book, *Children of the Second Birth*, was "Being a Narrative of Spiritual Miracles in a City Parish."[53] Shoemaker said the narratives in his book proved William James's statement that "self surrender . . . always must be regarded as the turning point of the religious life." Shoemaker wrote:

> We believe entirely that conversion is the experience which initiates the new life. But we are not fools enough to think that the beginning is the end! All subsequent life is a development of the relationship with God which conversion opened. For us its daily focal point is in what we call the "Quiet Time." As in all other private devotions, we pray and read the Bible. But the distinguishing element of a Quiet Time is listening for the guidance of God. "Speak, Lord, for Thy servant heareth" is the expectant mood of a Quiet Time.[54] The validity of what we believe to be God's guidance must show itself, in the long run, by more acute moral perception, more genuine human relationships, and increasing assurance of what one ought to do with every hour of the day.

---

[51] 1 John 2:17: "And the world passeth away, and the lust thereof: but he that doeth the will of God abideth forever."

[52] Compare A.A.'s Eleventh Step language and concept: "Sought through prayer and meditation to improve our conscious contact with God as we understood Him, praying only for knowledge of His will for us and the power to carry that out."

[53] Samuel Shoemaker, Jr., *Children of the Second Birth* (New York: Fleming H. Revell, 1927).

[54] See 1 Samuel 3:9.

Chapter by chapter, Shoemaker told the stories of people in his parish whose lives were transformed as they were born again. And each chapter seems to contain a point or a story which made its mark later in A.A. thinking. In fact, one can trace from its Oxford Group beginnings directly to A.A. the whole idea of telling stories; of relating one's experience, strength, and hope; of encouraging life-change by sharing experience; and of showing how a relationship with God was established. Many Oxford Group books took this tack.[55] Anne Smith commended these stories to AAs and their families in the workbook she read to them in the Smith's Akron home in early A.A. days.[56] And the Big Book followed this Oxford Group lead by using "Bill's Story" as chapter one; by including many personal stories in the back of the book; and then stating on page 29:

> Each individual, in the personal stories, describes in his own language and from his own point of view the way he established his relationship with God.

An earlier version, contained in the multilith copy of the Big Book which was circulated before the First Edition was printed, stated:

> This is a group of personal narratives. Then clear-cut directions are given showing how an alcoholic may recover. These are followed by more than a score of personal experiences. Each individual, in the personal stories, describes in his own language and from his own point of view the way he found or rediscovered God.[57]

---

[55] See, for example, Harold Begbie, *Twice Born Men* (New York: Fleming H. Revell, 1909); and *Life Changers* (New York: G.P. Putnam's Sons, 1927); Amelia S. Reynolds, *New Lives for Old* (New York: Fleming H. Revell, 1929); Samuel M. Shoemaker, Jr., *Children of the Second Birth* (New York: Fleming H. Revell, 1927); and *Twice-Born Ministers* (New York: Fleming H. Revell, 1929); and Arthur J. Russell, *For Sinners Only* (London: Hodder & Stoughton, 1932).

[56] See Dick B., *Anne Smith's Spiritual Workbook* (Seattle: Glen Abbey Books, 1993), pp. 12-13.

[57] Multilith copy of the original manuscript, available at A. A. Archives in New York.

Recall that A.A.'s Big Book states the alcoholic must be rid of the manifestations of self and self-centeredness which block him from God.[58] In his first *Children of the Second Birth* story, Shoemaker provided one of the many definitions of *sin* that can be found in his and other Oxford Group writings: "anything, and the only thing, that walled men away from God."[59] Then Shoemaker set forth a phrase we think could have found later expression in A.A.'s "God as we understood Him."[60] Shoemaker said that, as time had gone by, the man whose story Shoemaker told, had had his experience deepened and he had seen the whole Christ. At the beginning, however, that man had simply needed to "surrender as much of himself as he could, to as much of Christ as he understood" (pp. 25, 47). And this idea of surrendering as much of himself as one understands to as much of God as he understands found frequent expression in Oxford Group writings, and also in Anne Smith's Spiritual Workbook.[61] Shoemaker contended it would be far better if we would let men begin their discipleship where they honestly can, letting their experience develop until their theology comes straight, rather than cramming a creed down a person's throat and thinking that it means anything to swallow it

---

[58] Big Book, pp. 62, 64, 71.

[59] See Dick B., *The Oxford Group & Alcoholics Anonymous*, pp. 130-133, for the following definitions of "sin" found in Oxford Group writings: (1) "Sin was anything done contrary to the Will of God, as shown in the New Testament or by direct guidance;" (2) "The best definition of sin that we have is that sin is anything in my life which keeps me from God and from other people;" (3) "All selfishness is sin and all sin is a form of selfishness;" (4) "Sin is the thing which keeps us from being channels of God's power. Whatever keeps us from a living, loving relationship with other people—or from a vital and open relationship with God—is sin;" (5) "But if sin be looked upon as anything that puts a barrier between us and Christ, or between us and other people, then there are many things which we must call by the name of sin."

[60] For the Big Book expressions: "God *as we understood Him*," see Steps Three and Eleven on page 59, page. 60, and page 63.

[61] Stephen Foot, *Life Began Yesterday* (New York: Harper & Brothers, 1935), pp. 12-13, 175; James D. Newton, *Uncommon Friends* (New York: Harcourt Brace Jovanovich, 1987), p. 154; Samuel M. Shoemaker, *How To Become A Christian* (New York: Harper & Brothers, 1953), p. 72; and Dick B., *Anne Smith's Spiritual Workbook* (Seattle: Glen Abbey Books, 1993), p. 28.

whole without digesting it. In any event, the man in Shoemaker's chapter knelt in prayer and dedicated his life not only to belief in Jesus Christ, but also to His life and work. The man recorded in his diary: "I do feel reborn, born of the Spirit."[62] Shoemaker then quoted Romans 8:2-4:

> For the law of the Spirit of life in Christ Jesus hath made me free from the law of sin and death. For what the law could not do, in that it was weak through the flesh, God sending his own Son in the likeness of sinful flesh, and for sin, condemned sin in the flesh: That the righteousness of the law might be fulfilled in us, who walk not after the flesh, but after the Spirit (pp. 33-34).

Shoemaker's thinking, as exemplified in his third story, might well have been a stimulant to Bill Wilson's use of the phrase "power greater than ourselves." Bill deleted the word "God" from the original draft of the Second Step and substituted the word "Power" for "God."[63] Shoemaker had said:

> There were people in the world who had found a Power which could be transmitted into the lives of others. That Power was the one solution to all problems, and without it men go on the rocks (pp. 45-46).

Compare these two portions of the Big Book:

> The tremendous fact for every one of us is that we have discovered a common solution. We have a way out on which we can absolutely agree, and upon which we can join in brotherly and harmonious action (p. 17).

---

[62] See Big Book, p. 63: "as we became conscious of His presence, we began to lose our fear of today, tomorrow or the hereafter. We were reborn."

[63] See *Pass It On* at page 198, which quotes the original Second Step language: "Came to believe that God could restore us to sanity." The present language, found on page 59 of the Big Book, is: "Came to believe that a Power greater than ourselves could restore us to sanity."

> Lack of power, that was our dilemma. We had to find a power by which we could live, and it had to be a Power greater than ourselves. Obviously. But where and how were we to find this Power? Well, that's exactly what this book is about. Its main object is to enable you to find a Power greater than yourself which will solve your problem. . . . And it means, of course, that we are going to talk about God. . . . We found that as soon as we were able to lay aside prejudice and express even a willingness to believe in a Power greater than ourselves, we commenced to get results, even though it was impossible for any of us to fully define or comprehend that Power, *which is God* (pp. 45-46) [emphasis ours].

Shoemaker had told, in his third story, of a group which had prayed together to help the man find the "Power." Shoemaker said they prayed:

> Opening their minds to as much of God as he [the man] understood, removing first the hindrance of self-will allowing the Spirit to focus an impression upon the mind, like light upon a camera exposed (p. 47).

Shoemaker reported that the man lifted his own life to God; the everlasting miracle of second birth happened; and the man experienced a sense of liberty, of peace, an inward glow, and a sense of rightness. Compare the Big Book's description of what happened when the early AAs took the Third Step:

> As we felt new power flow in, as we enjoyed peace of mind, as we discovered we could face life successfully, as we became conscious of His presence, we began to lose our fear of today, tomorrow or the hereafter. We were reborn (p. 63).

Shoemaker's next story told of a parishioner's coming to realize that "surrender" meant a great and life-giving relationship to God. She became converted. She reported that, "The surroundings did not change, but my attitude did—and all the irksomeness went" (p. 54). She said that in her own room great decisions have been made, and great renunciations which grew out of saying to God:

"Nevertheless not my will, but Thine" (p. 58). Compare this Big Book language:

> As we go through the day we pause, when agitated or doubtful, and ask for the right thought or action. We constantly remind ourselves we are no longer running the show, humbly saying to ourselves many times each day "Thy will be done." We are then in much less danger of excitement, fear, anger, worry, self-pity, or foolish decisions (pp. 87-88).

Next, Shoemaker wrote of a friend who couldn't find "a personal God" (p. 61). So he tried an experiment. He decided to become honest about himself with the crowd. He confessed his lack of interest in finding God. Then he experienced a feeling of lightness. Then, said Shoemaker: "Before the weekend was over, he had made the greatest 'decision': of his life—to surrender himself unconditionally and for always to the will of God" (pp. 61-62).

Compare these lines from Bill's Story in the Big Book:

> With ministers, and the world's religions, I parted right there. When they talked of a God personal to me, who was love, superhuman strength and direction, I became irritated and my mind snapped shut against such a theory (p. 10).
>
> My friend suggested what then seemed a novel idea. He said, "Why don't you choose your own conception of God?" That statement hit me hard. It melted the icy intellectual mountain in whose shadow I had lived and shivered many years. I stood in the light at last. It was only a matter of being willing to believe in a Power greater than myself. Nothing more was required for me to make my beginning. . . . At long last I saw, I felt, I believed (p. 12).
>
> There [shortly thereafter at Towns Hospital] I humbly offered myself to God, as I then understood Him, to do with me as He would. I placed myself unreservedly under His care and direction. My friend promised when these things [the other steps Bill's friend,

> Ebby, took with Bill at Towns Hospital] were done, I would enter upon a new relationship with my Creator (pp. 13-14).

In Shoemaker's next chapter, he described a lady called "A Fool For Christ."[64] She gave her life to Christ. And she talked about God's plan for the universe; of His plan for individual people; of finding that plan and living under the dominance of the Holy Spirit; of the necessity for letting go of your own plans and desires of your own life; and of trusting that God could run it better than yourself, as He saw fit to use you, not as you saw fit to serve Him. In the act of self-giving, the lady said, one had to be willing to break with anything wrong one was doing. And she herself thought of a man to whom she must go with apology, and seek to create a new relationship.

Compare these ideas in the Big Book:

> Are we now ready to let God remove from us all the things which we have admitted are objectionable? Can He now take them all—every one? If we still cling to something we will not let go, we ask God to help us be willing. . . . When ready, we say something like this: My Creator, I am now willing that you should have all of me, good and bad. I pray that you now remove from me every single defect of character which stands in the way of my usefulness to you and my fellows. . . . Now we need more action, without which we find that "Faith without works is dead. . . ."[65] We have a list of all persons we have harmed and to whom we are willing to make amends (p. 76).

The following chapter told of a lady who suffered from inner fears and anxieties which, as Shoemaker put it, had walled her away from God. Then, as he described it: "She surrendered to God her groundless fears, and with them *turned over to Him her life for His direction.*" Note that the original language Bill Wilson used in A.A.'s Third Step read as follows:

---

[64] See 1 Corinthians 4:9-10.

[65] See James 2:14, 17, 18, 20, 22, 26—"faith without works is dead."

> Made a decision to turn our wills and our lives over to the care and direction of God.[66]

Shoemaker told of another parishioner, a young Englishman, who made his decision for Christ. According to Shoemaker, the resultant experience of Christ meant that he could *understand* such expressions as "Conversion, God-guidance, winning people, and Quiet Times" (p. 85).[67]

Shoemaker wrote much in this book about "Quiet Times" and Guidance. He pointed to the practical aspect: "Keeping a daily Quiet Time along with God, the first thing in the morning" (p. 57). He said the early morning is the best time for quiet time, but not the only time. Note the Big Book's statement:

> On awakening let us think about the twenty-four hours ahead. We consider our plans for the day. Before we begin, we ask God to direct our thinking, especially asking that it be divorced from self-pity, dishonest or self-seeking motives (p. 86).

Shoemaker described all aspects of Quiet Time—Bible study, prayer, and listening for Guidance.

In two different stories, Shoemaker mentioned that this or that person had said he or she "got religion" (pp. 113, 165). Note that Ebby Thatcher had used that precise expression when he came to Bill, carrying the Oxford Group message. Ebby had looked Bill straight in the eye and had said, "I've got religion" (Big Book, p. 9).

Children of the Second Birth seemed to introduce the concept of "willingness"—based on John 7:17 ("If any man will do his will, he shall know . . ."). See pages 145 and 147. And Shoemaker

---

[66] *Pass It On*, p. 198.

[67] Compare 1 Corinthians 2:13-14: "Which things also we speak, not in words which man's wisdom teacheth, but which the Holy Ghost teacheth, comparing spiritual things with spiritual. But the natural man [of body and soul, but lacking spirit] receiveth not the things of the Spirit of God: for they are foolishness unto him: neither can he know them, because they are spiritually discerned."

wrote much about the way to keep the "New Life," as he called it (p. 148). It involved daily Quiet Time, Bible study, prayer, listening, and the power of God to lead and guide those obedient enough to be led. Shoemaker stressed the power of confession; and he emphasized the power that "comes with self humiliation, of abject honesty and ungrudging apology" (p. 153). Note the Big Book's discussion of the need for Fifth Step confession after completion of the Fourth Step self-examination:

> They never completed their housecleaning. They took inventory all right, but hung on to some of the worst items in stock. They only *thought* they had lost their egoism and fear; they only *thought* they had humbled themselves. But they had not learned enough of humility, fearlessness and honesty, in the sense we find it necessary, until they had told someone else all their life story (p. 73).

An important concluding chapter is entitled "Thy Will Be Done" (pp. 175-187). In it, Shoemaker wrote of the importance of surrender and of using the words of surrender which Jesus Christ uttered at Gethsemane: "Nevertheless, not my will, but thine, be done" (p. 182). Shoemaker ended this chapter as follows:

> It will be a great day for the Christian cause when the world begins to realize that "Thy will be done" does not belong on tombstones, but ought to be graven into the lives of eager men and women who have enlisted in God's warfare beyond return and beyond recall (p. 187).

And this message must have echoed down the halls to A.A. For Bill Wilson used many variations of "thy will be done" in the Big Book.[68]

---

[68] In the Big Book, see: (1) pp. 67, 88: "Thy will be done;" (2) p. 63: "May I do Thy will always;" (3) p. 76: "Grant me strength, as I go out from here, to do your bidding;" p. 85: and (4) "Thy will (not mine) be done."

Religion That Works

In many ways, the collection of Shoemaker sermons in *Religion That Works* is the most powerful part of the legacy Shoemaker bequeathed to Alcoholics Anonymous.[69]

His first chapter was entitled, "What If I had but one Sermon to Preach?" His theme verse was John 17:3:

> And this is life eternal, that they might know thee the only true God, and Jesus Christ, whom thou hast sent (p. 9).

Shoemaker then spoke of the homesickness of the human soul for God. He said the senses world seems well enough until our "spirit" is awake, after which we feel a lonely sense of uneasiness and an increasingly sharper sense of incompleteness. He said if we were what that interior incompleteness craves for, we should be like Christ. He said the nearer we become like Christ, and through Him reach the Father, the more fully is that intense and invisible longing satisfied and completed, so that whatever happens to the outward life, the inward life is rich and vivid and believing. He quoted St. Augustine's familiar saying: "Thou has made us for Thyself, and our hearts are restless till they find rest in Thee" (p. 11). He concluded: "The admission of that fact is the first step . . . to a genuine solution of the problem of life. We are homesick as we stand" (p. 11). Interestingly, one often hears in A.A. meetings about the hole the speaker had inside and the misery with which it left him or her until he or she found God and "filled" that hole with God.

Shoemaker's next topic was sin—the barrier between us and our best and between us and God. He said that when man has sinned, "prayer and peace are both impossible" (p. 11). The solution? Shoemaker said it is salvation. We need the Cross, he said—"the medicine of the world" (p. 12). And the offer of the Cross is

---

[69] Samuel Shoemaker, Jr., *Religion That Works* (New York: Fleming H. Revell, 1928).

conversion—the means by which a human soul can be lifted into a region hitherto undiscovered, where the rift in man's soul can be healed and the disunity harmonized. Then, he said, peace takes the place of pain and strength of weakness. "Ye must be born again," said Shoemaker, quoting Jesus's message in John 3:3 (p. 14).[70] And the new life, the new birth begins, he said, "by utter self-dedication to the will of God" (p. 14). Then, said Shoemaker, there is the possibility of a guided life, influenced and led at every step by the Holy Spirit. For conversion is the beginning, not the ending, of an experience of God. That conversion experience continues when we use all the means Jesus put at our disposal for continuation—prayer, the Scriptures, the Church, the Sacraments, Christian fellowship, and worship.

Shoemaker said many situations in life are not covered by the Sermon on the Mount. Man needs special guidance and illumination. Shoemaker pointed to the infinite possibilities of learning the will of God through communion with Him. He said God is knowable in Christ. And we do not know Him, nor have we really found Him, because we have not surrendered ourselves to Him. There is something within us He hates, and we will not let it go. There is a plan He has for us bigger than our own plan, and we are afraid of it. Somewhere we hold back. Somewhere we keep control of our own destiny. Then, using words which can certainly be found in A.A., Shoemaker said at page 19:

> Let go![71]
> Abandon yourself to Him.[72]
> Say to Him, "Not my will but Thine be done."[73]

---

[70] John 3:3: "Jesus answered and said unto him, Verily, verily, I say unto thee, Except a man be born again, he cannot see the kingdom of God."

[71] A.A. is certainly familiar with the slogan, "Let go and let God." See, for example, *A.A. Comes of Age*, p. 48.

[72] Big Book page 154 says, "Abandon yourself to God as you understand God" (p. 164).

[73] Big Book page 85 states: "Thy will (not mine) be done."

> Live it. Pray for it. Put yourself at His disposal for time and for eternity.[74]

In his next chapter, Shoemaker spoke of "The Necessity of Christ" (pp. 21-30). And he quoted several Bible verses. The first is John 1:18:

> No man hath seen God at any time; the only begotten Son, which is in the bosom of the Father, he hath declared *him* (pp. 21-23).

That verse, said Shoemaker, shows that God is hard to know and that apart from authentic revelation of Himself, God is obscure and unknowable. The verse tells us that Jesus, the only begotten Son, declares God and makes Him knowable and known. Then, said Shoemaker, there is the inevitable rough going in life. Those who wish to turn from confusion and restlessness can turn to Christ. And when they do, said Shoemaker, they have "got something."[75] They believe in and trust God. Note that the Big Book proclaims at page 68, "All men of faith have courage. They trust their God." Shoemaker said men trust God because they have come to know Him. He pointed to sin—the barrier between us and our own best and between us and God—and said we need a solution for sin. He said Christ offers three parts of the solution: (1) Forgiveness for the past—holding out the heart of God as willing to forgive anyone who comes in honest penitence and says he is sorry and means to stop; (2) Power to stop sinning; and (3) The Cross to make up for the mass of unatoned, unforgiven,

---

[74] Big Book page 85 states: "Step Eleven suggests prayer and meditation. We shouldn't be shy on this matter of prayer. Better men than we are using it constantly."

[75] An interesting comparison can be made between this language and the language Bill used when he checked into Towns Hospital after making his decision for Christ at Calvary Rescue Mission. Bill told Dr. Silkworth he had "found something." See *Pass It On*, p. 120. In *A.A. Comes of Age*, Bill himself gave a few more details. He said he shouted at Dr. Silkworth: "Doc, I've found something!" He said, "I tried to explain the new thing I thought I had found" (p. 62). But Bill was inebriated, and Silkworth simply ran Bill off to bed.

unwashed sin. Finally, and certainly in addition, Christ offers the solution of eternal life over death.

Shoemaker concluded with these verses from the Bible which emphasize Christ's role as Christ himself put it (p. 22):

> I am the way, the truth, and the life.[76]
> I am the bread of life.[77]
> I am the door.[78]
> I am the good shepherd.[79]
> I am the resurrection and the life.[80]
> I am the Son of God.[81]
> No man cometh unto the Father but by me.[82]

Shoemaker said it is not enough to know the centrality of Christ in Christian thinking. If Jesus could only provide a way of life, He would stand on a level with Confucius and Moses and Socrates. We must, said Shoemaker, make Him the center of our lives in thankfulness for what He has done for us and for all men.

Next, Shoemaker dealt with the problem of unbelief as described in Mark 6:6: "And he [Jesus] marvelled because of their unbelief. . . ." (pp. 31-42). Shoemaker remarked that we often think unbelief means intellectual unwillingness to swallow ancient doctrines. But to Shoemaker, it meant the dark conclusion of men

---

[76] John 14:6: "Jesus saith unto him, I am the way, the truth, and the life: no man cometh unto the Father but by me."

[77] John 6:35: "And Jesus said unto them, I am the bread of life: he that cometh to me shall never hunger; and he that believeth on me shall never thirst."

[78] John 10:9: "I am the door: by me if any man enter in, he shall be saved, and shall go in and out, and find pasture."

[79] John 10:14: "I am the good shepherd, and know my *sheep*, and am known of mine."

[80] John 11:25-26: "Jesus said unto her, I am the resurrection, and the life: he that believeth in me, though he were dead, yet shall he live: And whosoever liveth and believeth in me shall never die. . . ."

[81] John 10:36: "Say ye of him, whom the Father hath sanctified, and sent into the world, Thou blasphemest; because I said, I am the Son of God?"

[82] John 14:6.

who have looked life square in the face and said that it (life) is insensate and meaningless. He said the unbelief of which Jesus was speaking was simply the rejection of spiritual power in the plain face of that power. Unbelief was the refusal to recognize and accept a spiritual power whose force was manifested to people where they could all see it. Bill Wilson's chapter to the agnostics called up this same picture when he said:

> We agnostics and atheists chose to believe that our human intelligence was the last word, the alpha and the omega, the beginning and end of all.[83] Rather vain of us, wasn't it? We, who have traveled this dubious path, beg you to lay aside prejudice, even against organized religion (p. 49).
>
> Leaving aside the drink question, they [thousands of worldly men and women] tell why living was so unsatisfactory. They show how the change came over them. When many hundreds of people are able to say that the consciousness of the Presence of God is today the most important fact of their lives, they present a powerful reason why one should have faith (p. 51).
>
> When we saw others solve their problems by a simple reliance upon the Spirit of the Universe, we had to stop doubting the power of God. Our ideas did not work. But the God idea did. . . . We agnostics and atheists were sticking to the idea that self-sufficiency would solve our problems. When others showed us that "God-sufficiency" worked with them, we began to feel like those who had insisted the Wrights would never fly (pp. 52-53).[84]

Dr. Bob was more outspoken. In his Big Book story, Dr. Bob wrote:

---

[83] For the Biblical expression "Alpha and Omega, the beginning and the end(ing)," see Revelation 1:8; 21:6; and 22:13.

[84] Compare 2 Corinthians 3:5: "Not that we are sufficient of ourselves to think anything as of ourselves; but our sufficiency is of God;"

> If you think you are an atheist, an agnostic, a skeptic, or have any other form of intellectual pride which keeps you from accepting what is in this book, I feel sorry for you. . . . [W]e know that we have an answer for you. It never fails, if you go about it with one half the zeal you have been in the habit of showing when you were getting another drink. Your Heavenly Father will never let you down! (p. 181).

In any event, Shoemaker said the primary factor in the refusal of people to believe in the face of plain evidence of power was moral. Sin, he said, is always calling us to doubt. The profoundest scientist has prejudices, loves, temperament, and dispositional tendencies, which affect all his work; and enter into all his large judgments. All men sin; and unbelief and sin are sworn and congenital allies. If sin can make a man lose faith in God, it can have its own way with him. If doubt can make sin its ally, together they can rob man of God and wreck his life. Similarly, said Shoemaker, the *way out* of unbelief (and of sin) is moral. Jesus said in John 7:17: "If any man will do his will, he shall know . . ." Shoemaker said this means, "If any man will begin by living up to as much as he understands of the moral requisites of God, he will later, in the light of his experience, come to see straight intellectually" (p. 86). Note how Bill Wilson treated the topic in his agnostic chapter. Bill said:

> When, therefore, we speak to you of God, we mean your own conception of God. . . . At the start, this was all we needed to commence spiritual growth to effect our first conscious relation with God as we understood Him. Afterward, we found ourselves accepting many things which then seemed entirely out of reach. That was growth, but if we wished to grow we had to begin somewhere. So we used our own conception, however limited it was (p. 47).

Shoemaker said, "A moral experiment is worth ten times an intellectual investigation in apprehending spiritual truth. Obedience is as much the organ of spiritual understanding as reason" (p. 86).

Our own unfaith, he said, may make it impossible for God to do the work He wants to do through us. Unbelief isn't doubting some fact of long ago—unbelief is acting and feeling as though there were no God in the daily conduct of our lives. You can believe in miracles in the New Testament and in the Old, Shoemaker said; but if you cannot believe in miracles in your own life, your faith is cold, intellectual assent, and not the warm and vibrant thing Christ meant faith to be. Shoemaker said we should ask ourselves honestly just how much sin enters into our doubt—the sin of intellectual pride, the sin of self-pity which loves to think itself injured in an unjust cosmos, the sin of laziness which will not really investigate, the sin of fear which will not face God lest He ask of us that which we are unwilling to grant. Someone, said Shoemaker, needs to take down this generation in the pride of its intellect, and humble it before God. Knowledge of God is worth more than all the wisdom of the world. This age needs to know how much of its unbelief is conceit at the bottom.

Shoemaker's next topic was "The Meaning of Self-surrender" (pp. 43-53). And he said there are two ways to go about such a surrender. The first involves largely a deliberate act of the will. Man takes the plunge and throws himself utterly upon God to do with as He will. And note that Bill Wilson's Big Book story says of Bill's own surrender at Towns Hospital, "There I humbly offered myself to God, as I then understood Him, to do with me as He would" (p. 13). Two of the Oxford Group mentors, Dwight Moody and Professor Henry B. Wright, used John 7:17 as the theme for this type of surrender.[85] "Just do it, and know" might be a way of describing their thesis. But Shoemaker said there are those who simply cannot take the kingdom of heaven by force. For them, a great effort is needed just to open the door to their life to God. Shoemaker was speaking of their need for an open, relaxed, and unstruggling mind as the medium through which God alone

---

[85] See Douglas C. Macintosh, *Personal Religion* (New York: Charles Scribner's Sons, 1942), pp. 355-56, 365; and Henry B. Wright, *The Will of God and a Man's Life Work* (New York: The Young Men's Christian Association Press, 1909), pp. 19, 119-59.

could come into their lives. For some, then, there is not only the effort of deliberate self-surrender, but also a cessation of effort so as not to interfere with God's dealing with us. And again Shoemaker quoted William James on the "turning point."

He said James was talking about a "crisis" of self-surrender, not a "process" (p. 48). Shoemaker then dwelt on the "process" which comes *before* the act of surrender—the long discovery that the way of self is no way at all, and leads nowhither—the lonely, despairing, feverish desire to be rid of oneself. Compare Bill's Big Book explanation of this as an alcoholic would understand it:

> The old pleasures were gone. They were but memories. Never could we recapture the great moments of the past. There was an insistent yearning to enjoy life as we once did and a heartbreaking obsession that some new miracle of control would enable us to do it. . . . As we became subjects of King Alcohol, shivering denizens of his mad realm, the chilling vapor that is loneliness settled down. It thickened, ever becoming blacker. Some of us sought out sordid places, hoping to find understanding, companionship and approval. Momentarily we did—then would come oblivion and the awful awakening to face the hideous Four Horsemen—Terror, Bewilderment, Frustration, Despair (p. 151).

Shoemaker spoke of the process after surrender and said it is the steady matching up of the actual with the ideal, the rethinking and remolding of life in accordance with the great decision. Note how Bill Wilson said in his story, "No words can tell of the loneliness and despair I found in that bitter morass of self-pity" (Big Book, p. 8). Then Bill Wilson told of the essential requirements for establishing and maintaining "the new order of things." He said, "Simple, but not easy; a price had to be paid. It meant the destruction of self-centeredness" (Big Book, p. 14).

Shoemaker spoke of four immediate results of surrender when one has wholly let go of one's life and is living continually with reference to God. We'll set them out below; and, with them, we will give an A.A. reference which seems related:

1. A wide sense of liberation, for self-will has killed the very thing it wants—freedom. Joy follows this freedom (pp. 43-49). [Bill Wilson's story concerning his "hot flash" conversion experience said: "There was a sense of victory, followed by such a peace and serenity as I had never known. There was utter confidence. I felt lifted up." Big Book, p. 24.]

2. An inquiry into one's life plans in the large, to see if they are such as God would choose as His first, best plan for us (p. 49). [Bill Wilson said his friend, Ebby Thatcher, had returned to visit him at Towns Hospital after Bill's religious experience. Bill said, "My friend had emphasized the absolute necessity of demonstrating these principles in all my affairs. . . . Faith without works is dead. . . . For if an alcoholic failed to perfect and enlarge his spiritual life through work and self-sacrifice for others, he could not survive the certain trials and low spots ahead." Big Book, pp. 14-15].

3. The retroactive element—righting past wrongs (p. 49). [Bill reported in his account of the surrender "process," that "We [he and Ebby] made a list of people I had hurt or toward whom I felt resentment. I expressed my entire willingness to approach these individuals, admitting my wrong. . . . I was to right all such matters to the utmost of my ability." Big Book, p. 13].

4. Growing victory over sin. Deliverance—mastery over the quick tongue, the disagreeable spirit, the resentments (p. 50). [Dr. Bob often spoke of guarding that "erring member," the tongue.[86] Bill wrote, in his Tenth Step discussion, "We have entered the world of the spirit. Our next function is to grow in understanding and effectiveness. This is not an overnight matter. It should continue for our lifetime. Continue to watch for selfishness, dishonesty, resentment, and fear." Big Book, p. 84].

---

[86] *The Co-Founders of Alcoholics Anonymous: Biographical sketches. Their last major talks* (New York: Alcoholics Anonymous World Services, 1972, 1975), p. 9; and *DR. BOB and the Good Oldtimers*, p. 338.

A.A.'s Eleventh Step language evidences its concern for knowing the will of God. It says:

> Sought through prayer and meditation to improve our conscious contact with God as we understood Him, praying only for knowledge of His will for us and the power to carry that out (Big Book, p. 59).

Shoemaker devoted an entire chapter to "How To Know The Will of God" (pp. 54-65). In it, he borrowed heavily from the Scotch evangelist, Professor Henry Drummond. He said that it was the love of Drummond's life to do the will of God and that Drummond had written on the fly-leaf of his Bible these eight points as to the "how." These were the eight points:

First, "Pray." Shoemaker added that we often seek God's approval, rather than His will. He cautioned that to pray for God's will to be revealed, we must be ready and willing to have it revealed, and come to Him with an open mind, in great honesty, having put our own wills behind us and seeking candidly the mind of the Lord. These ideas flooded into A.A. and are perhaps best and most succinctly expressed at page 570 of the Big Book, as follows: "Most emphatically we wish to say that any alcoholic capable of honestly facing his problems in the light of our experience can recover, provided he does not close his mind to all spiritual concepts. . . . Willingness, honesty and open mindedness are the essentials of recovery. But these are indispensable." Shoemaker referred to John 7:17, emphasizing that man must *will* to do God's will. A person must start his prayer with obedience to what he already knows of God's will. Note that the Big Book suggests the following prayer with the following comment:

> Every day is a day when we must carry the vision of God's will into all of our activities. "How can I best serve Thee—Thy will (not mine) be done." These are thoughts which must go with us constantly. We can exercise our own will power along this line all we wish. It is the proper use of the will (p. 85).

Second, "Think." Shoemaker added there is a moral obligation to be as intelligent as you can and to face all the facts you can, honestly and fearlessly. Compare the Big Book's Fourth Step language: "Made a searching and fearless moral inventory of ourselves."

Third, "Talk to wise people, but do not regard their decision as final." Shoemaker added, "Consult them for what they are worth, but make the decision your own. The discussion should be to clear the issue, not to settle it." This Shoemaker idea comprehends the much debated, and probably much misunderstood Oxford Group concept of "checking." Bill Wilson ultimately criticized it; while Dr. Bob continued to endorse the idea—perhaps because, as A.A.'s own history states, "Dr. Bob probably knew more than Bill did about Oxford Group principles."[87]

Fourth, "Beware of this bias of your own will, but do not be too much afraid of it." Shoemaker pointed out that it is a mistake to think that God's will is in the line of the disagreeable. He said, "you will never really be happy anywhere else" (p. 61). Bill Wilson seemed to adopt this idea in the Big Book statement: "We are sure God wants us to be happy, joyous, and free" (p. 133).

Fifth, "Meantime, do the next thing, for doing God's will in small things is the best preparation for knowing it in great things." Sometimes, Shoemaker added, God makes us wait for the full emergence of His plan; and if we have been faithful in a few things, He will make us master of many things—revealing as much truth as we can live up to. Note the Big Book's statement: "We realize we know only a little. God will constantly disclose more to you and to us. . . . See to it that your relationship with Him is right, and great events will come to pass for you and countless others" (p. 164).

[87] Bill's criticism of "checking" can be found in *Pass It On* at page 172. Dr. Bob's endorsement of the practice can be found in *The Co-Founders of Alcoholics Anonymous* at pages 12-13. The statement that Dr. Bob probably knew more than Bill did about Oxford Group principles can be found in *Pass It On* at page 142.

Sixth, "When decision and action are necessary, go ahead." Shoemaker said the more you trust God in critical situations, the more you will learn you can trust Him; and if you will throw the onus of the decision off yourself and onto Him, giving Him only a ready and obedient will, you will be amazed at the way things work out for you. We have already quoted portions from the Big Book on dealing with fear and the Big Book's statement that people commence to outgrow fear when they trust God and let him demonstrate what He can do (Big Book, p. 68).

Seventh, "Never reconsider the decision once it is finally agreed upon." Shoemaker pointed out that even if a decision is made selfishly, we make the best of a bad bargain. Go forward and banish fear, he said. God always has a substitute will which goes into the game when the first-string will is out.

Eighth, "You will probably not find out until afterward that you were led at all." Shoemaker concluded that prayer is the heart of the discovery of the will of God; but the prayer that asks that God make known His will cannot happen without radical and basic surrender to the will of God first. Speaking of the efficacy of a prayer that we be shown all through the day what our next step is to be, the Big Book later adds:

> We constantly remind ourselves we are no longer running the show, humbly saying to ourselves many times each day "Thy will be done." We . . . are not burning up energy foolishly as we did when we were trying to arrange life to suit ourselves. It works—it really does. We alcoholics are undisciplined. So we let God discipline us in the simple way we have just outlined (pp. 87-88).

Shoemaker concluded that there can be no other success than to do what God wants you to do. And he quoted two verses which were of major importance to him in establishing the importance of doing God's will (p. 65):

> Not every one that saith unto me, Lord, Lord, shall enter into the kingdom of heaven; but he that doeth the will of my Father which is in heaven.[88]

> And he trembling and astonished said, Lord, what wilt thou have me to do? And the Lord *said* unto him. Arise, and go into the city, and it shall be told thee what thou must do.[89]

Throughout his writings, and in this book in particular, Shoemaker made much of the "Fellowship of the Holy Ghost"—centering his discussion around 2 Corinthians 13:14 (pp. 66-76):

> The grace of the Lord Jesus Christ, and the love of God, and the communion of the Holy Ghost, *be* with you all. Amen.

Interestingly, the next to the last line in the basic text of the Big Book states on page 164, "We shall be with you in the Fellowship of the Spirit."[90]

Shoemaker felt that the fellowship, or communion, of the Holy Spirit had a very special meaning: It was the fellowship of believing people which was created by the Holy Spirit, rather than fellowship individually with the Holy Spirit himself. Shoemaker said there are two very different ideas: one is in an individual; the other is a corporate experience. One finds the Holy Spirit unmediated; the other, said Shoemaker, finds Him through group experience of men and women like-minded. We will not dwell on

---

[88] From Jesus Christ's Sermon on the Mount, Matthew 7:21.

[89] From the exchange between Jesus Christ and Saul (who, after his conversion, was called Paul) on the Road to Damascus, Acts 9:6.

[90] The terms "Holy Ghost" and "Holy Spirit" in the King James Version are both translations of the same two Greek words in the Greek New Testament. The Greek words are *pneuma hagion*, which are best translated in modern usage as "holy spirit." And Shoemaker usually spoke of the "Holy Spirit" rather than the "Holy Ghost." For the similarities between the terms "ghost" and "spirit" in the English language, particularly when they are used in the phrases "holy ghost" and "holy spirit," see Merriam-Webster's Collegiate Dictionary. Tenth Edition. (Mass: Merriam-Webster, 1993), p. 554.

this at any length. But Shoemaker held that the real first century Christian fellowship had a deep cause: the common discovery of spiritual truth which came from the fellowship of the Holy Spirit—an unmistakable mark of sheer vitality, of heightened power and amplified possibilities, which means they struck a whole new vein of truth about life. And it is the author's belief that Bill Wilson picked up on this idea in his statement of A.A.'s Tradition Two:

> For our group purpose there is but one ultimate authority—a loving God as He may express Himself in our group conscience.[91]

Shoemaker cited as authority for his idea the following declaration of Jesus Christ:

> For where two or three are gathered together in my name, there am I in the midst of them.[92]

Shoemaker believed the "Spirit" can communicate "His" truth to a spiritual fellowship of believers in ways He cannot communicate it to individuals. And it seems to the author that Bill Wilson held to this same idea that God communicates to a group in a special way, distinct from His communication to individuals in the group.

Shoemaker wrote a chapter on "Isaiah's Vision of God," where Isaiah and God had colloquy (pp. 88-99). Shoemaker referred particularly to Isaiah, Chapter 6, where the following is set forth:

> Also I heard the voice of the Lord, saying, Whom shall I send, and who will go for us? Then said I, Here *am* I; send me. And he said, Go, and tell this people. . . ."[93]

---

[91] Big Book, p. 564.

[92] Matthew 18:20.

[93] Isaiah 6:8-9. Interestingly, Henry Fitzhugh M. (one of the early AAs in New York who was very religious in his views and who also was a close friend of Bill and Lois) wrote in his Big Book story about a suggestion made to him about how to pray. He was

(continued...)

Shoemaker was speaking, he said, of an experience of hearing, seeing, feeling, or discovering—which causes a man or woman to acquire an absolute faith. This, said Shoemaker, is the faith described in Hebrews 11:6 (p. 88):

> But without faith *it is* impossible to please him: for he that cometh to God must believe that he is, and *that* he is a rewarder of them that diligently seek him.

Shoemaker and other Oxford Group writers often referred to the verse in Hebrews 11:6 to establish that faith comes only when one believes that God is and rewards those who diligently seek Him.[94] The author believes the counterpart of this idea can be found on page 60 of the Big Book, which states that its writers were "convinced" of three things:

> (a) That we were alcoholic and could not manage our own lives.
> (b) That probably no human power could have relieved our alcoholism.
> (c) That God could and would if He were sought.

Shoemaker had much to say about Isaiah's talk with God. He said Isaiah stood in the presence of God long enough to let God sink in. Isaiah confessed his own utter need, his desperate guilt and shame. And, said Shoemaker, to such honesty, God can respond with the gift of grace, with the helping hand of His extended power. Then, said Isaiah to God: "Here *am* I; send me."

---

[93] (...continued)
told to pray by saying, "God here I am and here are all my troubles. I've made a mess of things and can't do anything about it. You take me, and all my troubles, and do anything you want with me." See Big Book, p. 504.

[94] Samuel M. Shoemaker, *The Gospel According To You* (New York: Fleming H. Revell, 1934), p. 47; *National Awakening* (New York: Harper & Brothers, 1936), pp. 40-41; *Religion That Works*, p. 55; and *Confident Faith* (New York: Fleming H. Revell, 1932), p. 187; Leslie D. Weatherhead, *How Can I Find God?* (London: Hodder and Stoughton, 1933), p. 72; and Philip Leon, *The Philosophy of Courage or The Oxford Group Way* (New York: Oxford University Press, 1939), p. 19.

It was an offer, said Shoemaker, of self. Isaiah definitely asked for a commission when he responded to God's question by saying, ". . . Send me!" Shoemaker suggested that man put aside not the pride of presumption so much as the pride of false humility and say: "Here am I. Send me." Then, said Shoemaker, God says: "Go!" (p. 99).

Shoemaker's final chapter was on "The Higher Reaches of Christian experience" (pp. 119-28). He wrote:

> Religion is dedicated to the proposition that there is a spirit in man: and that however strong or evil his instincts may be, they can be brought into line with the high desires of the spirit. Christianity passionately believes that (p. 119).

He then suggested we all "lift up our eyes unto the hills" (p. 120).[95]

We need to consider several high places of the spirit. The first, he said, was the high place of "faith." And he was talking about the high hill of such trust in God as literally transfigures the earth. A faith which refuses ever to consider any situation a trap, but views each situation as a crucible in which some creative event may take place. This was the kind of faith which set Saint Paul to work in prison as effectively as in the marketplace. Shoemaker referred to Acts 16, where Paul and Silas were brought into the market-place before the magistrates, were then beaten, and were finally imprisoned. They sang praises to God and prayed. An earthquake occurred. The prison doors opened, and every one's bands were loosed. They then witnessed to the amazed keeper of the prison, promising salvation if he believed on the Lord Jesus Christ. The keeper and his house were saved; and they rejoiced—believing in God.[96]

Shoemaker said he was talking about the faith which is sure of the final conquest of good over evil—sure because the quantity of

---

[95] Psalm 121:1

[96] Acts 16:16-34.

evil is outweighed by the quality of good, and because God is God. Note that, in the chapter to the agnostics, the Big Book said, "We had to stop doubting the power of God. . . . We had to fearlessly face the proposition that either God is everything or else He is nothing. . . . [Having] arrived at this point, we were squarely confronted with the question of faith" (pp. 52-53). And the Big Book concludes this "faith" chapter by talking about the "miracle of healing," saying, "Even so has God restored us all to our right minds" (p. 57).

Shoemaker next spoke of living in the high places of "love." Though not mentioning 1 Corinthians 13, Shoemaker paraphrased its language and spoke of the love that rejoices in the success of rivals, is fair to the truth of critics, and is patient toward those who wilfully misunderstand us; the love that is the great reconciler. And it extends even to those who irritate. These definitions of love—some coming from the Sermon on the Mount and some from 1 Corinthians 13—seem to find expression in the Big Book's frequent mention of patience, tolerance, understanding, kindliness, and love.[97] That these basic principles in the Big Book probably came from the Bible—whether they came via Shoemaker, the Oxford Group, or the Bible itself—seems confirmed by Dr. Bob's statement that the Sermon on the Mount contained A.A.'s underlying philosophy, and that the Sermon on the Mount, the Book of James, and 1 Corinthians 13 were considered "absolutely essential" as an answer to AAs' problems.[98]

Shoemaker also spoke of the high place of "humility"—a topic that fills the pages of the Big Book.[99] He spoke of the vital importance of "prayer." He was speaking of the height a man reaches when prayer becomes the climate of his life. We have already mentioned the Big Book's stress on prayer.[100] And Shoemaker concluded with his oft-mentioned topic of

---

[97] Big Book, pp. 83, 118.

[98] *DR. Bob and the Good Oldtimers*, pp. 228, 96.

[99] Big Book, pp. 13, 57, 59, 63, 68, 73, 76, 85, 87-88, 164.

[100] See, for example, Big Book, pp. 85-86.

"witness"—the necessity of an individual's learning how to share his faith with others.

Twice-Born Ministers

In this fifth book, Shoemaker frequently spoke about "A First Century Christian Fellowship," of which he said he and his Calvary Church were very much a part.[101] He dedicated the book itself to the Fellowship's founder, Dr. Frank N. D. Buchman. And the name of Buchman's group—"A First Century Christian Fellowship"—found place on the announcements and programs of almost all Oxford Group "houseparties" that were held in the late 1920's and early 1930's.[102] Some of these houseparties were attended, at a later point, by Bill and Lois Wilson.[103] And, as we have mentioned previously, Dr. Bob said the members of "the alcoholic squad of the Oxford Group" were "a Christian Fellowship."[104]

The *Twice-Born Ministers* book itself tells the stories of a number of members of the clergy whose lives were changed by being born again. Their steps involved ideas which found their way into A.A. language and concepts.

In an early chapter, Shoemaker told of an organist in one minister's church who found that selfishness, pettiness, and temper had made it difficult for herself and others. These shortcomings were "blocking her from Christ" (p. 32). In this connection, compare the Big Book statement, "We hope you are convinced now that God can remove whatever self-will has blocked you off from Him" (p. 71). The organist made a decision for Christ and

---

[101] Samuel Shoemaker, Jr., *Twice-Born Ministers* (New York: Fleming H. Revell, 1929), pp. 23, 46, 90, 95, 101, 147, 148.

[102] Dick B., *The Akron Genesis of Alcoholics Anonymous*, pp. 147, 175.

[103] *Pass It On*, pp. 168-170; and *Lois Remembers*, p. 103.

[104] Dick B., *The Akron Genesis*, pp. 187-88.

became, said Shoemaker, a more loving and effective person. Another parishioner, an agnostic, was undergoing a miserably unhappy domestic situation. That woman was brought, through honest and deep sharing, and a decision for Christ, to "a real and glowing experience of Christ," said Shoemaker (p. 33).

Another chapter told of a minister's coming to realize the importance of honesty through telling another about oneself. The man said he "saw for the first time that honesty with others about oneself was the first step in knowledge of God" (p. 50). Compare the Big Book's discussion of the Fifth Step which states, "They had not learned enough of humility, fearlessness and honesty, in the sense we find it necessary, until they told someone else *all* their life story" (p. 73). Shoemaker said the minister realized the importance of sharing "to the limit of my own spiritual experience" (p. 56). And this idea that a spiritual experience must *shared* became much embedded in A.A. language.[105] Shoemaker concluded by stressing the importance of confiding one's troubles and sufferings, one's triumphs and hopes, and one's life experience of all sorts. He said, "The conspiracy of silence about sin, about deliverance, about spiritual experience has lasted long enough. This generation is frank about other things, and they want the truth about what God does for us" (p. 61). Note in this connection that Ebby Thatcher, fresh from his Calvary Church-Oxford Group indoctrination, was reported by Bill to have done the following: "My friend sat before me, and he made the point-blank declaration that God had done for him what he could not do for himself. . . . That floored me. It began to look as though religious people were right after all."[106]

In another chapter, Shoemaker dealt with Oxford Group Founder Dr. Frank Buchman's four absolute standards—the four absolutes of honesty, purity, unselfishness, and love (pp. 83-95). Standards that were so much a part of early A.A. and still persist in some

[105] Big Book, pp. 25, 27, 569-70.

[106] Big Book, p. 11.

present-day A.A. areas as "yardstick" principles to practice.[107] Shoemaker pointed to four things he said the person who was the subject of the story had learned from Frank Buchman (p. 92):

1. There was one person who had wronged me whom I would not forgive.[108]
2. There was a restitution which I would not make.[109]
3. There was a doubtful pleasure which I would not give up.
4. There was a sin in the long past which I would not confess.[110]

The person said that when the foregoing things were straightened out, he not only came to a new power and release, but for the first time began to get daily guidance which he knew could be relied and acted upon because his own life was disciplined. Here we are reminded of the so-called "promises" in pages 83 and 84 of the Big Book. The promises state that when the AAs have been painstaking about their first nine steps, which include making restitution, they will be "amazed" before they are half-way through. They will know "a new freedom and a new happiness." They will "comprehend the word serenity . . . and know peace;"

---

[107] See the discussion in Mel B., *New Wine: The Spiritual Roots of the Twelve Step Miracle* (Minnesota: Hazelden, 1991), pp. 21, 41, 64, 76, 95, 98, 138; *The Co-Founders of Alcoholics Anonymous: Biographical sketches; Their last major talks* (New York: Alcoholics Anonymous World Services, Inc., 1972, 1975), pp. 12-13; *DR. BOB*, pp. 54, 163; *Pass It On*, pp. 127, 172; *Alcoholics Anonymous Comes of Age*, pp. 75, 161; *The Language of the Heart*, pp. 196-100; *The Four Absolutes*, published by Cleveland AA, 940 Rockefeller Building, 614 Superior Avenue, N.W. Cleveland, Ohio 44113; the 1940-1942 issues of the *Cleveland Central Bulletin*, which bore the Four Absolutes on its masthead; and Ernest Kurtz, *Not-God: A History of Alcoholics Anonymous*. Expanded ed. (Minnesota: Hazelden, 1991), pp. 242-243.

[108] See the Big Book, pages 65, 67, 70, 77, which deals with listing the people we have harmed, straightening things out, and going about it in a helpful and forgiving spirit.

[109] See Big Book, p. 76, which deals with asking God for the willingness to go out to our fellows and repair the damage done in the past.

[110] See Big Book, p. 75, which points out that in A.A.'s Fifth Step—the confession step: "We pocket our pride and go to it, illuminating every twist of character, every dark cranny of the past, . . . withholding nothing."

and they "will suddenly realize" that God is doing for them what they could not do for themselves.

A subsequent chapter placed emphasis on "Let go and let God" (pp. 96-109). This expression, of course, is well-known in A.A. and elsewhere.[111] The family of one of early A.A.'s founders, Henrietta Seiberling, put the slogan "Let go and let God" on Henrietta's tombstone. In any event, Shoemaker's chapter described two ministers who were not facing themselves honestly and were in fear of losing direction in their lives. Both laid themselves open in the presence of a friend who laid his life alongside of theirs. And both found the beginning of a remaking.

Another chapter told of a minister suffering from fear and selfishness (pp. 110-127). He was choking on the idea that he could somehow make decisions without the guidance of God. He had decided that experience was experience even if it was experienced without God's will. Finally, the minister turned to God and spoke out loud, "O God, if Thou canst use me now, at last I am ready" (p. 120). There followed "a sudden, indescribable lightness of body and mind; and the joy. . ." (p. 120). This might be compared to Bill Wilson's description of his own spiritual experience when he cried out at Towns Hospital, "If there be a God, let Him show himself."[112] In the Big Book, Bill reported that the effect of this cry was electric: "There was a sense of victory, followed by such a peace and serenity as I had never known. There was utter confidence. I felt lifted up, as though the great clean wind of a mountain top blew through and through" (Big Book, p. 14).

Shoemaker's minister reported that he then began a steady practice of early morning Quiet Time and fellowshipping with friends at First Century Christian Fellowship houseparties, which was something Bill Wilson himself did after his release from

---

[111] *A.A. Comes of Age*, p. 48; and Jan R. Wilson and Judith A. Wilson, *Addictionary: A Primer of Recovery Terms and Concepts from Abstinence To Withdrawal* (New York: Simon & Schuster, 1992), p. 110.

[112] *Pass It On*, p. 121.

Towns Hospital. The minister reported that in the fellowship he discovered friends "who were being brought into a new and abiding consciousness of God's presence and His claims upon their lives" (p. 123). Compare Bill's statement in the Big Book that "many hundreds of people are able to say that the consciousness of the Presence of God is today the most important fact of their lives" (p. 51).[113] Shoemaker's minister began placing complete trust in God as to the future. And the minister said, "So long as the barriers of sin—rebellion, self-pity, the sins which fester in idleness—are faced and destroyed through confession, prayer, and forgiveness, spiritual growth need never stop. . . . This is the life that makes us free" (p. 127). Again, compare one of A.A.'s "promises": "That feeling of uselessness and self-pity will disappear" (Big Book, p. 84).

Another of Shoemaker's stories concerned a minister who was impressed by four people whose lives had changed (pp. 128-140). Of the first, the minister said that the man's honest sharing of his own need, and of the way Christ had helped him, enabled the minister to have confidence in ultimate victory over inner defeat. The second person's story of surrender to Christ had punctured the minister's pride. The third got across to him the power of disciplined and Christ-inspired love for one's fellow-men. And he said the challenge of the fourth man's story lay in his sheer life of guidance and faith.

The minister himself then tackled the problem of his relation to his father. He confessed to his father and restored for the wrong in his antagonism of five years's standing. Nonetheless, the minister continued to march to his own tune in his general life. Then he read an article entitled "The Conversion of a Sinner." In that article, he saw the fruit of *self-will* in that "sinner's" breakdown. He said it showed him that he himself was really

---

[113] See also the Big Book, pp. 56 ("overwhelmed by a conviction of the presence of God"); p. 63 ("we became conscious of His presence"); p. 85, ("To some extent we have become God-conscious"); p. 162 ("Many of us have felt, for the first time, the Presence and Power of God"), and p. 570 ("God-consciousness").

living independent of Christ's power and direction, really leaning on his own strength for every important decision.

The minister reported that he had then made "the decision to cast my will and my life on God" (p. 134). He said "There came an indescribable sense of relief, of burdens dropping away" (p. 134). And there are remarkable parallels between this story and Big Book language.

For one thing, the Big Book speaks of the alcoholic as "an extreme example of *self-will* run riot" (p. 62). It then says that "we had to quit playing God. It didn't work. . . . [W]e *decided* that hereafter . . . God was going to be our director" (p. 62) [emphasis ours]. Then the Big Book describes the decision to let God be God and says, "we enjoyed peace of mind." Summing it all up, the Big Book's actual Third Step decision is very similar in content to the decision just described in *Twice-Born Ministers*. Let's compare the two:

> I decided "to cast my will and my life on God."[114]

> We "[m]ade a decision to turn our will and our lives over to the care of God *as we understood Him*.[115]

Shoemaker's next story concerned a college freshman who had decided for the ministry (pp. 141-152). The man said he knew he needed to face a complete and unreserved surrender in his life; and he made it after being perfectly honest with another man about his own inner life as he knew God saw it. Soon, however, the freshman was back to his old ways and forgot about his surrender. Then, as he put it, he realized the abundant life was more than the conversion of the moment; for, he said, the implications of conversion "are the work of a lifetime, and he concluded there is need for daily surrender" (p. 149).

---

[114] Shoemaker, *Twice-Born Ministers*, p. 134.

[115] Big Book, p. 59.

He went to a room with another member of the First Century Christian Fellowship and said the man gave him the four absolute principles of Christ—honesty, purity, unselfishness, and love. Then the man asked the freshman how his life stacked up beside them. He also told the freshman about himself. Soon, said Shoemaker, the freshman reached what he called "a turning-point in my life" (p. 151). He confessed all of his secrets and shames, and felt a release and happiness he had not known before. The concept in this story—the concept of continuance, of the need for daily practice of principles—finds place in A.A.'s Tenth, Eleventh, and Twelfth Steps. Many in A.A. call them the "maintenance" steps. Others call them the "growth" steps. The Big Book introduces them with these statements:

> We have entered the world of the spirit. Our next function is to grow in understanding and effectiveness. This is not an overnight matter. It should continue for our lifetime. Continue to watch for selfishness, dishonesty, resentment, and fear. . . . (p. 84)
>
> It is easy to let up on the spiritual program of action and rest on our laurels. We are headed for trouble if we do, for alcohol is a subtle foe. We are not cured of alcoholism. What we really have is a daily reprieve contingent on the maintenance of our spiritual condition. Every day is a day when we must carry the vision of God's will into all our activities (p. 85).

Shoemaker's final chapter was entitled, "How shall I begin?" (pp. 181-98). And he was writing about how the message of his book about rebirth could be made effective in the lives of others. For his answer, he took the verse in 1 John 1:3 (pp. 181-82):

> That which we have seen and heard declare we unto you, that ye also may have fellowship with us: and truly our fellowship *is* with the Father, and with his Son Jesus Christ.

Shoemaker said he never learned more about religious work than he learned from Oxford Group Founder, Frank Buchman.

Buchman had said, "The first and fundamental need is ourselves" (p. 182). Shoemaker said the whole witnessing process must begin with a fresh sense of sin; a questioning of ourselves about professional ambition, discouragement and self-pity, grudges, our dispositions, our sins of the flesh, and our want of private prayer and Bible study. Shoemaker said there will never be effectual work with others except it begins in an experience of our own.

Bill Wilson put it this way in the Big Book:

> Ask Him in your morning meditation what you can do each day for the man who is still sick. The answers will come, *if your own house is in order*. But obviously you cannot transmit something you haven't got. See that your relationship with Him is *right*, and great events will come to pass for you and countless others (p. 164, emphasis ours).

Shoemaker said our own experience, our own work with others, must begin with a confession. Then with a surrender involving a break with our particular sins, and including restoration and restitution, confession and forgiveness. But, he said, the core of the new life must be the Holy Spirit. Guidance will not come without a definite time in the morning for sufficient prayer, Bible study, and listening for the Holy Spirit's direction. This, he said, requires digging out with our own minds [intuition]. And the Big Book speaks of asking God for "inspiration, an intuitive thought or a decision."[116] But Shoemaker makes the point that Quiet Time process involves "intuition" *plus* (p. 184). Then, he said, there must be the winning of another; telling that person what Christ has done for us. It means helping others to itemize surrender—facing problems together, remembering them; making a decision; then giving all their sins and problems to God; taking a different way for the rest of their lives; and trusting God for all that they cannot see at the time. Shoemaker said the greatest help in continuance, next to vital Quiet Time, is a *sharing fellowship*

---

[116] Big Book, p. 86.

(p. 190)—something that AAs seemed to have appropriated in their insistence on regular, continuing attendance at meetings of the A.A. Fellowship.

If I Be Lifted Up

Shoemaker said in the Foreword that he wrote *If I Be Lifted Up* to approach the central meaning of the Cross of Christ.[117] He took John 12:32 as his title and theme verse:

> And I, if I be lifted up from the earth, will draw all *men* unto me.

In the foregoing statement, Jesus was speaking to the people about his own glorification, his death and the fruit it would bear, and the way in which he would cast out the prince of this world—the devil. And one might ask why this Shoemaker book would be discussed in any analysis of Shoemaker and A.A. Surely there is no talk in the Big Book or Twelve Steps about the Cross of Christ or Atonement. Yet one must realize that neither Bill Wilson and his small band in New York, nor Dr. Bob and the alcoholic squad of the Oxford Group in Akron, were merely hearing in their meetings about "aggressive evangelism," "absolutes," being "maximum," "soul-surgery," or "checking," as might be inferred from reading Bill Wilson's later criticisms of the Oxford Group.[118] In fact, the author has seen very little evidence that Dr. Bob agreed with Bill's views. We believe the major reason for Bill's departure from the Oxford Group in New York in 1937, *as he saw it at that time*—after only two-and-a-half

---

[117] Samuel Shoemaker, Jr., *If I Be Lifted Up* (New York: Fleming H. Revell, 1931), pp. 7-8.

[118] See Bill's detailed criticisms of the Oxford Group and his assertions about "a vast and sometimes unreasoning prejudice. . . . all over this country against the O.G. and its successor M.R.A." *Pass It On*, pp. 171-73.

years of participation—was his uncomfortable feeling that his emphasis on working with drunks was not well received at Calvary Church.[119] And apparently Bill's approach was not welcome at Calvary—a fact verified by the apology Shoemaker later made to Bill.[120] However, the major focus of the Oxford Group meetings at the T. Henry Williams home in Akron *was* on helping drunks. Moreover, Dr. Bob's last major talk to A.A. in 1948 contained no recital of objections either to the Oxford Group or to its ideas. In fact, Dr. Bob then discussed the Oxford Group's Four Absolutes and said, "I think the absolutes still hold good and can be extremely helpful."[121]

Early AAs heard *much* in their Oxford Group meetings about Jesus Christ and the Cross of Christ. In fact, Dr. Bob's wife, Anne Smith, highly recommended Shoemaker's *If I Be Lifted Up* in the workbook she read to early AAs and the families in the Smith home.[122] Henrietta Seiberling read *If I Be Lifted Up*.[123] And it was on the Oxford Group Literature List in the *Calvary Church Evangel,* and thus was an Oxford Group book "of the day."[124] But we will not get into Shoemaker's theology of the Cross. Shoemaker said Jesus saw the prince of the world expelled while he, being lifted up on his Cross, would draw the world away after a new ideal of spiritual values. Far more important for our

---

[119] See *Pass It On* for a discussion of the tension which developed over Bill's focus on alcoholics and holding special meetings with and for them (pp. 168-171). The other reasons Bill gave for his distaste for the Oxford Group can be seen as later arguments as to why the break-off had been a good one, but several of his reasons seem to have been based on events which came into focus after Bill left the Oxford Group in 1937. See *Pass It On*, pages 171-173. In any event, that is how the author viewed it considering the fact that Dr. Bob never expressed such concerns, and was very reluctant and upset over the break-off when it occurred in 1939 in Akron. See *DR. BOB and the Good Oldtimers*, pp. 156-71.

[120] See *Pass It On*, p. 178 footnote.

[121] *Co-Founders*, p. 13.

[122] See Dick B., *Anne Smith's Spiritual Workbook* (Seattle: Glen Abbey Books, 1993), pp. 12-13, 17-18.

[123] Dick B., *The Akron Genesis of Alcoholics Anonymous*, pp. 85, 87.

[124] Dick B., *The Akron Genesis of Alcoholics Anonymous*, pp. 56-58.

study, Shoemaker mentioned a number of ideas which can be found in later A.A. language.

Shoemaker said he wanted to talk about "the quality in man which is farthest from the Cross and therefore needs spiritual treatment more than any of our moral ills" (p. 26). That, said Shoemaker, is our pride. Shoemaker called pride the deadliest sin of all (p. 27). He called the Cross God's "antidote to pride" (p. 33). On pages 34-35, he cited Philippians 2:6-8:

> Who [Christ Jesus], being in the form of God, thought it not robbery to be equal with God: But made himself of no reputation, and took upon him the form of a servant, and was made in the likeness of men: And being found in fashion as a man, he humbled himself, and became obedient unto death, even the death of the cross.

Interestingly, Shoemaker said the antidote to pride is not humility, but gratitude. He said humility means a person is still struggling with his own attitude. Gratitude means that the person has found something without, in the presence of which to forget himself and bow down in thankfulness. He said pride may hide unseen in humility, but pride is gone out of thankfulness.

Shoemaker cautioned:

> Do not marvel at what God has done *through* you, for you may wind up merely marveling at you: but marvel at what God has done *for* you, for He has had compassion on you and is saving you unto eternal life (p. 34).

Shoemaker concluded with a prayer that man be thankful for God's mercy, and humble for His Love through Jesus Christ. Dr. Bob appears to have grasped this Shoemaker humility concept, whether he got it from Shoemaker or not. Dr. Bob said in his last major address to A.A.:

> Another thing with which most of us are not too blessed is the feeling of humility. I don't mean the fake humility of Dickens's

> Uriah Heep. I don't mean the doormat variety; we are not called upon to be shoved around and stepped on by anyone; we have a right to stand up for our rights. I'm talking about the attitude of each and every one of us toward our Heavenly Father. Christ said, "Of Myself, I am nothing—My strength cometh from My Father in Heaven." If He had to say that, how about you and me? Did you say it? Did I say it? No. That's exactly what we didn't say. We were inclined to say instead, "Look me over, boys. Pretty good, huh?" We had no humility, no sense of having received anything through the grace of our Heavenly Father.[125]

And Dr. Bob ended his story in the Big Book: "Your Heavenly Father will never let you down!" (p. 181).

Shoemaker spoke of getting rid of fear and self-will (pp. 38-47). As to fear, he said man must face the worst in reality and in possibility, be honest with himself and those who have a right to know about it, and then expose himself to searching religious experience. As to self-will, Shoemaker called for man to crucify self to be brought to a new life through the death of self-will. Note Bill's Story in the Big Book, which says: "Belief in the power of God, plus enough willingness, honesty and humility to establish and maintain the new order of things, were the essential requirements. Simple, but not easy; a price had to be paid. It meant the destruction of self-centeredness" (pp. 13-14).

Shoemaker wrote a chapter on Christ's seven last words from the cross (pp. 73-116)—also the subject of a later book.[126] *If I Be*

---

[125] *Co-Founders*, pp. 14-15.

[126] This later book was Samuel Shoemaker's *Christ's Words From the Cross* (New York: Fleming H. Revell, 1933). The author will not review this book separately because of its particular focus on the Passion and because the material is well covered in *If I Be Lifted Up*. However, concepts in *Christ's Words* which *should be noted* are Shoemaker's reference to Jesus Christ as Savior and Lord (p. 11); honesty about ourselves (p. 12); estrangement from God (p. 18); trust in God, not self—with a believing, derivative life, instead of an effortful and self-propelled one (p. 35); finding a personal God who can truly be called Father (p. 43); humanity's homesickness for God (pp. 44-45); self-surrender to God to bring about a right relationship with God (p. 49); and, again, Paul's surrender through asking, "Lord, what wilt thou have me to do?" (p. 52).

Lifted Up covered these ideas: (1) God's forgiveness, assuring instantaneous companionship in the world beyond (pp. 76-79). (2) The necessity for conversion—the sudden kind, that occurred when the thief on the next cross turned to Christ a penitent (pp. 79-82), and the kind called for in Romans 10:9—a confession that Jesus is Lord and a belief that God raised him from the dead (p. 83). (3) Jesus's concern for human needs—those of his mother and his beloved disciple, John (pp. 85-91). (4) Jesus's acquiescence in God's will when he said, "Nevertheless, not my will, but thine, be done" (pp. 91-97). (5) Jesus's humanness in saying, "I thirst" (pp. 97-103). (6) Jesus's understanding of his real mission when he said, "It is finished" (pp. 103-09). (7) The natural ending of a life spent in doing God's will, exemplified by Jesus's words, "Father, into thy hands I commend my spirit" (pp. 109-16).

Shoemaker ended his "Last Words" chapter by pointing out that salvation comes through the mercy of God, not the merit of man. The Cross signifies not how little we can do for ourselves, but how much God has done for us. And how many times A.A.'s Big Book speaks of the grace of God and the realization that God has done for the alcoholic what he could not do for himself.[127]

Shoemaker's concluding chapters pointed out that man's deepest need is not for more instruction in moral principles, but for more inspiration; not for more knowledge of what to do, but for some liberated power in putting all that into effect. Then he used words that seem prophetic of A.A. ideas. He said:

> The fact is that I sin. I deliberately sin. With my eyes open. . . . There are moral lapses in me for which I can never hope to atone. . . . It [sin] makes a gap between myself and the Ideal which I am *powerless* to bridge. . . . Only God, therefore, can deal with sin. He must contrive to do for us what *we have lost the power to do ourselves*. . . .[128] The deepest meaning of the Cross is that God

---

[127] See, for example, Big Book, pp. 11, 25, 50, 57, 71, 84, 100.

[128] See the language of A.A.'s First Step: "We admitted we were powerless over alcohol—that our lives had become unmanageable."

> made reconciliation for us with Himself. . . . Something done for us—a gift to us. Grace comes first, then character. Salvation first, then service. . . . Our most serious problem today, I think, is not outbreaking sin, but pride. . . . It is God's utmost to shake us out of our independence. . . . Not only can we count upon the love of God at all times: but He has sealed and demonstrated that love in the Atonement of the Cross. As St. Paul says, "We have received the reconciliation."[129] The reconciliation is as much a spiritual fact as the estrangement from God. . . . "Beloved, if God so loved us, we ought also to love one another."[130] The forgiven must forgive. We cannot keep the reconciliation which has been given to us unless we become infinite extensions of that reconciliation into the world. We pray everyday that God will forgive us "as we forgive those who trespass against us"[131] (pp. 131-137) [emphasis ours].

In his chapter, "Our Need of Christ's Cross," Shoemaker urged in his conclusion that man must not merely be penitent about the common sins of sloth or impurity or crooked deals, but something which underlies and includes them all—"self-sufficiency and the independence of God" (p. 159). This, he said, is the major sin of all. It is pride par excellence, he said, to try to get along without God. And compare the Big Book statement, "We agnostics and atheists were sticking to the idea that "self-sufficiency" would solve our problems" (p. 52). Shoemaker said:

> The heart of Christianity is relationship with God, not ethics—they follow. . . . The deepest thing in the Christian religion is not anything that we can do for God, it is *what God has already done for us*. He has offered to us redemption, regeneration, a new nature through the Cross of Christ (pp. 161-62) [emphasis ours]. . . . God

---

[129] Compare Romans 5:10: "For if, when we were enemies, we were reconciled to God by the death of his Son, much more, being reconciled, we shall be saved by his life." Compare also 2 Corinthians 5:18-20; Ephesians 2:16; and Colossians 1:21.

[130] 1 John 4:11.

[131] See Matthew 6:12, 14-15.

in mercy strip us this day of the last vestiges of self-reliance, and help us to begin anew trusting to nothing but His Grace! (p. 166).

As to these words, see the number of times the Big Book speaks of a relationship with God.[132] And—as we have already discussed—the concept that God has done for man what man could not do for himself. Finally, the importance of recognizing that self-reliance can fail and does not go far enough; that it must be replaced with a different basis: trust and reliance upon God (p. 167).[133]

Shoemaker quoted the Apostle Paul, "By grace are ye saved through faith; and that not of yourselves: *it is* the gift of God:"[134] He said faith is a kind of leap out toward God, in which the will also is involved. Faith has become for us the function of the whole man: mind and heart and will. It is an attitude toward life and the unseen in which all our powers are implicated. Shoemaker told of sitting with a man who had never had a clean victory over sin and the fear of sin. After talking to him, Shoemaker said that if he would make an act of surrender in faith, he would find himself not the possessor of, but "possessed by a *Force outside himself, greater than himself*, independent of his moods and his sudden seizures of temptation" [emphasis ours].[135] Compare the language of A.A.'s Second Step: "Came to believe that a *Power greater than ourselves* could restore us to sanity"[136] [emphasis ours].

---

[132] Big Book, pp. 13, 28-29, 56, 100, 164.

[133] Big Book, p. 68.

[134] Ephesians 2:8.

[135] This language referring to "a Force outside himself, greater than himself" can be found in *If I Be Lifted Up* at page 176; and on that page very clearly refers to God.

[136] Big Book, p. 59.

Confident Faith

By the time 1932 rolled around, Sam Shoemaker was—without realizing it—putting together major elements of what would become the Twelve Steps of Alcoholics Anonymous. These elements were the steps—the "path" to a "relationship with God," a "vital religious experience," an "experience of God." All these expressions were used by Shoemaker, and all, in a variant form, became a part of A.A. language. The steps, or elements, that comprised the path can be found, though not in the order of the Twelve Steps of A.A., in various parts of Sam's 1932 book, *Confident Faith*.[137]

Dr. Bob owned, studied, and loaned this book to early AAs in Akron. The author personally found the book among the collection of books owned by Dr. Bob's children; and he verified that it was circulated by Dr. Bob.[138] Consequently, Dr. Bob probably was familiar with its Twelve Step elements. Similarly, those elements can be found on pages thirteen through fifteen of the Big Book, where Bill describes the path on which Ebby led him both before and after Bill's conversion experience at Towns Hospital in December of 1934. Did Ebby get these steps from *Confident Faith* or simply from the array of Oxford Group sources to which he had been exposed by the time he carried the message to Bill?[139] We do not know, but Ebby's earlier Oxford Group companions and mentors, particularly Rowland Hazard and Shep Cornell, were

---

[137] Samuel Shoemaker, Jr., *Confident Faith* (New York: Fleming H. Revell, 1932).

[138] See Dick B., *Dr. Bob's Library* (West Virginia: The Bishop of Books, 1992), pp. 48-52.

[139] Ebby's close relationship with his Oxford Group mentors, Shep Cornell and Rowland Hazard, is further exemplified by the evidence presented in Appendix 10 which shows that Shep Cornell sponsored Ebby as his godfather at the time of Ebby's baptism at Calvary Church.

thoroughly conversant with those Oxford Group ideas by the end of 1934—when Ebby carried the message to Bill.[140]

In one sense, Shoemaker had begun spelling out the first step—need, defeat, the unmanageable life, spiritual misery—long before he wrote *Confident Faith*. In *Realizing Religion*, Shoemaker had been writing about spiritual misery and man's restlessness and discontent due to estrangement from God. He also wrote about the reality of "sin"—the selfishness and self-centeredness that blocks man from God and leaves him defeated when his self-reliance fails him. Also, somewhere in this period, the little prayer—"God manage me because I can't manage myself"—began appearing at Calvary Church, in Oxford Group literature, and in Anne Smith's Spiritual Workbook.[141] And though Shoemaker did not articulate these A.A. First-Step elements in *Confident Faith*, he did write:

> I begin to turn towards Christ in a kind of despair of everything else, like Simon Peter when he said, "Lord, to whom shall we go? thou hast the words of eternal life" (p. 105)?[142]

Moreover, he wrote a chapter entitled "The Simplicity of Religion," in which he told the story of Naaman, found in 2 Kings, Chapter 5 (pp. 130-140). Shoemaker said, "Naaman knew he was sick [of leprosy]. . . . The story gets its whole point from that fact" (p. 130). Note that the Big Book says the First Step in recovery begins only when the newcomer has learned he must fully concede to his innermost self that he is sick—an alcoholic.[143] Bill Wilson variously phrased the disease problem in terms of

---

[140] *Pass It On*, pp. 113-16. And see Appendix 10 of our book, which further illustrates Ebby's close association with Shep Cornell, in that Shep was Ebby's godfather at the time of Ebby's baptism at Calvary Episcopal Church.

[141] See Dick B., *The Oxford Group & Alcoholics Anonymous*, pp. 149-50; and *Anne Smith's Spiritual Workbook*, p. 29.

[142] See John 6:68.

[143] Compare Big Book, pp. xiii and 30.

hopelessness, complete deflation, being "licked," and "powerlessness."[144]

Shoemaker spoke much more broadly in *Confident Faith*, and said our very society is leprous. He continued:

> We never were so unhappy. There never was so much nerve-strain. There never was so much fear, nor such a sense of futility. Never were so many tired people dragging themselves through life, and wondering why. Above all, never were so many assured at last that there is no final security in the heaping up of riches (p. 138).

In this book, as elsewhere, Shoemaker made it clear that man suffers when he relies on his own ways, rather than on God's. Interestingly, Bill's secretary, Nell Wing, wrote:

> Bill's definition of humility was willingness to seek God's will in your life and then follow it. I'm reminded of a statement I saw once posted on the bulletin board of an alcoholic rehabilitation facility. It read: "There is but one God, and today you are not him." That's pretty close to Bill's view of humility.[145]

In *Confident Faith*, Shoemaker elaborated on his earlier statements that the solution to spiritual misery is a vital religious experience leading to faith in Almighty God (pp. 17-18). His thesis was becoming: Start with a willingness to believe: (1) that God is, (2) that He has the answers, and (3) that He is a rewarder of those who diligently seek Him.[146] Of faith, Shoemaker wrote:

---

[144] See, Dick B., *The Akron Genesis of Alcoholics Anonymous*, pp. 256-58; "Bill W., " *The AA Grapevine*, March, 1971, p. 21; and Kurtz, *Not-God*, pp. 21-23, 34.

[145] Nell Wing, *Grateful To Have Been There* (Illinois: Parkside Publishing Corporation, 1992), pp. 44-45.

[146] See Hebrews 11:6, a verse upon which Shoemaker repeatedly drew: But without faith *it is* impossible to please him [God]: for he that cometh to God must believe that he is, and *that* he is a rewarder of them that diligently seek him.

> The trouble with the faith of to-day is that it is at one remove [sic] from faith in God. It is faith in laws, and moral principles, and ways of life: but it is not faith in God Himself. . . . Cease believing in the ways of God: believe in God, then life will take you by surprise (pp. 19-20).

Then, in language prophetic of material in A.A.'s Steps, Shoemaker told of how he began, in four simple stages, to find his own deepest experience of Christ (pp. 40-42).

First, Shoemaker said he met a man who had an experience of Christ—a person who knew how to discover the availability of Christ for himself and for other men. This kind of meeting, said Shoemaker, disturbs and challenges. It makes us dissatisfied and goads us to a much deeper satisfaction. This stage reminds the author of the Big Book's challenge at the beginning of the Steps. It says, "If you have decided you want what we have and are willing to go to any length to get it—then you are ready to take certain steps."[147]

Second, Shoemaker said many do not know what to do next, though they see that if Christ is to come in, wrong things have to go out. This, said Shoemaker, is the "how" of it. And he virtually forecast two of A.A.'s housecleaning steps. He said: (1) Face your sins.[148] (2) Go to someone you can trust and make a clean breast of them (p. 41).[149]

Third, Shoemaker said that you must then surrender your life to Christ in an act of commitment which gives God the opportunity to complete the process by His acceptance and forgiveness and restoration.[150]

Fourth, keep the experience alive, said Shoemaker. To accomplish this, Shoemaker found two things indispensable: (1) The grace of God—which, he said, comes through prayer, the

---

[147] Big Book, p. 58.

[148] Step Four.

[149] Step Five.

[150] See A.A. Steps Three, Six, and Seven.

Scriptures, and the Sacraments and worship of the Church; and (2) The help of other Christian people—which comes through the sharing of our experiences and knowing one another's hearts.

Shoemaker said that through these four simple ways Christ became a reality in his life. He likened the process to Paul's witness to the jailer, as recorded in Acts chapter 16. Paul and Silas had been imprisoned after Paul had cast a devil spirit out of a woman. Paul and Silas had prayed and sung praises to God; an earthquake occurred; the jail doors were opened; and the prisoners' bands were loosed. The jailer was baffled, trembling, inquisitive and humble. Shoemaker wrote of this:

> When the jailer asked St. Paul, "What must I do to be saved?", St. Paul had an answer for him, "Believe on the Lord Jesus Christ, and thou shalt be saved." People need to be told how. The "how" for most of us lies along some such way as this I have described. We must see the faith in a life that has it, we must give up the things in our lives which are contrary to it, we must give ourselves entirely to Christ, and we must use the means He has given us to go on . . . (p. 42).

Shoemaker spoke of an experiment of faith—an experiment very much to be found in A.A.'s step process. He wrote:

> The faculty of faith is required when you step from hypothesis to experiment. You can't tell whether the ice will hold till you step out on it. But faith is supplanted by knowledge when the experiment works. It is so in science, and it is so in life (p. 105).

As in previous books, Shoemaker turned to John 7:17 in teaching about his concept of "willingness" to believe in God. He wrote:

> He that willeth to do His will shall know of the doctrine. Anyone who loves anything else better than God cannot believe in God. Anyone who does not know God, and insists upon carrying over into faith some habit or attitude which comes before God for him, will never know God (p. 106).

Shoemaker told of a young man who was dissipating his life away in drink. The man was exposed to a group whose ideals were attractive to him. Shoemaker warned the man that merely "resolving" himself out of sin would inevitably cause him to fall back into it. The young man responded with a new look—first of guilt and then of dependence upon God. He gave up all notions that he could possibly live up to the ideals he admired, and he simply handed his life to God. Shoemaker said he saw the man find a growing victory and peace in Jesus Christ. He said that what the man had needed was not ethics and ideals. His experience came through the grace of God. Shoemaker concluded his book with words which found their way into A.A.'s Big Book almost verbatim. He wrote:

> Faith is not sight; it is a high gamble. There are only two alternatives here. God is, or He isn't. You leap one way or the other. It is a risk to take to bet everything you have on God. So is it a risk not to (p. 187).

Compare Bill Wilson's explanation that faith does not come from logic or "Reason." The Big Book said:

> When we became alcoholics, crushed by a self-imposed crisis we could not postpone or evade, we had to fearlessly face the proposition that either God is everything or else He is nothing. God either is, or He isn't. What was our choice to be? Arrived at this point, we were squarely confronted with the question of faith. We couldn't duck the issue. . . . Imagine life without faith! . . . Hence, we saw that reason isn't everything. Neither is reason, as most of us use it, entirely dependable, though it emanate from our best minds (pp. 53-55).

In previous books—*Children of the Second Birth* and *Twice-Born Ministers*—Shoemaker had elaborated on the *decision* which marks the beginning of the surrender path. He had spoken of the "turning point," just as the Big Book does. He had illustrated one means of making the decision to surrender to God by quoting Luke 22:42:

"Nevertheless not my will, but thine, be done." And the Big Book uses somewhat comparable language in its Third Step prayer (p. 63). Shoemaker had described the beginning of a surrender by using two different expressions which find counterparts in the Big Book—"Abandon yourself to God" and the "decision to cast my will and my life on God." In *Confident Faith*, he further explained the surrender process, employing Jesus Christ's teaching that "Ye must be born again." And Shoemaker stressed that this meant "conversion."

Stating that he (Shoemaker) wanted no other nor better heaven than to enjoy forever the development of a relationship with God, he pointed to the Apostle Paul's experience with Jesus Christ on the road to Damascus as an example of surrender.[151] Jesus appeared to Paul and admonished Paul for persecuting him. Paul responded by saying, "What shall I do, Lord?" (p. 110). Shoemaker wrote:

> From being a man who knew just exactly what he should do and was doing it for dear life, Saul became a man who asked another what to do. There Paul surrendered. There Paul passed over from being a self sufficient individual who was working out his own problems with a general feeling that God was helping him, to being a dependent individual who worked out his problems with the specific feeling that Jesus Christ was his master and Lord. A great deal else went beside his inward division and unhappiness. And perhaps the greatest thing he lost at the time was the pride which loves best to control one's life. We all know the great appeal of self-reliance. The world is filled with people who will not ask God for any help, because they are convinced they can do for themselves whatever is necessary. Saul left that behind in the dust of the road. He got up a dependent person. That is precisely what surrender means. The center of control is no longer self, but Christ. . . . It begins with asking just that question, "Lord, what shall I do?" (p. 110).

---

[151] See Acts 9:1-21; 22:1-21; and 26:1-23.

To see the influence of the foregoing Shoemaker language on A.A., one needs to examine and compare the following portions of the Big Book: (1) Bill's remarks on pages 28 and 29 concerning the forming of a relationship with God. (2) Bill's remarks on pages 52, 53, and 68 about the failure inherent in self-reliance and self-sufficiency and the success to be found in "God-sufficiency." (3) Bill's remarks on pages 98 through 100 about the necessity for depending upon God, rather than upon ourselves or other people.

In his chapter "Christ and Human Relations," Shoemaker set the stage for the A.A. Fourth Step's searching and fearless moral inventory, the honest facing of our faults. On page 23, Shoemaker listed, concerning the relationships which needed to be straightened out: (1) An enmity with a person who has wronged you, and from whom you feel estranged by that wrong. (2) A similar enmity with a person whom you have wronged. (3) A constant irritation and estrangement with a member of your own family. Shoemaker's list of mal-adjusted relationships reads much like A.A.'s "grudge" or "resentment" list.[152] And he said, "I am convinced that the very first thing that Jesus Christ wants to set right in the lives of all of us is our relationships. You cannot love God whom you have not seen without loving your brother whom you have seen" (p. 24).[153]

Shoemaker asked how this can be done. And he gives an answer which can be found in A.A.'s Fourth Step formula. He said we must begin by freely admitting the defects. Then we must share our own wrong in the situation. The Big Book phrases it thus: "Putting out of our minds the wrongs others had done, we resolutely looked for our own mistakes. . . . Where were we to blame?"[154] Several times, Shoemaker gives the same stress to an

---

[152] Big Book, p. 64-65, says, "In dealing with resentments, we set them on paper. We listed people, institutions or principles with whom we were angry. . . . On our grudge list we set opposite each name our injuries."

[153] See 1 John 4:20: "If a man say, I love God, and hateth his brother, he is a liar: for he that loveth not his brother whom he hath seen, how can he love God whom he hath not seen?"

[154] Big Book, p. 67.

honest facing of the facts, an honest facing of sins, that one finds in the Big Book. Thus Bill Wilson spoke on page 64 of a "fact-finding and a fact-facing process" and of taking "stock honestly." Shoemaker said, "We need a way of looking at life which begins with the facts of human selfishness" (p. 98). He said of those suffering from the moral factor in unbelief: "One wants to say to them that their lives are too self-centered, too dirty, too dishonest, too hard to believe in God. The pure in heart see God" (p. 106).[155] The Big Book says, at pages 62 through 67: "Selfishness—self-centeredness! That, we think is the root of our troubles. . . . Though our decision [to seek God] was a vital and crucial step, it could have little permanent effect unless at once followed by a strenuous effort to face, and to be rid of, the things which had been blocking us. . . . Where had we been selfish, dishonest, self-seeking and frightened?"

In his discussion of the Bible story about Naaman,[156] Shoemaker wrote:

> Now I think that our world, and we individuals in particular, are very much like Naaman. We know in the hearts of us that we are sick, sick with a dreadful moral and spiritual sickness (p. 134).[157]

He spoke of fear as an example of spiritual sickness and said:

> Fear is one of the most wasteful emotions. Fear is always on the lookout for something else to be afraid of, always wearing itself out about things which do not happen. . . . I do not doubt but that there are hundreds who have fallen ill, some who have committed suicide, because they had no faith to substitute for fear: and fear literally ate the heart out of them. And its antidote is faith in God.

---

[155] See from the Sermon on the Mount, Matthew 5:8: "Blessed *are* the pure in heart: for they shall see God."

[156] See 2 Kings 5:1-19.

[157] On page 64, the Big Book speaks of "all forms of spiritual disease." It speaks of spiritual sickness, and of a "spiritual malady."

> The emotion of worship, of trust, of faith, is strong enough to offset fear (p. 172).

The Big Book said:

> Notice that the word "fear" is bracketed. . . . This short word somehow touches every aspect of our lives. It was an evil and corroding thread; the fabric of our existence was shot through with it. . . . Sometimes we think fear ought to be classed with stealing. It seems to cause more trouble (pp. 67-69).
>
> We are now on a different basis; the basis of trusting and relying upon God. We trust infinite God rather than our finite selves. . . . The verdict of the ages is that faith means courage. All men of faith have courage. They trust their God. We never apologize for God. Instead we let Him demonstrate, through us, what He can do. We ask Him to remove our fear and direct our attention to what He would have us be. At once, we commence to outgrow fear (p. 68).

And what are the next steps on the path to faith, to the relationship with God? A.A.'s Fifth, Sixth, and Seventh Steps speak of confession, of becoming ready to have God remove the blocks, and then of humbly asking for His help. *Confident Faith* dealt with these same points. Speaking about young people, Shoemaker said:

> Then one day that young person sits down with you, and shares the inner struggles of the past, some of which you did not know or understand. . . . Then arises the question whether you will be fully honest with him or her, about yourself, your past, your present, your own inner life. . . . It might reveal your own timid half-surrender to God, or your hidden fears, or your selfishness. . . . Now if you have the courage to face the issues, you may get free of a lifetime of inhibitions and selfishness which have continued right along while you thought you were being quite a good Christian (pp. 123-24).

This Shoemaker language is similar to language found in A.A.'s Fifth Step discussion on pages 72-75 in the Big Book. And what followed?

For Shoemaker, the next steps had to do with the Oxford Group's Five C's and particularly with *Conviction* and *Conversion*. These "steps" required a strong personal conviction of sin—wanting to hate and forsake it; and then to repent, to be transformed, and to change. There had to be a deliberate turning to God for the answers. A.A.'s Sixth and Seventh Steps speak of a willingness to have God remove shortcomings and then of asking for His help in doing so.

Shoemaker spoke of convicting a person of sin and carrying his miserable self-will straight up under the eyes of Almighty God. Again, referring to Saul's conversion on the road to Damascus, he wrote:

> Where Saul asks for help, God gives help—help to recognize and choose the best. The minute Saul is really convinced that both his love and his hate are in the wrong place, the minute Saul is honest, God can flood his spirit with light, and speak truth into his soul. . . . But later I began to study religious experience in William James's great book *The Varieties of Religious Experience*. I found out that conversion was not a remote and isolated incident in the life of St. Paul, but a widespread and common experience. I learned that these experiences varied immensely in their details, but were often surprisingly alike in their essentials. I found that in its main outlines, St. Paul's conversion conformed to many others: namely in the need which preceded it, the divided life, sharpening into a sense of sin [*Conviction*] and the need for forgiveness. And in the willing surrender of the self to God and His mercy and His plan, as represented in the words, "What shall I do, Lord?" And in the action of God upon that open soul, the change God makes, the forgiveness He gives, the peace that follows. And in all the subsequent life, of inward unity and deep joy, of outward righteousness and service, of steady witnessing of that Power which has saved and kept, and of perpetual contact with Christ [*Conversion*]. . . . I want to assure . . . man of two things: first, that with God it is never too late, and that His grace is out after

> him, and has been seeking him all these wasted years; and second, that he can himself have some part in setting in effect the processes of grace—he can do his part—he can surrender whole-heartedly to the Christ Whom he longs to have in control of his life. He must be *willing* to give up the sins which beset, and to accept in full God's plan for his life. . . . The bright light, and the audible voice, and the journey to Damascus . . . are unimportant, but the consciously needy heart, and the surrender of the will, and the infilling of the living Christ are universal, and belong to us all, and are of utmost importance. This is Christ's way to faith and peace and abundant life (pp. 111, 115-18).[158]

Later, Shoemaker explained:

> [Paul] stopped struggling morally and handed himself over to God. He let God give him victory over the power of his sins (p. 159).

We believe that if the student of the Big Book will compare with the foregoing Shoemaker language the two short paragraphs on Big Book page 76, which comprise the suggestions for taking Steps Six and Seven, he will see the full impact of Shoemaker's influence. The last words in the two Big Book paragraphs are: "I pray that you [God] now remove from me every single defect of character which stands in the way of my usefulness to you and my fellows. Grant me strength, as I go out from here, to do your bidding."

That both Shoemaker and Wilson were talking about conversion experiences is exemplified by the frequency with which Shoemaker mentioned William James and by the fact that Bill Wilson specifically mentioned in the Big Book the influence of A.A.'s two great mentors—William James and Carl Jung. Of James, Bill wrote:

> The distinguished American psychologist, William James, in his book "Varieties of Religious Experience," indicates a multitude of ways in which men have discovered God (p. 28).

---

[158] See Acts 9:1-19. And compare Acts 22:1-21; and 26:1-23.

In previous pages of the Big Book, Bill speaks of Jung's solution for alcoholism—the religious or conversion experience (pp. 26-27). And then, years later, in writing to Jung, Bill conveyed the same idea that Shoemaker was conveying in the language we have quoted, namely, that conversion experiences were not limited to those such as the Apostle Paul had. Thus Bill said to Dr. Carl Jung: "This concept [of becoming the subject of a genuine conversion] proved to be the foundation of such success as Alcoholics Anonymous has since achieved. This has made conversion experience . . . available on an almost wholesale basis."[159]

Concluding as to the importance of conviction and conversion, Shoemaker said:

> Go back to the step of the new birth, with all that it means of giving up your sins and yourself to God in complete surrender. Pray that you will move forward, . . . for the honesty that really wants Him by intending to obey Him. . . . Some of you will need to relinquish your positive sins. The life in grace is an abidingly derivative life. It hangs upon God utterly. It is the saved and kept life; saved by the conversion to Christ, kept by His Holy Spirit (p. 165).

A reader will not find in *Confident Faith* an extended discussion of "amends" or "restitution"—the subjects of A.A.'s Eighth and Ninth Steps. For Shoemaker covered these subjects in other pre-Big Book writings. But *Confident Faith* nonetheless contains the hook. Shoemaker referred to a section of Scripture often used in Oxford Group writings, and later even in A.A. literature, to refer to the importance of straightening things out with one's brother. The verses are from the Sermon on the Mount, Matthew 5:23-24:

> Therefore if thou bring thy gift to the altar, and there rememberest that thy brother hath ought against thee; Leave there thy gift before

---

[159] *Pass It On*, pp. 382-383.

> the altar, and go thy way; first be reconciled to thy brother, and then come and offer thy gift.[160]

Shoemaker wrote:

> O God, Who has taught us that we may bring no gift to Thine altar if another still have aught against us; and that we cannot love Thee whom we have not seen, if we love not our brother whom we have seen: Teach us what the Christian spirit means in all our human relations (p. 33).

Continuation (also called *Conservation*) was the fifth of the Oxford Group's "Five C's," and it had to do with concepts that found their way into A.A.'s last three steps. Steps Ten, Eleven, and Twelve deal with maintaining, living, and growing in the life of grace. Shoemaker spoke more of these in other books. But in *Confident Faith*, he touched on the idea of daily spiritual growth in his chapter "Three Levels of Life." He said:

> Let us look again at our illustrations. The woman in love with the married man will do something more than renounce him, and promise to behave: she will want to turn the whole situation to the glory of God. She will face the sin in herself, repent of it, get clear of it. . . . The man with money in the bank will long ago have given that money to God; and he will anew ask God what He wants him to do with it. The woman with her eye on the fur coat surrenders afresh the whole idea to God and asks Him what He wants: she will test the guidance which comes by principles of honesty and unselfishness; and she will do what she is told gladly, and, if it mean renunciation of her desires, freely and without lingering regret. The man who thought of pushing his competitor to the wall will do something more than desist; he will probably go

[160] See *DR. BOB and the Good Oldtimers*, p. 308; and the concluding words in the *Grapevine* memorial issue for Dr. Bob, *RHS*. See also Dick B., *The Oxford Group & Alcoholics Anonymous*, p. 183, where footnote 207 lists the frequency with which these verses were cited in Oxford Group writings, and also shows the importance of the verses in Oxford Group discussions of restitution.

> and confess his meanness of spirit, make friends with the other man, and bring the relationship to a level of creative spiritual fruitfulness (p. 156).

These Shoemaker *Continuation* concepts can be identified in the Big Book's language on pages 84 and 86, having to do with daily efforts to eliminate selfishness, dishonesty, resentment, and fear. Also in its pages that speak of practicing principles of patience, tolerance, kindliness, love, and forgiveness.

The Conversion of the Church

Often using descriptive words which may have found their way into A.A. usage, Shoemaker said he wrote *The Conversion of the Church* to rediscover Christ's will for the Church.[161] He spoke much of a "Group," which he said is the Church on the march; and of "the Fellowship," which he said the original Church was often called. He said the "conversion" of the church meant the "transformation" of the church into that which Christ intended—the fellowship of his radiant followers, his brotherhood, and his body. A.A., of course, focuses on the *group* concept, calls itself a *fellowship*, and originally spoke much of a "conversion," "transformation," and "change," which would bring an individual into a relationship with God (Big Book, p. 29).[162]

The Conversion of the Church is of value to the student of A.A. in large part because of the amount of time Shoemaker devoted to discussing "sharing by confession and witness," and the process for bringing others to a life-changing spiritual awakening. In fact, Shoemaker concluded the book with these two statements:

---

[161] Samuel M. Shoemaker, *The Conversion of the Church* (New York: Fleming H. Revell, 1932).

[162] See also Big Book, Appendix Two.

> Nothing less than a God-inspired awakening, a "rushing mighty wind" from heaven, bearing upon its wings the fire of grace from the throne of God, is sufficient for the need of the world and the Church at this hour. . . . (p. 124).[163]

> Life-changing on a colossal scale is the one hope of the world today (p. 125).[164]

Shoemaker's first chapter was, as he conceded, negative about the Church. He said:

> I think the great practical apostasy of the Church in our time lies in her forsaking of the great function of "the cure of souls," so that this has fallen either into disuse or into other hands: while the Church is busy with other things (p. 12).

The "cure of souls," or "soul-surgery" as it was called in the Oxford Group, was the life-changing result that Frank Buchman's First Century Christian Fellowship sought.[165] Shoemaker said the Church needed to carry its message into an individual's life by telling the stories of living people—giving "news," not "views" (pp. 18, 73).[166] Shoemaker said the Church needed to learn the truth of Henry Drummond's statement that we do not need to *prove* things to people, but only to let them *see* things. Speaking then about service, Shoemaker wrote:

---

[163] See Acts 2:2 for the reference to the "rushing mighty wind" which occurred on the day of Pentecost when believers first received the gift of holy spirit and began speaking in tongues.

[164] The quote is from Dr. Frank N. D. Buchman, Oxford Group founder. Shoemaker had said earlier in the book that Buchman was "a man who knew how to deal with people—individuals."

[165] See, for example, Howard A. Walter, *Soul-Surgery*, 6th ed. (Oxford: at the University Press by John Johnson, 1940).

[166] Shoemaker, *The Conversion of the Church*, pp. 18 and 73. The "news, not views" expression which urged the sharing of experience, rather than opinion, was common in the Oxford Group and in early A.A. See Dick B., *The Akron Genesis of Alcoholics Anonymous*, pp. 99, 237-38.

> The *great* service, the service which exceeds all other services, is the impartation of transforming spiritual experience (p. 23).

Shoemaker's next chapter concerned the conversion of Christians, and he defined "conversion" as "a maximum experience of Jesus Christ" (p. 28). Shoemaker believed there were four elements for attaining such experiences; and he expressed the ideas as follows:

> Now I have a conviction that the will of God for every man, woman and child who calls himself a Christian is that our lives be dedicated to His will in utter surrender and consecration; that the Voice of God in prayer should be an abiding reality, to be depended on for every decision; that we be an integral part of a vital Christian fellowship; and that we be used to bring other people to Christ (pp. 28-29).

He then asked, "How can we gain back authentic inspiration [and] . . . know again so clearly the power of God in our lives" (p. 29)? He answered that there is "only one place to begin, and that is with ourselves. . . . '[W]e take hold of God by the handle of our sins'" (p. 29). Shoemaker recited a number of sins he said hold us back from fulness of spiritual power: pride, exclusiveness, hypocrisy, resting your case in a point of view, and emotional refuges which take the individual from a firm hold on God to the consequent clutching after secondary security.

Then he asked how to go the rest of the way with conversion. And he answered that we must start "by the sharing of these sins with another Christian who has found his way a bit farther than we have" (p. 35). He said this sharing, this confession idea, has a Scriptural basis in James 5:16—"Confess *your* faults one to another, and pray for one another, that ye may be healed" (p. 35). He then spelled out the confession idea which found place in A.A.'s Fifth Step:

> I am equally convinced that the Protestant notion of "confession to God only" ignores the deep spiritual and psychological fact that we

> almost always need a human hearer and witness to validate our confession to God and make it *real to us*. Of course confession in the absolute sense, is to God alone: but where there is a human listener, confession is found to be both more difficult and efficacious. It is, as a matter of fact and experience, a relatively uncostly thing to fall on our knees and confess our sins to God—it should not be, and perhaps would not be if we were closer to God and more sensitive to His will; but it is a very costly thing to say these things out in the presence even of a human being we can trust; and, as a matter of fact, this is extraordinarily effective in making the first break to get away from sins. . . . It is my conviction, and that of the Oxford Group with which I am associated, that detailed sharing should be made with one person only (pp. 36-37).

There are close parallels between the foregoing language and that found in the Big Book's discussion of the Fifth Step. For one thing, the Fifth Step language suggests: "Admitted to God, to ourselves, and to another human being the exact nature of our wrongs."[167] Then, at pages 72 and 74, the Big Book says:

> In actual practice, we usually find a solitary self-appraisal insufficient. . . . They took inventory all right, but hung on to some of the worst items in stock. They only *thought* they had lost their egoism and fear; they only *thought* they had humbled themselves. But they had not learned enough of humility, fearlessness and honesty, in the sense we find it necessary, until they told someone else *all* their life story. . . . We must be entirely honest with somebody if we expect to live long or happily in this world.

Shoemaker spoke much of a *practice* that later became common in A.A. It is the practice in which the sponsor or confessant shares his or her "sins" with the confessing alcoholic. Shoemaker believed that the sharing of sins is not likely to be effective unless the person who hears the confession also shares of himself or herself. The Big Book speaks little about this idea that the life-

---

[167] Big Book, p. 59.

changer should share about himself or herself in order to bring the new person to share more fully. It calls for careful thought in choosing the person with whom the "intimate" and "confidential" step is to be taken. It suggests that someone ordained by an established religion is a possibility, but may not always understand alcoholics. It also suggests "a close-mouthed, understanding friend," or possibly "our doctor or psychologist." But the author's own experience in A.A., in the area where he got sober, is that AAs usually share the results of their inventory and self-examination with their A.A. "sponsor." And the sponsor usually shares some of the sponsor's own shortcomings with the person who is "confessing" and taking the Fifth Step.

Shoemaker explained the sharing process as he saw it: "Detailed sharing should be made with one person only" (p. 37). The person to whom confession is made should be a "good listener" (p. 38). Shoemaker said, "The obvious way to make it easy for another person to share is to share yourself" (p. 38). Quoting from a story and then from the Bible, he said:

> Confess your sins one to another. I have confessed mine. Now you shall not stir till you have recounted yours. The difference between true sharing and formal confession lies primarily in the open willingness of the person who is trying to help, to share himself. St. Paul tells the Thessalonians, ". . . [W]e were willing to have imparted unto you, not the gospel of God only, but also our own souls" (1 Thess. 2:8). He may have reason to think that he knows about what your difficulty is, and he may share something parallel in his own life. Or he may share in general what sort of person he was before his conversion, and how Christ came to him and changed him. In any case, he will create the sort of atmosphere in which you can talk without fear, reserve, or hurry (p. 39).

The Big Book suggests: "We have a written inventory and we are prepared for a long talk. . . . We pocket our pride and go to it, illuminating every twist of character, every dark cranny of the past. Once we have taken this step, withholding nothing, we are delighted" (p. 75).

Shoemaker moved on from self-examination and confession to the next Oxford Group surrender "step"—decision. He said:

> Of course, the mere externalizing of these difficulties does not banish them, though it is apt to banish emotional tension about them. They must next be gathered up in a new decision of the will and handed over to God in a new surrender (p. 39).

Here Shoemaker set the stage for A.A.'s Sixth and Seventh Steps, which suggest what is to be done after the Fifth Step confession has been completed. The A.A. newcomer is to return home, review what has been done in the sharing, make sure that nothing was omitted, and then test himself or herself for readiness to have God remove all the things which were admitted to be objectionable. This Big Book process of making oneself ready for surrender is to be followed by the surrender to God of "every single defect of character which stands in the way of my usefulness to you and my fellows" (p. 76).

Shoemaker spoke of man's part in such a conversion, stating:

> There are a good many people who know that they need to be converted: but they have such an august conception of conversion that they have not learned that they may have a part in their own conversion. It is true that only the Spirit of God converts any man; it is His direct action on the soul that alone converts. But we may draw near and put ourselves in position to be converted by the simple act of self-surrender (p. 40).

Compare these two parallels: First, note from the Big Book:

> God had restored his sanity. What is this but a miracle of healing? Yet its elements are simple. Circumstances made him willing to believe. He humbly offered himself to his Maker—then he knew. Even so has God restored us all to our right minds. To this man, the revelation was sudden. Some of us grow into it more slowly. But He has come to all who have honestly sought Him. When we drew near to Him He disclosed Himself to us! (p. 57).

Then, note these verses from the Book of James, which we believe substantially influenced both Shoemaker *and* A.A.[168]:

> Submit yourselves therefore to God. Resist the devil, and he will flee from you. Draw nigh to God, and he will draw nigh to you. . . . Humble yourselves in the sight of the Lord, and he shall lift you up.[169]

Shoemaker next turned to the Oxford Group idea of *Continuance* (p. 41). He spelled out the elements of that process: (1) prayer; (2) a series of new relationships, including apologies and restorations; and (3) "a full experience of the Lord Jesus Christ." (p. 45) He said these elements mean we live in the open with people and ask their help in breaking the clutches of old habits. Miracles begin to happen. And Prodigals and Pharisees sit down with one another in sharing fellowship and laugh to think how blind and stupid they used to be.

"Living In Touch With God" is a foundational chapter when it comes to learning about Shoemaker's Biblical emphasis. He commenced:

> The Christian life consists in a current of spiritual electricity which runs through three angles of a triangle: God, myself, and other people. A block anywhere in the circuit will put a stop to the current (p. 47).

In this particular chapter, Shoemaker discussed the "current" as it runs between God and man. But he also pointed to two Bible verses as proof that an experience of God is all bound up inextricably with our human relationships between one person and another (p. 47). The Bible verses are:

---

168 For the influence of the Book of James on A.A., see *Pass It On*, p. 147.

169 James 4:7, 8, 10.

> If a man love not his brother whom he hath seen, how can he love God whom he hath not seen?[170]

> If thou bring thy gift to the altar, and there rememberest that thy brother hath ought against thee, first go and be reconciled unto thy brother, and then come and offer thy gift.[171]

Shoemaker said it is idle for us to try to be in touch with God, or keep in touch with Him, so long as there are human relationships which must be righted. He pointed out that God is there to guide us as to what we are to do. He said man lays hold of God through experience and not through definition. He said he agreed with the premise that God speaks in six great ways: in nature and in creation; in the moral law; in the Scriptures; in Jesus Christ; in human conscience; and in history (p. 49). He said that many of us do not believe in the practical Voice of God. And he pointed to our need and said we cannot carry on a conversation with God through nature, or the moral law. We find God's general will in the Scriptures, he said. We find God still more directly in Jesus Christ. But human conscience is no perfect reflector of God, and history only points to His existence and to His general will.

Shoemaker said we want something more direct. We want to know that God can and does speak directly to the human heart. He said the reason why some people, including himself, believe in guidance, at least in theory, is that the Old and New Testaments are full of instances of it. Instances as specific as you please. Innumerable times, people in the Bible said clearly that they were guided of God in this and that act and decision.

---

[170] The King James Version of 1 John 4:20 says: "If a man say, I love God, and hateth his brother, he is a liar: for he that loveth not his brother whom he hath seen, how can he love God whom he hath not seen?

[171] The King James Version of Matthew 5:23-24 reads: "Therefore if thou bring thy gift to the altar, and there rememberest that thy brother hath ought against thee; Leave there thy gift before the altar, and go thy way; first be reconciled to thy brother, and then come and offer thy gift."

On pages 50 and 51, he said there are conditions of guidance:

1. We must have first a surrendered will which wants God's will more than its own, and is ready to do what one is told, no matter whether it be to one's taste or not.
2. We must be relaxed from all tension, of haste or unbelief, or too impatient seeking. (Note on this subject, that the Big Book says at page 86: "We relax and take it easy. We don't struggle. We are often surprised how the right answers come after we have tried this for a while.")
3. We want faith, a leaning towards God, trusting that He who rolls the spheres can guide the human mind. (Note that the Big Book says at page 87: "We usually conclude the period of meditation with a prayer that we be shown all through the day what our next step is to be, that we be given whatever we need to take care of such problems.")
4. We need a regular time for waiting on God. . . . But guidance may come at any time, said Shoemaker, and the set times are only more protracted periods in which our minds are sensitized to the Holy Spirit. (Note that the Big Book says at pages 86-87: "On awakening let us think about the twenty-four hours ahead. We consider our plans for the day. Before we begin, we ask God to direct our thinking. . . . We usually . . . conclude with a prayer that we be shown through the day.

   . . . As we go through the day we pause, when agitated or doubtful, and ask for the right thought or action.")

Shoemaker asked how we know what *is* guidance. He said guidance always comes with an authority all its own. This varies in intensity; for guidance is sometimes the motion of a consecrated human mind, mobilized to do the will of God; and sometimes it is the clear shooting-in of God's thought above our own thought. Guidance tells you which of several right things you ought to do. But, he said, it must be tested by the spirit of Christ to avoid self-deception; and Shoemaker listed the means of "checking" to be sure there is no self-deception. Shoemaker's "checks" were very much used by all Oxford Group people. On pages 53 through 55, he suggested as to checking:

1. The Holy Spirit's guidance will never be contrary to the New Testament.
2. God's will is sometimes made clear also by circumstances. He guides by open and closed doors.
3. Guidance should be tested by the concurrence of other guided people.
4. Real, honest, dispassionate thinking should precede guidance. Shoemaker said: "We all know that intuition is better than reason . . . and some of us know that guidance far exceeds intuition."

Shoemaker often wrote about three levels of life on which he said men live: the level of instinct ["I want"], the level of conscience ["I ought"], and the level of grace ["I am guided"] (p. 57). He said that Jesus was just as anxious to get us up from the level of conscience to the level of grace as he was to get us from the level of instinct to the level of grace.

Shoemaker then said he would share his own experience as to how to seek a real hold on God, and a real knowledge by genuine revelation of God's will. He said religion today is largely the imitation of an example, while it ought to be the hearing of a Voice. And how is that brought about? Shoemaker said that something happened when he moved up out of the old conception of a "Morning Watch," which, he said, had a way of slipping round till evening, to the conception of a "Quiet Time" (p. 60). He said the "Quiet Time" emphasis was in a different place. Formerly he had sought to find his way up to God. Now he let God find His way down to him (Shoemaker). He said:

> Listening became the dominant note. Not the exclusive note: for there was Bible study first, taking a book [of the Bible] and studying it straight through; and there was also ordinary prayer, confession, petition, thanksgiving, intercession. But the bulk of the time was listening. Most of us find it indispensable to have a loose-leaf notebook, in which to write down the things which come to us. . . . We do not want to forget the slightest thing that God tells us to do: and I have sometimes had a rush of detailed guidance which came almost as fast as I could write it (p. 60).

> He may give us the conviction of sin that clears us of a stoppage and sends us to someone with restoration and apology. He may send us a verse of encouragement, like "Fear not," "Go in thy might, have I not sent thee?" "All is well." He may warn us against a wrong course, or a tedious and time-killing person, or a tendency in ourselves. He may send us to the telephone to call someone, or tell us to write a letter, or pay a visit, or take some exercise, or read a book. Nothing which concerns our lives is alien to His interest, or to the doing of His Will. He may give us guidance about how to help someone, or tell us what is the matter with them or us (p. 61).

The Big Book is filled with examples of similar searches for the guidance of God. We'll illustrate with examples from several Big Book chapters.

"Bill's Story" said of Bill:

1. "I placed myself unreservedly under His care and direction" (p. 13);
2. "I was to sit quietly when in doubt, asking only for direction and strength to meet my problems as He would have me" (p. 13); and
3. "I must turn in all things to the Father of Light who presides over us all" (p. 14).

"We Agnostics" said:

1. "there is an All Powerful, Guiding, Creative Intelligence" (p. 49);
2. "they found that a new power, peace, happiness, and sense of direction flowed into them" (p. 50); and
3. "When we drew near to Him, He disclosed Himself to us" (p. 57).

"How It Works" said:

1. "We asked God to help us show them the same tolerance, pity, and patience that we would cheerfully grant a sick friend" (p. 67);
2. "We ask Him to remove our fear and direct our attention to what He would have us be" (p. 68);
3. "We asked God to mold our ideals and help us to live up to them" (p. 69);
4. "In meditation, we ask God what we should do about each specific matter. The right answer will come, if we want it" (p. 69); and
5. "We earnestly pray for the right ideal, for guidance in each questionable situation, for sanity. . . ." (p. 70).

"Into Action" said:

1. "We ask that we be given strength and direction to do the right thing" (p. 79);
2. "Asking each morning in meditation that our Creator show us the way of patience, tolerance, kindliness, and love" (p. 83);
3. "Much has already been said about receiving strength, inspiration, and direction from Him who has all knowledge and power" (p. 85);
4. "We ask God to direct our thinking" (p. 86);
5. "Here we ask God for inspiration, an intuitive thought, or a decision" (p. 86);
6. "A prayer that we be shown all through the day what our next step is to be" (p. 87); and
7. "As we go through the day we pause . . . and ask for the right thought or action" (p. 87).

And there are many other examples in the Big Book of A.A.'s adoption of the guidance-of-God concepts Shoemaker espoused, whether they came from Shoemaker, the Oxford Group, the Bible, or other Christian literature.

Shoemaker's next chapter is "Living In Touch With People." And here he presented an idea that is popular in A.A. today: You cannot give away what you do not have yourself. On page 164, the Big Book states, concerning the helping of others who are still sick: "But obviously you cannot transmit something you haven't got." Shoemaker said: "The evangelists had forgotten to tell me that before I could give it away, I must have the experience of Christ myself" (p. 67). Shoemaker also said, "We have got to learn the *secret* of health, we have got to know the hindrances and the cure" (p. 69). Shoemaker spoke of what is needed for us to start working with others. He suggested:

> What really gets people at the outset? Only one thing—experience told with humor and enthusiasm. The ordinary processes of friendship must build sufficient confidence first, but the first gun to fire is a piece of news. It will probably be the story of your own experience of Christ, as you feel guided to tell it, adapted all the while to the sort of person you are talking to. It might be the story of someone else whose situation is more nearly parallel than your own. The Gospel was originally "news," not "views" (p. 73).
>
> We keep to fundamental *experiences* first, and let the truth follow (p. 76).
>
> You will never do effective work with individuals unless you have first fully caught their attention and made them want what you have; and unless next you have learned the secrets of their lives, and they have told you what kind of people they are underneath where most people do not see them (p. 77).

The Big Book's chapter, "Working With Others," contains many similar witnessing ideas. It says:

> When you discover a prospect for Alcoholics Anonymous, find out all you can about him (p. 90).
>
> See your man alone, if possible. At first engage in general conversation. After a while, turn the talk to some phase of drinking. Tell him enough about your drinking habits, symptoms, and experiences to encourage him to speak of himself. If he wishes to

> talk, let him do so. . . . If he is not communicative, give him a sketch of your drinking career up to the time you quit. . . . If his mood is light, tell him humorous stories of your escapades. Get him to tell some of his (p. 91).
>
> Keep his attention focused mainly on your personal experience. . . . Even though your protege may not have entirely admitted his condition, he has become very curious to know how you got well. Let him ask you that question, if he will. *Tell him exactly what happened to you*. Stress the spiritual feature freely (pp. 92-93).
>
> Simply lay out the kit of spiritual tools for his inspection. Show him how they worked with you. . . . Tell him that if he wants to get well you will do anything to help. . . . If he is to find God the desire must come from within (p. 95).

Shoemaker said the sharing of needs is not enough. There must be a decision in which the will gathers up the facts which the mind has collected, and the aspiration the heart has felt, and packs them into a moral choice. This is the act of self-surrender which is man's part in his own conversion, the step which puts him in position to receive the grace of God which alone converts. Of surrender, Shoemaker said:

> Surrender is a handle by which an ordinary person may lay hold of the experience of conversion. It is the first step, the step of the will. In order to make surrender the decision of the whole life, and not merely the emotion of a moment, it needs to be filled with practical content: we must help people to see just what they are surrendering to God, their fears, their sins, most of all their *wills*, putting God's will once and for all ahead of every other thing (p. 78).

Shoemaker then pointed to the maintenance and growth ideas in surrender. He said: "There is the need for rededication day by day, hour by hour, by which progressively, in every Quiet Time, the contaminations of sin and self-will are further sloughed off (for they do have a way of collecting) and we are kept in fresh touch with the living Spirit of God. A further surrender is needed when and whenever there is found to be something in us which offends Christ, or walls us from one another" (p. 79).

The Big Book states:

> The spiritual life is not a theory. *We have to live it*. . . . Every day is a day when we must carry the vision of God's will into all our activities. "How can I best serve Thee—Thy will (not mine) be done." These are thoughts which must go with us constantly. We can exercise our will power along this line all we wish. It is the proper use of the will (pp. 83, 85).

Shoemaker spoke of building "a solid spiritual roadway under people's feet" (p. 79). He said there were four next steps which they would need if they were to keep travelling.

The first was a daily Quiet Time. To him, this meant constant help, suggestions about how to study the Bible, where and what to read in it—probably starting with the Gospels. He recommended Donald Carruthers' pamphlet, *How to Find Reality in Your Morning Devotions* as a guide.[172] He warned that there is a constant tendency to drop back from the full faith that God's Holy Spirit can guide, and to say that the Bible is enough, or prayer is enough. He said:

> A full-orbed Quiet Time means Bible study, prayer, ample time to wait upon God in quiet, writing down what is given to us, and perhaps the sharing of what has come to us with those who are closest to us. . . . There are no people who "cannot get guidance" except those who will not, or have not fulfilled the conditions (p. 81).

The second step on the roadway to a healthy relationship with God will be partly dependent, he said, upon integration in a guided group, often called a "spiritual family" (p. 81). Again he spoke

---

[172] Donald W. Carruthers, *How To Find Reality In your Morning Devotions: A Laboratory Approach to- - - I. The Word of God "The Bible" II. The Power of God "Prayer" III "The Guide of God"* The Holy Spirit (State College, Pennsylvania, n.d.)

of the First Century Christian church concept of *koinonia*, the fellowship (p. 81).

The third step for continuation of the spiritual life in those we help is that they shall begin to help others (p. 82). The Big Book put it this way: "Our very lives, as ex-problem drinkers, depend upon our constant thought of others and how we may help meet their needs" (p. 20).[173]

Finally, said Shoemaker: "The real truth is that the depth of an experience of Christ may be measured by our inability to keep still about it. The real thing overflows. When a person finds Him [Christ] fully, they have a message about Him for other people" (p. 85). He said: We should "never forget that "it is God that worketh in us, both to will and to do," and the energy and light which we need for this kind of work is a gift from God.[174] Without guidance to initiate and continue it, we shall just be tinkering with human personalities" (p. 86). Shoemaker concluded with this prayer: "God help us to give freely, as He has given it to us" (p. 86). Interestingly, page 164 of the Big Book contains very similar language. And it ends:

> Abandon yourself to God as you understand God. Admit your faults to Him and to your fellows. Clear away the wreckage of your past. Give freely of what you find and join us.

Shoemaker's last two chapters dealt with fellowship and the "new" church. In the fellowship chapter, he elaborated on his idea of fellowship, in the spiritual sense, as the intimacy which springs up between human beings who are agreed on a spiritual ideal which they are working out together. He referred to the Book of Acts and the mighty group-movement of the First Century Christian Church, in which the believers were fused into a corporate organism called "the body of Christ" (p. 88). He said the real fellowship is the power to live and work with people on

---

[173] See also Big Book, pp. 14-15, 89, 159.

[174] See Philippians 2:13.

the basis of absolute love and honesty. It involves lending one's life to the brotherhood of Christ, living in the absolute open with others, and sharing sins, feelings, plans, mistakes, and possessions with those who can be trusted with maximum stewardship of these things. He said a true fellowship provides the climate for group-guidance. He pleaded for rediscovery of fellowship under the guidance of God's Holy Spirit. And we believe his ideas may have influenced A.A.'s Twelve Traditions which grew out of the need for unity in the recovery program. The Traditions contain concepts of common welfare, the guidance of the group by God, message carrying, and proceeding on the basis of spiritual principles (Big Book, p. 564).

As to the new church, Shoemaker said:

> Somewhere the new church will have a group for the sharing of experience, a working "*koinonia*." As those who are won increase, there will be the need for a meeting where they see and hear one another, where those who are discouraged are lifted up again, where those who have had victories can share them with others, where people can declare themselves. At first this will be small. It grows out of changed lives. Beware of "starting a group." Convert people, and the group will develop as you relate them (pp. 114-115).[175]

We see a possible Shoemaker influence in the A.A. idea that there should be groups for sharing experience, and that people should be able to come to be lifted up through hearing victories shared by others. The A.A. Preamble, which is read at almost every A.A. meeting, commences with these words: "Alcoholics Anonymous is a fellowship of men and women who share their experience, strength and hope with each other that they may solve their

---

[175] Compare the last page of Big Book text on page 164, including the following on fellowship: "Still you may say: 'But I will not have the benefit of contact with you who write this book.' We cannot be sure. God will determine that, so you must remember that your real reliance is always upon Him. He will show you how to create the fellowship you crave."

common problem and help others to recover from alcoholism."[176]

The Gospel According To You

The Big Book expresses the hope that its readers will find God *now*! (p. 59). And Sam Shoemaker said he put in *The Gospel According To You* a collection of his 1933-1934 sermons which seemed most likely to help real seekers after God.[177] We believe this Shoemaker book virtually lays out the steps which AA's adopted for their path to a relationship with God—their road to "finding God."

Gospels vary, said Shoemaker; and the question he posed for the reader is just how effective the reader's own gospel can be. He suggested:

> The real Gospel is not ours, but Christ's. The real recommendation of the Gospel lies not in our persuasive powers, but in the Holy Spirit's power to come through us when we are open. And the real opener of men's hearts and minds to the influence of the Gospel is the wonderful grace of God. . . . Let us declare the Gospel to the world, clothed, as it was at first, in the flesh and blood of life. And there will come to us the glorious experience that came to John the Baptist, "And the two disciples heard him speak, and they followed Jesus" (pp. 18-19).[178]

---

[176] This Preamble can be found at the beginning of every issue of A.A.'s *Grapevine*—its monthly publication.

[177] Samuel Shoemaker, *The Gospel According To You* (New York: Fleming H. Revell, 1934), p. 4.

[178] The Gospel of John, chapter 1, gives the account of John the Baptist and his foretelling of Jesus. Verse 29 states that John saw Jesus coming and said, "Behold the Lamb of God, which taketh away the sin of the world." In verses 32 and 33, John continues: "I saw the Spirit descending from heaven like a dove, and it abode upon him. And I knew him not:" Then he received revelation that Jesus was the Son of God. The

(continued...)

Shoemaker's second chapter asked if the reader is running away from life—if he is in flight from reality. And he pointed to two ideas which we believe can be found in A.A.'s First and Second Steps. He said:

> Real religion always begins by facing the facts, all the facts, pleasant and unpleasant—the facts about human nature, its rottenness and its potentiality, the facts about pain and suffering, the facts also about the way they sometimes bless us when we take them aright, the facts of faith and the difference it makes in life, the great fact of GOD. Any religion which pretends to reality, and does not begin with the data in experience, is pretending only. . . . Begin with the facts. Dwindling fortune, diminishing health, age creeping up, increasing temptation somewhere, a difficult decision to be made, the difficulty of life itself. Face it, and don't run from it. . . . But face the other facts, too—GOD, and faith, and the way believing in God and obeying Him turns life into clear sailing for those who believe and obey (pp. 29-31).

The Big Book said at page 57: "Circumstances made him willing to believe. He humbly offered himself to his Maker—then he knew. Even so has God restored us to our right minds."

Shoemaker's next chapter was on "doubt." And he examined the story of "doubting Thomas." He pointed out that Thomas had said to Jesus: "Lord, we know not whither thou goest; and how can we know the way (p. 34)."[179] Jesus answered and said: "I am the way, the truth, and the life: no man cometh unto the Father, but by me" (p. 34).[180] Thomas had been told that Jesus would be raised from the dead. But when Thomas saw him, he doubted the whole resurrection until he had been "convinced" by seeing Jesus's

---

[178] (...continued)
verses Shoemaker quoted are John 1:35-37: "Again the next day after John stood, and two of his disciples; And looking upon Jesus as he walked, he saith, Behold the Lamb of God! And the two disciples heard him speak, and they followed Jesus."

[179] John 14:5.

[180] John 14:6.

wounds. Shoemaker said doubt arises from several causes. Doubt, like that in Thomas' life, may arise out of a negative, melancholy nature. A vast amount of doubt comes, or is alleged to come, from the evil of life. Shoemaker said that "a very large part of human misery is of our own making" (p. 38).[181] He also said most of our trouble comes from our freedom, freedom to choose better or worse. But, he said, the most fruitful source of doubt is our own moral mediocrity. It does not take much imagination, he said, to see that definite, vulgar sin inhibits faith—a man in the grip of low animal passions of sensuality or greed is in no position to believe in God. His life is too foul a place for faith to dwell in (p. 39).

And what is Shoemaker's answer to such doubt. He said:

> First the desire to believe, so that life may have a reason; and then exposure to the faith of others, going where faith is, and is to be found. . . . Stay alone, like Thomas and feed your mind on negative thoughts, and you will doubt, of course you will. Go where the disciples gather, like Thomas afterward, let the thoughts of believing people filter through your mind and heart, and you will believe, as he did,—of course you will. . . . The cure for doubt is fellowship with the faith of others who believe. That asks of you at the beginning no acceptance nor agreement, merely honest self-exposure. It led Thomas to faith. God grant it may lead you (pp. 41-43).

Shoemaker's next chapter called for his readers to be doers of the word, not hearers only. On page 44, he first quoted the King James Version, and then, Moffatt's translation of James 1:22:

1. Be ye doers of the word, and not hearers only, deceiving your own selves.
2. Act on the Word, instead of merely listening to it and deluding yourselves.

---

[181] See Big Book, p. 62—a virtual quote of Shoemaker: "So our troubles, we think, are basically of our own making."

Shoemaker was talking about a subject very important in all his teachings—the experiment of faith. He said we have been living in a world of religious ideas, instead of a world of religious experience. His suggestion: Try it out by experiment, and prove it by its results; otherwise, you only fool yourself into believing that you have the heart of religion when you haven't.

Shoemaker said on page 47 that the experiment of faith must begin with the statement from the Word of God that God is, and that he is a rewarder of them that seek him.[182] Shoemaker said we must give God a chance to act directly in our own lives, to speak to us personally, and to assure us that God really is; for, he said, "the great thing that all of us long for in religion is the *reality of the Presence of God*" (p. 47, emphasis ours). And note how the Big Book confirms this reality in terms of what AAs acted upon, believing either that God is, or taking suggested action, based on a willingness to believe. The Big Book says:

> When many hundreds of people are able to say that the consciousness of the presence of God is today the most important fact of their lives, they present a powerful reason why one should have faith (p. 51).

> In a few seconds he was overwhelmed by a conviction of the Presence of God (p. 56).

> As we felt new power flow in, as we enjoyed peace of mind, as we discovered we could face life successfully, as we became conscious of His [God's] presence. . . . (p. 63).

> Many of us have felt, for the first time, the Presence and Power of God within its [an alcohol treatment hospital in an eastern city] walls (p. 162).

---

[182] Here Shoemaker again used the precise language of Hebrews 11:6. See also Samuel Shoemaker, Jr., *National Awakening* (New York: Harper & Brothers, 1936), p. 40. For another book about Oxford Group ideas which cited this verse, see Leslie D. Weatherhead, *How Can I Find God?* (London: Hodder and Stoughton, 1933), p. 72.

Shoemaker said we often labor for a mystical experience of God, when there is a much more simple way. He said if we will be honest with God about all our sins, and lay ourselves open to him, he will come to us, revealing his presence directly. Perhaps this Shoemaker idea is comprehended in this simple Big Book formula: "Burn the idea into the consciousness of every man that he can get well regardless of anyone. The only condition is that he trust in God and clean house."[183] Shoemaker said the next phase of the experiment of faith is simply discovering fellowship and teamwork with other Christians who know us, to offset our isolation or a spurious fellowship of cooperation without sharing.

He said he believed that the "Word" means any genuine coming to us of truth, comfort, or grace from God himself, especially the kind we hear, either with outward ear, or with the inward. Then he suggested looking at the ways in which the Word of God comes to us, to see whether we listen to it only, and delude ourselves, or whether we act on it, and so are made sure of it.

Shoemaker spoke first of a concept which we believe became embedded in A.A.'s Sixth Step—the conviction of sin. He said we often hear something that goes home to us, reveals a fact about ourselves that we have not faced, or perhaps have not wanted to face. It may be in a book that describes someone of our temperament. Or a word from a friend about ourselves. And he asked whether we let the remark run off like water on a roof, or do we "act on it." He said we should see these truths not so much as proof of guilt, but as the principle of growth—taking action to change.

He said the "Word" of God most assuredly comes to us through the Bible. The Bible can often have a direct message for us as touching a present situation, an encouragement, a rebuke, or a direction. Again, he asked, do we take it as meant for us now, and do we "act on it?" And he went further with the Bible. He said we need to find the way of life out of which it was born, and enter into it, because we have known at least the beginnings of the

---

[183] Big Book, p. 98.

experience which the Bible describes. He suggested the same thing about prayer. Do we listen to, and then debate, the Bible or the prayer; or, do we "act on it?"

Finally, he spoke of God's Word as it comes to us directly. He said he didn't contend that every unusual thought which comes into our minds is God speaking. But he did claim that God speaks to us more often than we admit and that He is always trying to make contact with us through God-given ideas. He said these ideas will be more trustworthy as we become more disciplined, trained in Christ, and instructed in God's written Word. "We shall be surer of them as we obey them, and, as St. John commands us, 'try the Spirits whether they are of God'—and that must be done both by checking them against the historic authority of Christ and His Church, but also by 'acting on' them, following the guidance we have" (pp. 52-53). In these concepts of listening for the Word, obeying it, trying it, and checking it, Shoemaker was teaching basic Oxford Group ideas reflected in any number of Oxford Group books of his time.[184]

Shoemaker said:

> I know some people who believe themselves to be cut off from direct communication with God, by some lack of mystical capacity. I do not believe a word of it. If they are cut off, it is by their own disobedience to the truth they knew somewhere in the past. If they will face that, admit it, act on it, ask God's forgiveness for it, be positive about what God gives them as they pray now, their doubt will disappear. Reasoning is no cure for doubt. Action is. Act on the word—and only so will you know that it *is* the word, God's Word to you (pp. 53-54).

---

[184] See, for example, Eleanor Napier Forde, *The Guidance of God* (Oxford: Oxford University Press, 1930); Cecil Rose, *When Man Listens* (New York: Oxford University Press, 1937); Howard J. Rose, *The Quiet Time* (New York: The Oxford Group at 61 Gramercy Park, North, 1937); W. E. Sangster, *God Does Guide Us* (New York: The Abingdon Press, 1934); Burnett Hillman Streeter, *The God Who Speaks* (London: Macmillan & Co., 1943); and Jack C. Winslow, *When I Awake* (London: Hodder & Stoughton, 1938).

Here, without specifically mentioning it, Shoemaker was expanding on his teaching about John 7:17—"If any man will do his [i.e., God's] will, he shall know." Shoemaker, the Oxford Group mentors, and the Oxford Group writers were forever teaching about obedience as the organ of spiritual knowledge.[185] As these writings show, the obedience began with "willingness;" and A.A. picked up on that idea. In the chapter to the agnostics (on how to find faith), the Big Book said:

> We needed to ask ourselves but one short question. "Do I now believe, or am I even willing to believe, that there is a Power greater than myself? As soon as a man can say that he does believe, or is willing to believe, we emphatically assure him that he is on his way" (p. 47).[186]

Shoemaker's next chapter really bears heavily on ideas to be found in A.A.'s Fourth Step—the moral inventory. He commenced by saying that Jesus "saw sin as the barrier between us and God, between us and fullness of spiritual life" (p. 58). Then he told the story of a man whose health and life were saved because he found an experience of Christ. Shoemaker said, "The basic problem of dissipation usually goes back to some kind of fear or pride; and his real sin is not dissipation but selfishness, and that selfishness has caused him to return to his dissipation" (p. 59). The Big Book discussion of the Fourth Step treats the "sin" issues in these ways: (1) "Being convinced that self, manifested in various ways, was what had defeated us, we considered its common manifestations" (p. 64). (2) "Resentment is the number one offender" (p. 64). (3) "Where had we been selfish, dishonest, self-seeking and frightened?" (p. 67). (4) "We reviewed our fears thoroughly" (p. 68). (5) "Now about sex. . . . Where had we been selfish,

---

[185] See discussion and citations in Dick B., *The Oxford Group & Alcoholics Anonymous*, pp. 19, 34, 48, 111-12, 127, 137, 186, 261.

[186] We have already quoted the conclusion of this same chapter which said: "Circumstances made him willing to believe. He humbly offered himself [acted on the belief]—then he knew" (p. 57).

dishonest, or inconsiderate?" (p. 69). At the beginning of this discussion, the Big Book said: "Our liquor was but a symptom. . . . When the spiritual malady is overcome, we straighten out mentally and physically" (p. 64). The Big Book discussion is filled with mention of "honesty."

Shoemaker said:

> The mischief in the world that is done by good people does not arise from their *blindness* to greater good, but from their dishonesty about it. Christ is that true Light that lightens the life of all of us. If we consult that light simply, and report our findings honestly, we should live different lives and make a different world. The light is often there, when we make it darkness by misrepresenting the light we have (p. 63).

Pleading for divine guidance—for being led by the Spirit of God—Shoemaker asked in his next chapter: "Head, Heart or Holy Spirit—Which Rules You?" He said of God:

> He knows where your heart is right, and where your head is right; and where they both be wrong. Do you ask Him? Do you pray long enough to come away sure about what He wants you to do (p. 70)?

He said, "Let us have a Quiet Time, and ask God" (p. 73). The whole chapter concerned asking God for guidance and the results that can come of that. For example, he said:

> How different it is when the Holy Spirit is at work, and we depend upon Him! Sometimes He tells us silence. Sometimes personal confession of wrong. Sometimes keeping off religion altogether. Sometimes ministry to another kind of need for a time. Sometimes He says to take a knife and cut deep. But deep within Him there is a smoothness, a clearness, a freedom from human suasion, that can only be achieved when God Himself is present. Then is when lives are changed, when our words are filled with power, when we are

channels and we know it, and the other person knows it; and we give God the glory (p. 79).[187]

In a chapter entitled "Hurdles," Shoemaker presented a step sequence that was to appear later in A.A. He discussed the "steps" to the Christian life. These, he said, involve overcoming hurdles—with God's help. He commenced with Psalm 18:29: "With the help of my God I shall leap over the wall."

He said: "And first we must say that the initial hurdle is *deciding* to run the Christian course at all" (p. 82) [emphasis ours]. This idea, we believe, parallels A.A.'s Third or "decision" step. Shoemaker continued: "The next hurdle for most of us arises when we begin to *face ourselves honestly*" (p. 83) [emphasis ours]. This idea, we believe, parallels A.A.'s Fourth Step concept of "self examination" or "inventory." Moving forward, Shoemaker said: "Then there is another hurdle that comes first for you; it is the hurdle of *letting another person with spiritual experience know that you consciously admit your need*, and want help (p. 84) [emphasis ours]. This seems to parallel A.A.'s Fifth Step confession idea.

Then Shoemaker covered an idea which A.A. originally termed "surrender," but which Bill Wilson appears later to have split into the initial act of decision in Step Three and the ultimate act of decision to clean house in Step Seven.[188] Shoemaker said: "Next there comes a hurdle familiar in the idea to many . . . the hurdle of surrender to God. . . . I think that, in this day especially, the heart of that decision lies in the entrusting of our lives to the

---

[187] At the conclusion of its Eleventh Step discussion, the Big Book says: "We constantly remind ourselves we are no longer running the show, humbly saying to ourselves many times each day 'Thy will be done.' We are then in much less danger of excitement, fear, anger, worry, self-pity, or foolish decisions. We become much more efficient. We do not tire so easily, for we are not burning up energy foolishly as we did when we were trying to arrange life to suit ourselves. It works—it really does. We alcoholics are undisciplined. So we let God discipline us in the simple way we have just outlined" (pp. 87-88).

[188] Big Book, pp. 62-64, 76.

security of God, as over against the false securities of this world" (p. 85). Shoemaker added: "The heart of surrender does not lie in asking God to take our problems and solve them for us because we have been unable to do so; it lies in *giving ourselves to Him for the doing of His will* (p. 88). Note that A.A.'s Seventh Step prayer says: "I pray that you now remove from me every single defect of character which stands in the way of my usefulness to you and my fellows. Grant me strength, as I go out from here, to do your bidding" (Big Book, p. 76).

Next, almost as if he were himself prophesying the order of A.A.'s steps, Shoemaker moved to the area of amends, found in A.A.'s Steps Eight and Nine. Shoemaker said: "For most people there is wrapped up in the decision to surrender to God the necessity to right all wrongs with men, and it generally means a specific wrong of act or attitude toward somebody in particular. This is the hurdle of *restitution*" (p. 87) [emphasis ours]. The Big Book starts its discussion of restitution in this way:

> Now we go out to our fellows and repair the damage done in the past. We attempt to sweep away the debris which has accumulated out of our effort to live on self-will and run the show ourselves (p. 76).

Shoemaker concluded the "Hurdles" chapter with a lead-in to A.A.'s Tenth and Eleventh Steps, which have to do with maintenance of, and growth in, the spiritual experience. Shoemaker spoke of this hurdle: the "fresh, vivid battle with returning, characteristic temptation" (p. 91). The Big Book expresses the task this way: "Continue to watch for selfishness, dishonesty, resentment, and fear;" and the Big Book gives a daily surrender/house-cleaning formula for dealing with these shortcomings (Big Book, p. 84).

Chapter Eight dealt with human pride and how God levels it. Shoemaker considered pride to be first on the list of seven deadly sins, partly because pride infuses and underlies almost all other sins, and also because of the power of its subtlety. Bill Wilson wrote much *in later years* about pride, but the subject is hardly discussed directly in the Big Book or in the Steps. However, Shoemaker's indirect influence seems apparent if one reads Shoemaker's language carefully. Thus Shoemaker told of the lesson of the great depression of the 1930's. He said:

> The net lesson for us of all this depression is something more than the need for a better established economic system; it says to us that we were meant to live in *conscious dependence upon God*, and not in the pride of our own independence (p. 97) [emphasis ours].

One A.A. counter-part of this idea can be found in the following, on pages 99 and 100 of the Big Book:

> Remind the prospect [the newcomer to A.A.] that his recovery is not dependent upon people. It is dependent upon his relationship with God. . . . When we look back, we realize that the things which came to us when we put ourselves in God's hands were better than anything we could have planned.

Certainly a central idea in A.A.'s Third Step is that man must make the decision to quit playing God, to let God be God, and to let Him become the Director of his life. Shoemaker said:

> You and I are impotent to help ourselves in our greatest need. Pride ought to die right there. And when it dies, man really turns to God (p. 105).

Shoemaker's next chapter dealt with a familiar theme: the joy that comes when man discovers or rediscovers God—to use one of Bill Wilson's earlier expressions.[189] Shoemaker said:

---

[189] See Dick B., *The Oxford Group & Alcoholics Anonymous* (Seattle: Glen Abbey Books, 1992), pp. 10-11; and *Alcoholics Anonymous* (New York: Works Publishing Co., 1939—Multilith Draft on file in A.A. Archives in New York), p. 13.

> If you know the joy which comes after a crisis, when one we love who is ill gets well; or when one from whom we have become estranged is restored to us, you will better understand how the deepest joy in all human experience arises when our estrangement from God gives place to our restoration in *His love* and His *companionship* (p. 106) [emphasis ours].

The Big Book tells on page 56 of a minister's son who finally and humbly turned to God. The account continues:

> The barriers he had built through the years were swept away. He stood in the Presence of Infinite Power and *Love*. He had stepped from the bridge to shore. For the first time, he lived in conscious *companionship with his Creator* [emphasis ours].

In language paralleling Sixth Step conviction ideas, Shoemaker wrote:

> We want to make the best of two worlds. We want God, but we want other things too. The sense of conflict, the sense of sin, is really a well-placed danger signal, telling us we are headed for trouble, perhaps nervous breakdown, because we are still two or more selves. And God made us to be one self, the self of His vision and His will for our life (p. 112).

> Let him [the estranged man] face all that is prodigal in him, all that is estranged from God, and offensive to God. Let him come back in honest penitence to God, like the son in the story, and all that misery will be left behind. Joy will come automatically as a by-product (p. 113).

A.A.'s Sixth Step discussion suggests: "If we still cling to something we will not let go, we ask God to help us be willing" (p. 75). We see in this phrase a strong trace of Shoemaker's "penitence," "repentance"—the desire to change!

Shoemaker's chapter on faith as the master of sorrow contained a dissertation on that hour when triumphant faith works something very near a miracle. Shoemaker wrote much on Romans, Chapter Eight. We quote the most significant portions Shoemaker used:

> Romans 8:35:
> Who shall separate us from the love of Christ? *shall* tribulation, or distress, or persecution, or famine, or nakedness, or peril, or sword?
>
> Romans 8:37-39:
> Nay, in all these things we are more than conquerors through him that loved us. For I am persuaded, that neither death, nor life, nor angels, nor principalities, nor powers, nor things present, nor things to come,
> Nor height, nor depth, nor any other creature, shall be able to separate us from the love of God, which is in Christ Jesus our Lord.

Shoemaker was talking about overcoming fear—a subject that comes up constantly in A.A. meetings and is discussed in the Big Book. The Big Book tenders faith as the antidote to fear. Shoemaker wrote:

> The real enemy of faith is not reason, but inexperience; it is not an overgrown mentality, it is an underdone experience. . . . You must begin with searching your own heart for the things that drive faith away. . . . You will be surprised the way your rational difficulties begin to clear up if you get your moral difficulties straightened out first. . . . Listen to the spiritually experienced, who have themselves tried the experiment, and you will find that it turns out for you the same way" (p. 127).

Shoemaker then talked about surrender. In effect a surrender to "God as you understand Him." He wrote:

> The true meaning of faith is self-surrender to God. . . . Surrender to *whatever you know about Him*, or believe must be the truth about Him. Surrender to Him, *if necessary, in total ignorance of Him*. Far more important that you touch Him than that you understand

> Him at first. Put yourself in His hands. Whatever He is, as William James said, He is more ideal than we are. Make the leap. Give yourself to Him (p. 128) [emphasis ours].

Did the A.A. language, "God as we understood Him," really result from a "compromise" with the God of the Bible that was made in Ruth Hock's office? A compromise with the atheists on one side, the minister's son on the other, and Bill Wilson in the middle? We believe Shoemaker's surrender-to-God-as-you-understand-him ideas were well in place and probably well understood by Ebby when he first carried the Oxford Group message to Bill. Ebby told Bill that God had done for him (Ebby) what he could not do for himself. He then suggested that Bill start overcoming his hostility to religion by choosing his own conception of God for a *beginning*.[190] We believe Ebby was giving Bill a straight Oxford Group message about how to come to believe in God, the Creator, the Maker—to whom Bill surrendered, first at the Calvary Rescue Mission, and again at Towns Hospital. Either Ebby or Bill, or both, could very well have found the God-as-you-understand-Him idea in any of several Shoemaker writings or teachings. Witness the foregoing quote from Shoemaker's *The Gospel According To You*—published in 1934.

Shoemaker wrote a chapter entitled "Jesus' Temptation and Ours." In it, he discussed the record in which Jesus Christ resisted the temptations of the Devil by quoting to the Devil, and standing on, several scriptures from the Old Testament.[191] When the Devil made offers to Jesus—even quoting Scripture—Jesus answered the Devil with the Word of God. Jesus told the Devil to take a hike. He said, "Get thee hence, Satan. . . ."[192] Every time the Devil made Jesus an offer or challenged him, Jesus

---

[190] Big Book, p. 12.

[191] See Matthew 4:1-11.

[192] Matthew 4:10.

simply answered by accurately quoting the Word of God in context. He repeatedly responded, "It is written."[193]
Shoemaker explained:

> Temptation is a real crisis, always, for it marks a direction according to the way we meet it. If we live in the will of God consistently, then the Spirit will go with us into the wilderness, and help us to fight our battle with the powers of darkness. If we go in alone, with no knowledge of God, the outcome is uncertain. We have God to call on, as Christ had. We have from Christ the vision of God's will in the world, and what it might mean if all men looked up to Him for their light, and dwelt with one another as His sons (p. 142).

Shoemaker wrote on "Our Counterpart of the Cross." He asked if it was simply suffering. Or service generously given. Or sacrifice freely made. Interestingly, Shoemaker explained with a concept later found in A.A.'s Step Five. He said: "It is my own conviction that the truest counter-part of the Cross is the sharing of our sins" (p. 146). He felt it is not service. He said that the most important contribution is a real word of apology, an admission of need, or an acknowledgement of failure. All these level pride and show the real need of a holy and loving Father. Shoemaker quoted the verse from the Sermon on the Mount that we have already discussed—reconciling with one's brother before bringing one's gift to the altar.[194] He discussed the idea of sharing our part in a wrong—an idea later to be found in A.A.'s Fourth and Ninth Steps. And he discussed the Twelfth Step idea of sharing for witness. He said Christ died on the Cross to forgive us our sins and save us from them, but he also died to show us true values and the way of life. Shoemaker said: "When we confess, we tell of something that has taken place before Christ's

---

193 Matthew 4:4,7,10.

194 See Matthew 5:23-24.

cure: when we witness, we tell of the cure and of Him Who works it" (p. 151).

Shoemaker wrote of "Christ and Human Sin." He quoted 1 Timothy 1:15:

> This *is* a faithful saying, and worthy of all acceptation, that Christ Jesus came into the world to save sinners; of whom I [i.e., the Apostle Paul] am chief.

He also quoted 1 John 2:1-2:

> My little children, these things write I unto you, that ye sin not. And if any man sin, we have an advocate with the Father, Jesus Christ the righteous: And he is the propitiation for our sins: and not for ours only, but also for *the sins of* the whole world.

And then Shoemaker wrote of the redemptive action of Christ. He said:

> Whatever theory you hold about the Fall of Man, that story and doctrine are utterly true to what we most deeply feel about ourselves when we are honest. Contact with God is our normal condition, as normal as water is for fish. Sin and estrangement mean we have lost something, rejected something we ought to have accepted. We feel both responsible and guilty for our separation from God, because we *are* both responsible and guilty. So far as justice is concerned, it would have been no more than was coming to us if God had closed the door and been through with us forever. . . . But . . . He came to us . . . and identified Himself with us, by sending His Son in the likeness of our flesh, to live life under precisely our conditions and to transform it from within. From within that same identified Life, He challenged us, giving Christ a message to human sin, a message of conviction but also of hope, a message of warning and rebuke which was also a message of faith and salvation. "Christ Jesus came into the world to save sinners." That is God's eternal attitude toward humankind in its waywardness, sinfulness and estrangement (pp. 159-60).

Shoemaker then touched on the need for self-examination and confession—the heart of A.A.'s Fourth and Fifth step ideas. Shoemaker said:

> The reason why we do not conquer the obvious sins, but go on half-slave and half-free, is that the great sin of ego is unrecognized and therefore unsurrendered. . . . The deepest fault in any of us, the meek ones as well as the proud, is the self-assertion in self-made plans. Christ came to get at that in you and me. He came with a Gospel to change us and keep us changed (p. 161).

Note that the Big Book said at pages 61-63:

> The first requirement is that we be convinced that any life run on self-will can hardly be a success. . . . Our actor is self-centered—ego-centric. . . . Neither could we reduce our self-centeredness much by wishing or trying on our own power. We had to have God's help. . . . First of all, we had to quit playing God. It didn't work.

Shoemaker said, "You can't change life, but you can change yourself. That is why it is anything but morbid to face your sins; it is the one healthy and hopeful thing any of us can possibly do" (p. 166). He also said:

> We know that Christ Jesus came into the world to save such as you and me—to save us from the sins we hate, to save us from the sins we love, to save us from the sins we do not know, to save us from the one great, all-inclusive sin of God-less, self-filled, self-directed, self-ridden lives (p. 167).

The Big Book set forth a rather simple formula for obtaining God's help in eliminating selfishness, self-centeredness, and self-will. It said:

> Next, we decided that hereafter in this drama of life, God was going to be our Director. He is the Principal; and we are His agents. He is the Father, and we are His children. . . . Being all

> powerful, He provided what we needed, if we kept close to Him and performed His work well (pp. 62-63).

Shoemaker's last two chapters had to do with the receipt of power from on high. The power that was promised prior to, and received at, Pentecost. The power received when one makes Jesus Christ one's personal Lord and Savior. His last chapters also had to do with Christ's mission in this world. Relevant though they are for the Christian, these passages simply lost any possible direct influence when the Big Book was put in its final form.

National Awakening

National Awakening is a Shoemaker book that was published in 1936, just about the time A.A.'s original Step ideas were beginning to take shape and work.[195] The book followed by only a year the Oxford Group book which Shoemaker's good friend from Princeton, Professor Philip Marshall Brown, completed in 1935. Brown's book was *The Venture of Belief.*[196] Both books focus largely on the initial surrender ideas that lead to the religious experience. They speak of an experiment of faith involving willingness to believe, belief that God is, and the self-surrender decision that leads to a new birth and a religious or conversion experience.

Shoemaker's first chapter is "National Awakening" and speaks about the significance of Easter. He commenced by stating, "This is Easter Day. Christ is risen" (p. 1). And he said Easter manifests the absolute power of God. He said: "Our light is come in the Risen Christ; the glory of the Lord is risen upon us. How may we

---

[195] Samuel Shoemaker, Jr., *National Awakening* (New York: Harper & Brothers, 1936).

[196] Philip Marshall Brown, *The Venture of Belief* (New York: Fleming H. Revell, 1935).

as a people arise?" (p. 2). He asked: "Do you think a moral and spiritual awakening might be the answer to our needs?" (pp. 2-3). Then he quoted President Franklin D. Roosevelt who said he doubted "if there is any problem—social, political, or economic—that would not melt away before the fire of such a spiritual awakening" (p. 3). These are potent and relevant words for the A.A. history student who will remember that "The Solution" in the Big Book is a "spiritual awakening."

Shoemaker then defined the problem in achieving such an awakening. He said:

> If we were different, the world would be different. And the heart of that problem is that many of us are wrong with God and wrong with each other: and what we need is to be right with God, and right with each other. Towards God we need repentance, and towards man we need restitution. The first step is not resurrection, it is crucifixion. . . . It is the crucifixion of pride, narrowness, stupidity, ignorant prejudice, intolerance, fixed viewpoints about other people, laziness, lack of vision, self-satisfaction, conventionality that we need. There is no resurrection without crucifixion. . . . [W]e have got to stand for the answers to those problems, security in the will of God, faith instead of inferiority, dependence on God instead of pride: the personal direction of God in the life of every man, woman and child (pp. 6-7).

Though it may not seem immediately apparent, this is the approach of A.A.'s "house-cleaning" Steps. Following A.A.'s Third Step decision are its Steps that lead to "repentance" and "change" of self (Four through Seven) and then to restitution (Eight and Nine). The objective of the Third Step decision and of the house-cleaning Steps (Four through Nine) is to reach the maintenance and growth Steps (Ten through Twelve). These last three Steps are to enable: (a) daily house-cleaning, (b) the daily seeking of God's will and reliance upon it, and (c) a resultant spiritual awakening.

Shoemaker suggested five ideas for a national resurrection. The first is that we face our responsibility. Next, that we recognize only God can make us different; and that only He can give us a sharpened sense of sin. Third, that we need someone to help us see ourselves as we are. Fourth, that we must make a decision. And finally, that "we need training in the next steps of obeying God in everything, and so we need company" (p. 10).

Shoemaker's second chapter was "Christianity: Service, Or Spiritual Power." He drew a distinction between two ideas in Christianity: (1) Service, (2) Spiritual Power. The first idea is that Christianity is human service; and that "faith without works is dead." The "faith without works" verse is from the Book of James and is very much repeated in the Big Book.[197] But Shoemaker said the idea that "service" and "works" exemplify Christianity missed the point. He said:

> Our friend, the ordinary man, is mixing up roots and fruits. The fruit of Christianity is service, but the root of it is touch with the living God, which brings spiritual power into life. One of the places where that power overflows is in service. Our modern world wants to take a desirable fruit of Christianity and say that it is Christianity itself. This is not the service which overflows from a relationship with God through Christ; this is a substitute for that relationship. Humanity then becomes our god, and service our religion (pp. 12-13).

How important it is to keep these Shoemaker words in focus as one views the Twelve Steps of A.A.! The Big Book says its main purpose is to help people to find power (p. 45). The Twelfth Step then announces that the previous steps have enabled access to that power. It begins: "Having had a spiritual awakening as the result of these steps . . ." (p. 60). Only then does the idea of service enter the Twelfth Step. It continues: "[W]e tried to carry this message to alcoholics and practice these principles in all our affairs." The end of the Twelve Steps was not service; it was power. The power having been received, the message of awareness

---

[197] See James 2:20. For examples of references to this expression in the Big Book, see pp. 14-15, 76, 88, 93, and 97.

of the power was to be conveyed through service and was to be implemented through "works." Shoemaker said:

> I believe that that is precisely what our modern religion needs: to be lifted up and purged from the dead works of human self-effort, and begin to serve the living God by power which He offers us, rather than by service without that power which we offer to Him (p. 15).

What is the focus of the Big Book? The reader can consider these sentences having to do with restitution:

> At the moment we are trying to put our lives in order. But this is not an end in itself. Our real purpose is to fit ourselves to be of maximum service to God and the people about us (p. 77).

But the next few pages say:

> We will suddenly realize that God is doing for us what we could not do for ourselves. . . . Much has already been said about receiving strength, inspiration, and direction from Him who has all knowledge and power. It we have carefully followed directions, we have begun to sense the flow of His Spirit into us. To some extent we have become God-conscious (pp. 84-85).

Shoemaker said Christ sought primarily to release the power of God in people's lives. He spoke of Jesus's healings and his lifting of fear. Shoemaker said Christ's service ". . . lay primarily in being able to communicate to people a certain quality of living based on His own faith and experience of God. He deeply changed the people about Him, and then He welded them into a company who should continue His work and transmit that same power to people throughout the world" (pp. 20-21).

Shoemaker's next chapter was entitled "When God Comes." He said:

> Every so often in human history, the Spirit of God comes into the world in fresh manifestation of power. We notice a kind of cycle in the spiritual life of mankind; somewhere a great Reality is born, which brings a new discovery of God and new tides of life (p. 23).

Compare this Big Book language:

> We finally saw that faith in some kind of God was a part of our make-up. . . . Sometimes we had to search fearlessly, but He was there. He was as much a fact as we were. We found the Great Reality deep down within us. In the last analysis it is only there that He may be found. It was so with us (p. 55).

Shoemaker asked, "What do we do with questioners?" (p. 28). He replied:

> One argument in religion is about as good as another; but an experience beats any argument. Men run from your arguments about God, they will not listen to your elaborate explanations; but when you tell them what it is with Him, their hearts, as John Wesley said, are "strangely warmed," and their minds are strangely persuaded. . . . Jesus gave His answer to John. . . . He just gathered up in a cascade of living words the living deeds He and they had been seeing, and said, "Go your way, and tell John what things ye have seen and heard; how that the blind see, the lame walk, the lepers are cleansed, the deaf hear, the dead are raised, to the poor the gospel is preached."[198] It was proof by evidence (p. 28).

Shoemaker's next three chapters were a powerful introduction to his often-mentioned experiment of faith, and they seem to forecast the A.A. approach to it. The first chapter was entitled, "Finding Real Security today"—which, of course, was in God. The second chapter was entitled, "How To Find God"—and the answer, in substance, was "surrender!" The third chapter was

---

[198] See Matthew 11:4-5.

"How." The answer was: to be born again, as Jesus had taught Nicodemus in the third chapter of the Gospel of John.[199]

Let's return to the "security" chapter which outlined the faith experiment. Shoemaker said:

> All of us seek security in some form, because we need it and must have it. . . . That applies to the highest life imaginable on earth. It applies to Christ. . . . His ultimate security was in God. And we must honestly ask ourselves where lies our final security; whether it lies in people and things or whether it lies in God (p. 35).

As we have pointed out, Dr. Bob said to the AAs assembled at his last major address:

> Another thing which most of us are not too blessed with is the feeling of humility. . . . I'm talking about the attitude of each and every one of us toward our Heavenly Father. Christ said, "Of Myself, I am nothing—My strength cometh from My Father in heaven." If He had to say that, how about you and me?[200]

Here's what Shoemaker said about real security:

> And where is it? It lies in a faith in God which includes an experiment. It lies in believing that God is, that He has a plan, and that He will reveal that plan to us. It lies in fitting in with that plan ourselves, and finding that God will take care of us when we dare to make that experiment (p. 40).[201]

He said there are three basic elements in making an experiment like that; and he continued:

> The first is a belief in God. . . . Real faith begins when we trust a God Who works into modern life through individuals. . . . You will

---

[199] See John 3:1-21, and compare Romans 10:9,10.

[200] *Co-Founders*, pp. 14-15.

[201] Compare Big Book, pp. 99-100.

> never find it by believing in a God Who sits still. A God with a plan—with definite, accurate information for people who want to see that plan fulfilled—that is the groundwork of true security (p. 41).[202]

> The second thing is utter preoccupation with God's plan. "Seek ye first the Kingdom of God, and his righteousness. . . ." Ordinarily we think that if we look after our needs, God will take care of His plan. The truth is that if we look after God's plan, He takes care of our needs. . . . Christ put this very concretely, "Your Father knoweth that ye have need of all these things."[203]

> The third thing is that God can tell you your part in that plan. The whole thing lies perfect in His mind. . . . In some sense we grasp something of the *whole* plan. . . . That whole plan can be fulfilled only as each of us fulfills his God-guided part in the whole, like weavers weaving different parts of a patterned rug (pp. 42-43).

Shoemaker concluded this chapter as follows: "And if our security, and that of all men, lies in believing in God, devoting ourselves to His plan and waiting on Him for direction, then we must seek that security with all our hearts" (p. 43).

Now as to the way to find God. Shoemaker set forth two versions of Psalm 46:10 (p. 45):

> Be still, and know that I *am* God: I will be exalted among the heathen, I will be exalted in the earth [King James Version].

> "Give in," he cries, "admit that I am God, high over nations, high over the world" [Moffatt's Translation].

He said the concept of "giving in" (as reflected in Moffatt's Translation) is the gateway to a true faith; and the command shows us the way to find God. Shoemaker said the words assume in us

---

[202] See Hebrews 11:6.

[203] See the Sermon on the Mount, Matthew 6:32-33.

a natural capacity for God and that it is unnatural not to believe in Him, not to be in touch with Him. He said: "The emptiness, loneliness, homesickness, wistfulness, wonderment which all men feel at some time is a hollow place in the human soul that God is meant to fill." He again quoted St. Augustine's "Thou hast made us for Thyself, and our hearts are restless till they find rest in Thee" (p. 46). Shoemaker said of God:

> We hear him saying to us, "Give in, admit that God is, and that He is the great Answer to your life, and that your life never is nor will be complete without Him. . . ." We want God because He created the hunger within us for Him. We want Him from dependence, from fear, from loneliness, from the craving for perfection in our souls. We want Him from bewilderment, confusion and darkness. We want Him from innate love for Him, for insatiable preoccupation with the invisible Reality of the world (p. 47).

Shoemaker added some comments which seemed to touch A.A.: God is God, and self is not God. He said:

> I see in these words ["give in . . ."], too, not only the truth of our capacity for God and of our estrangement from Him, but a vigorous emphasis on God's lordship over every man. God is God, and self is not God—that is the heart of it. It is an actual fact that we become God to ourselves unless we have God to believe in: the final reference becomes ourselves (p. 48).

And note the progression in the Big Book's Third Step discussion: First, we must be convinced that self-propulsion doesn't work. Next, that we are self-centered. Then, that we must decide to quit playing God. And finally, that God shall be our Director, our Father, the Principal. Shoemaker said: "He [God] does not wish us to have no wills at all, but continually to conform our wills with His. . . . The same self which has resisted God must be the self which freely cooperates with Him" (pp. 48-49). Note that the Big Book says on page 85: the thoughts "Thy will (not mine) be done" must go with us constantly. "We can exercise our will power along this line all we wish. It is the proper use of the will."

Shoemaker said what the Big Book later also said, in effect:

> [T]he deepest, toughest stumblingblock in the way of faith is not intellectual skepticism, but moral confusion and personal self-will; and the place to take hold may not be the place of immediate intellectual difficulty, but the place of moral independence and self-will . . . *pride* in the form of self-sufficiency (pp. 49-50).

Shoemaker therefore said: "Give in!" Compare the following two statements—one from Shoemaker and one from the Big Book:

> And then [when people give in] He discloses Himself as they honestly seek and obey (Shoemaker, p 50).

> But He has come to all who have honestly sought Him. When we drew near to Him He disclosed Himself to us! (Big Book, p. 57).

Shoemaker then asked, "How is it done?" (p. 51). How do we "give in?" He said the whole thing centered in giving of the will to God. This meant surrender. And as to surrender, Shoemaker said:

> There are two surrenders for most of us: one where we give ourselves to God to get out of a scrape, and another where we give ourselves to God that He may use us to help the world get out of a scrape. The first surrender is necessary, but will become selfish and die unless it moves on to the second. No man is truly redeemed who does not become part of Christ's whole redemptive process in the world. . . . God give us all grace today to still the other voices and influences about us, to look in the one necessary direction, to

> leave behind us all self-sufficiency and pride, to "give in" to Him with all our hearts (p. 54).[204]

Shoemaker quoted the following from John 3:3-4 to show the "how" of the "give-in" process:

> Jesus answered and said unto him, "Verily, verily I say unto thee: Except a man be born again, he cannot see the kingdom of God." Nicodemus saith unto Him, "How . . . ?" (p. 55).

Shoemaker spelled out his answer from the Gospel of John. He said Nicodemus began by recognizing Christ's power, stating that he knew Christ was a teacher from God and could not do the miracles "except God be with him."[205] Then Shoemaker said:

> A man is born again when the control of his life, its center and its direction pass from himself to God. You can go to church for years without having that happen. . . . We shall begin by knowing the need of a new birth when we begin knowing that it is the sins of people like you and me that have made the world into the hell it is today. And the thing to do with sin is to do what Nicodemus did: go and search out someone with whom we can talk privately and frankly. Tell them of these things, and, with them as witness, give these sins and our old selves to God. . . . I said I was going to do that for years, but it never happened until I let a human witness come in on my decision. That is the "how" of getting rid of sin if you are in earnest about doing it at all: face it [Step Four], share it [Step Five], surrender it [Steps Three, Six, and Seven]. Hate it [Step Six], forsake it [Step Seven], confess it [Steps Five, Eight and Nine], and restore for it [Step Nine] (pp. 57-58).

The foregoing "Step" annotations are, of course, ours. But we see in Shoemaker's statement as to the "how" of being born again a

---

[204] For Big Book comments on self-sufficiency versus "God-sufficiency," see pp. 52-53. In the Bible, see 2 Corinthians 3:5: "Not that we are sufficient of ourselves to think any thing as of ourselves; but our sufficiency *is* of God."

[205] See John 3:1-21.

definite format for the procedures set forth in A.A.'s Steps Four through Nine. We believe Shoemaker's words give evidence of Shoemaker's impact on these six A.A. steps. Shoemaker went on to emphasize and elaborate upon the necessity of getting straight with other people—making amends.

In a later chapter, Shoemaker articulated ideas he developed from 1 Samuel 3:9—"Speak, Lord; for thy servant heareth." Shoemaker expressed the belief that simon-pure religion is being in touch with God. It is not theology, nor sociology, nor a fine code of ethics. Religion, he repeated, is being in touch with God (p. 79). And note how often A.A. speaks of a "conscious contact with God"—particularly in the language of its Eleventh Step. Shoemaker spun out his thesis from the story of Samuel. He said he was going to follow the child Samuel through the first experience he ever had of being in touch with God.[206] He said God found a ready spirit in the child Samuel. To this open child, God spoke.[207] When Samuel was instructed by Eli, the priest, that the Lord was trying to talk with him (Samuel), Samuel followed Eli's instructions and put himself in an obedient stance. He said, "Speak, Lord; for thy servant heareth." Shoemaker said that man so often declines obedience, and tells God to listen. The theme is often: "Hear, Lord, for thy servant speaketh." Shoemaker said of this account about Samuel:

> This, then is a complete story of how we can be in touch with the living God. We need to come to Him with the child's openness and simplicity. God always meets such an approach more than halfway, and takes the initiative with an open life (p. 86).

Shoemaker concluded *National Awakening* with two chapters on the importance to God of having people with whom He can work.

---

[206] See the account in 1 Samuel 3:1-21.

[207] One is reminded of Dr. Frank Buchman's oft-repeated statement: "When man listens, God speaks." The second half of this expression was: "When man obeys, God acts." See Buchman, *Remaking The World*, pp. 35, 29.

This because they are open and believing. Once people are open and believing, they must then listen and obey. Shoemaker cited Moses as an example. His closing prayer in the next-to-last chapter was: "God forgive us all, and send us the light, and help us to live by it" (p. 98).

His concluding chapter spoke of the importance of man's disciplining himself to heed the Spirit of God. Shoemaker said he was concerned about whether we were going to find enough disciplined men and women to work together under God in a divinely-led fellowship to restore the sovereignty of God in the world. Perhaps Bill's words in the concluding portion of the Big Book reflect an awareness of this need. Bill wrote:

> Abandon yourself to God as you understand God. . . . Give freely of what you find and join us. We shall be with you in the Fellowship of the Spirit, and you will surely meet some of us as you trudge the Road of Happy Destiny (p. 164).

The Church Can Save The World

The Church Can Save The World was completed in April of 1938, about the time Bill Wilson began his drafts of the Big Book.[208] War clouds were looming in Europe, and Shoemaker wrote: "I have written this book because I believe the only answer to the mounting needs and perils of the world is a spiritual answer—God's answer" (p. vii). Shoemaker said he believed Christendom faced the practical question whether anyone could show people how to stem the tide of atheistic materialism by a strong united church.

In his first chapter, Shoemaker said he felt the ordinary power of men and of nations to lift, correct, and right themselves is

---

[208] Samuel Shoemaker, Jr., *The Church Can Save The World* (New York: Harper & Brothers, 1938).

estopped by a paralysing influence—the force of antichrist.[209] He pointed out that antichrist is an old Biblical concept; that it once meant a natural force of darkness and chaos; and finally the Devil, or some man peculiarly in his grip with evil power over other men. He said: "Whatever attacks any strong Christian force anywhere is itself a part of the force of antichrist" (p. 11). He said there was need for a vast host—a combined force of the world's united decency, conviction, faith, and personal responsibility—if the world was to be changed.

The next chapter was "The Church Has the Answer." Shoemaker said the real church that God recognizes is that force, wherever recruited, that sees, and joins, and helps to win the war for God against antichrist" (p. 19). The true church, he said, unites all churches in the one supreme task of defeating antichrist and bringing the nations under God's control. His concern was the dilution of the church's message and gospel. He said a number of the clergy had set out to clip and whittle that message to fit and suit the minds of men. They had jibbed at fundamental Biblical concepts. Comparative religion had attempted to make all religions "comparative," especially Christianity. He said the emphasis on the "Bible as literature," upon what one did *not* believe rather than upon what Christianity establishes, and the whole trend humanizing Christ and his message, have destroyed all real authority in whole areas of Protestant Christianity. He said the last stage was a gospel of "kindness." A gospel with no answer for genuine human tragedy or sin; with no covering enshelterment for a life which cannot find forgiveness within itself; with no objective truths to believe; and with no real answer for a despairing, selfish, materialistic society. He suggested that even the real Jews, the "true Israel," might want rise to their spiritual heritage, join the allies in the war for God, and say to God, with the prophets:

---

[209] For a discussion of the Biblical concepts of antichrist, see 1 John 2:18, 22; 4:3; 2 John 7; and compare John 5:43 and 2 Thessalonians 2:3-9. See also Robert Young, *Young's Analytical Concordance to the Bible*, Newly Revised & Corrected (New York: Thomas Nelson, 1982), "Universal Subject Guide to the Bible," p. 16 ["antichrist"].

"Speak, Lord, for thy servant heareth" (a verse so often quoted by Shoemaker).[210]

The Church's answer, said Shoemaker, was that American voices needed to speak authoritatively for the living God, telling in simple, vivid language that: (1) God can change human nature; (2) He has a plan for every hour of every life; and (3) He will reveal it to them that wait on Him. Shoemaker suggested that the highest act of worship is the moment when each individual comes into "direct contact with God."[211] He referred to Isaiah's vision. There was a clear thought from God: "Whom shall I send, and who will go for us?" (p. 37). And the supreme and worthy end of the worship was Isaiah's response: "Here *am* I, send me" (p. 37).[212] The church's answer, said Shoemaker, was "God-guided personalities to make God-guided nationalities to make a new world" (p. 42).

In a chapter on "The Home and Spiritual Revolution," Shoemaker and his wife (who co-authored the chapter) wrote much about discovering the true meaning of the word "love" as Jesus Christ taught it by showing us *how* to love. The thrust of their message was that we need to ask God to show us how to help our families and our neighbors. Reverend and Mrs. Shoemaker wrote: "When the establishment of God's reign in the nation is every man's primary thought and commitment, his business and his home will throw off the germs of selfishness" (p. 51). In this matter of God's "reign," Bill Wilson often spoke of God as the "Father of Light who *presides* over us all" [emphasis ours].[213]

---

[210] 1 Samuel 3:9.

[211] A.A.'s Eleventh Step and related discussion speak about making a "conscious contact with God." See Big Book, pp. 47, 51, 55- 56, 59, 87.

[212] See Isaiah 6:8.

[213] Big Book, pp. 14, 568; and see *Bill Wilson's Original Story*, a manuscript bearing no date, in which each line is numbered from line 1 to line 1180, a manuscript located by the author, and of which he was given a copy, at Stepping Stones Archives, Bedford Hills, New York. The quote appears at page 30 of this manuscript. For the probable Biblical source, see James 1:17: "Every good gift and every perfect gift is from above,

(continued...)

Shoemaker spoke of the evil of a "dominating self-will" in the home (p. 55); and he said the home is often a battlefield "in which everyone is captain and nobody is crew—planless, higledy-piggledy, self-seeking" (p. 55). These same evils of "self," namely "self-will" and "self-seeking" also receive condemnation in the Big Book (p. 62). As to the family, Shoemaker said:

> God has a plan for you as individuals and as a family. If you learn how to obey Him, He will build real security into the nation through you. Imagine the families of America gathering every morning before breakfast to listen to God and get from Him His blueprint for the day (p. 57).

Compare the Big Book's discussion of morning meditation, with the suggestion that it might include wives and friends (p. 87). And, of course, such meditation did include wives and friends in early A.A.—both in Dr. Bob's home, in Bill's home, and in the homes of most early AAs.[214]

Shoemaker's next chapter discussed "The Church and the Nation." As in a previous book, he quoted President Roosevelt's statement that there was no problem that would not melt before the fire of a spiritual awakening (p. 67). Shoemaker said: "True patriotism . . . believes a country's . . . best exports are changed lives and life-changers who can bring God's control to other lands as well" (p. 69). He called for a "swing up to God," stating:

---

[213] (...continued)
and cometh down from the Father of lights, with whom is no variableness, neither shadow of turning."

[214] See Dick B., *The Akron Genesis of Alcoholics Anonymous*—particularly the portions at pages 203-15, entitled "What the Akron AAs Did in Their Homes for Recovery." Bill Pittman's *A.A.: The Way It Began* (Seattle: Glen Abbey Books, 1988), p. 183, reports that Lois Wilson informed Bill Pittman, the author, that she and Bill Wilson frequently used one particular devotional. And, in her own memoirs, Lois reported the *daily* Quiet Times that Bill, she, and some early AAs frequently had. *Lois Remembers*, p. 101.

> America should turn to God. Thousands and millions of Americans remembering the God of their fathers, and getting down on their knees again in repentance for the years of neglect and indifference. . . . Thousands and millions of Americans being absolutely honest with their families, with their companies, with their creditors, with their neighbors, and making every wrong right. Thousands and millions of American homes where the day begins with the Bible and listening to God, and His Word as the decisive factor in every problem. . . . (p. 72).

And, how many of these Shoemaker exhortations seemed to find place in the Big Book—(1) "grasping and developing a manner of living which demands rigorous honesty" (p. 58), (2) becoming "ready to let God remove from us all the things which we have admitted are objectionable" (p. 76), (3) going "out to our fellows and repair[ing] the damage done in the past" (p. 76), and (4) "on awakening" considering "our plans for the day" and asking "God to direct our thinking" (p. 86).

Shoemaker next wrote a chapter on "The Quality of a Spiritual Revolutionary." He said that spiritual revolution begins in ourselves, in you and in me; and it begins with dissatisfaction. He said most of us have a petty sense of sin, but he added:

> The worst of all sins is failing to have God's answer, for ourselves, for the people we know, for our nation. The real blackness of personal sin only comes when we see how ineffective we are. It is our inadequacy, our lack of a plan, our paucity of thinking (pp. 82-83).

And the Big Book speaks about the failure of self-reliance and the success that comes from relying on the power of God (p. 52). Shoemaker spoke of the qualities that block us from being spiritual revolutionaries: indifference, inferiority, sentimentality, pride, affectional frustration and defeat, and ambition. He said: "We must be changed, in a much deeper sense than we have ever been changed before. It is not enough to repent; each time we truly repent, we must be changed anew" (p. 93).

This need for change, he said, arises our of the intolerable pain of the crucifixion of self. About this, he said:

> The daily and hourly renewal of the crucifixion of our selves, and the implantation of the will of God where our wills used to be, comes by seeking the mind of God through listening. . . . How many of us are grown up enough to remember that the important thing in prayer is not to change the will and mind of God, but to find them. What we want is not to influence God this way or that, but to let Him influence us (pp. 96-97).

Note how A.A.'s Eleventh Step says: "Sought through prayer and meditation . . . praying only for the knowledge of His will for us and the power to carry that out" (Big Book, p. 59).

Shoemaker added words which explain the Oxford Group ideas of leaving things in God's hands, listening, writing down leading thoughts, and checking them with guided people (p. 98).

Shoemaker's chapter "Extending the Revolution" contains many expressions relevant to A.A. step ideas; and it may indicate just how many of those ideas were firmly fixed by 1938—the year that Bill began writing the Big Book and completed writing the Twelve Steps. The important part of the chapter, for our purposes, begins when Shoemaker asked what must be done with those whom God leads us to change.

And he started by referring to his "favorite" verse—John 7:17, stating:

> When a man comes in to discuss the nature of the Holy Trinity with me, or the theory of the Atonement, he may be wanting theological light, but the chances are there are other needs in his life which obscure his understanding of the intellectual convictions of Christianity. "If any man will do his will, he shall know of the doctrine."[215] We must get to the point of whether the man is

[215] Shoemaker cited John 7:17.

> "willing to do his will" in all areas.[216] Take the four standards of Christ: absolute honesty, absolute purity, absolute unselfishness, and absolute love.[217] When people's lives are wrong, they are usually wrong on one or more of these standards. Many quite respectable people have hidden things in their past and present that need to come out in confidence with someone.[218] A sin often does not appear in all its "exceeding sinfulness" until it is brought into the light with another; and it almost always seems more hopelessly unforgivable, and the person who committed it more utterly irredeemable, when it remains unshared. The only release and hope for many bound and imprisoned and defeated people lies in frank sharing. It is not costly to share our problems, or even our comfortable sins, but it is costly to share the worst thing we ever did, the deepest sin in our life, the besetting temptation that dogs us.[219]

Explaining the confession or "sharing" process further, Shoemaker added:

> By our own frank honesty about ourselves, and our willingness, under God as He guides, to share anything in our own experience that will help the other person, and by the willingness to ask God-

---

[216] Note the Big Book discussion at pages 46 and 47 which speaks of "willingness to believe" as the starting point in defining and comprehending "that Power, which is God." It says if we believe, or are even willing to believe, that there is a Power greater than ourselves, we are on our way. As we have noted before, the Big Book says on page 57 that *circumstances* make a desperate person "willing to believe." Then he offers himself to God. And then he knows there is a God.

[217] Here Shoemaker is referring to the "Four Absolutes" which were Oxford Group principles very much spoken of and utilized in early A.A.

[218] Here Shoemaker appears to make reference to the first "C"—*Confidence*—in the Oxford Group's "soul-surgery" or "life-changing" practice.

[219] Here Shoemaker is making reference to the second "C"—*Confession*—the idea which became embodied in A.A.'s Fifth Step and had its roots in James 5:16 ("Confess your faults one to another"). The Big Book talks about the darkest secrets, stating the alcoholic "is revolted at certain episodes he vaguely remembers" (p. 73). And the Big Book calls for "illuminating every twist of character, every dark cranny of the past . . . withholding nothing" (p. 75). See also *Pass It On*, p. 138, n. 2.

> inspired questions of them that carry the matter right down to the roots, we shall get deep enough to know the real problems. . . . If the person is honest with himself and with God, he will be honest also with us and be ready to take the next step, which is a decision to surrender these sins, with himself, wholly to God (p. 111).

Note that A.A.'s Fifth Step says: "Admitted to God, to ourselves, and to another human being the exact nature of our wrongs" (Big Book, p. 59).

The Oxford Group had neither Twelve Steps nor "six" steps.[220] Therefore, as we have said before, it is hard to draw a specific parallel between an Oxford Group "surrender," and A.A.'s two "surrender" steps, its Third Step and its Seventh Step. In early A.A. in Akron, the whole surrender process was simply called "surrender."[221] In the Oxford Group, and in A.A., that process involved a "decision" on one's knees. In A.A., this "decision" idea became embodied in A.A.'s Third Step.[222] The surrender of sins became Step Seven. However, when Shoemaker and other Oxford Group people spoke of a surrender, they lumped the "decision" and the "surrender of will and break with sin" together. Thus Shoemaker wrote:

> For those who look right into the light [after sharing], the next step is a decision which we ought to help them make. William James said long ago that "self-surrender has been and always must be regarded as the vital turning-point of the religious life." We need to help people see what goes into a decision of surrender: a complete break with sin, which we have spoken of in detail with them, so that it is quite specific what they give to God—temper, fear, sex, inferiority, pride, etc.; the readiness from now on to listen to God, and take adequate time for it each day, with the Bible, prayer, listening, and recording what God tells us; the

---

[220] See *Pass It On*, p. 206, n. 2.

[221] See Dick B., *The Oxford Group & Alcoholics Anonymous*, pp. 134-41.

[222] Big Book, p. 59: "Made a decision to turn our will and our lives over to the care of God. . . ."

> complete giving to God of the great trend of our lives (pp. 113-14).[223]

People have often asked the author how the Oxford Group people did a "Fourth Step" or took a "moral inventory." The answer is that the Oxford Group did not have a "fourth step;" nor, as far as the author can tell, did it call the self-examination process a "moral inventory." But it certainly did advocate fact finding, "making the moral test," and examining one's life, as measured against Christ's standards—the "yardsticks" of the Four Absolutes, as Dr. Bob called them.[224] And just as the Big Book advocated putting on paper separate lists of resentments, fears, selfish sex, and harms, so too did the Oxford Group people advocate working with paper lists. In the Oxford Group, one's life was examined as to its conformity with the four absolutes or four standards, as they were also called. Thus Shoemaker said:

> I asked Him whether he had had a Quiet Time about the four standards: absolute honesty, purity, unselfishness, and love. He said he had, and produced a piece of yellow-fool's-cap from his pocket, neatly divided into four quarters, one for each standard, on which he had written down all the places where he had fallen down on them. The paper was quite full. I shared honestly with him about my own sins. He said he wanted to make a decision and give himself completely to Christ, so we got down on our knees and he did it. We had a Quiet Time, and more guidance came to him.

---

[223] Note how Shoemaker focuses on virtually the same major "character defects" the Big Book covers in its Fourth Step inventory discussion—resentment, fear, selfish sex, dishonesty, and harms (pp. 64, 68-70).

[224] See Frank N. D. Buchman, *Remaking The World* (London: Blandford Press, 1961), pp. 24, 28, 46, 38; H. A. Walter, *Soul-Surgery* (Oxford at the University Press by John Johnson, 1940), pp. 41-48, 69; Clarence I. Benson, *The Eight Points of the Oxford Group* (London: Oxford University Press, 1936), pp. 44, 162, 18, 7; Cecil Rose, *When Man Listens*, pp. 17-19; Hallen Viney, *How Do I Begin?* (The Oxford Group, 1937); Olive Jones, *Inspired Children* (New York: Harper & Brothers, 1933), pp. 47-68; and *Inspired Youth* (New York: Harper & Brothers, 1938), p. 4; Shoemaker, *Twice-Born Ministers*, p. 182; and *How To Become a Christian*, pp. 56-67. See also Dick B., *Anne Smith's Spiritual Workbook*, pp. 4, 14; and *Co-Founders*, pp. 32-33.

> There were various people he must make restitution to, and others he must help (pp. 119-20).

In Shoemaker's remarks, we can see a progression similar to that in A.A.'s steps. There was self-examination by making a list of shortcomings (Step Four). There was confession to God and another person (Step Five). There was a desire to change with God's help (Step Six). There was a decision and a surrender to God (Steps Three and Seven). And there was the making of restitution (Steps Eight and Nine).

Shoemaker's next chapter was called "Turning The World Right Side Up." And here was Shoemaker's six point "programme" for accomplishing the turnabout: (1) Change—finding out precisely what the sin is that stands between us and Christ, and surrendering it to him. (2) Listen—finding "possible ways out" in a Quiet Time with God, and writing down what He says to you. (3) Obey—asking God what he wants, and, by obedience, often clearing up a relationship, paying a debt, healing an old sore. (4) Combine—maintaining a fellowship with the person through whom you found conviction, change, and light. (5) Demonstrate—showing people examples, rather than theories, of what a changed life has accomplished. (6) Lead—recognizing that God has a plan and that he will give appropriate parts of that plan to those who ask Him responsibly.

We see in Shoemaker's six points a good many Twelve Step elements: (1) Using self-examination and confession to ascertain blocks from God and others (Steps Four and Five). (2) Seeking guidance (Step Eleven). (3) Making restitution (Steps Eight and Nine). (4) Working with another ("a sponsor") who takes the confessing person through the self-examination, confession, conviction, and surrender process (Steps Four through Seven). (5) Carrying the message as to the spiritual awakening and change (Step Twelve). (6) Accepting responsibility for leading a changed life (Steps Ten, Eleven, and Twelve).

Shoemaker's last chapter bespoke the ongoing need for spiritual growth that one can also find in A.A.'s last three steps. Shoemaker said:

> We need steady life-changing as the main drive of our work. The spiritual front is not alone a show of conviction, it is a force of persuasion. We need to know how to recognize sin, how to get it shared, surrendered, forgiven, restored for, and then used to help others in like case. We need to know how people behave under conviction of sin: how they lie and fight back. We need to know what goes into a spiritual decision, and how to bring men to it. Equally we need to know how to mobilize our people's deepest spiritual experiences; for often we have grounded them in futile and secondary activity. . . . We need, not only individual life-changers, but a network of them everywhere—friendly, open, realistic people who can point others to the answer as it is in Christ and are constantly doing it (p. 154).

This language seems relevant when one considers the last two elements of A.A.'s Twelfth Step. The Twelfth Step says that, "having had a spiritual awakening," the alcoholic is to carry the message of that awakening and (in a very real sense) witness to that message by "practicing the principles in all his affairs" (not a direct quote). And Shoemaker indicates what A.A. also appears to believe: that fellowship and teamwork are necessary for the life-changing process to be effective. He calls for "complete passion with complete giving under complete control" (p. 157).

Some Other Pre-1939 Books

Some of our readers will know that, prior to 1939, Shoemaker wrote much more than is contained in the aforementioned books. His articles in the parish publication—*The Calvary Evangel*—were voluminous; and many of his materials were put out in pamphlet form. We found several of these pamphlets at Bill Wilson's

Stepping Stones home in a binder there which contained a copy of Anne Smith's spiritual workbook.

One little Shoemaker book that definitely made its mark on A.A. was *One Boy's Influence*.[225] Anne Smith was much impressed with this 1925 booklet and discussed it in her spiritual workbook.[226] For one thing, Shoemaker's book told how people generally go wrong when they get away from God. He stated that sin then walls them away still more. Shoemaker called this situation "being out of touch with God" (pp. 6-7). He suggested testing transgressions by measuring them against the four absolute standards—absolute honesty, absolute purity, absolute unselfishness, and absolute love. He suggested to the boy in his story that we are "to give ourselves to Christ—to surrender entirely to Him . . . and have done with all this compromise and live a full out Christian life" (p. 11). The boy in the story gave himself to Christ and asked for the strength to keep going and for help to win another. The boy asked Shoemaker how to "keep going." Shoemaker suggested the "Morning Watch"—with twenty minutes for Bible study, five or ten minutes for prayer, then asking God for what he really needed, and then listening for God's direction. Shoemaker talked to the boy about getting religion across to another. He suggested: "Strike deep, talk honestly about sin, aim for complete surrender, and make them in turn winners for others" (p. 15). The rest of the story is about the boy's change and his working with and successfully influencing others.

Shoemaker wrote another small book, *The Breadth and Narrowness of the Gospel*, which was published in 1929.[227] But we will not cover it in this study because we do not feel its contents had significant impact on A.A. Similarly, we have only

---

[225] S. M. Shoemaker, Jr., *One Boy's Influence* (New York: Association Press, 1925).

[226] See Dick B., *Anne Smith's Spiritual Workbook*, p. 17.

[227] Samuel Shoemaker, Jr., *The Breadth and Narrowness of the Gospel* (New York: Fleming H. Revell, 1929).

briefly mentioned *Christ's Words From The Cross*.[228] Most of its relevant contents were covered in a previously published Shoemaker book that we have discussed.[229] Also, we reviewed the contents of *Christ's Words* at some length in our own previous book, *The Oxford Group and Alcoholics Anonymous*.[230] We have not reviewed *Calvary Church Yesterday and Today* in this chapter because its contents are more relevant to Shoemaker's biography, to his Oxford Group activities and connections, and to his relationship with Bill Wilson, all of which are covered elsewhere in our book.

We will have more to say about the significance of Shoemaker's pre-1939 books when we reach our conclusion. But we can say that originally we found much in these books which seemed to have spilled over directly into A.A.'s Big Book; and our review for this study simply amazed us as we saw page after page and phrase after phrase in the Shoemaker books which seemed duplicated, sometimes almost verbatim, in the Big Book.

We will see shortly why this still leaves a puzzle in the light of the dearth of evidence as to whether, where, when, and how Bill Wilson ever read *any* of Shoemaker's books. Bill did not mention them. His wife, Lois, did not mention them. With the exception of one late Shoemaker book, they are not in the library, or in any other part, of Bill's home at Stepping Stones. The author was provided nothing about them at A.A. Archives in New York. And they are not mentioned in the reminiscences of Bill's former secretary, Nell Wing.[231]

Did Bill read Shoemaker at all? If so, would it have been at the Calvary House bookstore? At an Oxford Group meeting at Calvary

---

[228] Samuel Shoemaker, Jr., *Christ's Words From The Cross* (New York: Fleming H. Revell, 1933).

[229] See Shoemaker, *If I Be Lifted Up*, pp. 73-116.

[230] See Dick B., *The Oxford Group & Alcoholics Anonymous*, pp. 190-92.

[231] In fact, in a telephone interview with the author from her home in New York on September 11, 1993, Nell specifically said to the author that Bill Wilson simply was not a reader of books and that she knew of nothing specific from Shoemaker that Bill had read.

House, in New York, in Maryland, or elsewhere? At an Oxford Group houseparty? At the Smith home in Akron? At T. Henry's? At other Akron meeting places? In the homes or places of business of, or in gatherings with, such Oxford Group stalwarts as Rowland Hazard, Shep Cornell, Hanford Twitchell, Irving Harris, and other Calvary Church and Oxford Group people with whom Bill kept much company? At meetings of the Oxford Group businessmen's team? In Shoemaker's study or office? At a New York bookstore or library?

We don't know, and we haven't the answers. But we are still searching; and in a later part of this book, we will show how all the foregoing were definite possibilities. In fact, it seems highly improbable that Bill failed to look at Oxford Group and Shoemaker literature somewhere. Why is this issue important? Perhaps it would not have been if Bill hadn't given Shoemaker so much credit, if Bill had not left the specifics about the Shoemaker influence in darkness, and if the specifics we've set out above didn't seem to establish that Bill did borrow language and ideas from Shoemaker. For the specifics we have set out above do seem to confirm Bill's statements that Shoemaker was a major source of A.A. ideas. And the specifics do help to explain Bill's A.A. ideas.

5

Sam's Remarks to and about A.A.

Addresses to A.A.

At St. Louis in 1955

Sam Shoemaker made a number of speeches to AAs, sometimes on the same platform with Bill Wilson. His best known address was the one he made at A.A.'s Twentieth Anniversary Convention in St. Louis in 1955. The speech is reproduced in full in *Alcoholics Anonymous Comes of Age*.[1] We will not cover all its points here, but we do wish to give the flavor of Shoemaker's observations about the organization of which he was given credit as a founder.

Shoemaker commenced his talk by saying he always felt Bill gave him a great deal more credit for helping to get A.A. started than he should have been given. But, he said, Bill's perceptions were deep and his memories sharp.

Shoemaker said that the first thing Bill got in his mind as offering any real hope for his alcoholism was talking with men and women in whom there was the beginning of a real religious experience. Shoemaker alluded to the fact that Ebby Thatcher was one of these people and was also present at the Twentieth Anniversary Convention. He said these people had begun to find

---

[1] *Alcoholics Anonymous Comes of Age* (New York: Alcoholics Anonymous World Services, Inc., 1957), pp. 261-270.

this religious experience through the Oxford Groups, much of whose work was centered in those days at his old parish at Calvary Church on Gramercy Park in New York.

He referred to the contributions to A.A. of Dr. Carl Jung, Dr. William Silkworth, and Professor William James, but said there was need for a spiritual factor that would create a kind of synthesis and offer a kind of positive dynamic. He then referred to the Book of Acts and said people had to acknowledge that the Apostles had effected miraculous healings whether the people understood or agreed with Christianity or not. He said he felt A.A. had been wise in avoiding theology; and in just pointing to its own spiritual experiences.

But he dealt with the agnostics and atheists who came to A.A. He quoted a Roman Catholic Spanish philosopher, who said:

> Those who deny God deny Him because of their despair at not finding Him (p. 263).

He said AAs had chosen to relate their inescapable experiences, tell people to turn their wills and lives over to the care of God *as they understood Him*, and leave the theory and theology to the churches, where they belong. Shoemaker added that people who belonged to no church and could hold no consistent theory could give themselves in A.A. to the God they saw in other people—an idea which, we would add, has probably given many Christians a good deal of difficulty with A.A. *and* its ideas.

But Shoemaker then moved forward with Christian words and ideas in speaking about his experiment of faith. He said if God is what Christ said He is, He is more eager to help us than we are to be helped. He quoted William James for the statement that self-surrender is the vital turning point of the religious life and added: "One may say that the whole development of Christianity in inwardness has consisted of little more than the greater and greater emphasis attached to this crisis of self-surrender."

Shoemaker stressed the importance of going to God for help since God is the only source of effective help. He said each alcoholic must grow up and stop *using* God and begin to ask God to *use him*. He said the alcoholic must stop asking God to do what *he* (the alcoholic) wants, and begin to find out what it is that God wants. He said many people say they have given up faith because they have prayed for something they wanted and it didn't come. This, they said, established either that there is no God or else that He has no interest in them. Shoemaker said, "What childish nonsense! How can anybody expect God to acquiesce in the half-baked prayers that a lot of us send up to Him" (p. 265).

He added:

> Real prayer is not telling God what *we* want. It is putting ourselves at His disposal so that He can tell us what He wants. . . . It is vital for us to listen as well as talk when we pray. Everybody that is away from God and tries to do his own will in defiance of God is half-crazy. Till our own clamorous, demanding voices quiet down we cannot hear the voice of God (p. 266).

Then he spoke of "surrender." He said it is not weakness. People may think they have overcome, or never really had, disreputable sins. But, he challenged: "Who of us avoids selfishness and self-centeredness and the love of adulation and the love of power and pride?" (p. 266). He said these things got non-alcoholics into difficulties and are just as bad as anything that got alcoholics into difficulties. Nobody, he said, is strong. Character and good behavior are not the end of all existence. "The real questions in life which underlie these matters of behavior are definitely of a religious nature. And they have only a religious answer, an answer that comes from God" (p. 266). He said that when we get through to God, or let Him get through to us, we begin finding light.

Shoemaker felt the great need of his time was for a vast, world-wide spiritual awakening. He said Western man is gradually getting it through his head that he owes the greatest of all human blessings, the blessing of liberty, to God and religion.

He spelled out what he believed to be four universal factors in all genuine spiritual awakenings: conversion, prayer, fellowship, and witness. He said conversion meant turning to God—the search for perfection. Prayer is the place where we get in touch with God and God's power. We do not so much "get what we want" as find out what we should do. As to fellowship, he said the church is a community consisting of people who know they have a great need and are gathered to find its answer in worship toward God and fellowship with one another. He said the church is not a museum; it is a hospital; and that is why we can all belong to it and should. He said the last item in an awakening is witness by life and by word. He said every real believer shares in Twelfth Step work; and every real believer wants to get his belief across to other people and will take the trouble to try to learn to do it by life and by word.

He said A.A. people need the church for personal stabilization and growth; and the church needs A.A. as a continuous spur to greater aliveness and expectation and power. He said he believed A.A. had derived its inspiration and impetus indirectly from the insights and beliefs of the church.

At Long Beach in 1960

Perhaps the most important address Shoemaker ever gave to A.A. was the one he delivered at A.A.'s Third International Convention. The occasion was A.A.'s Twenty-fifth Anniversary, at Long Beach, California, on July 3, 1960. Shoemaker shared the podium with the Right Reverend Monsignor John J. Dougherty, President of Seton Hall University. After the monsignor had concluded his remarks, Bill Wilson said that the two benefactors (Dougherty and Shoemaker) could bring to AAs the facts that: (1) "God is the ultimate reality." (2) "He is among us." And we have (3) "the consciousness of His presence." All three of Bill's expressions could be found in the Big Book Bill had written some twenty years before. At Long Beach, Bill suggested he had first seen Shoemaker in church. He said: "I shall never forget my first sight of him there in his pulpit." And then Bill introduced Shoemaker as "Sam."

Here are some of the highlights of Shoemaker's speech.

Shoemaker's whole address was focused on the importance to A.A. of an experiment of faith. He said this concept enabled A.A. to open its doors to believers, to people of all faiths, and to atheists, agnostics, and skeptics.

First, Shoemaker spoke of God, and stated:

> Now . . . [A.A.'s] program of recovery turns, as we all know, on the faith in a Power greater than ourselves. Willpower, and the appeal to it as sufficient to get any of us out of his troubles, are a snare and a delusion. . . . When you think you're able to manage your life without God, you add pride to whatever other sins you may have. . . . Many people's problems begin to be solved the minute they know they cannot solve them themselves. That puts pride right out of the driver's seat. . . . Nobody but God is big enough to tell the human ego to move over.

Then Shoemaker posed a question: How do you present the importance of God to a fellowship such as A.A. that encompasses such a wide diversity of belief and unbelief? Of this problem, Shoemaker said:

> But now how is that . . . [the necessity for God] going to be suggested in a program that was to reach, not only Catholics and Protestants and Jews, but skeptics and agnostics and atheists and total non-believers in any kind of God? Some people have had unhappy experiences with churches, and many think they have.

Shoemaker said he felt the use, in the Twelve Steps, of the phrases *Power greater than ourselves* and *God as we understood Him* was truly inspired. He made these important observations about the phrases:

1. If anybody came into A.A. with already-formed loyalties, such as those to a Christian body, those loyalties would not be interfered with and would in fact be *strengthened*. He said:

> The God that is, is a great deal more than we can ever understand of Him; and we learn more of Him by experience than ever we do by argument or futile discussions with the belief as to whether our own church is better than some other church. Now, if we are satisfied with the beliefs that our church tells us to hold, then we will go along with them and grow as that church encourages us to do.

2. As to those who come into A.A. with little or no faith, he said:

> Our initiation does not begin by being asked to swallow a lot of doctrine that we are not prepared to swallow. A.A. says begin with as much faith as you've got—there is Something. . . . What we have to deal with is the God that really is and not our human concepts of Him. It is much better for anyone to pray to the God that is, he with no name and we with no words, than to pray to your own creation of God, with words prettier than a poem, but fictitious.

3. Then, seemingly aware of the absurd names for God that he had heard in A.A. and elsewhere, Shoemaker made several points which we consider confusing, but which certainly pointed Shoemaker's listeners toward his often-taught *experiment of faith*. He said:

> Sometimes for beginners, suggestion is better than explication. Some of the often absurd modern names of God, like the Man upstairs, are crude attempts to use an easily grasped picture to suggest God, rather than to use theological language to dogmatize about Him. Beginners need all kinds of practical self-starters and courage to experiment. For nobody ever found faith sitting in a chair reading a book and wishing he had it. We often begin by acting as if faith were true, in order to find out whether it is true. . . . I have always thought the first steps toward it ought to be severely experimental, and put within the reach of the greatest skeptic, provided he's got an open and honest mind.

But Shoemaker certainly didn't leave the subject in the experimental stage. He said he believed the experimental approach to faith was a good one. But, he said:

> There will come a time when you cannot leave it at just an experiment. You've got to grow as the Monsignor has been telling you. You've got to go on and think out what has happened and use your mind about it. You will probably be a good deal stronger if you link up, as he suggested, with some outfit that exists to help people definitely with their religious faith; for we need to grow in the spiritual dimension and we certainly do not want to make a church out of A.A. That would cause trouble. But as a precursor to the Church, what St. Paul called the Law to the Gospel, a tutor, a schoolmaster to get us ready for the church, I think A.A. stands second to none.[2]

Note the significance of Shoemaker's language. Early A.A. favored and *encouraged* church attendance. The Big Book spoke approvingly of it. Bill Wilson called A.A. a spiritual *kindergarten*, implying the need for moving on and growing. And Dr. Bob, of course, pursued the growth path through extensive Bible study, spiritual reading, and successive membership in two Christian churches during his fifteen years of sobriety. Shoemaker, then, was applauding the experimental, the *as if* approach, as the place for the atheistic, agnostic, or skeptical *beginner*. But he certainly did not leave either the acquisition of, or the growth in, faith at that. In fact, Shoemaker concluded this portion of his address by saying, "Thank God for the amount of cooperation that there is between the churches and A.A." A thankfulness, we might add, that he might not be able to express if he saw A.A. as it exists today. For that cooperation is not at all evident, at least not to this author.

---

[2] See Galatians 3:24-26: "Wherefore the law was our schoolmaster *to bring us* unto Christ, that we might be justified by faith. But after that faith is come, we are no longer under a schoolmaster. For ye are all the children of God by faith in Christ Jesus."

Shoemaker said A.A. must always allow for some people who continue to say that they don't believe in God in any conventional way. But he certainly encouraged an understanding of God as a power to whom you go when you have need of what is called grace. He said the whole world, Christian and non-Christian, owes an unspeakable debt to Jesus Christ for revealing to us a God who is loving, patient, forgiving, eager to help, while yet expecting us to live according to His laws. He said:

> Before anything else is suggested about a change and a cure, the first impression that people of God ought to give is the impression of what Masefield called "The Everlasting Mercy."
> . . . When we know ourselves to be beyond the reach of any merely human help, the first Face of God we need to see is the Face of Love.
> . . . Now there is just one answer for any sin and any need on the face of this earth. And that lies in the forgiveness of God for the past and the Grace of God for the future. I take that to be the spiritual angle of A.A. because it is the spiritual angle of all mankind.

Shoemaker's *A.A. Grapevine* Articles

[*And So From My Heart I Say . . .*]

In the September, 1948, issue of the *AA Grapevine*, Shoemaker told of the work at the old Calvary Mission down in the Gas House District where some of his "gentleman-drunk" friends were living together in a kind of simple spiritual community. He said they made a lot of mistakes in those days, helping some upwards and some downwards. But he said, they showed some of the ways not to do it.

Shoemaker said Wilson saw something in the work there. Wilson said that if a few men could find sobriety through what William James called "a firmer hold on religious realities," then many might. And Shoemaker said Bill set to work learning the laws and making them available to more people. He said he felt there was something working "way beyond Bill" in the way Bill gained insight into alcoholics, into eternal spiritual laws, and into ways in which one can bring men and women into touch with God without raising needless religious prejudices and creating unnecessary spiritual divisions.

Shoemaker said Bill had sent him one of the early prospectuses of the book, *Alcoholics Anonymous*. And Shoemaker said he knew then that Bill had a potent start. But he said the ability of Bill's idea to take root and grow depended on many factors. Shoemaker felt there was something bigger than Bill and his associates at work. An idea must grow warm in your own mind, and then in the minds of others. But, he said, faith exercises its mighty part with its belief that the unlikely or even impossible can take place. Love mediates faith to others, said Shoemaker, by caring what happens to them, by patience, by persistence, by humor—particularly regarding oneself. Shoemaker said it is by "contact with the Author of all life" that the gifts are received and which include the right idea and the dynamics of its transmission.

He said A.A. represented a genuine *kairos* ("a fullness of time") which, he said, according to the New Testament use of the word, describes the moment in which the Eternal breaks into the temporal and the temporal is prepared to receive it.[3] He said A.A. represents such a *kairos* in which the Eternal came into time with the right message for one kind of human need. And Shoemaker said when he came into one of A.A.'s companies of men and women, so lovable, so honest about themselves, so modest in their claims, and yet so sure of their actual experience, he felt he was experiencing something much like the gatherings of the early church.

Shoemaker said, "Paying lip-service to God is one thing—experiencing the power of God to give a whole new outlook

---

[3] See Galatians 4:4: "But when the fulness of the time was come, God sent forth his Son, made of a woman, made under the law;" and Ephesians 1:10: "That in the dispensation of the fulness of times he might gather together in one all things in Christ, both which are in heaven, and which are on earth, *even* in him."

on life, to know victory instead of defeat, and adventure instead of despair is another."

He said he believed he had just seen the beginning of what A.A. can do, not only for alcoholics, but for all who need a change of heart and first begin to get it as they see it in others.

[*The Spiritual Angle*]

In 1955, Shoemaker wrote for AA's *Grapevine* that A.A., at its inception, had three answers and an incomplete. He said: (1) Dr. Carl Jung had shown that science knew no answer to alcoholism; (2) Dr. William Silkworth had given the medical perspective on the problem; and (3) Professor William James had provided proof that spiritual answers worked. What was missing was a spiritual factor which would enable translation of the spiritual experience into universal terms without letting it evaporate into mere ideals and generalities.

He said Step Two suggested a belief that a Power greater than ourselves could provide the answer. And the belief was not based on theory, but on evidence. There were people in A.A. in whose lives the beginning of a change had occurred. And he said you could question the interpretation of the experience, but not the change itself.

He gave as an example the account in Acts 3 and 4, where Peter and John healed the man lame from birth. People questioned how it came about. The apostles told them it was through the name of Jesus Christ. And the people were confronted with the healing they saw. Shoemaker said, "You can fight a theory about an experience, but you have to acknowledge the experience itself."

Shoemaker applauded A.A.'s staying away from the theological business. He said there was evidence of a Power and what had occurred. And A.A. left it at that. He said the mistake would have been to say a great deal more and define God. He said this would have turned away those unhappy with their religion and those agnostics and atheists who either did not know or disbelieved. He said the founders were wise to stick with inescapable *experience*.

They left the theory and the theology—"*very i*
are"—to the churches or to the God people saw
Shoemaker argued for the psychological soun
approach. He said that anyone seeking genuine s
only go so far with reasoning. Then he must decide and act. He propounded his idea "act as if it were true, and see whether it is true."[4] He said: "It is when you let truth go into action, and hurl your life after your held conception of truth that things start to happen. If it is genuine truth, it will accomplish things on the plane of actual living." And the belief will come because things are seen. Here Shoemaker was back to his familiar theme of John 7:17: Take the suggested spiritual action by obeying what you know of God's will, and you will know God and His will.

As was the case in so many of the books Shoemaker had written before the publication of A.A.'s Big Book, Shoemaker was continuing to say: (1) Open the door on a spiritual search with your whole life thrown into it. (2) God is always there, ready to receive our feeblest approaches, our most selfish and childish prayers, and our always entirely unworthy selves, and ready to get down to business with us. Shoemaker was arguing for the experimental approach. He was citing William James and the crisis of self-surrender which involves throwing our conscious selves on the mercy of the powers that be, which are more ideal than we are and make for our redemption. He said we need first to lean on a human being who seems to be finding the answer, and then come to lean on the "Higher Power" who stands behind him. He said this is the heart of all religion—"Most of us come to God in the

---

[4] Shoemaker wrote an article for the October, 1954, *Christian Herald*. It was entitled *"Act As If—" The First Step Toward Faith*. It advocated the experiment of faith. The experiment could begin with a cry on the knees: "O God, if there be a God, send me help now, because I need it." He said you can "get religion" by acting as if you have faith, making a prayer to God as you understand Him. He suggested acting as if God *were*, praying to find God's will, rather than trying to get Him to change it in favor of your own. And he said there would be the sense of added strength, some insight about the problem, and a realization that you are in touch with more Power than ever before in your life.

st instance from a need." And he asked where in the world a defeated person can possibly go, if he doesn't go to God.

Shoemaker had a theme about prayer: "One begins a mature religion at the point where he stops trying to get God to do what he wants, and begins asking God to show him what God wants." He said prayer is meant to *find* the will of God and to align or realign ourselves with His purposes. Thus it requires that we *listen* as well as *speak*. Note here how Shoemaker was spelling out for AAs the Oxford Group idea of receiving guidance by listening—a theme Shoemaker emphasized so often when he cited 1 Samuel 3:9 in his books ("Speak, Lord, for thy servant heareth"). Then Shoemaker talked about quieting down for prayer. Here was an allusion to the Oxford Group's Quiet Time.

Shoemaker spoke of the surrender of sins—particularly those of selfishness and self-centeredness and pride. Note that he had long before spoken of these in his books; and that A.A. had adopted the precise phrases—"selfishness, self-centeredness"—in its Big Book.[5]

In his article on the clergy, Bill Wilson spoke of his questions as to where he came from, where he was going, and what he was doing here on earth. Bill said religion had the answers that science and philosophy could not provide. Shoemaker wrote about these same points in *his Grapevine* article. Then Shoemaker spoke of faith as the candle in the darkness of life's mystery. He said that when we get through to God, by whatever name we call him, or rather when we let him get through to us, we begin finding light.

Shoemaker repeated what he had said at A.A.'s St. Louis Convention in 1955: that there are four elements in a spiritual awakening: conversion, prayer, fellowship, and witness. And we have already seen how he covered these subjects voluminously in his pre-1939 books. He said he felt conversion is the place where one turns toward God. Prayer is the place where we get in touch anew with God and his power. Prayer turns on the switch. An "awakening," he said, includes discovering the power that is in

---

[5] Big Book, p. 62.

prayer. As to fellowship, he said we can never do the job alone. We need people who know they have a great need, are gathered to find its answer in worship toward God, and fellowship with one another. And, as to witness, he said it comes by life and by word. A spiritual experience changes us deeply on the inside, and begins to show on the outside. Then, said Shoemaker, is the time to open up and witness.

Each of these four "awakening" elements—conversion, prayer, fellowship, and witness—had been thoroughly discussed in the books Shoemaker wrote prior to 1939. In his *Grapevine* article, he said, "The parallels between these four ideas and A.A.'s Twelve Steps must be obvious to anybody." The author felt that way about *many* of the Shoemaker ideas he found in his review of the Shoemaker books. The difference is that Shoemaker himself—in his *Grapevine* article of 1955—seemed to be looking back and seeing what Bill had extracted from all of his (Shoemaker's) teachings.

Shoemaker said A.A. is experimental and experiential; but none can doubt, he said, that God is what made A.A. what it is and inspired it and keeps it growing. He concluded:

> I believe that AA will go on serving men and women as long as it may be needed *if* it keeps open to God for inspiration, and open to people for service.

[*Those Twelve Steps As I Understand Them*]

In a January, 1964, *A.A. Grapevine* article, Shoemaker said he felt the wisdom and experience packed into the Twelve Steps were a good example of one of those hours when men's powers are at high pitch and tension and the Spirit of God hovers near, making suggestions.[6] He said he doubted the Steps could have been the mere product of human insight and observation and still have

---

[6] The article has been reprinted in full in *Best of the Grapevine, Volume II* (New York: The A.A. Grapevine, Inc., 1986), pp. 125-134..

changed the course of existence for so many lives. He marked the Twelve Steps as "morally and spiritually and psychologically and practically" sound.

He said the *First Step* involves what Christianity has taught from the beginning: that the "whole range of human defeat" cannot be dealt with by simply "exerting more will power." He said the first step towards sobriety and toward self-understanding and the knowledge of life requires the concession that "our lives have become unmanageable." And, as the author found in his research, the prayer "O, God, manage me because I cannot manage myself," was part of the Shoemaker—Oxford Group—Anne Smith heritage which Bill Wilson received in A.A.'s formative period.

Of the *Second Step*, Shoemaker said belief does not come by calling out to some nameless power, or by reading long books of philosophy or theology; it comes by seeing thousands of wretched lives transformed. Here Shoemaker was espousing the "knowing" that comes from joining others in the experiment of faith—an experiment that begins with the "doing" covered by John 7:17 and James 1:22—and about which he had written in earlier books.

Speaking of the *Third Step*, Shoemaker referred to William James and the "turning point" quote which appeared so many times in his books. He affirmed that surrender begins with a "decision." He said "all spiritual experience must begin decisively if it is going to happen at all." The decision is like screwing the light bulb in tight enough to touch the place where the current comes out.

Those who have read Shoemaker will be familiar with what he said of *Step Four*: "Face yourself as you really are." Bible Christian that he was, Shoemaker referred to the Ten Commandments and the Sermon on the Mount as guides. He said alcoholism may force honesty about oneself, and the deepest thing to look for will be pride in some form.

Referring to *Step Five*, Shoemaker said confession is an old idea. And he had in mind the verse from James 5:16, which he had often quoted on the subject. He spoke, as he had spoken so often before, on the subject of laying aside pride and opening up ourselves to another human being.

As to *Step Six*, Shoemaker said, as he had said in his books, that it involved *repentance*. He said this involved not just ending the inconveniences of wrong-doing, but leaving behind the wrongdoing itself. This, he said, requires a vision of how much better the new life is than the old, and understanding the need for help from the "Higher Power." He said, as Oxford Group people always said about the "Higher Power": We need God and we need each other. God alone can give us this new mind and keep us in it.

Step Seven involves a beginning, by asking God to change us. Shoemaker suggested doing it in the quiet of our own homes, by kneeling in church, or by praying with another person (as the early church did in the Book of James and as early AAs did in Akron). He said we need help, Grace, the lift of a kind of divine derrick.[7] He said the help from God is a much needed part.

Step Eight calls for action: making a list and willingness. This is not just regret expressed to God, but willingness to go to others in honesty and humility. Here one can recall the portions Shoemaker often quoted from the Sermon on the Mount about leaving gifts at the altar and first going to, and becoming reconciled with, the brother we have harmed.

As to *Step Nine*, Shoemaker did discuss how to make amends, but he also spoke much about keeping a tight lip when it comes to telling all we know and revealing something about the sins of another. He said: "What is known in confidence should be kept in confidence until or unless the person involved gives permission to speak of it." The Big Book makes this same suggestion.[8]

His *Step Ten* discussion talked of sin, pride as the root-sin, and conviction of sin. He spoke of *continuance*—an Oxford Group practice the author identified with A.A.'s last three steps. Shoemaker said we must "keep open to facing ourselves afresh and

---

[7] Compare James 4:10: "Humble yourselves in the sight of the Lord, and he shall lift you up."

[8] Big Book, pp. 79-80.

making things right where they have gone wrong." In other words, daily surrender and restitution are part of the new life.

As to *Step Eleven*, Shoemaker quoted his old friend, the Apostle Paul, and the verse from Acts: "Lord, what wilt thou have me to do?" He repeated his idea that "Prayer does not seek to change God's will, but to find it."

Pointing to *Step Twelve*, Shoemaker spoke of "spiritual rebirth." And we recall his many teachings on being born again and the new birth. He said the Twelfth Step involved the spread of the awakening to others and a deepening and continuation of the awakening in ourselves. He said, "This was surely the secret of the Twelve Apostles and all the early Christian disciples." He epitomized the Twelfth Step by referring to the old phrase: "Out of Self into God and Others."

Concluding, Shoemaker said the Twelve Steps are one of the very great summaries and organic collections of spiritual truth known to history. He said they offer "a way out" (a phrase Sherry Day used in his description of Oxford Group Bible principles and one often heard in A.A.). And Shoemaker pointed to "the way" (and here is a reference to Jesus Christ as the way, the truth, and the life).[9] Shoemaker said: "Thank God for the Twelve Steps and for a man wise enough and open enough to God and to the observation of human experience to receive these truths, and transmit them to the world."

Comments about A.A. in Later Books

Now and then, in the books he wrote after A.A.'s Big Book was published, Shoemaker would make comments about A.A. and its principles. Here are a few examples.

---

[9] John 14:6: "Jesus saith unto him, I am the way, the truth, and the life; no man cometh unto the Father, but by me."

In 1948, Shoemaker's *Revive Thy Church Beginning With Me* was published.[10] He said:

> Alcoholics Anonymous are giving a great lead in practical witness to spiritual truth and power, and are often what St. Paul said the law was, a "tutor" to bring people to Christ and His Church.[11] One must be with these people to feel and know the power of it all—the men and women, some of them still bearing on their faces the marks of defeat and degradation, men and women who have known the depths of loneliness and despair, laughing and talking together, eager for any helpful truth and experience one can bring them. It all grew from the fact that one man saw a change in two other men; he found the same answer himself—then he universalized it with the help of doctors, ministers, psychiatrists and reclaimed alcoholics. There are too few places where one can take a listless, conventional religionist, or a skeptical, unbelieving pagan, and have him "stabbed broad awake" as he will be at an open meeting of A.A. (pp. 78-79).

Shoemaker then listed the Twelve Steps, stating there is much wisdom in them about "the cure of souls" (pp. 79-80).

Shoemaker's *The Church Alive* was published in 1951.[12] He wrote about the need of the Church to create *place of exposure* where you can take people to let them see and feel the "work of God's Spirit actively at work in individuals and in companies" (p. 146). He illustrated by saying this of A.A.:

> Alcoholics Anonymous is such a place of exposure. More than a hundred thousand men and women in this country alone are "dried up." Why? Because those who are being changed through the truths discovered and made available through that extraordinary movement gather weekly in small companies, where they give testimony and

---

[10] Samuel Shoemaker, Jr., *Revive Thy Church Beginning With Me* (New York: Harper & Brothers, 1948).

[11] The reference seems to be to Galatians 3:24: "Wherefore the law was our schoolmaster *to bring us* unto Christ, that we might be justified by faith."

[12] Samuel Shoemaker, Jr., *The Church Alive* (New York: E. P. Dutton, 1951).

> witness to what has happened to them, being alcoholics. When an alcoholic (or for that matter any other human being with a need in his life) listens to what is said, he is powerfully exposed to a faith that can change and save him. These are not lectures, though there is teaching in what they say: they are testimonies, backed by the lives and life story of those who speak. In my opinion, "A.A." has superbly related simple Christian truths to the problem of alcohol. The "open" meetings are places of exposure for those seeking an answer to that need (pp. 146-47).

In *How To Become a Christian*, Shoemaker said most people owe their Christian faith to other persons.[13] He said he had recently listened to a man give his story at an A.A. meeting. The man said he was a proud materialist and that it took a long time for him to get the spiritual angle of A.A. or to admit that God had anything to do with his recovery. This man "took the program" for several months, as Shoemaker put it, and then spoke at a meeting. An English seaman came up to the man and said: "You didn't say a thing about God in the meeting" (p. 139). The man made an excuse. But the Britisher grabbed his lapels and said: "You are evading Him!" The man went off on another drinking spree, but returned with his pride broken. Shoemaker said, "He had to admit that he needed God, that God and God alone had the answer for Him" (p. 139). Shoemaker cited the Seaman's word as a word of simple, friendly witness—which produced results.

His Remarks about What the Church Can Learn from A.A.

After he had attended and spoken at length at A.A.'s Twentieth Anniversary Convention in St. Louis in 1955, Shoemaker preached

---

[13] Samuel Shoemaker, Jr., *How To Become A Christian* (New York: Harper & Brothers, 1953).

a sermon entitled, *What The Church Has To Learn from Alcoholics Anonymous*. Thousands of copies of the sermon were requested, reprinted, and disseminated. And it is reprinted in full in . . . *And Thy Neighbor*.[14]

Shoemaker wrote that Bill had found his initial spiritual answer at Calvary Church in New York, when Shoemaker was rector there in 1935.[15] Shoemaker then briefly recounted the story of A.A.'s founding in Akron, Ohio. He said he had remarked at the A.A. Convention that he thought it had been wise for A.A. to confine its activity to alcoholics, but had added that we might see an effect of A.A. on medicine, psychiatry, correction, the ever-present problem of human nature, and not least on the Church. He said, "AA indirectly derived much of its inspiration from the Church. Now perhaps the time has come for the Church to be re-awakened and re-vitalized by those insights and practices found in AA" (p. 25). He said many might be asking what they could learn from a lot of reconstructed drunks. And he gave as his text 1 Corinthians 1:26, quoting "God chose what is foolish in the world to shame the wise, God chose what is weak in the world to shame the strong." He pointed to the "sarcasm" in the verse since he said it was evident that anything God can use is neither foolish nor weak. Then he recited his points as to what the church needs to learn from A.A.

His first point was that "nobody gets anywhere till he recognizes a clearly-defined need" (p. 26). He said people come to A.A. because they are desperate, not just to find religion. They are in

---

[14] Cecil Cox Offill, . . . *And Thy Neighbor: Sam Shoemaker talks about creative living* (Texas: Word Books, 1967), pp. 23-31.

[15] See Chapter 6 of this book for an indication that Shoemaker was probably mistaken in his recollection that Bill "found his initial spiritual answer at Calvary Church . . . in 1935." There are strong indications in A.A.'s own literature and in Bill's recollections that he had "found something" at Calvary Rescue Mission in 1934 when he made his decision for Christ before he checked into Towns Hospital. Also that he had found "the God of the preachers" between December 11 and December 18, 1934, when Bill had his "hot flash" experience at Towns Hospital and concluded, as well, that he had been "born again." In both cases, Bill had made a surrender; and at Towns Hospital, he had taken the Oxford Group "steps" with Ebby prior to 1935.

search of redemption. They are willing to tell somebody of their need if there is the least chance it can be met. Shoemaker said there is a great relief in being accepted by one who has himself been unaccepted. He said there were no good Christians in the first church, only sinners. Thus the Book of James said, "Confess your faults one to another."[16] He said the last place today where one can be candid about one's faults is in church. He said that is a stinging and miserable situation, just as hideous as anybody's drunkenness can ever be.

In his second point, he said: "Men are redeemed in a life-changing fellowship" (p. 27). He says AAs don't expect to let anybody stay as he is. They live to extend and keep extending help. When a person takes his place in this redemptive, life-changing fellowship, he may be changed today and out working tomorrow, giving away what he has got. He said the Church ought to be bringing other people into redeeming, life-changing fellowship.

His third point concerned the "necessity for definite personal dealing with people" (p. 28). He said AAs know all the stock excuses; they've used them and heard them a hundred times. And they know how to put the blame on others. He said he had heard AAs laboring with one another, sometimes patient as a mother, and sometimes savage as a prize-fighter, now explaining, and now pounding in heavy personal challenge, but always knowing the desperate need and the sure answer. He said Church people need to see themselves as they are before God, not as they would like to appear before others. The "fearless moral inventory" of A.A. gets at pride, which many in the Church have never recognized, let alone faced or dealt with.

Fourth, he said the Church "needs to learn from AA. . . the necessity for a real change of heart, a true conversion" (p. 29). He said we need to be in a process of transformation; and AAs are. At every meeting, there are people seeking and in conscious need. Everybody is pulling for the people who speak, and looking for

---

[16] James 5:16.

more insight and help. They are pushed by their need and pulled by the inspiration of others who are growing. He said many Church people may not really want to find God because finding Him would change them from their habitual ways; and they really don't want to endure the pain of change. He said change must begin somewhere, and it ought to begin with us.

Finally, he said: "One of the greatest things the Church should learn from AA is the need people have for an exposure to the living Christian experience" (p. 30). He pointed out that AAs can go and hear recovered alcoholics speak about their experiences and watch the process of new life and onlook taking place before their very eyes. He said the attraction of A.A. is due to hearing people with problems like your own. They speak freely about the answers they are finding. And you realize that such honesty and change is what you need. He said the ordinary Church service cannot produce this. He advocated establishment of informal companies where people who are spiritually seeking can see how faith takes hold on others. He said this process needs to be established and multiplied.

Shoemaker said he stood at the A.A. Convention Auditorium in St. Louis and said to himself that he would like to see the Church like what he saw: people with a great need who have found a great Answer, and do not hesitate to make it known wherever they can. He repeated a theme he had uttered at the Convention itself: that the Church needs to learn its need for honesty, for conversion, for fellowship and for honest witness.

Part 3

The Shoemaker Relationship with A.A.

6

Shoemaker's Relationship with Bill Wilson

The Shoemaker "puzzle" no longer seems to the author to be a question of *whether* Bill Wilson got most of his spiritual language from the teachings of Sam Shoemaker, but *how*. And we believe we've found some substantial pieces of evidence that may answer the "how." In this chapter, we will summarize the facts and, in many cases, reproduce in somewhat more detail, in our appendices, the evidence itself.

Bill and Sam

One can speculate that Bill Wilson might have met Sam Shoemaker personally prior to, or possibly at the time of Bill's decision for Christ at Calvary Rescue Mission. For Bill once remarked that Sam began teaching him "way back in 1934." But such an assumption would require reliance on some very scanty remarks in Al-Anon literature and elsewhere. For example, in *Lois Remembers*, there is, on page 197, a chronology of "Al-Anon and A.A. Historical Events."[1] Lois Wilson's book records, in its November, 1934, entry, "Ebby tells Bill of his 'release' from

[1] *Lois Remembers* (New York, Al-Anon Family Group Headquarters, 1987), p. 187.

alcohol." Did Ebby actually put Bill in touch with Shoemaker or bring him to a meeting led by Shoemaker at some time after this first Thatcher-Wilson meeting, but prior to Bill's going to the Rescue Mission altar?

Lois said she came home in the late fall of 1934, and found "sober Ebby" earnestly talking with Bill.[2] She said Bill had continued to drink after that meeting with Ebby, but that "his urge to hear more about Ebby's new source of strength had drawn him to Calvary Mission on Manhattan's East 23rd Street, where Ebby was staying" (p. 88). While the historical evidence about this period is somewhat muddled, it appears that Bill might have been drawn first either to Calvary Church or to the Rescue Mission. For Bill said he had seen Ebby get up in the "pulpit" on the "previous Sunday night" and give witness to the fact that, with the help of God, he (Ebby) had been sober a number of months.[3] Was this "pulpit" at Calvary Church, or was it at the Rescue Mission? Was Shoemaker there when Ebby gave *his* testimonial? We do not know. But it seems clear that Bill *later* went to Calvary Rescue Mission when Ebby was *not* there.[4]

At that time, Bill went to the altar, knelt down, and made a decision for Christ.[5] Sam Shoemaker's wife, Helen Smith Shoemaker, told the author in a phone conversation from her home on October, 1991, that she was present at Calvary Mission when Bill made this decision for Christ.[6] Was Sam Shoemaker there? We do not know. However, Bill did write of this general period

---

[2] *Lois Remembers*, p. 87.

[3] *Pass It On* (New York: Alcoholics Anonymous World Services, 1984), p. 119; and see Dick B., *The Akron Genesis of Alcoholics Anonymous* (Seattle: Glen Abbey Books, 1992), pp. 156-158.

[4] A number of A.A. accounts have indicated that Ebby was present when Bill made his decision for Christ. But the archivist at Stepping Stones pointed out to the author that Bill Wilson was drunk when this occurred and that Ebby was drunk when people later asked him for his recollection. However, Billy Duvall was present at the event and reported that Ebby was *not* present.

[5] Dick B., *The Akron Genesis of Alcoholics Anonymous*, p. 157.

[6] See Dick B., *The Akron Genesis of Alcoholics Anonymous*, p. 157.

in *A.A. Comes of Age*: "How well I remember the first day I caught sight of him [Shoemaker]. It was at a Sunday service at his church. . . . I can still see him standing there before the lectern."[7] When was this? Was it before Bill entered Towns Hospital? We do not know.

There is a partially erroneous account in an Al-Anon publication which suggests that Bill might have gone to Oxford Group meetings prior to his entry into Towns Hospital on December 11, 1934. Al-Anon's *First Steps* said:

> When Bill left Towns Hospital for the last time on December *8*, 1934, never to drink again, he and Lois *returned* to Calvary House at Calvary Church to attend Oxford Group meetings. Dr. Sam Shoemaker was a leading figure in the Oxford Group movement at the time (emphasis ours).[8]

We believe *First Steps* meant to give the date as December *18* rather than December *8*. But the book does speak of Bill and Lois' *returning* to Oxford Group meetings. Had they gone to Oxford Group meetings *before* Bill entered Towns Hospital on December 11, 1934?

We know the statement in *First Steps* is partly erroneous because *Pass It On* contains a picture of Bill's last admission and discharge from the Charles B. Towns Hospital; and it fixes those dates at December 11, 1934 (for entry) and December 18, 1934 (for discharge).[9] But there is the suggestion in *First Steps* that Bill and Lois might have attended Oxford Group meetings led by Sam Shoemaker, and that the meetings occurred prior to Bill's December 11th hospitalization at Towns. We doubt that possibility since Lois seemed to say, in *Lois Remembers*, that she really

---

[7] *Alcoholics Anonymous Comes of Age* (New York: Alcoholics Anonymous World Services, 1957), p. 157.

[8] *First Steps: Al-Anon. . . 35 years of beginnings* (New York: Al-Anon Family Group Headquarters, 1986), p. 15.

[9] *Pass It On*, p. 104.

wasn't familiar with what had been happening to Bill since his visit with Ebby until Bill phoned her, at which time Bill apparently announced to her that he was going to tell her of his Calvary Rescue Mission experience (p. 88). And we deduce that Bill was more or less drunk from the time he first met with Ebby until the time he checked into Towns Hospital after his Rescue Mission conversion. It therefore seems unlikely that he and Lois were attending Oxford Group meetings or hearing from or about Shoemaker in that brief period.

The picture changed dramatically once Bill was released from Towns Hospital on December 18, 1934; and all historical accounts seem agreed that Bill immediately surged forth to Oxford Group meetings, mostly in Lois's company. And some of these meetings were led by Sam Shoemaker.[10] Lois stated:

> It was an ecstatic time for us both. With Ebby and another alcoholic, Shep C., as our companions, we *constantly* went to Oxford Group meetings at Calvary Episcopal Church on Fourth Avenue (now renamed Park Avenue South) at 21st Street in New York. Shep not only was a fellow grouper, but also worked in Wall Street and summered in Manchester.[11]

We have now located some very reliable evidence as to the details of Bill's personal relationship with Sam during the six month period between December 18, 1934, and May of 1935, when Bill met Dr. Bob in Akron. And there is one very dramatic evidentiary link that tells us that Bill *must* have been in fairly close touch with Sam from almost the moment he left Towns Hospital on December 18, 1934. Before we get to that evidence, we should see what *else* Bill was doing in those early days right after his release from Towns, and which might have attracted Shoemaker's attention. Lois Wilson wrote about this period:

---

[10] *Lois Remembers*, p. 91, 94; *Pass It On*, p. 127, 132; Ernest Kurtz, *Not-God: A History of Alcoholics Anonymous*. Expanded ed. (Minnesota: Hazelden, 1991), pp. 24-25; and Robert Thomsen, *Bill W.* (New York: Harper & Row, 1975), pp. 228-32.

[11] *Lois Remembers*, p. 91 (emphasis ours).

> As far as I am concerned, A.A. began in *1934* in my father's old house on Brooklyn Heights where Bill and I were living. When Bill came home to 182 Clinton St. from Towns' Hospital in New York after his spiritual awakening, he began immediately bringing drunks to the house (emphasis ours).[12]

Moreover, within ten days of his release from Towns on December 18, 1935, Bill began meeting at Stewart's cafeteria in New York with a little group of ex-drunks.[13] Little noticed, has been the fact that Rowland Hazard was among the group that met with Bill at Stewart's.[14] So, at a very early period, possibly between December 18, 1934, and January 22, 1935, we have Bill Wilson going to Oxford Group meetings which were sometimes led by Sam Shoemaker. Furthermore, he went in the company of Ebby Thatcher and Shep Cornell. And he was meeting with alcoholics at Stewart's Cafeteria, sometimes with Rowland Hazard. We mention this because, as we have shown, Rowland and Shep were not only ardent Oxford Group members, but also were much involved in Shoemaker's Calvary Church as vestrymen. In fact, our very recent inspection of Shoemaker's journals shows repeated hand-written references by Shoemaker in his daily journals to Rowland and to Shep.[15] Moreover, as Charles Clapp, Jr., told in his story, *The Big Bender*, Shep Cornell and Sam Shoemaker worked with drunks.[16]

Now we are ready for the first concrete evidence that Sam Shoemaker was, from the very beginning of Bill's sobriety, in personal touch with Bill and knew of his work with drunks. And

---

[12] See the Brooklyn, New York A.A. newsletter, *the Junction*, for June, 1985, a copy of which was provided to the author by archivist Dennis C., and which is in the author's possession.

[13] Thomsen, *Bill W.*, p. 232; Kurtz, *Not-God*, p. 25; and *Lois Remembers*, p. 94.

[14] Thomsen, *Bill W.*, p. 230.

[15] See Appendix Five.

[16] Charles Clapp, Jr., *The Big Bender* (New York: Harper & Brothers, 1938). Shoemaker also frequently mentions Charles Clapp, Jr., in his journals; and his name is mentioned in connection with Rowland Hazard and Shep Cornell.

work with them Bill did! Lois said Bill was bringing drunks home in 1934. Many accounts, including one given to the author by Bill's secretary, state that Bill immediately began visiting drunks at Towns Hospital, Calvary Rescue Mission, and Oxford Group meetings. Bill had been out of Towns Hospital just a little over a month. He had been sober less than two months. But he was helping drunks, and Sam Shoemaker knew it.

On January 22, 1935, Shoemaker wrote a letter addressed to "Dear Bill." He signed it "Sam S." We have set the letter out in full in Appendix Three. In that letter, Shoemaker wrote Bill of Bill's "guidedness" in having known "Jim," whose wife was a full-time member of the Oxford Group. Shoemaker said "Jim" had held out [from getting sober] a long time, but that Bill might be "just the person that cracks the shell and brings him over." Shoemaker said Jim drank a lot, was desperately unhappy and inferior, and "needs what you [Bill] have got for him." Then Shoemaker expressed gratitude for what Bill had done to help another man—apparently also an alcoholic.[17]

This seems to the author to be dramatic evidence. Bill had been sober just a short time. But, by all accounts, he was on fire with the idea of helping drunks. Shoemaker personally recognized that fact and called on Bill for help—when Bill was less than two months sober!

Until the writing of this book, we had discovered little evidence of Bill's personal contacts with Shoemaker between January of 1935 and May of 1935 (when Bill went to Akron and first met Dr. Bob) or between September of 1935 (when Bill returned from his

---

[17] See Appendix 10. When the author visited the archives at Calvary/St. George's in November, 1993, he discovered in the parish register and in *The Calvary Evangel* much more about this "alcoholic." The man's full name was Frederick E. Breithut. Not only had Bill Wilson apparently helped this man with his drinking problem sometime in late 1934 or early 1935, but Wilson had sponsored Breithut as his godfather at the baptism of Breithut at Calvary Church on March 14, 1935. Wilson then was present at the church on March 24, 1935, when Breithut and Bill's sponsor, Ebby Thatcher, were confirmed as communicants of Calvary Episcopal Church. Shoemaker was present and officiating on both occasions.

three month stay with Dr. Bob) and October of 1935. But the picture changed when Shoemaker's daughters provided us with access to Sam Shoemaker's journals.[18] We discovered, for example, that Shoemaker was, on March 7, 1935, concerned about leading Wilson into becoming a communicant at Calvary Episcopal Church.[19] We also discovered other journal entries which—though they did not clearly indicate that Shoemaker was referring to Bill Wilson—nonetheless mentioned a man named "Bill" and linked "Bill" with people who were recovered alcoholics and were friends of, and worked with, Bill Wilson. These people were: Rowland Hazard, Victor Kitchen, Charles Clapp, Jr., and Shephard Cornell. Bill's Oxford Group friend, John Ryder, was also mentioned in these same entries.[20]

There are some additional facts about this period which also have been corroborated.

First, as we have said, Bill, Lois (his wife), Ebby Thatcher, and Shep Cornell (the Oxford Group member who had rescued Ebby) were "regularly" and "constantly" attending Oxford Group meetings together.[21] Shoemaker led a good many of these meetings.[22] We have described, in our other books, the form that

---

[18] See Appendix 10 for complete details as to what the author found on his inspection of Shoemaker's personal journals.

[19] See Appendix 10 of this book which contains the evidence we obtained in our visit to the Calvary Church archives in New York in November of 1993. The parish records show that Sam Shoemaker baptized Frederick Breithut at Calvary Church in March, 1935, with Bill Wilson present and sponsoring Breithut as one of Breithut's godparents. Later in March of 1935, Frederick Breithut and Ebby Thatcher were, in the same ceremony, confirmed as communicants of Calvary Church. As can be seen from Shoemaker's personal journal entries (reproduced in Appendix 5 of our book), Shoemaker was, about the same time, asking in March of 1935, whether Bill Wilson had as yet been "confirmed" into Calvary Church membership.

[20] See Appendix Five for details.

[21] *Lois Remembers*, p. 91, 98.

[22] *Lois Remembers*, p. 94.

these Oxford Group meetings followed; and they involved participation by those attending, and specifically by Bill.[23]

Second, Lois stated, in a context that made it clear she was talking of this early period: "Bill and Sam Shoemaker of the Oxford Group were very good friends."[24]

Third, Reverend Irving Harris, a very close friend of Sam Shoemaker's for many years, and one of Shoemaker's assistant ministers at Calvary Church, prepared a typewritten memorandum entitled, "Bill Wilson and Sam Shoemaker;" and we have included in Appendix Four the full text of that memorandum. Harris made these points about the Wilson-Shoemaker relationship: (1) Wilson frequently talked to Sam about the "early formulations of the Twelve Steps and the principles of the New Testament." (2) Wilson was familiar with the seven Biblical principles of the Oxford Group that Reverend Sherwood Day had written for the Oxford Group back in the 1920's and which Sam had asked Day to reproduce for *The Calvary Evangel* in one of its 1926 issues. (3) Bill and Sam discussed these seven Biblical principles. (4) The talks "took place in Sam's book-lined seventh floor study at Calvary house with the door closed and the telephone switched off." (5) Others in the Oxford Group were persuaded that Bill should be involved in Oxford Group "traveling teams," but Shoemaker was never personally persuaded that Bill should participate in this general team travel that was then going on.[25]

---

[23] Dick B., *The Oxford Group & Alcoholics Anonymous* (Seattle: Glen Abbey Books, 1992), pp. 73-109; and Dick B., *The Akron Genesis of Alcoholics Anonymous*, pp. 169-178; and see *Lois Remembers*, where Bill's wife tells, at page 94, of a Sunday afternoon Oxford Group meeting, probably led by Shoemaker, where Bill had been chosen to "share" or "witness" and recounted his alcoholic story, ending with his dramatic spiritual awakening.

[24] *Lois Remembers*, p. 103.

[25] There is now additional evidence concerning Harris's comments about Bill Wilson, Oxford Group traveling teams, and the attitudes of other group members about Bill and the Oxford Group's world outreach. Thus: (1) In a four-hour interview with the author at Highstown, New Jersey, in November of 1993, Parks Shipley, Sr., stated to the author that he had been much involved with Oxford Group traveling teams, particularly in 1935,

(continued...)

(6) Shoemaker became Bill's "special ally and comforter, enabling him to withstand the pressures to conform."

Fourth, although much more needs to be learned about the "team" and Bill's participation in it, Bill definitely belonged to an Oxford Group team at Calvary; and the "team" was probably the Oxford Group businessmen's team, of which Shoemaker was very much the inspired leader, and of which we shall have more to say in a moment. Lois specifically recalled: "Bill belonged to a team for a while."[26]

The evidence as to what Bill and Sam were doing together becomes even clearer, commencing about November 2, 1935; and the evidence has only recently come to light as both the author and Shoemaker's daughters began a detailed study of Shoemaker's daily journals for the period from November, 1934, through January of 1936. In Appendix Five, we have quoted five specific journal entries in which Sam Shoemaker mentions Bill Wilson by name. And we have quoted five additional entries which very probably refer to Bill Wilson and his relationship and activities with Sam Shoemaker and his associates during the year 1935. For example, almost as soon as Shoemaker had returned from abroad in the Fall of 1935, he was speaking about telephoning and meeting with Bill Wilson. Moreover, at Thanksgiving time, in November of 1935, Shoemaker spoke of Bill Wilson in connection with a major team event in New York involving Wilson, Shoemaker, Frank Buchman, and a number of other well-known Oxford Group leaders.

---

[25] (...continued)
that he knew Bill Wilson as one of the business team members, and that the team members were expecting "more" of Bill Wilson in participation in Oxford Group life-changing work than Wilson's preoccupation with helping drunks. (2) Sam Shoemaker's personal journal entries for November of 1935 show that Wilson was not only a member of the team and was given leadership work in connection with the visit of League of Nations President Carl Hambro to the United States, but also was being considered for Oxford Group work in other countries.

[26] *Lois Remembers*, p. 93.

The *New York Times* for Thursday, November 21, 1935, reported that Carl Joachim Hambro, President of the Parliament of Norway and chief spokesman of the smaller powers in the League of Nations, was addressing an Oxford Group meeting of three hundred bankers, lawyers, and businessmen at the Bankers Club. In attendance were such luminaries as Paul D. Cravath, William Randolph Hearst, Richard Whitney, William A. Harriman, and Lieutenant General Robert Lee Bullard.[27] The Hambro events also involved a meeting attended in Boston by some 1,500 of its citizens. This Oxford Group event even received favorable mention in a Jewish publication.[28] The Hambro visit occasioned major meetings during the Thanksgiving period in 1935; and Shoemaker specifically recorded in his journal that Bill Wilson had a leadership role in the event. Wilson is mentioned by name, sometimes as "Bill W." and sometimes as "Bill Wilson," on November 2, November 18, and November 20, 1935. Other entries which link Shoemaker and Wilson during the 1935 period are included, and discussed further, in our Appendix Five. Regrettably, the Shoemaker daughters have been unable thus far to locate Shoemaker's journals for the critically important period from January of 1936 to, and including, the date of the Big Book's publication in the Spring of 1939. However, as a random sample of Shoemaker's journal entries, the 1935 quotations certainly establish the substantial degree to which Shoemaker was involved with Bill Wilson.

The next evidence concerns the Oxford Group houseparties which Bill attended, both alone and with Lois. Bill went to his first houseparty in Richmond, Virginia, in December, 1935. Lois then went with him to at least three more: (1) Stockbridge, Massachusetts, in June, 1936; (2) Poconos in Pennsylvania, in

---

[27] This article was supplied to the author by Michael Hutchinson of Oxford, who has been with the Oxford Group as an activist since 1931 and lives in the same complex as Buchman's biographer, Garth D. Lean.

[28] Again, material on an article in *The Jewish Advocate* for January 11, 1936, covering this same visit to the United States by the president of the Norway parliament was supplied to the author by Michael Hutchinson.

December, 1936; and (3) West Point, New York, in January, 1937.[29]

When the author visited the archives at the Bill and Lois Wilson home at Stepping Stones in Bedford Hills, New York, he found much additional evidence about these houseparties. In *The Akron Genesis of Alcoholics Anonymous*, we set out the details of Lois Wilson's Oxford Group Notebook, which the author found at Stepping Stones.[30] In Appendix 7 of this book, we have listed the entries Lois made concerning Oxford Group houseparties. The important thing is that Lois specifically mentions the people she and Bill met at the "Pocono House Party Dec 4-6" [1936]. She lists Irving Harris (who was Shoemaker's assistant minister), Ray Purdy (who had been associated with Shoemaker since Princeton days and had been General Secretary of the Philadelphian Society there), and Cleveland Hicks (who taught Bible at the houseparties)—all clergy with whom Shoemaker was closely associated. And, as to "Houseparty at West Point-Jan 10/37," she specifically mentions Sam Shoemaker and Frank Buchman. The author personally obtained from Mr. and Mrs. James D. Newton—both long-time Oxford Group activists and personal friends of Shoemaker and Buchman—many houseparty programs and invitations of those days. Almost always, Shoemaker and Buchman were listed prominently as participants. Hence Bill was exposed to Shoemaker views during Oxford Group houseparties held throughout Bill's Oxford Group "membership."

Finally, Shoemaker wrote a letter to H. H. Brown of Fort Worth, Texas on March 13, 1952, which touched on Shoemaker's early close relations with Bill. Shoemaker said:

> Bill Wilson found his spiritual change in this House [Calvary House] when the Oxford Group was at work here many years ago.

---

[29] See *Lois Remembers*, p. 103.

[30] Dick B., *The Akron Genesis of Alcoholics Anonymous*, pp. 150-155.

> I have had the closest touch with Bill *from that day* to this (emphasis ours).[31]

As of the date of the writing of this book, there is now very clear evidence that Bill Wilson and Sam Shoemaker were in fact in the closest touch from Bill's earliest Oxford Group days. There is also ample evidence of Bill's contacts and relationship with Shoemaker in the years after the Big Book was written. Shoemaker wrote for the *Grapevine*. He spoke on the same stage with Bill. He addressed A.A. Conventions. And the two exchanged a good deal of correspondence after 1942.[32] But the puzzler, for the author, concerned the evidence prior to 1940—the evidence of what took place in A.A.'s formative years.

To summarize, all students of A.A. history can see from the evidence that Bill Wilson was in a position to learn a great deal from Sam Shoemaker personally, from at least December 18, 1934, to the date of Shoemaker's death. The evidence has come through Paul L., archivist at Stepping Stones; Mrs. W. Irving Harris; Dr. Charles Knippel; Nell Wing, Bill Wilson's secretary; The Reverend Stephen Garmey, Vicar at Calvary Episcopal Church; and Shoemaker's two daughters—Sally Shoemaker Robinson and "Nickie" Shoemaker Haggart. It has also come through Oxford Group leaders Jim and Eleanor Forde Newton, Garth Lean, Michael Hutchinson, George Vondermuhll, Jr., Parks Shipley, Sr., Charles Haines, and Reverends Harry J. Almond, Howard C. Blake, and T. Willard Hunter. We add, however, that much more could still be hoped for. Is there any document in which either Bill or Shoemaker precisely detailed the ideas they exchanged? Is there any evidence as to whether and where Bill might have read Shoemaker's books and other writings? Is there any evidence as to whether and in what manner Bill and

---

[31] From a letter quoted at page 69 of the thesis by Charles Taylor Knippel, *Samuel M. Shoemaker's Theological Influence On William G. Wilson's Twelve Step Spiritual Program of Recovery* (St. Louis University; 1987, Unpublished Ph.D. dissertation).

[32] See Knippel, pp. 63-88.

Shoemaker discussed either the Big Book or the Twelve Steps prior to their writing? Unfortunately, we have no answers. Therefore, much of any belief that Shoemaker influenced Wilson's specific Big Book language must still rest merely on the evidence that the two had much personal contact prior to the Big Book's publication and that their writings are remarkably similar.

The Shoemaker Circle

One cannot overlook Shoemaker's influence on Bill via the wide circle of people with whom Shoemaker worked, and with whom Bill had many contacts in A.A.'s pre-Big Book years. We have covered much of this material in other books, and we therefore list it here, more or less in outline form.

Personalities

First, of course, come the persons involved in the Oxford Group meetings attended by Bill and often held at Calvary House. We know these meetings were led by Calvary clergy, of whom we will speak in a moment. But they were also led by good friends Bill had in the Oxford Group. An example is F. Shepard Cornell. "Shep" was much involved in the Oxford Group with Ebby Thatcher, Hanford Twitchell, Rowland Hazard, Victor Kitchen, and a good many others in the businessmen's team. He was very close to both Shoemaker and Buchman, helped sponsor and lead Oxford Group houseparties, and served on the Calvary Church vestry as its clerk when Twitchell was church Treasurer and Hazard also was on the vestry. Shep met at the Wilson home meetings which were held on Tuesday nights beginning in the fall of 1935.[33]

---

[33] *Pass It On*, p. 162.

Then there was Rowland Hazard, who met at Stewart's Cafeteria with Bill after the Tuesday night Oxford Group meetings.[34] Rowland had first carried the Oxford Group message to Ebby. As an ex-problem drinker, Rowland was also involved with Shep Cornell in helping drunks; and he was very much involved with Shoemaker's church as a vestryman.

Also, there was Hanford Twitchell, Treasurer of Calvary Church and Oxford Group leader, who did Twelfth Step work with Bill. Twitchell was involved in Shoemaker's businessmen's team and was a frequent participant in Oxford Group houseparties.[35]

All these people were very close to Shoemaker, thoroughly conversant with Oxford Group and Shoemaker ideas, and very much involved in helping drunks to recover.

The Oxford Group Businessmen's Team

Another Shoemaker circle which influenced Bill was the Oxford Group businessmen's team. Actually, the team included businessmen, clergy, and full time Oxford Group volunteers. Also, it had no organized "membership" as such. But it contained a powerhouse of men who worked personally with Shoemaker and were very much influenced by him. Recent efforts by Jim and Eleanor Newton, George Vondermuhll, Jr., Parks Shipley, and Mrs. Irving Harris have enabled the author to come up with a list of the men who belonged to this team. In many cases, these men

---

[34] A.A. historian Mel B., author of *New Wine* and a substantial contributor to A.A.'s *Pass It On*, supplied the author with news articles from *The Providence Journal* which were written at the time of Rowland's death. They report that Rowland Hazard died December 19, 1945. He had been a member of one of Rhode Island's oldest and most prominent families. He died in his sixty-fifth year and was, at that time, Vice President and General Manager of the Bristol Manufacturing Company. He had served in the Rhode Island Senate and been a Captain in the United States Army in World War I. And he was a graduate of Yale University. We have also learned that Rowland Hazard maintained continuous sobriety throughout his participation in the Oxford Group, and in activities at Calvary Church and with Sam Shoemaker.

[35] See, as to Hanford Twitchell, Nell Wing, *Grateful To Have Been There* (Illinois: Parkside Publishing Corporation, 1992), p. 68.

were in the business world that Bill Wilson loved. In Appendix Six, we have listed the members thus far identified. The important thing is that Sam Shoemaker was the "guru" of the businessmen's team and its inspirational leader.

The team included the following: (1) Jim Newton, the Firestone executive who helped bring the Oxford Group to Akron in 1933 and whom Lois mentioned meeting at a houseparty; (2) Howard Davison, a business executive Lois mentioned meeting at a houseparty; (3) Shep Cornell, a businessman who helped carry the Oxford Group message to Bill, who attended Oxford Group meetings with Bill and Lois, and whom Bill and Lois met at houseparties; (4) Reverend Cleveland Hicks, who taught Bible at houseparties and whom Bill and Lois met there;[36] (5) Victor Kitchen, an advertising executive whom Bill and Lois met at a houseparty and who specifically mentions the businessmen's team in his book, *I Was A Pagan*;[37] (6) Ray Purdy, a clergyman closely associated with Shoemaker from Shoemaker's Princeton days, and whom Bill and Lois met at a houseparty; (7) Sam Shoemaker; (8) Garrett Stearly, a clergyman, who made the explicit statement to Jim Newton that Shoemaker had told him (Stearly) that Bill Wilson had asked Shoemaker to write the Twelve Steps;[38] (9) Charles Haines, a steel company executive, whom Lois mentioned in connection with Bible teaching, and who was, for years, closely associated with both Shoemaker and

---

[36] In a telephone interview with the author in November, 1991, Mrs. W. Irving Harris stated that Hicks had taught Scripture at Oxford Group houseparties.

[37] See Victor C. Kitchen, *I Was A Pagan* (New York: Harper & Brothers, 1934). In his book, Kitchen relates how he recovered from alcoholism through his Oxford Group experiences. At page 123, he describes the businessmen's team of which we have been speaking. In her Oxford Group Notebook, Lois Wilson mentions meeting Kitchen and notes that he was in "advertising." Kitchen wrote articles for *The Calvary Evangel* in this mid-1930 period and conceivably could have met, or at least participated in meetings with, Dr. Bob, Anne Smith, Henrietta Seiberling, and T. Henry and Clarace Williams when Kitchen visited Akron in 1934 with an Oxford Group Team. See Appendix 10 of our book.

[38] In two different phone conversations with the author in 1992 and 1993, Jim Newton told and repeated this statement that Stearly had made to him.

Buchman;[39] (10) Charles Clapp, Jr., a businessman, who wrote *The Big Bender*,[40] and recounts in it how he recovered from alcoholism with the assistance of Shep Cornell and Sam Shoemaker; (11) Parks Shipley, a senior partner at Brown Brothers, who well remembers Bill Wilson as a member of the team; and (12) T. Henry Williams of Akron, whom Bill had, of course, come to know very well through the meetings he attended at the Williams home both during his stay with Dr. Bob in the summer of 1935 and in the next few years.[41] As to all these team members and those whom we have listed in Appendix Six, Reverend T. Willard Hunter of the Oxford Group wrote the author that they were all key players in the Oxford Group's team activities. In a telephone conversation in September, 1993, Hunter said that Jim Newton and Charles Haines were the business team sparkplugs; and he said he was not surprised to learn that Bill Wilson had been given a leadership role in the team during the period he was active in the Oxford Group.

The First Century Christian Fellowship Houseparties

Still another Shoemaker circle, already mentioned above, was the group of Shoemaker friends and associates who were very much involved in the Oxford Group houseparties. These houseparties were also often billed as meetings of "A First Century Christian Fellowship." Over and over on the programs and invitations of these houseparties, there appeared the names of Buchman,

---

[39] The information as to the close connection between Haines and both Shoemaker and Buchman was provided to the author by George Vondermuhll, Jr., long-time corporate secretary of Moral Re-Armament. Then Haines himself confirmed these facts in a telephone interview with the author in December, 1993.

[40] Charles Clapp, Jr., *The Big Bender* (New York: Harper & Row, 1938).

[41] This connection of Williams with the Oxford Group businessmen's team in New York does not appear to have been recorded in A.A. history and came to the author's attention when he interviewed James D. Newton in Florida in August of 1992.

Shoemaker, Rowland Hazard, Professor Philip Marshall Brown,[42] Hanford Twitchell, F. Shepard Cornell, Reverend Cleveland Hicks, and others whom Lois mentioned meeting at the houseparties.[43] All of these houseparty people were well acquainted with Sam Shoemaker, his ideas, and his books.[44] Almost all these men were part of Shoemaker's circle of church people, businessmen, and Oxford Group team members.

Eleanor Napier Forde

Last but not least comes the name of Eleanor Napier Forde Newton. For details about her Oxford Group connection, her service to both Dr. Frank Buchman and to Dr. Samuel Shoemaker, see our title, *The Akron Genesis of Alcoholics Anonymous*, pp. 22-27. Miss Forde, who later became the wife of Oxford Group activist, James D. Newton, wrote what was virtually the first American Oxford Group pamphlet, other than those written by Shoemaker. In 1930, she wrote *The Guidance of God.*[45] Anne Smith mentioned Miss Forde's ideas in Anne's spiritual

---

[42] See Philip Marshall Brown, *The Venture Of Belief* (New York: Fleming Revell, 1935). Shoemaker wrote an introduction to this book. It contains much information pertinent to A.A.'s Second and Third Steps and "religious experiences." In 1954, Bill Wilson did a taped interview of Cebra Graves, who had helped Rowland Hazard and Shep Cornell carry the Oxford Group message to Ebby Thatcher. During Bill's interview, Cebra Graves several times mentioned Rowland Hazard's friend, Professor Philip Marshall Brown of Princeton, an Oxford Group writer, scholar, and frequent Oxford Group speaker. Graves mentioned that he and Hazard had had many conversations with Brown. The point is that Brown was a colleague of Shoemaker's, and each apparently influenced the other in the matter of Oxford Group principles and practices.

[43] See Dick B., *The Akron Genesis of Alcoholics Anonymous*, pp. 147, 150-155.

[44] Almost all were frequently mentioned in the 1934-1936 Shoemaker journal entries which the author examined.

[45] Eleanor Napier Forde, *The Guidance of God* (Oxford: Printed at the University Press, 1930).

workbook.[46] And Lois Wilson mentioned that she and Bill met Eleanor Forde at a houseparty. Miss Forde had worked with Reverend Sam Shoemaker and lived at Calvary House; and, at Shoemaker's suggestion, she also began, in the 1920's, working full-time with Dr. Buchman and the Oxford Group.

Calvary Church

It would be hard to claim that Shoemaker's Calvary Church *itself* exerted an influence on Bill Wilson. One account of Bill Wilson's Oxford Group days suggests that he actually went to the Calvary Episcopal Church for meetings.[47] Shoemaker himself made it clear that the Church was very much involved with the First Century Christian Fellowship known as the Oxford Group. But despite some variations in language, the fact is that Bill and Lois attended Oxford Group meetings, some of which were held at Calvary House, adjacent to the Church, and some of which may have been held in the Church on Sunday evenings.[48] From what we have been able to piece together, the Calvary-sponsored Oxford Group meetings were held on Tuesdays, Thursdays, and

---

[46] See Dick B., *The Akron Genesis of Alcoholics Anonymous*, pp. 22-23. The author has a copy of the Anne Smith workbook in his possession and personally noted several references by Anne Smith to the thoughts and teachings of Eleanor Forde.

[47] *Lois Remembers*, p. 91.

[48] See *Lois Remembers*, p. 91: "We constantly went to Oxford Group meetings at Calvary Episcopal Church;" *First Steps* at page 15: "he [Bill] and Lois returned to Calvary House at Calvary Church to attend Oxford Group meetings;" *Pass It On*, p. 127: "After Bill's release from Towns on December 18, he and Lois started attending Oxford Group meetings at Calvary House, adjacent to Calvary Episcopal Church;" *Lois Remembers*, p. 94: "The Oxford Group meetings on Sunday afternoons were usually led by Sam Shoemaker or one of his two assistants [Reverend J. Herbert ('Jack') Smith and Reverend John P. Cuyler, Jr.], and various members of the congregation were asked to speak."

Sundays—the latter possibly in the sanctuary itself.[49] But they were probably *not church services*.[50]

On the other hand, Shoemaker's clergy very definitely were in touch with Bill Wilson. The clearest example is Reverend W. Irving Harris, Assistant Minister at Calvary Church. Of Harris and his wife, Julia, Bill Wilson wrote:

> In our early days there were those who actually infused the breath of life into us. Speaking in the language of the heart, they brought us much of the grace in which our society today lives and has its being. There was my own doctor, William Southworth [sic]. . . . There was Dr. Carl Jung. . . . From William James we learned. . . . But these cornerstones were only part of the needed foundation. Who could furnish us the wherewithal to construct this spiritual edifice which today houses our world-wide brotherhood? Sam Shoemaker and his wonderful co-workers, among whom were Irving and Julia Harris, were the people who were given this critical assignment.[51]

Irving Harris was a resident of Calvary House, a regular staff-member of Calvary Church, and was in charge of the Oxford Group office at Calvary House.[52] He later was editor of *The Calvary Evangel*.

Note that, in the foregoing remarks about Irving and Julia Harris, Bill Wilson mentioned Shoemaker's *other* co-workers. One of these was Reverend J. Herbert (Jack) Smith, Associate Rector of Calvary Church, who was very much involved in working with

---

[49] Thomsen, *Bill W.*, pp. 229, 252; *Lois Remembers*, pp. 94, 98; *Pass It On*, pp. 132, 162; Irving Harris, *The Breeze of the Spirit* (New York: The Seabury Press, 1978), pp. 24, 47; and John Potter Cuyler, Jr., *Calvary Church in Action* (New York: Fleming Revell, 1934), pp. 49, 55-58.

[50] James and Eleanor Newton told the author in a personal interview in September, 1993, that the Oxford Group meetings were never church services. However, Shoemaker said of this same period that his church services were Oxford Group services.

[51] From an article in *Faith At Work* magazine, July-August, 1963.

[52] Cuyler, *Calvary Church in Action*, p. 53.

Shoemaker and in running the parish in Shoemaker's absences.[53] A good deal of the work in bringing people to Christ was in Smith's hands and in the hands of Shoemaker's Assistant Minister, Reverend John Potter Cuyler, Jr.[54] *Pass It On* indicates Smith may have had substantial contact with Bill Wilson.[55] Shoemaker spoke much about the work of both Smith and Cuyler.[56] Though we have found no direct evidence at this point that either man directly conveyed Shoemaker ideas to Wilson, that seems quite probable since both were Shoemaker's assistants; and Oxford Group meetings at Calvary were often led either by Shoemaker *or* by these assistants at the Church.[57] Walter T. Biscoe was still another person connected with the church. He led some of the Oxford Group meetings; was a member of the Oxford Group businessmen's team; and apparently had a good deal of experience dealing with people at Calvary.[58] Thus he too might have been involved in working with Wilson and conveying Shoemaker ideas.

Other Sources of Shoemaker Impact

As we move away from Bill's personal contacts with Shoemaker; with Shoemaker's clergy; and with Oxford Group meetings, business team gatherings, and houseparties, we move more into the

---

[53] Cuyler, *Calvary Church in Action*, pp. 30-44.

[54] Cuyler, *Calvary Church in Action*, p. 33.

[55] *Pass It On*, p. 169. Compare Harris, *The Breeze of the Spirit*, p. 27; and see Mel B., *New Wine* (Minnesota: Hazelden, 1991), p. 90.

[56] Samuel Shoemaker, Jr., *Calvary Church Yesterday and Today* (New York: Fleming Revell, 1936), pp. 259-260, 262, 272-274, 276, 279.

[57] See, for example, *Lois Remembers*, p. 94. Parks Shipley confirmed to the author in a telephone conversation in September, 1993, that Smith and Cuyler led Oxford Group meetings.

[58] See Cuyler, *Calvary Church in Action*, p. 57; Shoemaker, *Calvary Church Yesterday and Today*, p. 277. In June of 1993, Mrs. W. Irving Harris wrote the author that Biscoe was a member of the businessmen's team.

realm of speculation as to where Shoemaker ideas could have impacted on Bill. Yet there *is* other evidence, and it is important because we are still unable to explain where and how Bill got such intimate acquaintance with language found in Shoemaker's books.

What else do we know?

We know that there was an Oxford Group Literature List, regularly published in *The Calvary Evangel*. We have published this list in full in Appendix Two, and the important thing is that almost every significant Shoemaker book prior to 1939 is listed there. This suggests that, whether Shoemaker's books were available at Oxford Group meetings, whether they were read by Oxford Group members, or whether Bill might simply have sought out the books, he certainly had a ready Oxford Group bibliography available to tell him about the books Shoemaker had written.

We also know about the Oxford Group bookstore or book-room in the basement of Calvary House. Shoemaker wrote the following about it:

> Downstairs [in Calvary House] is the book-room from which were sent out 144 orders, or 3291 items in a typical month to all parts of this country—this does not include what is sold locally in New York; and the press room where a team of people is working constantly on public relations, sending out positive and constructive views of nationally significant character to every kind of publication.[59]

In a telephone interview with the author in October, 1991 from her home in New Jersey, Reverend Irving Harris's wife, Julia, told the author that she had been in charge of the Oxford Group "book-room" in the basement of Calvary House. She said the book-room carried all of the books on the Oxford Group literature list, which was published in the March, 1939 issue of *The Calvary Evangel* and is reproduced in Appendix Two of our book. She said all the

---

[59] Samuel Shoemaker, Jr., *God's Control* (New York: Fleming H. Revell, 1939), p. 72.

books on the list, which certainly included Shoemaker's, were being disseminated by the American Headquarters of the Oxford Group at Calvary House in the later 1930's when Mrs. Harris was in charge. We noted above that Bill Wilson gave much credit to Reverend and Mrs. Harris as well-springs of spiritual enrichment; and we think it fair to assume that Bill might have peered into the book-room at Calvary House during the two-and-a-half years he was associated with the Oxford Group, was present at Calvary House, and was preaching "the Oxford Group message to anybody who would listen."[60]

There was another point of Shoemaker impact. That was Calvary Rescue Mission. Ebby Thatcher had lived there. Bill had made a decision for Christ there. And, upon his discharge from Towns Hospital, Bill spent an enormous amount of time there working with drunks.[61] As his secretary recalled, he did this, many times, in the company of Hanford Twitchell, Treasurer of Calvary Church. Also, the staff at Calvary Mission, were under the direction of Shoemaker and his church.[62]

The bottom line here is that Bill Wilson was in close touch with many people who greatly admired Reverend Sam Shoemaker. These were people closely connected with Shoemaker, Calvary Church, the Oxford Group, and all of the Oxford Group outreach through books, meetings, houseparties, and teams. We know their names, and we have ample evidence of their familiarity with Oxford Group-Shoemaker principles. These people included the Reverends Cuyler, Harris, Hicks, Purdy, Smith, and Stearly. They included Mrs. Julia Harris and Eleanor Forde, and perhaps even Miss Olive Jones, who was a principal staff member at Calvary

---

[60] See *Pass It On*, pp. 131-133 for this phrase and further discussion of Bill's "preaching."

[61] See *Pass It On*, p. 131; Thomsen, *Bill W.*, pp. 231-232; *Lois Remembers*, pp. 91-92; and Nell Wing, *Grateful To Have Been There*, p. 68.

[62] Dick B., *The Oxford Group & Alcoholics Anonymous*, pp. 106-109; Cuyler, *Calvary Church in Action*, p. 67; Harris, *The Breeze of the Spirit*, p. 49; and *Pass It On*, p. 117.

Church and the author of two Oxford Group books.[63] They included Rowland Hazard, F. Shepard Cornell, Hanford Twitchell, Victor Kitchen, and Charles Clapp, Jr. And they included Oxford Group people that Bill met in company with Sam Shoemaker in Maryland and at houseparties.[64]

Then there is the whole Akron story we have told elsewhere in *The Akron Genesis of Alcoholics Anonymous*. While the Akron people, other than T. Henry Williams, possibly did not meet with Sam Shoemaker in A.A.'s formative days, they certainly read his books. There is ample evidence that Dr. Bob, his wife, Anne, T. Henry and Clarace Williams, and Henrietta Seiberling all read Shoemaker books and passed them around.[65] And we believe these A.A. "founders" probably utilized them in forming their recovery ideas. In other words, the Akron influence on Bill is not to be overlooked—even when it comes to Shoemaker; for Bill lived in Akron for three months and imbibed the Akron ideas while he and Dr. Bob were talking recovery. And that went on throughout the years before the Big Book was published. Moreover, we have previously mentioned, and Appendix 10 reports, that a large Oxford Group team from Calvary Church descended upon Ohio and also upon Akron in 1934, the year after the famous Firestone meetings and testimonials of 1933. These 1934 Oxford Group team activities in Akron provide new evidence that there may have been much more direct Oxford Group influence, literature, and

---

[63] Olive M. Jones, *Inspired Children* (New York: Harper & Bros., 1933); and *Inspired Youth* (New York: Harper & Bros., 1938).

[64] See, for example, as to James W. Houck, Dick B., *The Akron Genesis of Alcoholics Anonymous*, pp. 148-149; as to John Ryder, *Pass It On*, pp. 173-174 and Nell Wing, *Grateful To Have Been There*, p. 69.

[65] See the frequent references to the reading of Shoemaker books in all our books: Dick B., *Dr. Bob's Library* (West Virginia: The Bishop of Books, 1992); *Anne Smith's Spiritual Workbook* (Seattle: Glen Abbey Books, 1993); *The Oxford Group & Alcoholics Anonymous* (Seattle: Glen Abbey Books, 1992); *The Akron Genesis of Alcoholics Anonymous* (Seattle: Glen Abbey Books, 1992); and *The Books Early AAs Read For Spiritual Growth* (Seattle: Glen Abbey Books, 1993).

Shoemaker sway directly from the East Coast then has previously been thought.

7

Shoemaker and His Bible

We've seen the Bible in every book and on almost every page that Shoemaker wrote. And Dr. Bob said A.A. got its basic ideas from the Bible. Question: Did A.A.'s basic ideas from the Bible come from Sam Shoemaker, or partly from Shoemaker? And the answer is that they certainly could have. But whether Dr. Bob was referring to that fact is highly questionable, for the Akron AAs—including Bill Wilson when he was there—studied the Bible itself; and they also studied a huge amount of Biblically-oriented literature, a part of which was Shoemaker's, but most of which was neither Shoemaker nor Oxford Group writing.[1]

In a study of Shoemaker, one could devote endless pages to the Biblical quotes and ideas that Shoemaker used in his books, sermons, and teachings. But we believe he had a rather simple message from the Bible which he used, and which was largely adopted by Bill, as far as A.A.'s steps are concerned. We believe Shoemaker taught three basic ideas from the Bible, and that these were used by Wilson as he put his Big Book together: (1) How to find and know God through self-surrender to Him and removal of the barrier or blockage of sin. (2) How to maintain and grow in the experience of God, through seeking God's plan and guidance, and living in harmony with spiritual principles taught by His Son, Jesus Christ. (3) How to keep the experience through giving the

[1] See Dick B., *The Books Early AAs Read For Spiritual Growth* (Seattle: Glen Abbey Books, 1993).

experience away by witness, fellowship, and teamwork. In short, just as the Oxford Group was doing, Shoemaker was advocating life-changing through the power of, guidance from, and witness for God. And we will examine his use of the Bible from this perspective to see the sources in the Bible Shoemaker used to teach these messages.

Finding and Knowing God Through Surrender of Self

Shoemaker believed in the efficacy of an experiment of faith. For him, that experiment usually began out of necessity and often out of hopelessness. He put this idea forward in the first chapter of his first book and quoted Proverbs 16:25:

> There is a way that seemeth right unto a man, but the end thereof *are* the ways of death.[2]

From that point of commencement, Shoemaker was quite specific in citing Biblical references he felt showed a "way out." First, he said one must start with a belief that God is, and rewards those who diligently seek Him. He cited and referred to Hebrews 11:6:

> But without faith *it is* impossible to please *him* [God]: for he that cometh to God must believe that he is, and *that he* is a rewarder of them that diligently seek him.[3]

---

[2] Samuel Shoemaker, Jr., *Realizing Religion* (New York: Association Press, 1923), p. 7; and compare Big Book, p. 8 ["No words can tell of the loneliness and despair I found in that bitter morass of self-pity. Quicksand stretched around me in all directions. I had met my match. I had been overwhelmed. Alcohol was my master."].

[3] Samuel Shoemaker, Jr., *The Gospel According To You* (New York: Fleming H. Revell, 1934), p. 47; *National Awakening* (New York: Harper & Brothers, 1936), p. 40;
(continued...)

Next, one must *seek* God. And Shoemaker cited Matthew 6:33 from the Sermon on the Mount:

> But seek ye first the kingdom of God, and his righteousness; and all these things shall be added unto you.[4]

For those who did not or could not believe, or were still wondering about belief, Shoemaker suggested relying on the principle in his favorite verse, John 7:17:

> If any man will do his will, he shall know of the doctrine, *whether* it be of God, or whether I speak of myself.[5]

Man was to take the leap of faith by simply assuming that God is, and then seeking Him through obedience to His known will—living according to His precepts set forth in the Bible.

For the starting point in *obedience*, which was the act of decision to do God's will, Shoemaker often referred to four verses which he believed typified a surrender to God's will:

---

[3] (...continued)
Religion That Works (New York: Fleming H. Revell, 1928), p. 55; *Confident Faith* (New York: Fleming H. Revell, 1932), p. 187; and compare Big Book, p. 53 ["God either is, or He isn't"].

[4] Samuel Shoemaker, Jr., *National Awakening*, p. 41; *A Young Man's View of the Ministry* (New York: Association Press, 1923), p. 80; *Religion That Works*, p. 64-65; Compare *Confident Faith*, p. 107; Dick B., *The Akron Genesis of Alcoholics Anonymous* (Seattle: Glen Abbey Books, 1992), p. 109; *DR. BOB and the Good Oldtimers* (New York: Alcoholics Anonymous World Services, 1980), pp. 144, 192; and Big Book, p. 60 ["That God could and would if He were sought"].

[5] Samuel Shoemaker, Jr., *Religion That Works*, pp. 36, 46, 58, 64, 86; *Twice-Born Ministers* (New York: Fleming H. Revell, 1929), p. 56; *A Young Man's View of the Ministry*, p. 41; *The Church Can Save The World* (New York: Harper & Brothers, 1938), pp. 110-112; *God's Control* (New York: Fleming H. Revell, 1939), p. 35; *The Experiment of Faith* (New York: Harper & Brothers, 1957), p. 35; *Living Your Life Today* (New York: Fleming H. Revell, 1947), pp. 101-109; *How You Can Help Other People* (New York: E. P Dutton, 1946), p. 61; *How To Find God* (Reprint from *Faith at Work Magazine*, n.d.), pp. 5, 6, 15; *Under New Management* (Michigan: Zondervan Publishing House, 1966), p. 46; and compare Big Book, p. 47 ["Do I now believe, or am I even willing to believe. . . he is on his way"].

> Give in, admit that I am God [From Moffatt's Translation of Psalm 46:10].[6]

> Thy will be done in earth, *as it is* in heaven [From Matthew 6:10 in the Sermon on the Mount].[7]

> Nevertheless not my will, but thine, be done [From Luke 22:42].[8]

> Lord, what wilt thou have me to do? [From Acts 9:6].[9]

The next part of obedience involved the *action* that carried out the decision, namely, self-examination, confession, conviction, and conversion which moved a new person into a relationship with God and eliminated the barrier of sin. As to these action steps, Shoemaker mentioned the verses covered below:

> 1. [*Self-examination*] And why beholdest thou the mote that is in thy brother's eye, but considerest not the beam that is in thine own eye? Or how wilt thou say to thy brother, Let me pull out the mote out of thine eye; and behold, a beam *is* in thine own eye. Thou hypocrite, first cast out the beam out of thine own eye: and then shalt thou see clearly to cast out the mote out of thy brother's eye [From Matthew 7:3-5 in the Sermon on the Mount].[10]

---

[6] Shoemaker, *National Awakening*, pp. 45-46, 48, 51; and compare Big Book, p. 62 ["This is the how and why of it. First of all, we had to quit playing God. It didn't work."].

[7] See Samuel Shoemaker, Jr., *Children of the Second Birth* (New York: Fleming H. Revell, 1927), pp. 58, 175-187; *If I Be Lifted Up* (New York: Fleming H. Revell, 1931), p. 93; *How To Find God*, p. 10; and compare Big Book, pp. 67, 88, 85, 83.

[8] Shoemaker, *A Young Man's View of the Ministry*, p. 70; *Children of the Second Birth*, p. 58; *Religion That Works*, p. 19; *If I Be Lifted Up*, p. 93; and compare Big Book, p. 85.

[9] Shoemaker, *A Young Man's View of the Ministry*, pp. 80, 86; *Religion That Works*, p. 65; *Confident Faith*, pp. 107, 110, 115.

[10] Shoemaker, *The Church Can Save The World*, pp. 81-121; *God's Control*, pp. 62-72.

> 2. [*Confession*] Confess *your* faults one to another [From James 5:16].[11]
>
> 3. [*Conviction*] This is a faithful saying, and worthy of all acceptation, that Christ Jesus came into the world to save sinners; of whom I am chief [1 Timothy 1:15].[12]
>
> 4. [*Conversion*] Except a man be born again, he cannot see the Kingdom of God [From John 3:3].[13]

The last step in the life-changing surrender process was making restitution or restoration; and Shoemaker referred to these verses from the Sermon on the Mount:

> Therefore if thou bring thy gift before the altar, and there rememberest that thy brother hath ought against thee; Leave there thy gift before the altar, and go thy way; first be reconciled to thy brother, and then come and offer thy gift [Matthew 5:23-24].[14]

Maintaining and Continuing in the Experience of God

There certainly were two ideas from the Bible that Shoemaker considered to be a vital part of what he and the Oxford Group

---

[11] Samuel Shoemaker, Jr., *The Conversion of the Church* (New York: Fleming H. Revell, 1932), pp. 35, 36, 39; and see A.A.'s Fifth Step and *Pass It On* (New York: Alcoholics Anonymous World Services, 1984), p. 128.

[12] Shoemaker, *The Gospel According To You*, pp. 157-167; *Realizing Religion* (New York: Association Press, 1923), pp. 21, 82; *The Church Can Save The World*, pp. 153, 93-94; and compare A.A.'s Sixth Step and Mel B., *New Wine* (Minnesota: Hazelden, 1992), pp. 34-35.

[13] Shoemaker, *National Awakening*, pp. 55-66; *Children of the Second Birth*, p. 32; *Realizing Religion*, pp. 21, 35; *God's Control*, p. 137; and compare Big Book, p. 63.

[14] Shoemaker, *The Conversion of the Church*, pp. 47-48; *The Gospel According To You*, p. 149; and Steps Eight and Nine.

called "Continuance" or "Conservation." The first had to do with the guidance of God and Quiet Time; and the second had to do with living by Christ's standards as Dr. Robert E. Speer had expressed them in the "four absolutes" or "four standards"—honesty, purity, unselfishness and love.

(1) [*The Guidance of God and the Will of God*] Quiet Time primarily involved Bible study, prayer, and listening for leading thoughts from God, all of these to determine the general and the particular will of God. As to Bible study, there are many verses in the Bible which call for "searching the Scriptures;" Shoemaker touched on this one:

> Search the scriptures; for in them ye think ye have eternal life: and they are they which testify of me [John 5:30].[15]

Similarly, though he could have cited endless verses to support his stress on *prayer*, including James 5:16 (which was a favorite in early A.A.), he did not seem to feel it necessary to support this point with Bible citations.

When it came to "listening to God," however, it was a different story. Over and over, Shoemaker suggested that man must listen for the voice of God, citing 1 Samuel 3:9:

> Speak, LORD, for thy servant heareth.[16]

Another verse he used to illustrate this idea was:

> What shall I do, Lord? [Acts 22:10].[17]

---

[15] Shoemaker, *Realizing Religion*, p. 60.

[16] Shoemaker, *Children of the Second Birth*, p. 16; *National Awakening*, pp. 78-88; *The Church Can Save The World*, p. 30; *God's Control*, pp. 115-116.

[17] Shoemaker, *Confident Faith*, pp. 107, 110, 115.

And he certainly believed that, as Jesus promised, God's Holy Spirit will guide us into all truth. He referred, in this connection, to John 16:13:

> Howbeit when he, the Spirit of truth, is come, he will guide you into all truth; for he shall not speak of himself; but whatsoever he shall hear, *that* shall he speak: and he will shew you things to come.[18]

He continually stressed the importance of doing the will of God, citing, for example, the following from the Sermon on the Mount:

> Not every one that saith unto me, Lord, Lord, shall enter into the kingdom of heaven; but he that doeth the will of my Father which is in heaven [Matthew 7:21].[19]

And Shoemaker fervently believed that the Holy Spirit would reveal God's thoughts and will to the minds of men.[20]

(2) [*The Four Absolutes*] For Shoemaker, the will of God required reaching out to, and endeavoring to live up to the Four Absolutes—the standards of Christ. We did not find him citing any particular verse for the idea of *honesty*; though he certainly referred to 1 Corinthians 13, which included honesty in its definition of love.[21] For *purity*, he quoted Matthew 5:8: "Blessed *are* the pure in heart: for they shall see God."[22] For *unselfishness*, he referred to 1 Thessalonians 2:8:

---

[18] Shoemaker, *The Conversion of the Church*, pp. 52-53.

[19] Shoemaker, *A Young Man's View of the Ministry* (New York: Association Press, 1923), p. 86; *Children of the Second Birth*, p. 182; *Religion That Works*, p. 65.

[20] Samuel Shoemaker, Jr., *With the Holy Spirit and With Fire* (New York: Harper & Brothers, 1960), pp. 30-32.

[21] Shoemaker, *Realizing Religion*, p. 50. See 1 Corinthians 13:6: [Love] "rejoiceth in the truth."

[22] Samuel Shoemaker, Jr., *The Experiment of Faith* (New York: Harper & Brothers, 1957), p. 36.

> So being affectionately desirous of you, we were willing to have imparted unto you, not the gospel of God only, but also our own souls, because ye were dear to us.[23]

And, while he made many references to verses on *love*, he cited 1 John 4:20 with particular force:

> If a man say, I love God, and hateth his brother, he is a liar: for he that loveth not his brother whom he hath seen, how can he love God whom he hath not seen?[24]

Giving the Experience Away to Keep It

Shoemaker utilized several verses to point up witnessing, fellowship, and teamwork.

Witnessing

Bill Wilson himself had early caught, from his Oxford Group association, the idea of "fishing for men."[25] And Shoemaker often used this expression in referring to Jesus's invitation to his first apostles:

> And he [Jesus] saith unto them, Follow me, and I will make you fishers of men [Matthew 4:19].[26]

---

[23] Shoemaker, *Realizing Religion*, p. 83; *The Conversion of the Church*, p. 39.

[24] Shoemaker, *The Conversion of the Church*, p. 47.

[25] *Lois Remembers* (New York: Al-Anon Family Group Headquarters, 1987), p. 88.

[26] Samuel Shoemaker, Jr., *Twice-Born Ministers*, p. 16; *Realizing Religion*, p. 82; *Revive Thy Church Beginning With Me* (New York: Harper & Brothers, 1948), p. 113. See also Garth D. Lean, *On The Tail of A Comet* (Colorado Springs: Helmers & Howard, 1988), p. 157.

As a correlative verse, Shoemaker mentioned the manner in which the early apostles witnessed to one another. They did not argue or preach; they simply said: "Come and see.":

> Philip findeth Nathanael, and saith unto him, We have found him, of whom Moses in the law, and the prophets did write, Jesus of Nazareth, the son of Joseph. And Nathanael said unto him, Can there be any good thing come out of Nazareth? Philip saith unto him, Come and see [John 1:45-46].[27]

Fellowship

Shoemaker believed the best base for witnessing is a working fellowship of witnessing Christians. He cited as an example 1 John 1:3:

> That which we have seen and heard declare we unto you, that ye also may have fellowship with us: and truly our fellowship is with the Father, and with his Son Jesus Christ.[28]

In two early books, Shoemaker placed great emphasis on *fellowship* as a critical factor in spiritual growth and witnessing. In *Religion That Works*, he wrote a chapter on "The Fellowship Of The Holy Ghost;" and his theme verse was 2 Corinthians 13:14:

> The grace of the Lord Jesus Christ, and the love of God, and the communion of the Holy Ghost, *be* with you all. Amen.[29]

In *The Conversion of the Church*, he wrote a chapter which was entitled "The Genius Of Fellowship;" and it was largely devoted to an account of the way the Communion of Saints worked

---

[27] Shoemaker, *Realizing Religion*, p. 74.

[28] Shoemaker, *Twice-Born Ministers*, pp. 181-182.

[29] See Shoemaker, *Religion That Works*, pp. 66-76; and note that Shoemaker used a translation of this verse that rendered the word "fellowship" instead of "communion."

together in the First Century Church. He cited whole portions from the Book of Acts.[30]

In *They're On The Way*, Shoemaker expressed again an idea he had taught many times before—an idea which caught hold in A.A. He said:

> The best way to keep what you have is to give it away, and no substitute has ever been found for personal Christian witness.[31]

Teamwork

We pointed out earlier that Reverend "Sherry" Day had written of seven primary New Testament principles which represented the Biblical principles of the Oxford Group and which also were part of the credo which Day shared with Shoemaker. One of the principles was "teamwork." Shoemaker's assistant minister, Irving Harris, summarized this Biblical principle as follows:

> Jesus Christ practiced teamwork. He gathered a small group of workers about Him and in this respect set an example for His followers. He believed that the highest light for the individual is to be found in association with others, in the group, in His church. When His followers were "of one mind, of one accord, in one place," the Spirit came. His teachings emphasized corporate life; the individual was to play his all-important part in a well-coordinated whole.[32]

---

[30] See also Samuel Shoemaker, Jr., *With The Holy Spirit and With Fire*, pp. 51, 58, 79; *They're On The Way* (New York: E. P. Dutton, 1951), pp. 158-159.

[31] Samuel Shoemaker, Jr., *They're on The Way*, p. 159; *How To Become A Christian* (New York: Harper & Brothers, 1953), p. 80; *The Church Alive* (New York: E. P. Dutton & Co., 1951), p. 139; *One Boy's Influence* (New York: Association Press, 1925), p. 15.

[32] Irving Harris, *The Breeze of the Spirit* (New York: The Seabury Press, 1978), p. 20.

The Biblical foundations for this statement are not hard to find. Thus Philippians 2:2,5 state:

> Fulfil ye my joy, that ye be likeminded, having the same love, *being* of one accord, of one mind. . . . Let this mind be in you, which was also in Christ Jesus.

And, in that great account of the birth of the Christian Church on the Day of Pentecost, Acts 2:1 states:

> And when the day of Pentecost was fully come, they were all with one accord in one place.

We have previously pointed to Shoemaker's emphasis on the First Century Christian Fellowship idea of the Spirit's guiding through a corporate experience.

Several of the "teamwork" concepts seem to be present in the language and ideas of A.A.: (1) a "Fellowship." (2) the "Group." (3) the idea of "a loving God as He may express Himself in our *group* conscience [emphasis ours]."[33] (4) the A.A. Legacy of *Unity*.[34] (5) The fact that each of the Twelve Steps either expressly or by implication begins with the word "we." (6) The fact that AAs frequently speak of their program as a "we" program. (7) A.A.'s Tradition Five which defines each group's primary purpose as being to help others who still suffer.[35]

---

[33] A.A. Tradition Two; see Big Book, p. 564.

[34] See *Alcoholics Anonymous Comes of Age* (New York: Alcoholics Anonymous World Services, Inc., 1957), pp. 49, 79-137 (discussing the legacy of "Unity").

[35] See Tradition Five; Big Book, p. 564.

8

The Striking Shoemaker Language in A.A.

By now the reader certainly has seen the large number of Shoemaker words, phrases, and ideas that have parallels in A.A.'s Big Book and Twelve Steps. Shoemaker himself observed the parallels. In Appendix 9 of our book, *The Akron Genesis of Alcoholics Anonymous*, we set out a large number of words, phrases, and ideas from Oxford Group, Shoemaker, and other Christian writings that were used by early AAs and which seem to have a counter-part in the Big Book.[1] In this portion of our Shoemaker book, we will simply highlight some of the clearest parallels between Shoemaker's language and that in A.A. We hope this will entice the reader to return to other examples we have covered earlier in this book and elsewhere.

The reader might justifiably conclude that some of the parallel expressions were not the peculiar property either of Shoemaker or the Oxford Group; but the reader must note the limited spiritual community in which Bill Wilson was hearing and developing his spiritual tools and spiritual recovery program. The expressions we have set forth below were the expressions Bill *was* hearing as he was learning Oxford Group ideas, learning how to find God, and learning how a spiritual experience could be achieved.

---

[1] Dick B., *The Akron Genesis of Alcoholics Anonymous* (Seattle: Glen Abbey Books, 1992), pp. 359-367.

Here are some very probable sources of Big Book language as they were expressed by Shoemaker:

1. I've got religion.[2]
2. What you want is simply a vital religious experience.[3]
3. Spiritual awakening.[4]
4. Spiritual experience.[5]
5. Relationship with God.[6]
6. A Personal God.[7]
7. Selfishness . . . self-centeredness.[8]
8. Self-will seems the blackest sin of all.[9]
9. You need to find God.[10]
10. For most men, the world is centered in self.[11]
11. God is and is a Rewarder of them that seek Him.[12]
12. Marvel at what God has done for you.[13]

---

[2] Shoemaker, *Children of the Second Birth* (New York: Fleming H. Revell, 1927), p. 118, 165. Big Book, p. 9.

[3] Shoemaker, *Realizing Religion* (New York: Association Press, 1923), p. 9. Big Book, p. 28.

[4] Shoemaker, *National Awakening* (New York: Harper & Brothers, 1936), p. 3. Big Book, p. 60.

[5] Shoemaker, *Twice-Born Ministers* (New York: Fleming H. Revell, 1929), p. 61. Big Book, p. 25.

[6] Shoemaker, *Children of the Second Birth*, p. 16. Big Book, p. 29.

[7] Shoemaker, *Children of the Second Birth*, p. 61; *Christ's Word's From The Cross* (New York: Fleming H. Revell, 1933), p. 43. Big Book, p. 10.

[8] Shoemaker, *Twice-Born Ministers*, p. 154. Big Book, p. 62.

[9] Shoemaker, *Realizing Religion*, p. 31. Big Book, p. 60.

[10] Shoemaker, *Realizing Religion*, p. 9. Big Book, p. 59.

[11] Shoemaker, *Realizing Religion*, p. 11. Big Book, p. 64.

[12] Shoemaker, *Religion That Works* (New York: Fleming H. Revell, 1928), p. 68; *The Gospel According To You* (New York: Fleming H. Revell, 1934), p. 47. Big Book, p. 60.

[13] Shoemaker, *If I Be Lifted Up* (New York: Fleming H. Revell, 1931), p. 34. Big Book, pp. 11, 84.

13. God is, or He isn't.[14]
14. Self-sufficiency . . . God-sufficiency.[15]
15. Self-pity, self-will, self-centeredness.[16]
16. Abandon yourself to Him [God].[17]
17. As much of God as he understood.[18]
18. The turning point.[19]
19. A vast Power outside themselves.[20]
20. That Power was the one solution.[21]
21. Nevertheless, not my will but Thine.[22]
22. I do feel reborn.[23]
23. Turned over to Him her life for His direction.[24]
24. Thy will be done.[25]
25. He made his decision.[26]
26. Let go and let God![27]

---

[14] Shoemaker, *Confident Faith* (New York: Fleming H. Revell, 1933), p. 187. Big Book, pp. 11, 84.

[15] Shoemaker, *If I Be Lifted Up*, p. 107. Big Book, p. 52-53.

[16] Shoemaker, *God's Control* (New York: Fleming H. Revell, 1939), p. 57. Big Book, p. 62.

[17] Shoemaker, *Religion That Works*, p. 19. Big Book, p. 164.

[18] Shoemaker, *Children of the Second Birth*, pp. 47, 25; *The Gospel According to You*, p. 128. Big Book, pp. 67, 88.

[19] Shoemaker, *Realizing Religion*, p. 30. Big Book, p. 59.

[20] Shoemaker, *A Young Man's View of the Ministry* (New York: Association Press, 1923), p. 42. Big Book, p. 46.

[21] Shoemaker, *Children of the Second Birth*, p. 45. Big Book, p. 45.

[22] Shoemaker, *A Young Man's View of the Ministry*, p. 70. Big Book, p. 85.

[23] Shoemaker, *Children of the Second Birth*, p. 25. Big Book, p. 63.

[24] Shoemaker, *Children of the Second Birth*, p. 82. This is very similar to the language of A.A.'s Third Step as it was written in the multi-lith copy that preceded publication of the First Edition of the Big Book.

[25] Shoemaker, *Children of the Second Birth*, pp. 175-192. Big Book, pp. 67, 88.

[26] Shoemaker, *Children of the Second Birth*, p. 125. Big Book, pp. 62, 64.

[27] Shoemaker, *Religion That Works*, p. 19; *Twice-Born Ministers*, p. 20, 106. A popular A.A. slogan, also used by Bill Wilson in *Alcoholics Anonymous Comes of Age* (New York: Alcoholics Anonymous World Services, 1957), p. 48.

27. Sharing to the limit of my own experience.[28]
28. There was a restitution I would not make.[29]
29. Consciousness of God's presence.[30]
30. The decision to cast my will and my life on God.[31]
31. Make things right with people I had wronged.[32]
32. A Force outside himself, greater than himself.[33]
33. Confess your sins one to another.[34]
34. God is God, and self is not God.[35]
35. We had given up self-will and put God's will in its place.[36]
36. We must share our own fault.[37]
37. An overwhelming sense of the Presence of God.[38]
38. There is a good deal of sorrow in our life of our own making.[39]
39. If the person is honest with himself and with God, he will be honest also with us.[40]
40. A very large part of human misery is of our own making.[41]

---

[28] Shoemaker, *Twice-Born Ministers*, p. 56. Big Book, pp. 92-93.

[29] Shoemaker, *Twice-Born Ministers,* p. 92. Big Book, p. 76.

[30] Shoemaker, *Twice-Born Ministers*, p. 123. Big Book, p. 51.

[31] Shoemaker, *Twice-Born Ministers*, p. 134. Big Book, p. 60.

[32] Shoemaker, *Twice-Born Ministers*, p. 166. Big Book, p. 76.

[33] Shoemaker, *If I Be Lifted Up*, p. 176. Big Book, p. 46.

[34] Shoemaker, *The Conversion of the Church* (New York: Fleming H. Revell, 1932), p. 35. A.A. Step Five.

[35] Shoemaker, *National Awakening*, p. 48. Big Book, p. 62.

[36] Shoemaker, *God's Control*, p. 68. Big Book, pp. 68, 71.

[37] Shoemaker, *Confident Faith*, p. 26. Big Book, p. 67.

[38] Shoemaker, *Confident Faith*, p. 57. Big Book, p. 56.

[39] Shoemaker, *Confident Faith*, p. 149. Big Book, p. 62.

[40] Shoemaker, *The Church Can Save The World* (New York: Harper & Brothers, 1938), p. 112. Big Book, p. 72.

[41] Shoemaker, *The Gospel According To You* (New York: Fleming H. Revell, 1934), p. 38. Big Book, p. 103.

9

Shoemaker Ideas That "Took" in A.A.

One could reach any number of conclusions as to where the real impact from Shoemaker can be found in A.A. Also conclude that Shoemaker had no corner on the market. Many A.A. ideas which can be identified in Shoemaker writings can also be found in the Bible early AAs studied. They can be found in the Oxford Group literature (other than Shoemaker's) AAs read. They can be found in many other Christian books that were making the rounds in A.A. They can be found in the writings of Dr. Bob's wife, Anne; and, to a *very* limited extent, in the writings of Emmet Fox, which some early AAs read.

But we have been looking at Bill's personal involvement with Shoemaker and the Shoemaker circle. We've reviewed the specific Shoemaker words and phrases in A.A.; and we have quoted Bill's and Shoemaker's own remarks about their relationship. All these items have led the author to believe that about a dozen Shoemaker concepts hit Bill Wilson hard. We phrase the Shoemaker ideas in our own words and refer the reader to our foregoing chapters for specific supporting references. Here, we believe, among others, are a dozen Shoemaker ideas that "took" in A.A.:

1. **Start from necessity**. People seek to find and know God and His power because of necessity—a necessity arising from their estrangement from God, the spiritual misery coming from that, their need for relief, and the unmanageable circumstances in their lives. Shoemaker often spoke of the estrangement from a loving

God that exists in people whom He meant to be His companions. And the Big Book, and particularly its earliest drafts, spoke much about seeking, finding, and "rediscovering" God, and also of the necessity for doing it. Shoemaker defined people's spiritual misery in terms of their self-made religion or lack of it, and their making or wanting to make "self" God or like God—a problem that Adam and Eve encountered. And the Big Book not only defined man's spiritual misery in terms of focus on self, self-will, and self-centeredness, but also suggested that the suffering person needs to make a decision to quit playing God. Playing God didn't work, said the Big Book. Shoemaker believed people turn to God out of their own necessity for help. And the Big Book speaks specifically of the alcoholic's need for divine help—God's help—with the alcohol problem and with ego problems such as anger, fear, and dishonesty that arise from self-centeredness.

Whence came the idea that AAs needed to admit that their lives had become unmanageable? In answer, we'd point to the "unmanageability prayer" that appeared at Dr. Frank Buchman's Oxford Group meetings, in Oxford Group writings, in Anne Smith's spiritual workbook, and in Shoemaker's own Calvary Church. The *necessity and longing* for God, plus an unmanageable life brings man *to* God, taught Sam Shoemaker. He said there was a gap that man was *powerless* to bridge.

A.A.'s First Step is founded upon the *powerless* and *unmanageable* ideas.

2. **Utilize an experiment of faith**. In their quest for God's help and power, people can either turn to the God in which they believe and about whom they have some understanding; or they can start with an experiment of faith. They *must* start with the belief that God IS, said Shoemaker. God either is or He isn't, he taught. So said Bill Wilson in the Big Book. On the other hand, if people have no belief or are unbelievers, they may start with an experiment. They can "surrender as much of themselves as they know to as much of God as they understand." Not much understanding may exist or be possible for many, said Shoemaker,

but start they must. And Shoemaker and many AAs have said such people can *begin* to believe when they "see God or Power" in the life of someone else. They can then "act as if," to use Shoemaker's expression. They can commence by choosing their own idea of that power *for a beginning*, take the action that successful believers took, and find God through their own experience—an experience sure to produce consciousness of the power and presence of God. Either believe and pray; or be *willing to believe*, *act*, *then pray and see* the experience of God happen. Shoemaker and A.A. seemed agreed on that.

3. **Make self-surrender the turning point**. The experiment of faith begins with a crisis of self-surrender. William James made that point. Shoemaker espoused it over and over. Both Shoemaker and the Big Book characterized the surrender to God as an act in which the declarant humbly "gives in," and admits that God is God and says: *Thy* will, not mine, be done. This is the turning point.

4. **Use the Bible as the source for God's universal will**. Where do you find the will of God? There was no question in Shoemaker's mind. You look first in the Bible. Then, as we mention in the next point (Five), you pray, and you "listen" for revelation from God of His particular will. Dr. Bob and Anne Smith did all three. So did Bill Wilson at the beginning. There was *daily* Bible study, prayer, and Quiet Time during Bill Wilson's three month stay with Dr. Bob and Anne Smith in Akron in the summer of 1935. Some very important spiritual principles, acknowledged by early AAs to constitute the will of God, were found in the Four Absolute Standards of Jesus Christ (culled from Dr. Robert E. Speer's views of the teachings of Jesus Christ in the Bible). "Essential" principles, to use Dr. Bob's expression, were also found in the Sermon on the Mount, 1 Corinthians 13, and the Book of James. Shoemaker taught on these. And these ideas became lodged, early in A.A., in its concepts of honesty, purity,

unselfishness, love, forgiveness, patience, tolerance, kindness, and the need for making restitution.

5. **Stress prayer and listening**. What was the place of prayer? Shoemaker taught that man's big job was to ask God what He wants and expect to hear from Him, instead of telling Him what man wants and then asserting God doesn't exist or won't help when that person doesn't get what he or she asked for. A.A. embodied this idea in its "prayer and meditation" language and in the concept of "praying only" for a knowledge of God's will and the power to carry it out. "Speak, Lord, thy servant heareth," was the stance Shoemaker urged. "Lord, what wilt thou have me to do?" was the approach Shoemaker taught. Then, said he, say to God: "Thy will be done." This language, of course, came directly from the Bible, and it often appears in the Big Book.

6. **Eliminate the blocks to God**. People must eliminate the blockage from and barriers to God. "*Sins*," Shoemaker called them. And so did early A.A. Sin, said both, involved those defects or weaknesses in human character—primarily centered in self—which kept man from seeing, knowing, and experiencing God. Spiritual misery, Shoemaker called it. A spiritual malady, the Big Book called it. All the same, *blockage*. The blocks were the common manifestations of self, the unsuccessful king. And the most objectionable blocks were resentments or grudges, fears, dishonesty, self-will or self-seeking, and *pride*. The last (and deadliest), said Shoemaker, simply meant that man was standing in the place of God instead of standing aside for Him.

7. **Follow a surrender path**. How did you eliminate the sin, the barriers, the blocks? In his very first book, *Realizing Religion*, Shoemaker talked about employing the Oxford Group's Five C's—"confidence, confession, conviction, conversion, and continuance." Did these conceptions involve "works" instead of God's "grace?" We leave an analysis of that theological question to others, but we did discuss it in our previous book on the Oxford

Group and A.A. However, *action* was considered, both by Shoemaker and in the language of the Big Book, to be necessary for bringing a person into a relationship with God and moving his life from sin into harmony with God's will. In the Oxford Group and in Shoemaker's view, you accomplished this through a life-changing process which involved the help of another. A changed person gained the *confidence* of the initiate in need; led that person to share or *confess*; brought him or her to a *conviction* that he or she had fallen short of God's plan and must change; helped with the *conversion*, through a surrender to God of the initiate's will, sins, and ego; and then helped that person *continue* the experience. This continuance meant drawing on God's power and guidance and then making things right with others, continuing to eliminate sins, trying to live by spiritual principles, and passing the experience *and* the principles on to others. There are clear parallels in A.A.

8. **Have a conversion experience or spiritual awakening**. What was the end result? A conversion experience, a religious experience, a spiritual experience, a maximum experience of Jesus Christ, God-consciousness, a spiritual awakening—all basically synonymous terms used by Shoemaker and, with the exception of the "Christ" experience, by the Big Book.

9. **Acknowledge that it was God's doing, not yours**. Realize that the life-change resulted from a miracle from God, not simply from man's work. Marvel at what God has done for you, said Shoemaker, not at what you have done for yourself. Realize that a miracle has occurred and that God has done for you what you could not do for yourself, said the Big Book in several ways.

10. **Belong to a fellowship**. Recognize the importance of Fellowship. AAs often point to the fact that the Twelve Steps begin with the word "we." Whether one is talking about the Fellowship of the Holy Spirit, as Shoemaker did; or a "koinonia" like that in the First Century Church, to which Shoemaker often referred; or simply a "Fellowship of the Spirit," of which the Big

Book speaks on page 164, Shoemaker and A.A. were both talking about fellowship as a vital medium for sharing experience, strength, and hope.

11. **Focus on a group**. Accept the importance of a "group." One might question whether the idea of a small group's importance was transmitted by Shoemaker to A.A. We can only say that Shoemaker came down hard on the importance of a "group" or "cell" within the church as being the place for dynamic life-changing to occur. And one need only read A.A. traditions and examine A.A. structure to see that AAs focus on the "group" as the means by which members of their fellowship can maintain their own awakening and help others to achieve that experience.

12. **Witness—pass it on**. Focus on witness, helping others, passing the life-change experience on. In one sense, the largest "Step" chapter in the Big Book is entitled, "Working With Others." The major focus of A.A. is on the "group's" having but one primary purpose—carrying the message; and on the individual's being responsible for reaching out with that message to, and helping, the alcoholic who still suffers.

10

Conclusion

Sam Shoemaker, and the "First Century Christian Fellowship" of which Shoemaker was an important American leader, were indispensable elements in the development of A.A.'s spiritual program of recovery and the spiritual tools A.A. uses today. And we have set out the relevant evidence about Shoemaker and his background, his Oxford Group status, his specific links with A.A., the relevant details in his writings and teachings, and the traces of his ideas in A.A.

For a moment, we propose to turn to the program of recovery Dr. Bob used at the height of early A.A.'s development and success in Akron. And for these three reasons: First, one could very easily show that—without any Shoemaker connection at all—the basic elements of the Akron program can be found in the Bible and in the practices of the Oxford Group. Second, one could make a strong case that Shoemaker's writings, and his part in the A.A.-Oxford Group link on America's East Coast, certainly put flesh on every one of the basic recovery ideas Akron used. Finally, whether its roots sprang from the Bible, the Oxford Group, Shoemaker, or all three, the Akron program was the recovery program that really enabled Bill Wilson to sell A.A.'s ideas to others and to publish the Big Book.

On these points, let's see what Bill himself said. Of Dr. Bob's work, Bill wrote:

> It had been decided that Bob would attend mostly to the questions of hospitalization and the development of our Twelfth Step work. . . . Dr. Bob became the prince of all twelfth-steppers. Perhaps nobody will ever do such a job again.[1]

At a much earlier date, Bill wrote:

> At Akron, Ohio, there is a physician, Dr. Robert H. Smith, who has been responsible during the last four years for the recovery of at least 100 chronic alcoholics of types hitherto regarded by the medical profession as hopeless. . . . The possible recovery among such cases has suddenly been lifted from almost nil to at least 50 percent, which, quite aside from its social implications, is a medical result of the first magnitude. Though, as a means of our recovery, we all engage in the work, Dr. Smith has had more experience and has obtained better results than anyone else.[2]

The Big Book itself states, at page 171:

> To 1950, the year of his death, he [Dr. Bob] carried the A.A. message to more than 5,000 alcoholic men and women, and to all these he gave his medical services without thought of charge.

And the fact is that A.A.'s co-founder, Dr. Bob, was, in the early days, basically "in charge" of personal outreach, employing a very

---

[1] *The Co-Founders of Alcoholics Anonymous. Biographical sketches. Their last major talks* (New York: Alcoholics Anonymous World Services, 1972, 1975), p. 27.

[2] *DR. BOB and the Good Oldtimers* (New York: Alcoholics Anonymous World Services, Inc., 1980), pp. 173-74.

simple program for recovery from alcoholism.[3] And he used it to help over 5,000 alcoholics in the fifteen years he was sober.[4]

Anne Ripley Smith, Dr. Bob's wife, was called the "Mother of A.A."[5] She and Dr. Bob believed in God, and virtually the first question Dr. Bob asked a newcomer was: "Do you believe in God?"[6] The Smiths believed that God is love.[7] They believed in the power of prayer. Dr. Bob prayed three times a day; he prayed for others; and morning prayer and Bible sessions in the Smith home were regular fare.[8] Dr. Bob and his wife studied the Bible to learn about God, to learn about His "rules of the road," and to learn about prayer.[9]

Dr. Bob utilized the Oxford Group concepts of moral inventory, confession, and restitution to help alcoholics to remove "sin" and shortcomings from their lives.[10] He was always a firm advocate of using the Oxford Group's Four absolutes–honesty, purity, unselfishness, and love–as "yardsticks" to bring a person's

---

[3] For one description of that program, see the story of Earl T. at page 292 of the Big Book. Earl described Dr. Bob's Six-Step program as follows: (1) Complete deflation; (2) Dependence and guidance from a Higher Power; (3) Moral inventory; (4) Confession; (5) Restitution; and (6) Continued work with other alcoholics. The program was summarized and presented in a bit more detail by John D. Rockefeller's aide, Frank Amos, as follows: (1) Admit to being a medically incurable alcoholic; (2) Surrender absolutely to God, admitting that there is no hope in yourself; (3) Remove sins from your life; (4) Engage in daily Quiet Time with prayer, Bible study, and spiritual reading; (5) Help other alcoholics; and, (6) though not required, meet frequently with other recovered alcoholics in a social and religious fellowship, and attend some religious service at least once weekly. See *DR. BOB*, p. 131.

[4] Big Book, p. 171.

[5] As to Anne Ripley Smith's being called by Bill Wilson, and others, the "Mother of A.A.," see Bob Smith and Sue Smith Windows, *Children of the Healer* (Illinois: Parkside Publishing Corporation, 1992), pp. 29, 43, 132; and Dick B., *The Akron Genesis of Alcoholics Anonymous* (Seattle: Glen Abbey Books, 1992), pp. 107-109.

[6] *DR. BOB*, p. 144.

[7] *DR. BOB*, pp. 110, 117; and see 1 John 4:8, 16.

[8] Dick B., *The Akron Genesis of Alcoholics Anonymous*, pp. 204-08.

[9] Dick B., *The Akron Genesis of Alcoholics Anonymous*, pp. 111, 127-28, 208-12.

[10] Big Book, p. 292.

behavior into line with the will of God.[11] He emphasized that early AAs got their basic ideas from their study of the Bible—the "Good Book," as he called it.[12] He named the parts of the Bible he considered "absolutely essential": the Sermon on the Mount, 1 Corinthians 13, and the Book of James.[13] All Dr. Bob's simple recovery tools—(1) belief in God, (2) prayer, (3) listening for God's guidance, (4) inventory, (5) confession of faults, (6) making restitution, and (7) service to others—can certainly be found in the Good Book, mostly in the parts Dr. Bob specifically mentioned.[14]

On the practical side, Dr. Bob said in his farewell address to A.A.: "Our Twelve Steps, when simmered down to the last, resolve themselves into the words 'love' and 'service.'"[15] Dr.

---

[11] *DR. BOB*, p. 54.

[12] *DR. BOB*, pp. 96-97.

[13] *DR. BOB*, p. 96.

[14] (1) As to belief in God, see Hebrews 11:6. (2) As to prayer, see James 5:16; Matthew 6:5-13; and *DR. BOB*, pp. 228, 111. (3) As to the guidance of God, see, for example, Psalm 32:8 and Proverbs 3:6; Henry Drummond, *The Ideal Life* (New York: Hodder & Stoughton, 1897), p. 282; Wright, *The Will of God*, pp. 19, 131; B. H. Streeter, *The God Who Speaks* (London: MacMillan & Co., 1943), pp. 141, 191; Clarence I. Benson, *The Eight Points of the Oxford Group* (London: Oxford University Press, 1936), pp. 80-81; and Philip Marshall Brown, *The Venture of Belief* (New York: Fleming H. Revell, 1937), p. 40. (4) As to "inventory"—looking for the log in your own eye—see Matthew 7:3-5. (5) As to confession—confessing faults one to another—see James 5:16. (6) As to restitution, see Matthew 5:23-24; Luke chapter 15; Luke 19:1-10; Numbers 5:6-7; and Dick B., *The Oxford Group & Alcoholics Anonymous* (Seattle: Glen Abbey Books, 1992), pp. 180-86. (7) As to the importance of helping others, see the story of the "Good Samaritan" in Luke 10:25-37. At the end of the story, Jesus commands: "Go, and do thou likewise" (Luke 10:37). See also the Big Book, p. 97.

As to God's being love, see 1 John 4:8.

As to the four "absolute" standards of love—honesty, purity, unselfishness, and love, see Robert E. Speer, *The Principles of Jesus* (New York: Fleming H. Revell, 1902), pp. 33-35; Henry B. Wright, *The Will of God and a Man's Lifework* (New York: The Young Men's Christian Association Press, 1909), pp. 167-218; Samuel Shoemaker, Jr., *How To Become A Christian* (New York: Harper & Brothers, 1953), p. 57; and Dick B., *The Oxford Group & Alcoholics Anonymous*, pp. 219-30.

As to the ingredients of "love," see 1 Corinthians 13; Henry Drummond, *The Greatest Thing In The World* (London: Collins, 1953); and *DR. BOB*, pp. 310, 96.

[15] *DR. BOB*, p. 338.

Bob was often quoted as saying of A.A.'s program, "Keep it simple."[16] And one distinguished historian concluded that this "keep it simple" advice exemplified a wariness of argument, analysis, and explanation; and constituted Dr. Bob's chief contribution to A.A.[17] We prefer to say, however, that—after an immense amount of Bible study, prayer, spiritual reading, and experience in working successfully with drunks—Dr. Bob's program *evolved* into a simple one.

Further, Dr. Bob's remarks about simplicity often had to do with toning down Bill Wilson's seemingly grandiose ideas and also with a concern that A.A. might "louse it [A.A.] up with Freudian complexes and things that are interesting to the scientific mind, but have very little to do with our actual A.A. work."[18] In contrast to his disdain for the program's becoming involved in *scientific* matters, Dr. Bob never shirked investigation and growth in *spiritual* subjects. He studied the Bible every day.[19] He continually read spiritual literature.[20] He urged, without pushing, that others do likewise.[21] And Dr. Bob's simple *program*, coupled with his intense interest in spiritual growth—through Bible study, prayer, and reading—is what brings us back to Sam Shoemaker in our conclusion.

One might ask why—if early AAs had the Bible in front of them, were praying, and were listening to God for their guidance—they would need the Oxford Group *or* Shoemaker. One answer is that they had a lot to learn, concerning what Shoemaker

---

[16] See the comments about this in *The Co-Founders of Alcoholics Anonymous*, at pages 4-5, with a partial quote from Dr. Bob's final remarks about keeping it simple.

[17] See Ernest Kurtz, *Not-God*, Expanded ed. (Minnesota: Hazelden, 1991), p. 103.

[18] Dr. Bob put the "simplicity" idea in precisely the foregoing language in his farewell address to A.A. See *DR. BOB*, p. 338.

[19] Dick B., *Dr. Bob's Library* (West Virginia: The Bishop of Books, 1992), pp. 5-14.

[20] See Dick B., *Dr. Bob's Library*, in its entirety, and particularly the Foreword by Dr. Ernest Kurtz, pp. ix-x.

[21] *DR. BOB*, pp. 310, 150-51.

later called "the spiritual angle."[22] Bill Wilson, for example, had scarcely seen a Bible or been inside a church until he encountered the Shoemaker circle in New York and A.A.'s Bible students in Akron.[23] Dr. Bob was a Christian and had received excellent training in the Bible in his younger years. Further, he began, or resumed, intense spiritual reading when he became affiliated with the Oxford Group in 1933. But the author has not yet discovered any significant evidence that this co-founder was either a great Bible student or an avid churchgoer during his long drinking career before 1933.

In short, the two founders needed help with medical facts and with what Dr. Silkworth called the "moral psychology" necessary to bring about an essential "psychic change."[24] Far more important, however, for their life-changing program, they needed help with religious ideas, with Biblical interpretation, and with tools for spiritual growth. The two founders were novices when it came to theological ideas, religious practices, evangelism, the structure of a religious fellowship, and personal work.[25] And they

---

[22] See Samuel Shoemaker, Jr., "The Spiritual Angle," *The A.A. Grapevine* (New York: The AA Grapevine, Inc, November, 1992), pp. 21-27—reprinted from the October, 1955, issue of the *A.A. Grapevine*.

[23] See Dick B., *The Akron Genesis of Alcoholics Anonymous*, p. 64. Bill said in a tape, "I hadn't looked in the Bible, up to this time [the time he arrived in Akron] at all." See also Nell Wing, *Grateful To Have Been There* (Illinois: Parkside Publishing Corporation, 1992), where his former secretary said at page 48: "Bill was not a churchgoer and avoided joining any particular denomination." Kurtz's *Not-God* states at page 16: "Of Bill's earlier exposure to religion, little is known—probably because there is little to know. . . . [T]he young Bill Wilson had 'left the church' at about age twelve—on 'a matter of principle.'"

[24] See Silkworth's "Doctor's Opinion" at pages xxv, xxvii, and xxix.

[25] While the following remarks certainly do not seem applicable to Dr. Bob, Anne Smith, Henrietta Seiberling, T. Henry and Clarace Williams, and a good many of the early *Akron* AAs, they do represent Bill Wilson's appraisal of at least his own shortcomings in the religious area. An Episcopal rector, John F. Woolverton, came across a letter from Bill Wilson to Sam Shoemaker, dated February 15, 1945; and Woolverton made the following observations: "Yet the 'initial spiritual answer' to Wilson's problem of alcoholism did not stick. Exposure to the First Century Christian (continued...)

certainly had no particular skills or experience when it came to bringing atheists and agnostics to a faith in God.

All these were realms in which both the Oxford Group and Shoemaker had developed specific ideas and practices. And, for Bill Wilson on the East Coast, Sam Shoemaker was the man of the hour. In Akron, Sam's writings were available to, and read and recommended by, Dr. Bob and Anne Smith, Henrietta Seiberling, and T. Henry and Clarace Williams.

At this point, we need not again recount or summarize what Shoemaker gave to A.A., its Big Book, and Twelve Steps. But we do want to review three major items.

1. **Shoemaker's experiment of faith**. As stated, *Dr. Bob and Bill had no specific program for bringing atheists and agnostics to a faith*. Yet Bill seemed surrounded by such people. Though it seems to have been overlooked or underplayed—even by Bill—Bill himself was apparently an atheist before he began recovery in the Oxford Group.[26] More important, Bill's friend and partner in the

---

[25] (...continued)
Fellowship [the Oxford Group] was, by Shoemaker's own candid admission, a matter of 'temporary inspiration' with Wilson. . . . What went wrong? What made Wilson declare in 1945 that aside from Catholic members of AA 'and a few others, we are as a group pretty deficient on the prayer and meditation side'?" See John F. Woolverton, "Evangelical Protestantism and Alcoholism 1933-1962: Episcopalian Samuel Shoemaker, The Oxford Group and Alcoholics Anonymous." Historical Magazine of the *Protestant Episcopal Church* 52:1, March, 1983, pp. 60-61. It is the author's view that Woolverton was urging a look back at what Shoemaker had, in the beginning, given Wilson and perhaps indirectly Dr. Bob, Anne, Henrietta, and the other Akron AAs in the realm of prayer, Bible study, and meditation practices. For these items of emphasis in Shoemaker's teachings and in those of the Oxford Group were very definitely heeded at A.A.'s birthplace and can most appropriately be deemed keys to early A.A.'s success. One need only listen to the tapes, examine the transcripts, and review the reading of Akron oldtimers for proof. See Dick B., *Dr. Bob's Library*, *Anne Smith's Spiritual Workbook*, *The Oxford Group & Alcoholics Anonymous*, *The Akron Genesis of Alcoholics Anonymous*, and *The Books Early AAs Read for Spiritual Growth*.

[26] Bill said in the Big Book at page 10, "I was not an atheist." Nonetheless, Bill's wife, Lois, informed Reverend T. Willard Hunter, in a taped interview she gave Hunter toward the end of her life, that Bill had been an atheist "at the beginning." The author has a copy of this tape in his possession.

Big Book publication scheme was Hank P.; and Hank had been, or was, an atheist, as was their vociferous newcomer friend, Jim B. In fact, Jim B. appeared at very early East Coast A.A. meetings *denouncing God*![27] We might add that, for whatever reason, Bill Wilson's success rate in New York was very low in those early days.[28]

Fortunately for Bill, Shoemaker had several important ideas which, we believe, made it possible for Wilson to put together A.A.'s approach to faith, and particularly to write the Big Book's chapter to the agnostics.[29] Shoemaker's concepts can be summarized by his own words for them—"the experiment of faith"—an approach to moving people from a condition of estrangement from God, with little feeling of contact with Him, into a *relationship with Him*.[30]

For the elements in his proposed experiment, Shoemaker used some simple Biblical tools as he saw them: You start by believing God IS.[31] If you don't believe, you become willing to obey what is known of God's will.[32] You seek God by utter preoccupation with His plan, acting as if God *will* guide and provide.[33] You ask Him to tell you His plan.[34] You surrender, or give in, to as much of God as you understand.[35] You "clean house" of your sins

---

[27] *Alcoholics Anonymous Comes of Age* (New York: Alcoholics Anonymous World Services, 1957) contains Bill's discussion and characterization of these two men at page 163.

[28] *Pass It On* (New York: Alcoholics Anonymous World Services, Inc., 1984), p. 166. See also Kurtz, *Not-God*, pp. 41, 56, 62-63.

[29] See Big Book, pp. 44-57, Chapter 4: "We Agnostics."

[30] See, for example, Samuel Shoemaker, Jr., *The Experiment of Faith* (New York: Harper & Brothers, 1957), particularly at page 10; *National Awakening* (New York: Harper & Brothers, 1936), pp. 40-41; and Big Book, p. 29.

[31] Hebrews 11:6.

[32] John 7:17.

[33] Matthew 6:33: "Seek ye first the kingdom of God. . ."; and compare the Big Book's "God could and would if he were sought" (p. 60).

[34] 1 Samuel 3:9: "Speak, Lord; for thy servant heareth."

[35] Psalm 46:10 (Moffatt): "Give in, admit that I am God."

through the process of self-examination, confession of faults, readiness to change, conversion (letting God change you), and restitution. Then you find—or know, or are conscious of, or are awakened to—God, His power, His plan, and His presence, through *experience*. And we believe Shoemaker's suggested experiment became a major part of A.A. thinking. It was one of Shoemaker's major contributions to A.A.

2. **Shoemaker's suggestions on prayer**. Shoemaker probably made a substantial contribution to A.A.'s thinking about prayer. The approach was hardly invented by Shoemaker. Nor was it unique with Shoemaker. Nonetheless, Bill's biographer said of Shoemaker's influence in this area:

> Perhaps the most important contribution Shoemaker made in Bill's life was in giving him a new interpretation of prayer. Prayer, Bill came to see, could be more than a listing of personal needs and desires, more than an attempt to influence the will of God. It could also be a method of discovering that will, and for this reason he [Bill] began to believe that it was as important to listen as to speak in prayer.[36]

Shoemaker's emphasis on "Thy will be done" may have become the touchstone for A.A. in its technique of praying "only" for a knowledge of God's will, and then surrendering to it.[37] And to this day, the Lord's Prayer—with its "Thy will be done"—is still the dominant way the world round for closing an A.A. meeting, just as it was in the Oxford Group.

3. **Shoemaker's suggestions on morning devotions**. Though one could hardly belong to the Oxford Group without hearing ideas about a "Morning Watch" and "Quiet Time," and though the

---

[36] Recall that Shoemaker often quoted 1 Samuel 3:9 ("Speak, Lord"); Isaiah 6:8 ("Here *am* I"); and Acts 9:6: "Lord, what wilt thou have me to do?"

[37] For "Thy will be done," see Matthew 6:10; and Big Book, pp. 67, 85, 88, 63, 76.

Quiet Time was standard fare in Akron A.A., it seems that Shoemaker's own repeated teachings on the subject had much to do with the fact and form of its inclusion in the Big Book by Bill Wilson. Wilson, of course, deleted all mention of the Bible from the basic text of the Big Book and hence eliminated mention of it as part of morning devotions. But the Big Book's discussion of morning devotions still reads much like the suggestion and remarks Shoemaker made about his own way of starting the day. Consider the very first radio talk Shoemaker gave on the subject on October 4, 1945:

> Good morning! . . . The morning sets the tone of the day. . . . how the day starts in the morning is not only an indication of what kind of life you are living, and what direction you are going in. . . . I'll tell you a secret: meet God first in the day, before you meet anybody else; and then you'll meet them in a different spirit.
>
> May I tell you what we do in our home? When my wife and I get up, the first thing we reach for is our Bibles—not a cigarette, nor a drink, nor the morning paper—but our Bibles, We read a chapter or two. The we get quiet and spend some time in prayer. Our older daughter usually comes in for this time of devotion with us. In quietness we pray for the people, the causes, the immediate responsibilities of the day, and ask God to direct us and to use us to do His work and His will. We ask Him for direction. We work out our plans together, we get clear if anything has gotten between us, we include our daughter in our plans and talk about any decisions she may have to make. The family prayer-time ought to be a kind of crucible in which human tensions are washed out and human problems solved by the advice and help of one another, as we all wait upon god. Bring the family and business problems before Him, ask Him about them, and trust Him to tell you. Begin the day that way, and I think you really will have a "good morning", and a good afternoon, and a good evening—and a good life.[38]

[38] "Gems for Thought," A presentation of the American Broadcasting Co., No. 1, Thursday, October 4, 1945, from the first "Morning Radio Talk by the Rev. Samuel M. Shoemaker."

Now note the Big Book's suggestions for starting the day:

> On awakening let us think about the twenty-four hours ahead. We consider our plans for the day. Before we begin, we ask God to direct our thinking. . . . In thinking about our day we may face indecision. We may not be able to determine which course to take. Here we ask God for inspiration, an intuitive thought or a decision. . . . We usually conclude the period of meditation with a prayer that we be shown all through the day what our next step is to be, that we be given whatever we need to take care of such problems. . . . If the circumstances warrant, we ask our wives or friends to join us in morning meditation. . . . There are many helpful books also. Suggestions about these may be obtained from one's priest, minister, or rabbi (pp. 86-87).

Is there a correlation between Shoemaker's radio suggestions and those found in the Big Book's suggestions as to morning meditation? We think so; and one can find similar suggestions by Shoemaker dating from his earliest books and pamphlets through 1938 and after. Whether the Big Book adopted the teachings of Shoemaker, or simply the many similar suggestions and practices from other Oxford Group sources, the basic theme seemed remarkably similar in both the Oxford Group Quiet Time practice and the Big Book's morning meditation suggestions. This was a major contribution to A.A. practice and persists to this day through the widespread use of Hazelden's *Twenty-Four Hours a Day* and A.A.'s own and newly-published *Daily Reflections*. The point here is that recovering people have reached, and still are reaching, outside the Big Book for daily spiritual inspiration and growth.

All this by way of history. But what is the importance of Shoemaker in relation to A.A. today? Just this. Bill Wilson claimed that Shoemaker inspired *both* Dr. Bob and himself with respect to the spiritual ideas that were essential to recovery. And early A.A. in Akron, Ohio, was phenomenally successful. No one before had achieved much long-range success with the "seemingly hopeless," and "incurable" real alcoholic prior to the work which came to fruition in Akron's alcoholic squad of the Oxford Group, led by Dr. Bob. Consequently, what Shoemaker taught must have relevance to what can be expected to succeed if one hopes to see a change in the plummeting success rate that exists in today's A.A. We believe there was nothing wrong with the Shoemaker ideas, nor with Dr. Bob's implementation of them. What, if anything, is wrong today, we believe, is the lack of a cadre in A.A. that is knowledgeable about, and can explain, the successful ideas Shoemaker taught.

Shoemaker had a message that could reach people in all the early stages of recovery. It was a message of openness, compassion, and strong principles—coupled with a demand that there be honesty and a willingness to try.[39]

For people with strong religious beliefs, Shoemaker taught: "Stand fast!" He never stopped talking to A.A. in terms that Bible students, Christians, or people of any belief could understand. He spoke with conviction of God, of Jesus Christ, of the Holy Spirit, and of the Bible. He declared, in a major speech to A.A., that any person with a belief in God and with particular religious convictions could feel comfortable in A.A. because "God as we understood Him" could definitely be the God of their understanding. If we accept Shoemaker's lead, there is plenty of room in today's A.A. for people with an understanding of God as He is described in the Bible, in the Christian faith, and in other religions.

For those of little or no faith, Shoemaker suggested some ideas about "acting as if" and seeing the God, or Power, "in other people." Such language might disturb those who believe in the God of the Bible.[40] But Shoemaker essentially was pointing out that many who enter A.A. have no religion, no faith, or no

[39] See John 7:17.

[40] Biblically, people who have not come to the Father through Jesus Christ are dead in trespasses and sins, and are without God and without hope. See, for example, John 14:6: "Jesus saith unto him, I am the way, the truth, and the life: no man cometh unto the Father, but by me;" John 3:16; Romans 10:9; and Ephesians 2:1-12.

tolerance of religion as they knew it. He felt they could and should be helped to faith *at the start* by choosing, for a beginning, their own conception of God. On the other hand, he often said that AAs needed church. And early A.A. encouraged, but certainly did not require, such affiliation.

But what of a group in today's A.A. which is seemingly increasing in numbers? Members who do not favor church attendance. Members who are not tolerant of the mention of religious views in A.A. And members who do not like to hear that the A.A. program is directed toward a belief in God Almighty—the One with all power—however one understands Him. It would seem from the little story below that Shoemaker's views may have had, and could still have, some impact on these people as well.

Bill Wilson told this story at a major A.A. gathering:

> A fellow came to Dr. Bob and said, "I'm an alcoholic; here is my history. But I also have this other 'complication.' Can I join A.A.?" Bob threw it out to all the other deacons, while the poor guy waited.
>
> Finally, there was some kind of hearing on it among the self-appointed elders. I remember how perfectly Bob put it to them. He reminded us that most of us were practicing Christians. Then he asked, "What would the Master have thought? Would He have kept this man away?" He had them cold! The man came in, was a prodigious worker, and was one of our most respected people.[41]

Shoemaker never wavered in his belief that AAs should know where they came from. And he never avoided mentioning God or Jesus Christ to AAs. He simply felt that A.A. should not attempt to spell out theological doctrine; and that theology should be left to the churches where it belonged and where, he also felt, AAs

---

[41] From Bill W.'s last major A.A. talk in 1969 at a dinner at the New York Hilton sponsored by the New York Intergroup Association, with more than 3,000 A.A.'s and their families and friends in attendance to honor Bill. See *The Co-Founders of Alcoholics Anonymous*, p. 23.

individually should belong. Also, the author found nothing in Shoemaker's approach to, or later comments about, A.A. to suggest Shoemaker accepted the idea that just "any god" would do, or that an A.A. could survive on the idea that all he or she had to do was "just not pick up that first drink" or "not drink and go to meetings."

The author believes A.A.'s Big Book teaches, and that Shoemaker would confirm, that if a real alcoholic in A.A. could, by himself or herself, just "not drink and go to meetings," he or she would not need God *or* A.A.

The Big Book makes clear that the first step in recovery requires AAs to concede to their innermost selves that they are alcoholics; that they have lost the ability to control their drinking; and that neither self-knowledge nor fear nor willpower, nor any other human power, can overcome their problem. Real alcoholics suffer from *powerlessness* and *unmanageability*, suggests the A.A. Fellowship. And Shoemaker's and the Oxford Group's "O God manage me, for I cannot manage myself" prayer covers just that point. The "manage me" prayer suggests to unbelievers that if they have reached the point where alcohol has become their master, their lives have become a wreck, and they believe or are even willing to believe that God can change that situation, they are ready for the experiment of faith that Shoemaker taught about. We believe Shoemaker, and the A.A. program that followed him, were suggesting that the newcomer throw himself or herself into the experiment with utter dedication and expect to emerge "happy, joyous, and free."[42]

In A.A. today, there seems to the author to be a widening circle of those who have no religious convictions, want no religious convictions, and apparently believe they need no religious convictions to recover from alcoholism. In fact, some believe that either mention or study in A.A. of its earlier Christian roots is personally offensive, violative of A.A. Traditions, or just plain irrelevant. But that was not the position Shoemaker took when he

---

[42] See Big Book, p. 133.

taught, spoke to, and spoke of, A.A. Nor is it the view, in the author's experience, of a great many in today's A.A. who—with A.A.'s current archivist—share the belief that whenever a civilization or society declines, there is always one condition present—they forgot where they came from. We would add that if AAs forget their roots, they may well lose sight of where to go in the future. We therefore conclude with a discussion of the A.A. Fellowship, the A.A. Solution, and the application of that solution in today's A.A. and in the various Twelve Step programs it has spawned.

The Fellowship of A.A.

From the author's own experience, there are some convictions that most AAs share. First, that there is a distinction between the A.A. Fellowship and the A.A. "program of recovery." One clear expression of this idea can be found in the Big Book's Chapter "There Is A Solution." It speaks of the fellowship *and* the solution. And it uses Shoemaker's own "way out" language. On page 17, the Big Book states:

> But there exists among us a fellowship. . . . The feeling of having shared in a common peril is one element in the powerful cement which binds us. But that in itself would never have held us together as we are now joined. The tremendous fact for every one of us is that we have discovered a common solution. We have *a way out* on which we can absolutely agree, and upon which we can join in brotherly and harmonious action [emphasis ours].

As to its *fellowship*, A.A. is wide open! There is no membership roster, mailing list, membership badge, or sergeant-at-arms to evict. Anyone—alcoholic, addict, believer, or atheist—can come to a fellowship meeting. Even "closed" meetings have no guard at the door. As A.A.'s Tradition Three expresses it: "The only requirement for A.A. membership is a desire to stop drinking."

And A.A. really has no "membership" as such. But it certainly does stress fellowship just as Shoemaker did.

The Solution

The program of recovery is a different story. The "common solution" in A.A. is a spiritual experience or, in the modified language of today's A.A., a "spiritual awakening."[43] As the Big Book puts it, you attain a spiritual awakening only when you "thoroughly follow our path"—the path described in the Twelve Steps. The path which helped early AAs find God and utilize His power to overcome powerlessness and unmanageable lives. Thus, on page 25, the Big Book describes the "simple kit of spiritual tools" (the Twelve Steps) and says of the solution:

> The great fact is just this, and nothing less: That we have had deep and effective spiritual experiences which have revolutionized our whole attitude toward life, toward our fellows and toward God's universe. The central fact of our lives today is the absolute certainty that our Creator has entered into our hearts and lives in a way which is indeed miraculous. He has commenced to accomplish those things for us which we could never do by ourselves.

At the conclusion of this chapter, the Big Book adds:

> Each individual, in the personal stories, describes in his own language and from his own point of view the way he established his relationship with God (p. 29).

Shoemaker certainly taught the steps to such a spiritual experience. They were Oxford Group steps, taken from Biblical ideas.

---

[43] See Big Book, pp. 25, 27, 569-70 (Appendix Two).

In fact, the Big Book was written primarily to enable others to learn and share in the success early AAs had experienced in their program of recovery. The Foreword to the First Edition states:

> To show other alcoholics *precisely how we have recovered* is the main purpose of this book (p. xiii).

Interpretation and Application of the Program Today

From his own experience in A.A., the author has found that there are a number of interpretations of the language and ideas in the first 164 pages of the Big Book—the "basic text," as it is called. Many A.A. newcomers are told, in their earliest days of sobriety, to get a dictionary to help them understand Big Book language. And well they should if they don't understand the sophisticated words Bill Wilson used. Further, as to the authority of the Big Book, the author holds with those in A.A. who regard the basic text of the Big Book as A.A.'s authoritative statement on how to recover from alcoholism via the A.A. recovery program.

Yet the dictionary alone seems far from sufficient when it comes to understanding the Big Book; for the Big Book's language has given rise to the characterization of God as a door knob, Santa Claus, and "Good Orderly Direction." Shoemaker himself spoke of "half-baked prayers," "absurd modern names of God," and self-made religion which people throw up as a bluff.[44] Such "childish nonsense," as Shoemaker sometimes called it, comes from free-lance creation of theological ideas by people with little knowledge or guidance as to where to start an experiment of faith.

---

[44] As to Shoemaker's remarks about "half-baked prayers," see *A.A. Comes of Age*, p. 265; as to "absurd names of God," see the remarks Shoemaker made in his 1960 address to A.A.'s Third Convention; and as to one's "own religion," or self-made religion, see Shoemaker, *Realizing Religion* (New York: Association Press, 1923), p. 2.

We repeat what Shoemaker said in his 1960 address to A.A.'s International Convention:

> It is much better for anyone to pray to the God that is, He with no name and we with no words, than to pray to your own creation of God, with words prettier than a poem, but fictitious.

But not everyone in A.A. reads Shoemaker, or wants to, or can even find his books of sixty years ago. In fact, most in present-day A.A. have difficulty getting to a study of the first 164 pages of the Big Book. So the opportunity for varied interpretations of A.A., its language, and its steps is great. AAs no longer have Dr. Bob or the early oldtimers leading their meetings with Bible in hand.[45] Nor are they privileged to sit in the Smith home on Ardmore Avenue in Akron and be a part of the prayer, meditation, and study sessions with Anne Smith reading to them and teaching from her spiritual workbook.[46] Unfortunately, many of the half-baked prayers, absurd notions, and self-made religions floating about the rooms of A.A. result from very sincere, even desperate, "interpretations" of the words in the Big Book. All reached with little knowledge of A.A.'s roots.

What is the challenge? First, in today's A.A., one must accept the fact that all are welcome. Second, that the points of entry for A.A. newcomers are today as varied as the nations, religions, and customs of the world. Third, even within the United States, new AAs come from recovery centers, physicians, psychologists, counselors, law enforcement agencies, churches, clergy, correctional institutions, courts, probation officers, AAs themselves, and other people genuinely concerned about the alcoholic's plight. Fourth, with such varied referral points, one must expect varied interpretations of A.A. ideas. And also expect to find an informed cadre of oldtimers that is relatively small in

---

[45] For a specific description of these meetings, see Dick B., *The Akron Genesis of Alcoholics Anonymous* (Seattle: Glen Abbey Books, 1992), pp. 189-90.

[46] See Dick B., *The Akron Genesis of Alcoholics Anonymous*, pp. 109-10.

size. Many in A.A. in fact say that A.A.'s weakest link is the sponsor who knows little or nothing about the program of recovery. With two million members spread around the globe, and one-third of all newcomers walking in and out of A.A. within ninety days, one would not expect a thoroughly experienced cadre or a well informed group of sponsors.

In fact, one of the mothers of a man the author sponsored once asked: "Where do you get your training as to sponsorship?" A flippant answer could have been: by drinking too much for too long, by coming into the rooms of A.A., and by passing on my failures and ill-conceived ideas about God and religion to someone else! For many of us, the failures did include a lack of understanding of, and certainly an unsatisfactory relationship with, God as we understood Him. Hardly something you would be proud to give away in order to keep it!

What then of Shoemaker? How can a knowledge of Shoemaker's relationship with Alcoholics Anonymous help today? The author believes several truths are becoming clearer: (1) Shoemaker probably *did* directly inspire Bill Wilson and possibly Dr. Bob concerning most of their spiritual ideas. (2) The early program in Akron, inspired at least by Shoemaker's teachings, *did* achieve a remarkable success rate—a rate far above anything in today's Twelve Step programs. (3) Shoemaker's teachings *do* aid materially in understanding the words and ideas in A.A.'s program. (4) AAs, and others involved in and with Twelve Step programs, *do* need help in understanding and interpreting the spiritual language and ideas in the Big Book, the Twelve Steps, and the A.A. Fellowship. (5) These people *need* that help just as much, if not far more today, than Bill and Dr. Bob did when they were reading the Bible and Oxford Group literature, and seeking inspiration and teaching from root sources such as Shoemaker. (6) There is little to be said for a cadre of oldtimers and sponsors in future A.A. who have no familiarity with A.A.'s spiritual roots, and even less respect for them.

For the author, a study of Shoemaker has been rewarding. It can be rewarding for AAs and Twelve Step people, and for the government, recovery, and religious communities seeking to help those involved in Twelve Step programs. And all can profit from knowing how, why, and where early A.A. experienced success through cooperation with religion. By contrast, there can be little profit in learning within A.A. multi-faceted philosophies and approaches developed by hordes who don't know, or who have forgotten, where A.A. came from.

A.A. worked. And A.A. works. How it works, or used to work, with a great *rate* of success, can be learned not only from A.A.'s Big Book, but also from its spiritual history. And the teachings, writings, and remarks of the Reverend Doctor Samuel Moor Shoemaker, Jr., are a rich and vital part of that history.

The New Light on Alcoholism

What is the new light on alcoholism that this study of Sam Shoemaker's legacy can shed?

It really comes from an ancient and universal lamp.[47] As the Master taught in the Sermon on the Mount—upon which A.A.'s philosophy was based—the light was not meant to be put under a bushel or a bed.[48] It is the light of the truth of God's power.

So let us return to the language which A.A.'s co-founders, Bill W. and Dr. Bob, used to describe that light and power, and, with God's help, to fashion their spiritual program of recovery.

Bill gave evidence in his own Big Book story, to the point of demonstration, that he was a real and seemingly hopeless alcoholic. So too Dr. Bob in his Big Book story. Dr. Bob and his wife, Anne, had both read the Bible and all the significant Oxford Group literature, including that of Sam Shoemaker, of that day. So had the others in Akron, including early teachers such as Henrietta

---

[47] "For thou *art* my lamp, O LORD: and the LORD will lighten my darkness." 2 Samuel 22:29.

[48] Matthew 5:15-16; Mark 4:3-23.

Seiberling. And, though Bill may not have *read* either from Shoemaker, the Oxford Group, or the Bible, he certainly had *heard* from all aplenty. To the point that he and Dr. Bob were racing all over Akron "oxidizing" drunks in those early, heady days.

Their message was simple: Believe in God and the power of God! Some might question: Was this really their message? Let us again look at their own words as recorded in the Big Book. Bill said in his story:

> My friend promised when these things were done I would enter upon a new relationship with my Creator; that I would have the elements of a way of living which answered all my problems. *Belief in the power of God*, plus enough willingness, honesty and humility to establish and maintain the new order of things, were the *essential* requirements (Big Book, pp. 12-14) [emphasis ours].

Dr. Bob said in his story: "If you think you are an atheist, an agnostic, a skeptic, or have any other form of intellectual pride which keeps you from accepting what is in this book, I feel sorry for you" (Big Book, p. 181). The Big Book itself said: "We had to stop doubting the power of God" (p. 52).

The Big Book was written to help alcoholics find God and establish a relationship with Him. Thus Chapter 5 states: ". . . There is One who has all power—that One is God. May you find Him now!" (p. 59). Page 29 of the Big Book states: "Each individual, in the personal stories, describes in his own language and from his own point of view the way he established his relationship with God."[49] And Dr. Bob wrapped up the reason for it all: "Your Heavenly Father will never let you down!" (p. 181).

Now what about Sam Shoemaker? What did he teach?

---

[49] The original multilith draft spoke of "finding or rediscovering God."

First, in effect, he asked: (1) Are you powerless?[50] (2) Has your life become unmanageable?[51] (3) Are you, or have you become, estranged from God?[52]

Second, where the reply was "yes," he suggested as a solution: (1) You need a power or force outside of, or greater than, yourself.[53] (2) You need a vital religious experience.[54] (3) You need to find God.[55] (4) You need a relationship with God.[56]

Finally, he taught—as to the means for meeting the needs: (1) Believe that God IS.[57] (2) Seek Him first.[58] (3) Surrender yourself to God.[59] (4) Make a decision to cast your will and your life on God.[60] (5) To as much of God as you understand.[61] (6) Examine yourself.[62] (7) Get honest with yourself, with God, and with another.[63] (8) Repent and desire change.[64] (9) Throw yourself on God's mercy and, by his grace, be transformed.[65] (10) Set things right with those you have harmed.[66] (11) Learn to pray effectively by seeking God's will, not just seeking answers for your own self-made designs.[67] (12) Study the Bible for this

---

[50] Shoemaker, *If I Be Lifted Up*, p. 131.

[51] Harris, *The Breeze of the Spirit*, p. 10.

[52] Shoemaker, *Realizing Religion*, p. 5.

[53] Shoemaker, *A Young Man's View of the Ministry*, p. 42; *If I Be Lifted Up*, p. 176.

[54] Shoemaker, *Realizing Religion*, p. 9.

[55] Shoemaker, *Realizing Religion*, p. 9.

[56] Shoemaker, *Children of the Second Birth*, p. 16.

[57] Shoemaker, *National Awakening*, p. 40.

[58] Shoemaker, *National Awakening*, p. 41.

[59] Shoemaker, *Realizing Religion*, p. 30.

[60] Shoemaker, *Twice-Born Ministers*, p. 134.

[61] Shoemaker, *Children of the Second Birth*, p. 47.

[62] Shoemaker, God's Control, pp. 104-05.

[63] Shoemaker, *The Church Can Save the World*, p. 112.

[64] Shoemaker, *Realizing Religion*, p. 19.

[65] Shoemaker, *Realizing Religion*, pp. 30-31.

[66] Shoemaker, *Twice-Born Ministers*, p. 32.

[67] Shoemaker, *Religion That Works*, pp. 64-65.

information, and all else will fall in its place.[68] (13) Live the spiritual principles of the Sermon on the Mount.[69] (14) Awaken to what God has done for you.[70] (15) Fish for men.[71] (16) Pass your discovery on and help others through sharing your successful experience.[72]

Did it work? It surely did. Even before there was an A.A.!

Bill Wilson's friends, Rowland Hazard, Shep Cornell, Vic Kitchen, and Charles Clapp, got sober, stayed sober, and helped other alcoholics get sober by these principles before A.A. was born. And all were close associates of Sam Shoemaker's. The point is not that A.A. was unnecessary, but rather that it was based on verities, on the light of the power of God, that had already been shed by the Bible, the Oxford Group, Shoemaker, the other Christian writers of that day, and by the experience of A.A.'s own co-founders.

Bill and Bob applied the Biblical truths. Anne Smith had written them down in her spiritual workbook and shared them with the many, including Bill Wilson, who visited and sometimes lived in the Smith home in Akron where A.A. was born. And the ideas worked. They worked for fifty percent (50%) of the drunks who really tried; and that record stands unequaled.

Those basic ideas can work today without fail if the light is not hid under a bushel. They have worked for the author and the many AAs he has sponsored. And they will work today for you if you choose to give your all to the service of God and other people, and receive the deliverance and peace God promises. We hold, with Dr. Bob: Your Heavenly Father will never let you down!

The End

---

[68] Shoemaker, *Realizing Religion*, pp. 58-62.

[69] Helen Shoemaker, *I Stand by the Door*, p. 24.

[70] Shoemaker, *If I Be Lifted Up*, p. 34.

[71] Shoemaker, *Realizing Religion*, p. 82.

[72] Shoemaker, *Twice-Born Ministers*, p. 56.

Appendix 1

Twenty-Eight Oxford Group Principles That Influenced A.A.

The following are the twenty-eight Oxford Group ideas; and our footnotes identify the places in the Bible, in Oxford Group books, in Shoemaker's writings, in Anne Smith's workbook, and in A.A. literature where the ideas can be found:

The Twenty-Eight Oxford Group Ideas

In the beginning, God.

1. *God*—Biblical descriptions of Him as Creator, Maker, Father, Spirit, Love, Living God.[1]

[1] a) Oxford Group writers gave the following as their Biblical authority (henceforth, "**Bible**"): "Creator" (Isaiah 40:28); "Maker" (Psalm 95:6); "Father" (Matthew 5:45); "Spirit" (John 4:24); "Love" (1 John 4:8); Living God (Acts 14:15). b) Oxford Group writings (henceforth, "**Oxford Group**"): Philip M. Brown, *The Venture of Belief* (New York: Fleming H. Revell, 1935), pp. 24-25; Geoffrey Allen, *He That Cometh* (New York: The Macmillan Company, 1933), pp. 222-223; Clarence I Benson, *The Eight Points of the Oxford Group* (Oxford: Oxford University Press, 1936), p. 73; Frank Buchman, *Remaking The World* (London: Blandford Press, 1961), p. 13. c) **Shoemaker**: *The Conversion of the Church* (New York: Fleming H. Revell, 1932), pp. 33, 49, 50, 51, 124; *National Awakening* (New York: Harper & Brothers, 1936), pp. 48, 55, 97, 107, 108; *Confident Faith* (New York: Fleming H. Revell, 1932), pp. 38, 54, 59, 74, 83, 96, 106, 107, 152, 183; *Realizing Religion* (New York: Association Press, 1921), p. 35; *Children of the Second Birth* (New York: Fleming H. Revell, 1927), p. 42; *Christ's Words From The Cross* (New York: Fleming H. Revell, 1933), p. 43. d) **Anne Smith**: Dick B., *Anne Smith's Spiritual Workbook*, p. 21. e) In A.A. (henceforth, "**A.A.**"), see in the Big Book: Creator (p. 13), Maker (p. 57), Father (p. 62), Spirit (p. 84); Living God (An early draft of the Big Book contained this phrase, which was later modified to "God" at page 29). See also *DR. BOB*, pp. 117, 110; *Pass It On*, p. 121.

2. *God has a plan*—His will for man—and provides definite, accurate information for the individual who wants the plan fulfilled.[2]

3. *Man's chief end*—To do God's Will, thereby receiving the blessings God promises to those who align their lives with His Will.[3]

4. *Belief*—We must start with the belief that God IS.[4]

Sin—Estrangement from God—The Barrier of Self.

5. *Sin is a reality*—The selfishness and self-centeredness that blocks man from God and from others.[5]

---

[2] a) **Bible**: Jeremiah 7:23; Isaiah 14:5; Proverbs 3:5-6. b) **Oxford Group**: Buchman, *Remaking The World*, pp. 8, 48; Horace Bushnell, *The New Life* (London: Strahan & Co., 1868), pp. iii, 1; Henry B. Wright, *The Will of God and a Man's Lifework* (New York: Young Men's Christian Association Press, p. 3; Brown, *The Venture of Belief*, p. 40. c) **Shoemaker**: *Children of the Second Birth*, p. 27; *Religion That Works* (New York: Fleming H. Revell, 1928), p. 19; *National Awakening*, pp. 41, 83, 89-98. d) **Anne Smith**: Dick B., *Anne Smith's Spiritual Workbook*, p. 23. e) **A.A.**: *DR. BOB*, p. 45; compare *Lois Remembers* (New York: Al-Anon Family Group Headquarters, 1987), p. 100; Big Book, pp. 208-209; 302-303.

[3] a) **Bible**: Acts 13:22; Matthew 6:32-33. b) **Oxford Group**: Henry Drummond, *The Ideal Life* (New York: Hodder & Stoughton, 1897), pp. 227-243; Wright, *The Will of God*, p. 9; Benson, *The Eight Points of the Oxford Group*, pp. 12-13; B. H. Streeter, *The God Who Speaks* (London: Macmillan, 1943), p. 11. c) **Shoemaker**: *National Awakening*, pp. 42, 47; *Christ's Words From The Cross*, p. 50. d) **Anne Smith**: Dick B., *Anne Smith's Spiritual Workbook*, pp. 22-23. e) **A.A.**: Big Book, Step Eleven, and pp. 164, 77.

[4] a) **Bible**: Hebrews 11:6. b) **Oxford Group**: Brown, *The Venture of Belief*, p. 24; Philip Leon, *The Philosophy of Courage or The Oxford Group Way* (New York: Oxford University Press, 1939), p. 19; The Layman with a Notebook, *What Is The Oxford Group?* (New York: Oxford University Press, 1933), Foreword. c) **Shoemaker**: *National Awakening*, pp. 40-41; *Children of the Second Birth*, p. 40; *Religion That Works*, p. 55; *Confident Faith*, p. 187. d) **Anne Smith**: Dick B., *Anne Smith's Spiritual Workbook*, p. 24. e) **A.A.**: Big Book, p. 53—a virtual quote of Shoemaker's *Confident Faith* language.

[5] a) **Bible**: Romans 3:23. b) **Oxford Group**: A. J. Russell, *For Sinners Only* (London: Hodder & Stoughton, 1932), p. 61. c) **Shoemaker**: *They're On The Way* (New York: E.P Dutton & Co., 1951), p. 154. d) **Anne Smith**: Dick B., *Anne Smith's Spiritual Workbook*, p. 26. e) **A.A.**: *Pass It On*, p. 197; Big Book, pp. 60-64, 66, 71, 76.

Finding or Rediscovering God.

6. *Surrender*—The turning point which makes it possible for man to have a relationship with God by surrendering his will, ego, and sins to God.[6]

7. *Soul-Surgery*—The "art" or way which enables man through the steps of Confidence, Confession, Conviction, Conversion, and Conservation (the 5 C's) to have the sin or spiritual disease cured.[7]

8. *Life-change*—The result in which man, through a spiritual experience, becomes God-centered instead of self-centered and focuses on helping others.[8]

The Path They Followed To Establish a Relationship With God.

9. *Decision*—The action by which man verbalizes his surrender and gives in to God, saying, essentially, "Thy will be done."[9]

10. *Self-examination*—A "moral" inventory in which man takes stock of his sins and their consequences.[10]

---

[6] a) **Bible**: Acts 3:19. b) **Oxford Group**: Benson, *The Eight Points*, p. 5. b) **Shoemaker**: *The Church Can Save The World* (New York: Harper & Brothers, 1938), pp. 113-114. d) **Anne Smith**: Dick B., *Anne Smith's Spiritual Workbook*, pp. 28-29. e) **A.A.**: Big Book, p. 59.

[7] b) **Oxford Group**: Howard A. Walter, *Soul-Surgery: Some Thoughts On Incisive Personal Work* (Calcutta India: Association Press, 1919). c) **Shoemaker**: *The Conversion of the Church*, p. 12; *Realizing Religion*, pp. 79-80. d) **Anne Smith**: Dick B., *Anne Smith's Spiritual Workbook*, pp. 30-31. e) **A.A.**: *DR. BOB*, p. 54; Kurtz, *Not-God*, pp. 48-49, 228; Richmond Walker, *For Drunks Only: One Man's Reaction To Alcoholics Anonymous* (Published in 1945; Reprinted by Hazelden), pp. 45-46.

[8] a) **Bible**: John 3:3. b) **Oxford Group**: Harold Begbie, *Life Changers* (New York: G. P. Putnam, 1927). c) **Shoemaker**: *The Church Can Save The World*, p. 153. d) **Anne Smith**: Dick B., *Anne Smith's Spiritual Workbook*, p. 29. e) **A.A.**: Big Book, pp. 63, 569-570.

[9] a) **Bible**: Matthew 6:10. b) **Oxford Group**: *What Is The Oxford Group?*, pp. 46-48. c) **Shoemaker**: *Children of the Second Birth*, pp. 58, 175-187. d) **Anne Smith**: Dick B., *Anne Smith's Spiritual Workbook*, p. 32. e) **A.A.**: Big Book, pp. 60, 63.

[10] a) **Bible**: Matthew 7:3-5. b) **Oxford Group**: Buchman, *Remaking The World*, pp. 3, 24, 28, 38, 46; Walter, *Soul-Surgery*, pp. 41-48, 69; Benson, *The Eight Points*, pp. 44, 162, 18, 7; Cecil Rose, *When Man Listens* (New York: Oxford University Press, 1937), pp. 17-19. c) **Shoemaker**: *The Conversion of the Church*, pp. 30-34; *Twice-Born Ministers* (New York: Fleming H. Revell, 1929), p. 182; *How To Become A Christian* (New York: Harper & Brothers, 1953), pp. 56-67; *God's Control* (New York: Fleming

(continued...)

11. *Confession*—Sharing with God and another person the inventory results.[11]

12. *Conviction*—Readiness to change resulting from man's conviction that he has sinned and that Christ miraculously can cure.[12]

13. *Conversion*—The New Birth, Change, namely, that which occurs when man gives himself to God, is regenerated, has part of God's nature imparted to him, and finds the barrier of sin gone.[13]

14. *Restitution*—Righting the wrongs and enabling man to cut the cord of sin that binds him to the past.[14]

Jesus Christ

15. *Jesus Christ*—The source of power as the Divine Redeemer and Way-Shower by whose transforming power man can be changed.[15]

---

[10] (...continued)
H. Revell, 1939), pp. 104-105. d) **Anne Smith**: Dick B., *Anne Smith's Spiritual Workbook*, pp. 32-33. e) **A.A.**: Big Book, pp. xvi, *Alcoholics Anonymous Comes of Age*, p. 39.

[11] a) **Bible**: James 5:16. b) **Oxford Group**: J. P. Thornton-Duesbury, *Sharing* (Pamphlet of the Oxford Group, published at Oxford University, n.d.), p. 5; Benson, *The Eight Points*, p. 18. c) **Shoemaker**: *The Conversion of the Church*, p. 35. d) **Anne Smith**: Dick B., *Anne Smith's Spiritual Workbook*, pp. 33-34. e) **A.A.**: *Pass It On*, p. 128; Big Book, Step 5.

[12] a) **Bible**: Psalm 65:3. b) **Oxford Group**: Walter, *Soul-Surgery*, pp. 64-78. c) **Shoemaker**: *Realizing Religion*, p. 81. d) **Anne Smith**: Dick B., *Anne Smith's Spiritual Workbook*, pp. 34-36. e) **A.A.**: See Mel B., *New Wine*, pp. 34-35; Big Book, Step 6.

[13] a) **Bible**: John 3:3-4. b) **Oxford Group**: Allen, *He That Cometh*, pp. 19-43. c) **Shoemaker**: *National Awakening*, pp. 55, 57-58. d) **Anne Smith**: Dick B., *Anne Smith's Spiritual Workbook*, pp. 36-37. e) **A.A.**: Big Book, pp. 63, 76; *Pass It On*, pp. 381-386.

[14] a) **Bible**: Numbers 5:6-7; Matthew 5:23-24. b) **Oxford Group**: Russell, *For Sinners Only*, p. 119. c) **Shoemaker**: *The Conversion of the Church*, pp. 47-48. d) **Anne Smith**: Dick B., *Anne Smith's Spiritual Workbook*, p. 42. e) **A.A.**: Big Book, Steps 8 and 9.

[15] a) **Bible**: John 14:6. b) **Oxford Group**: Brown, *The Venture of Belief*, p. 49. c) **Shoemaker**: *With the Holy Spirit and With Fire* (New York: Harper & Brothers, 1960), pp. 29-33. d) **Anne Smith**: Dick B., *Anne Smith's Spiritual Workbook*, pp. 54-56. e) **A.A.**: Compare Kurtz, *Not-God*, p. 50, Dick B., *The Oxford Group & Alcoholics Anonymous*, pp. 197-198; *Dr. Bob's Library* (WV: The Bishop of Books, 1992), pp. ix, 12, 37, 39-42; and *DR. BOB*, pp. 53-54, 141, 148, 163, 183.

Spiritual Growth—Continuance.

16. *Conservation*—Continuance as an idea, by which man maintains and grows in his life of grace.[16]

17. *Daily Surrender*—A process in which man engages in daily self-examination and surrender to get rid of newly accumulated sin and selfishness.[17]

18. *Guidance*—The walk by faith in which the Holy Spirit gives Divine Guidance to a life that is changed from sin to God.[18]

19. *The Four Absolutes*—Christ's standards, the standards of absolute honesty, purity, unselfishness, and love, by which man's life can be tested for harmony with God's will.[19]

20. *Quiet Time*—A period in which man can receive Divine Guidance and be sensitive to the sway of the Spirit.[20]

---

[16] a) **Bible**: Galatians 2:20; Romans 12:1-2. b) **Oxford Group**: Walter, *Soul-Surgery*, pp. 89-100; H. J. Rose, *The Quiet Time*, p. 2. c) **Shoemaker**: *Realizing Religion*, p. 80; *Religion That Works*, pp. 14-15. d) **Anne Smith**: Dick B., *Anne Smith's Spiritual Workbook*, pp. 37-43. e) **A.A.**: Big Book, pp. 83-85.

[17] a) **Bible**: Matthew 26:41; John 16:13-16. b) **Oxford Group**: Benson, *Eight Points*, pp. 45-46; Rose, *The Quiet Time*, p. 3. c) **Shoemaker**: *The Gospel According To You* (New York: Fleming H. Revell, 1934), pp. 81-91. d) **Anne Smith**: Dick B., *Anne Smith's Spiritual Workbook*, pp. 42-43. e) **A.A.**: Big Book, pp. 84-88.

[18] a) **Bible**: Psalm 32:8. b) **Oxford Group**: Benson, *The Eight Points*, p. 80. c) **Shoemaker**: *With The Holy Spirit and With Fire*, pp. 30-31; *The Conversion of the Church*, p. 86; *Twice-Born Ministers*, pp. 184-185. d) **Anne Smith**: Dick B., *Anne Smith's Spiritual Workbook*, pp. 50-52. e) **A.A.**: Big Book, Step Eleven.

[19] a) **Bible**: John 8:44; Matthew 5:5; Luke 14:33; John 13:34. b) b) **Oxford Group**: Robert E. Speer, *The Principles of Jesus* (New York: Fleming H. Revell, 1902), pp. 33-34; Garth Lean, *On The Tail of a Comet* (Colorado Springs: Helmers & Howard, 1988), p. 76. c) **Shoemaker**: *Twice-Born Ministers*, p. 150; *The Church Can Save The World*, p. 110; *How To Become a Christian*, p. 57. d) **Anne Smith**: Dick B., *Anne Smith's Spiritual Workbook*, pp. 56-58. e) **A.A.**: *DR. BOB*, pp. 54, 163; *Pass It On*, pp. 114, 172; *Alcoholics Anonymous Comes of Age*, pp. 68, 161; *The Language of the Heart*, pp. 198-200; *The Co-Founders of Alcoholics Anonymous* (New York: Alcoholics Anonymous World Services, Inc., 1972), pp. 13-14; Mel B., *New Wine*, pp. 76, 138; Kurtz, *Not-God*, pp. 242-243.

[20] a) **Bible**: Psalm 46:10. b) **Oxford Group**: Benson, *The Eight Points*, pp. 58-73. c) **Shoemaker**: *Realizing Religion*, pp. 65-66. d) **Anne Smith**: Dick B., *Anne Smith's Spiritual Workbook*, pp. 44-46. e) **A.A.**: Big Book, p. 86.

21. *Bible study*—Meditation which enables man daily to feed his soul on God's revelation of His Universal Will in the written Word.[21]

22. *Prayer*—Talking to God.[22]

23. *Listening to God for Leading Thoughts and Writing Down Guidance Received*—The means of receiving revelation of God's Particular or Private Will for a man.[23]

24. *Checking*—Testing thoughts to be sure they represent God's Guidance and not just self-deception.[24]

The Spiritual Experience or Awakening.

25. *Knowledge of God's will*—Attaining, with the Guidance of the Holy Spirit, a knowledge of God's Universal Will as revealed in the Bible, and receiving knowledge of His particular Will through obedience to His Universal Will.[25]

---

[21] a) **Bible**: 2 Timothy 2:15. b) **Oxford Group**: Streeter, *The God Who Speaks*; Russell, *For Sinners Only*, p. 94. c) **Shoemaker**: *Realizing Religion*, pp. 58-62; *The Conversion of the Church*, pp. 49, 60, 79; *Children of the Second Birth*, p. 97; *Twice-Born Ministers*, p. 184. d) **Anne Smith**: Dick B., *Anne Smith's Spiritual Workbook*, pp. 12-13. e) **A.A.**: *DR. BOB*, pp. 71, 96-97, 102, 111, 116, 136, 139, 140, 144, 148, 151, 162, 183, 187, 198, 218, 224, 228, 252, 261, 276, 306, 308, 310, 311, 314.

[22] a) **Bible**: James 5:16. b) **Oxford Group**: *What Is The Oxford Group?*, p. 69. c) **Shoemaker**: *Realizing Religion*, pp. 63-65; *National Awakening*, p. 53; *Children of the Second Birth*, p. 149. d) **Anne Smith**: Dick B., *Anne Smith's Spiritual Workbook*, pp. 48-49. e) **A.A.**: Big Book, p. 85.

[23] a) **Bible**: Jeremiah 30:1-2; 1 Samuel 3:9. b) **Oxford Group**: Buchman, *Remaking The World*, p. 36; Howard Rose, *The Quiet Time* (New York: The Oxford Group, 61 Gramercy Park North, n.d.). c) **Shoemaker**: *The Conversion of the Church*, pp. 60-66; *Children of the Second Birth*, p. 47. d) **Anne Smith**: Dick B., *Anne Smith's Spiritual Workbook*, pp. 52-53. e) **A.A.**: Big Book, pp. 86-87.

[24] a) **Bible**: John 16:13. b) **Oxford Group**: Russell, *For Sinners Only*, p. 94. c) **Shoemaker**: *The Conversion of the Church*, pp. 51-57; *Twice-Born Ministers*, p. 125. d) **Anne Smith**: Dick B., *Anne Smith's Spiritual Workbook*, pp. 53-54. e) **A.A.**: *Alcoholics Anonymous Comes of Age*, p. 74; *Pass It On*, p. 172; *Co-Founders*, pp. 12-13.

[25] a) **Bible**: John 7:17; Acts 9:6. b) **Oxford Group**: Wright, *The Will of God*, p. 137. c) **Shoemaker**: *The Conversion of the Church*, pp. 49-50; *Twice-Born Ministers*, pp. 184-185; *A Young Man's View of the Ministry* (New York: Association Press, 1923), pp. 78, 80; *Religion That Works*, p. 36. d) **Anne Smith**: Dick B., *Anne Smith's Spiritual Workbook*, pp. 61-63. e) **A.A.**: Big Book, Step Eleven.

26. *God-consciousness*—The total change resulting from the experience of God when His will is known, lived, and witnessed.[26]

Fellowship with God and Believers and Witness by Life and Word.

27. *Fellowship*—The Fellowship of the Holy Spirit in which believers maintain fellowship with God and mutually sacrifice to win others to the fellowship of the love of God revealed by Jesus Christ.[27]

28. *Witness by Life and Word*—Sharing with others by personal evangelism the fruits of the life changed and the proof of God's forgiveness and power.[28]

---

[26] a) **Bible**: John 3:7; Matthew 10:39; Matthew 6:33; Acts 2:1,4. b) **Oxford Group**: Dick B., *The Oxford Group & Alcoholics Anonymous*, pp. 265-278. c) **Shoemaker**: Dick B., *The Oxford Group & Alcoholics Anonymous*, pp. 265-278. d) **Anne Smith**: Dick B., *Anne Smith's Spiritual Workbook*, pp. 63-64. e) **A.A.**: Big Book, Step Twelve, pp. 569-570.

[27] a) **Bible**: 1 John 1:3; Ephesians 2:1-22. b) **Oxford Group**: Benson, *The Eight Points*, pp. 102-113; c) **Shoemaker**: *Religion That Works*, pp. 66-76. d) **Anne Smith**: Dick B., *Anne Smith's Spiritual Workbook*, pp. 58-59. e) **A.A.**: Big Book, p. 164.

[28] a) **Bible**: Acts 5:32; 26:22-23. b) **Oxford Group**: *What Is The Oxford Group?*, pp. 36, 26. c) **Shoemaker**: *One Boy's Influence* (New York: Association Press, 1925), p. 15; *They're On The Way*, p. 159; *How To Become A Christian*, p. 80. d) **Anne Smith**: Dick B., *Anne Smith's Spiritual Workbook*, pp. 60-61. e) **A.A.**: Big Book Step Twelve.

Appendix 2

The Oxford Group Literature Read by AAs

The Oxford Group Literature List in *The Calvary Evangel*

The following is the list of Oxford Group literature, with publication information added, that was included in the March, 1939, issue of *The Calvary Evangel. The Calvary Evangel* was the regular, monthly, parish publication of Sam Shoemaker's Calvary Episcopal Church in New York. In the 1930's, Calvary House, which was located adjacent to the church at 81 Gramercy Park, North, in New York City, was called by many the American Headquarters of the Oxford Group and its successor, Moral Re-Armament. In the later years, just before Sam Shoemaker evicted Oxford Group founder, Dr. Frank Buchman, from Calvary House, *The Calvary Evangel* had become virtually the "house organ" of Moral Re-Armament. Following is "The Oxford Group Literature List, published in the March, 1939 *Evangel* issue:

Allen, Geoffrey Francis. *He That Cometh*. New York: The Macmillan Company, 1933.
Brown, Philip M. *The Venture of Belief*. New York: Fleming H. Revell, 1935.
Foot, Stephen. *Life Began Yesterday*. New York: Harper & Brothers, 1935.
Forde, Eleanor Napier. *The Guidance of God*. Oxford: Printed at the University Press, 1930.
Holmes-Walker, Wilfred. *New Enlistment* (no publication data available to author).
Jones, Olive M. *Inspired Children*. New York: Harper & Brothers, 1933.
———. *Inspired Youth*. New York: Harper & Brothers, 1938.
Kitchen, V. C. *I Was A Pagan*. New York: Harper & Brothers, 1934.
Lean, Garth, and Martin, Morris. *New Leadership*. London: William Heinemann, 1936.
Rose, Cecil. *When Man Listens*. New York: Oxford University Press, 1937.
Rose, Howard J. *The Quiet Time*. New York: The Oxford Group at 61 Gramercy Park North, 1937.
Russell, A. J. *For Sinners Only*. London: Hodder & Stoughton, 1932.
Shoemaker, Samuel Moor, Jr. *Children of the Second Birth*. New York: Fleming H. Revell, 1927.
———. *Confident Faith*. New York: Fleming H. Revell, 1932.
———. *If I Be Lifted Up*. New York: Fleming H. Revell, 1931.
———. *National Awakening*. New York: Harper & Brothers, 1936.
———. *Realizing Religion*. New York: Association Press, 1921.
———. *Religion That Works*. New York: Fleming H. Revell, 1928.
———. *The Church Can Save The World*. New York: Harper & Brothers, 1938.

———. *The Conversion of the Church*. New York: Fleming H. Revell, 1932.
———. *The Gospel According To You*. New York: Fleming H. Revell, 1934.
Streeter, Burnett Hillman. *The God Who Speaks*. London: Macmillan & Co., 1943.
The Layman with a Notebook. *What Is The Oxford Group?* London: Oxford University Press, 1933.
Viney, Hallen. *How Do I Begin?* New York: The Oxford Group at 61 Gramercy Park North, 1937.
Walter, Howard A. *Soul-Surgery*. 6th ed. Oxford: Printed at the University Press by John Johnson, 1940.
Winslow, Jack. *Church in Action* (no publication data to the author).
———. *Why I Believe in the Oxford Group*. London: Hodder & Stoughton, 1934.

Oxford Group Books Known to Have Been Read By AAs, But Not on *The Calvary Evangel* List

The following are Oxford Group books known to have been read by one or more of A.A.'s founders, but not included in the *Evangel* list.

Begbie, Harold. *Life Changers*. New York: G. P. Putnam's Sons, 1927.
———. *Twice-Born Men*. New York: Fleming H. Revell, 1909 (Begbie wrote the book before the Oxford Group was underway, but his book was quite popular with Group people).
Leon, Philip. *The Philosophy of Courage*. New York: Oxford University Press, 1939.
Macmillan, Ebenezer. *Seeking and Finding*. New York: Harper & Brothers, 1933.
Nichols, Beverley. *The Fool Hath Said*. Garden City: Doubleday, Doran, 1936.
Reynolds, Amelia S. *New Lives For Old*. New York: Fleming H. Revell, 1929.
Russell, A. J. *One Thing I Know*. New York: Harper & Brothers, 1933.
Weatherhead, Leslie D. *Discipleship*. London: Student Christian Movement Press, 1934 (Weatherhead was not actually a "member" of the Oxford Group, but he wrote widely and sympathetically about it. His books were read by the founders).

Other Oxford Group Books That AAs Probably Read

Other books by or about the Oxford Group are listed in our Bibliography. It is probable that many were read by the early AAs in the case where the books bear publication dates prior to 1940. Dr. Bob said he had done an "immense amount" of the reading the Oxford Group had recommended. According to her son, John, Henrietta Seiberling read "all" the Oxford Group books of the 1930's. According to his daughter, Dorothy, T. Henry Williams had tables in the "furnace room" of his house, where boxes of Oxford Group books and pamphlets were available to those attending meetings at the Williams home. For a summary of the author's findings concerning all the spiritual books read by early AAs, see Dick B., *The Books Early AAs Read For Spiritual Growth* (Seattle: Glen Abbey

Books, 1993). And see Appendix 10 for other books which were included in and recommended as part of Calvary Church's recommended "Book List" in various issues of *The Calvary Evangel* during the 1930's. Among them were Carruthers' *How to Find Reality in Your Morning Devotions*; Grensted's *The Person of Christ*; Begbie's *Life Changers*; Reynolds' *New Lives for Old*; Duesbury's *Sharing*; Day's *Principles of the Group*; Cuyler's *Calvary Church in Action*; Smith's *The Meaning of Conversion* [not located by this author as yet]; MacMillan's *Seeking and Finding*; and Shoemaker's *Twice-Born Ministers* and *Christ's Words from the Cross*.

Appendix 3

The January 22, 1935, Letter from Sam to Bill

The following is a copy of the contents of a letter from Sam Shoemaker to Bill Wilson, dated January 22, 1935. At this date, Wilson had been sober less than two months and had been working with alcoholics from the beginning of his discharge from Towns Hospital on December 18, 1934. The author discovered the letter, mis-filed and not among other Shoemaker-Wilson correspondence, during the author's visit to Stepping Stones Archives at Bedford Hills, New York, in 1992. The archivist permitted the author to make the copy of the letter which is reproduced here:

Calvary Rectory
61 Gramercy Park, North
New York City
January 22, 1935

Dear Bill:

I hope you realize the guided-ness of your having known Jim Williams previously, as I understood you did, in business. His wife, Margaret, is full time in the Group and he has held out for a long while. You may be just the person that cracks the shell and brings him over. He drinks a lot and is desperately unhappy and inferior and needs what you have got for him. I am grateful for what you did for Breithut.

Yours ever,

s/ Sam S.

Mr. William Wilson
c/o Walter J. Fahys & Co.
29 Broadway
New York City

[Note: For further details as to Sam Shoemaker, Bill Wilson, and Frederick E. Breithut at Calvary Church, see Appendix 10.]

Appendix 4

The Irving Harris Memorandum Regarding Bill and Sam

In April, 1992, the author received a letter from Mrs. W. Irving Harris, dated April 7, 1992. The letter was accompanied by a typewritten copy of a manuscript Mrs. Harris had just found in going through her husband's papers in connection with her intended move from her New Jersey home to her daughter's home in Ohio. Of the manuscript, Mrs. Harris wrote:

> I thought it might confirm your thinking in the Bill-Sam relationship. It's an eye witness account as I know Irv's [her husband, Rev. W. Irving Harris's] way of writing.

Harris lived with his wife, Julia, at Calvary House, where Shoemaker also lived. Harris was an assistant minister at Shoemaker's Calvary Church, and a long-time associate and friend of Sam Shoemaker's.

The typewritten Harris manuscript, now in the author's possession, is entitled, "Bill Wilson and Sam Shoemaker." Reverend Harris typed the following memorandum:

> WHILE BILL never spent a single night at either Calvary House or at the Mission which Calvary Church maintained on East 23rd Street, New York, he owed much to the spiritual life generated at these places and even more to Sam Shoemaker, the man who headed up and fostered the activities at both centers.
>
> It was at a men's meeting at 61 Gramercy Park [Calvary House] that Bill's buddy, Ebbie Thatcher [sic] felt the power of fellowship and experienced the inner assurance that he could "move out of the dark tunnel" of alcoholism; and it was at a meeting at Calvary Mission that Bill himself was moved to declare that he had decided to launch out as a follower of Jesus Christ.
>
> Then as he was establishing guidelines which he believed to be basic in *maintaining* sobriety, he frequently turned to Sam Shoemaker to talk over the relation between these early formulations of the Twelve Steps and the principles of the New Testament. Sam's friend, "Sherry" Day, had already outlined several

principles of basic Christian living with which Bill was familiar.[1] As he discussed his counterparts to these he found that Sam's patient, quiet agreement put a seal on Bill's hope that these represented God's own truth. With a chuckle Sam would say something like, "Sounds like good old-fashioned Christian faith, Bill." And Bill would perhaps reply, "Yes, it looks that way . . . almost too good to be true." These talks took place in Sam's book-lined seventh floor study at Calvary House with the door closed and the telephone switched off.

At that time in New York the usual result of a full-blown experience like Bill's consisted of full-time participation in the activities of one of the several Oxford Group traveling teams. And Bill's new friends in the Group frequently urged him to get going in the customary team activity. Having shaken off the deadly grip of alcohol, he was consumed with a desire to spend his time not in general evangelism, or "life-changing," but in helping other alcoholics. He knew that many, many obsessive drinkers could find the same release and freedom which had come to him and it was to this work that he felt compelled to devote himself. And it was right here that Sam's counsel and backing proved so helpful. As one of the top American leaders of the old Group, Sam often had a deciding voice about where newly changed laymen might best tie in with the ever-extending work of the revival which was then taking place. And Sam was never personally persuaded that Bill should participate in the general team travel which was going on. He was impressed by the sincerity of Bill's own convictions about what he should do and advised him to follow his own deepest convictions even to the extent of incurring the disapproval of other leaders in the Group. In this Sam became Bill's special ally and "comforter," enabling him to withstand the pressures to conform. And by this, in God's providence, Sam shared in the steps which shortly led to the founding of Alcoholics Anonymous.

Several points need to be made about the foregoing vital manuscript written by Reverend Irving Harris. First, it bears no date. Second, Mrs. Harris stated it was an "eye witness" account. Third, the account had to be of events that took place subsequent to November of 1934 and prior to December of 1938 (the date the actual Twelve Steps were written). Fourth, in all likelihood, the events described took place after Bill's return from his three month stay in Akron in the summer of 1935 and before the fall of 1937 since Bill and Lois severed their connection with the Oxford Group in the summer of 1937. Fifth, there is a clear statement that Bill was familiar with Sherry Day's seven, biblical "Principles of the Group." Sixth, Bill and Sam Shoemaker were definitely discussing and comparing notes on Christian-Bible principles. Seventh, there is mention of Bill's involvement in Calvary House to the extent that his lay work on a team was considered; and Lois Wilson recalled that "Bill belonged to a team for a while."[2] L. Parks Shipley, Sr., had a similar but very specific recollection of Bill's participation in

---

[1] See the seven principles of the Bible that Day had written at the request of Shoemaker. Harris included them in his book, *The Breeze of the Spirit* (New York: The Seabury Press, 1978), at pages 18 to 21.

[2] *Lois Remembers* (New York: Al-Anon Family Group Headquarters, 1988), p. 93.

the Oxford Group business team. And this recollection was related to the author both in a phone interview and later in a personal interview with Shipley in the Fall of 1933 at Shipley's New Jersey home. Eighth, there is no suggestion that Sam Shoemaker *personally* "taught" Bill Wilson anything substantial, or that they discussed Sam's teachings, or that Sam "wrote," "participated in the writing of," "reviewed," or was in any way involved in the writing either of the Big Book or the Twelve Steps. In fact, Lois recalled that "Sam Shoemaker *ultimately* became an admirer of Bill's work and apologized for the lack of understanding by members of his staff and others in the OG [Oxford Group]"[3] Contrast with Lois's recollection the very clear recollection of Jim Newton, expressed to the author personally and on the phone during several conversations in 1992 and 1993, that Reverend Garrett Stearly told Newton on two different occasions that Bill Wilson had actually asked Sam Shoemaker to write the Twelve Steps, that Shoemaker had declined, and that Shoemaker told Bill that he (Bill) was the one to do it. Stearly was not only a member of Shoemaker's staff at Calvary Church in early years, but also a leader in the Oxford Group, and a frequent co-worker with Shoemaker on Calvary Church-Oxford Group affairs.

---

[3] *Lois Remembers*, p. 103 (emphasis added).

Appendix 5

Entries in Sam Shoemaker's Journals (1934-1939) about Bill Wilson

Sam Shoemaker kept a daily journal from at least the mid-1920's to the end of his life. Dr. Shoemaker's daughters, Sally and Nickie, made available to the author a large portion of these journals for inspection and, where relevant, for copying. The author inspected Shoemaker's journals at Nickie Shoemaker Haggart's home in Florida over the period from September 22 through September 25, 1993. The journals consisted of a large number of loose-leaf, lined, notepages tied together with strings. To date, the Shoemaker daughters have been unable to locate journals covering a very critical period from February of 1936 to April of 1939. This is unfortunate because the Shoemaker entries for the period of November, 1934, through January 31, 1936, contain so many entries concerning Bill Wilson that it seems equally probable there are similar entries throughout the period of the Shoemaker-Wilson friendship subsequent to January, 1936, and prior to the Big Book's publication in April, 1939. The likelihood seems even greater in view of the comments made by Reverend Irving Harris in his memorandum of the Shoemaker-Wilson relationship in this period. Also, because of Shoemaker's statement that he had received a copy of the Big Book manuscript before it was published and because of Reverend Garrett Stearly's twice-made statement to Jim Newton that Bill had asked Shoemaker to write the Twelve Steps.

Before we list the entries as to Wilson, we call attention to several facts: (1) Though Shoemaker was abroad for a majority of the year 1935 and though Wilson was in Akron with Dr. Bob throughout the summer of 1935, Wilson's name appears frequently in the journal of the busy Episcopalian rector during those months when both were in New York. (2) Not all the Shoemaker entries pertain to names, addresses, dates, or events because the journals also contain "guidance" which Shoemaker wrote down as he listened each day for God's leading thoughts. (3) Bill Wilson, and his associates and friends, are actually mentioned in the year-and-a-quarter period with more frequency than the many others who figured in the busy life of Calvary's rector. Thus there is frequent mention, not only of Bill Wilson, but also of Rowland Hazard, Shep Cornell, Victor Kitchen, Professor Philip Marshall Brown, Charles Clapp, Jr., Spoons Costello, as well as others on the Oxford Group businessman's team. And, of course, Dr. Frank Buchman is mentioned with much frequency. (4) In the few months in 1935 when Shoemaker and Wilson were both in New York, Bill Wilson is mentioned by name five times. And there are five additional entries which, taken in the context and in company with other mentioned names, seem probably to refer to Bill Wilson. Below we have set forth those 1935 entries that pertain to Shoemaker's comments about Bill Wilson:

1935 Entries Naming Bill Wilson

Below, we list the date of the entry, the specific words Shoemaker used, and our own remarks about the context. We will put our remarks in brackets so that they can be easily distinguished from the journal entries.

3/7/35: "Bill Wilson confirmed?"

[The quoted language is accompanied by mention of two of Wilson's friends, Victor Kitchen and Shep Cornell. Shoemaker's daughter, Nickie, and Mr. and Mrs. James D. Newton agree that Shoemaker was speaking of the possibility of Bill Wilson's being "confirmed" and becoming a communicant in Calvary Episcopal Church.]

11/2/35: "Bill W telephone since mine comeback?"

[Shoemaker's journals make it clear that he had been abroad in Europe from at least August 28 through October 15, 1935. One of Shoemaker's first concerns appears to have been a telephone contact with Bill Wilson.]

11/2/35: "Bill Wilson"

[Shoemaker again mentions Bill on this same date, this time calling him "Bill Wilson."]

11/18/35: "Bill Wilson . . . notify police and escort."

[Shoemaker here wrote at length of a huge gathering during the Thanksgiving period celebrating the visit of Carl Hambro, President of the League of Nations and the Norwegian Parliament. The event is covered in the newspapers for that period; and Bill Wilson's name is mentioned in Shoemaker's journal in company with the names of President Roosevelt, Dr. Frank Buchman, former Cabinet Secretary Carl Vrooman, and the Reverends Sherry Day and Cleve Hicks.]

11/20/35: "Bill Wilson . . . work in 50 countries telling what Group is & way it works."

[Shoemaker's journal entries for that day also contain the names of Carl Hambro, Frank Buchman, Carl Vrooman, Cleve Hicks, and James D. Newton.]

1935 Entries Probably Referring to Bill

In addition to the foregoing specific mentions of Bill Wilson by name, there are five other references to "Bill" and, though Shoemaker often refers in his journals to other persons by the name of Bill, the particular name "Bill" which we list below appears in company with the names of other associates and friends of Bill Wilson's.

1/10/35: "Bill"

[The reference also mentions Bill Wilson's friends, John Ryder, Rowland Hazard, Victor Kitchen, and Shep Cornell.]

1/21/35: "Men's meeting. Small . . . formal Bill . . . to win world Bill . . . Wilson's letters."

[The name "Bill" is mentioned with the name "Tex." In this early 1935 period, Bill Wilson was very much involved in working with alcoholics at Calvary Rescue Mission, of which "Tex" Francisco was superintendent. We are not convinced that the reference to "Wilson's letters" pertains to Bill Wilson, although that seems a possibility.]

1/24/35: "Keep all negatives out of this meeting . . . Maybe "you can be in touch with God" . . . Teams for Sinners . . . Bill Francisco may well . . . May let some of them talk in team meeting tonight . . . Plaza meeting . . . Spoons—racketeers . . . Bill."

[These notes seem very probably to refer to Bill Wilson because of their mention of Oxford Group teams, and of Tex Francisco and Spoons Costello. Tex and Spoons were connected with the Calvary Rescue Mission where Bill was working with drunks.]

6/25/35: "Sent Bill Venture of Belief"

[We cannot be sure that the reference is to Bill Wilson because Shoemaker was abroad and Bill Wilson was in Akron. However, Bill Wilson's friend, Rowland Hazard, was meeting during this period with Professor Philip Marshall Brown of Princeton, who was the author of *Venture of Belief*. And *Venture of Belief* contains a Foreword by Sam Shoemaker. The book uses a number of words and phrases which appear to have impacted on A.A.]

12/9/35: "What do Bill and John do best? . . . And Bill this p.m."

[There is nothing in the context that assures Shoemaker was referring to Bill Wilson. However, the entry appears in the same general time period when Bill was involved in Oxford Group team work, and the journal entry mentions Irving and Julia Harris, whom Bill Wilson had said had greatly inspired him. Hence, it is possible, however, that the entry refers to Bill Wilson and his Oxford Group friend, John Ryder. It is equally possible that the entry refers to some other Bill (possibly Bill Wood or Bill Houston, who are also mentioned with frequency in this period).]

Appendix 6

The Oxford Group Businessmen's Team

The author first learned about the Oxford Group Businessmen's Team in a personal visit and interview with James D. and Eleanor Forde Newton at their home in Fort Myers Beach, Florida. The interview took place in August, 1992. Newton related to the author that there had been a businessmen's team, led by Shoemaker. Newton said it met on Fridays and Saturdays. Their purpose was to inventory their shortcomings, apply Christian principles in their lives, obtain God's guidance in business situations, and achieve an "abundant life." Oxford Group leader, Dr. Frank Buchman, procured for the team the services of a Bible teacher named Miss Mary Angevine. Buchman wanted the team to have a greater knowledge of the Bible; and Miss Angevine taught them Scripture and also taught at Oxford Group houseparties. Newton specifically recalled to the author that the team included Hanford Twitchell, Charles Clapp, Jr., F. Shepard Cornell, Victor Kitchen, Rowland Hazard, and Professor Philip Marshall Brown of Princeton among its members. Later, Newton recalled that T. Henry Williams, and occasionally Russell Firestone—both of Akron—attended meetings on the East Coast. Newton himself was a member, but was often away on business for Firestone Tire & Rubber Company. Newton cannot recall Bill Wilson's presence. But the names Newton then recalled were all friends and associates of Sam Shoemaker's and, for the most part, of Bill Wilson's.

In further research, the author found that Lois Wilson had mentioned Bill's membership on a team, but she herself did not belong and related nothing more about the team.[1] Then the author discovered that Victor Kitchen had specifically written about the team.[2] Later, on examining Lois's Oxford Group Notes, the author found mention of Kitchen and others now known to have been team members. But the author was still unable to verify that Bill had been a member of this particular team. For sure, it consisted of Shoemaker's people. For sure, its members included many of Bill's closest Oxford Group friends. For sure, it was composed largely of businessmen in the business area Bill frequented. To date, however, the author has located only one still-living team member (Parks Shipley, Sr.) who can recall Wilson's participation in the team. Most of the members still alive are in their late eighties.

However, two additional pieces of evidence turned up in the author's research for this book.

---

[1] *Lois Remembers* (New York: Al-Anon Family Group Headquarters, 1987), p. 93.

[2] Victor C. Kitchen, *I Was A Pagan* (New York: Harper & Brothers, 1934), p. 123.

First, Jim and Eleanor Newton continued to search for details about the team. Finally, in the Spring of 1993, Eleanor Newton turned up a photo of the team; and the photo showed many more members than Newton had previously mentioned. Then Jim Newton set about identifying as many of the team members whose names and faces he and his wife could recall. He sent the photo to George Vondermuhll, who is a New England resident, long associated with these people; and Vondermuhll identified some additional names and faces. Finally, the photo was sent to Mrs. Irving Harris, who added to the list of names recalled. The author is still in search of further identities. But the confirmation of Newton's recollections about the team is now available.

Next, Shoemaker's younger daughter, Nickie Haggart, began searching Shoemaker's journals and came up with Shoemaker remarks about the team concerning events during the Thanksgiving period in 1935. And he specifically mentioned Bill Wilson's participation and responsibilities. And the journal entries show that Bill Wilson was very much involved with prominent businessmen, including Jim Newton of Firestone Tire & Rubber, in connection with the 1935 events. As a consequence, the author is sure that "more will be revealed," as the AAs say; and that this businessmen's circle will be found to be one of several Shoemaker influences on Bill in the late 1930's.

Meanwhile, we list below those members whose names and faces have been identified in the picture. The date of the photo is unknown, but Jim and Eleanor Newton believe the picture was taken at Briarcliffe.

The identified members are:

1. Michael Barrett
2. Alec Beck
3. John Beck
4. Walter Biscoe
5. Francis Bradley
6. Nort Brotherton
7. Shep Cornell (Bill's good friend, and Lois mentions)
8. John Cummings
9. Howard Davison (Lois mentions)
10. Charles Haines (Lois mentions)
11. Gilbert Harris
12. Cleve Hicks (Lois mentions)
13. Victor Kitchen (Lois mentions)
14. Morris Martin
15. Jim Newton (Lois mentions)
16. Bert Olsen
17. Ray Purdy (Lois mentions)
18. Norman Schwab
19. Parks Shipley (recalls Bill's team participation)
20. Samuel Shoemaker (Bill's good friend)
21. Murray Skinker
22. J. Herbert (Jack) Smith (Calvary Associate minister)
23. Garrett Stearly (Lois mentions)

24. Chris Story
25. Bill Wilkes

Mrs. Harris recalled that the following people were connected with the team:

1. Barclay Farr
2. Tom Page
3. John Ryder (Bill's good friend)
4. Fred Wilkens

Jim and Eleanor Newton added the names of the following people known to have been a part of the businessmen's team:

1. Charles Clapp, Jr. (Bill's good friend)
2. Rowland Hazard (Bill's good friend)
3. DuBois Morris
4. John Riffe
5. Hanford Twitchell (Bill's good friend)
6. C. Scoville Wishard
7. Loudon Hamilton (Lois mentions)
8. Philip Marshall Brown (Lois mentions)

The purpose in giving these names is that the author would like to learn all that he can about this important team. And he has already found some people who recall bits and pieces about the team and its members. For example, Vondermuhll recalled Haines's close connections with Shoemaker and with Buchman. Charles Haines personally verified this close relationship by a telephone interview with the author in November, 1993. Mrs. Harris recalled that Reverend Cleve Hicks taught Bible at houseparties. The name of Shep Cornell comes up repeatedly in connection with Wilson. Lois Wilson mentioned she had met Purdy, Newton, Hicks, Kitchen, Davison, Stearly, and Professor Brown at houseparties. She also made a specific notation about Charles Haines and the Bible. She mentioned Shep Cornell as a leader at a houseparty she and Bill attended. Another AA remembered the depth of involvement by the Beck family in Oxford Group activity. Reverend Jack Smith is specifically mentioned in several books about A.A. literature as having had contact with Wilson. Several things can be said about John Ryder: (1) He is well-remembered by Bill Wilson's secretary, Nell Wing, for his supportive letters and visits to Bill Wilson. (2) Irving Harris points out that Ryder was an advertising executive who was active in the Oxford Group, close to Sam Shoemaker, knew Bill Wilson in the days of Calvary Mission, and was involved with the men's group and Alcoholics Anonymous. Ryder had a daily Bible study group for the businessmen in his Madison Avenue office. (3) Ryder is quoted at some length in an A.A. Conference approved book. See Nell Wing, *Grateful To Have Been There* (Illinois: Parkside Publishing, 1992), p. 69; Irving Harris, *The Breeze of the Spirit* (New York: The Seabury Press, 1978), p. 150; and *Pass It On* (New York: A.A. World Services, 1984), pp. 173-74.

If you have, or someone you know might have, any information about the team, please contact the author via the address and telephone number provided in the back of this book.

Appendix 7

Lois Wilson's Oxford Group Notebook

In the author's most recent visit to the archives at Bill and Lois Wilson's home at Bedford Hills, New York, Paul L., the archivist at Stepping Stones, made available a small notebook that was kept by Lois Wilson during the years of her Oxford Group involvement between December, 1934 and August of 1937. The notebook in no way resembles Anne Smith's workbook. It commences with the notation that it is for the period 1935-1936. It contains, in Lois's own words, "Oxford Group Notes," and was kept by "Lois B. Wilson, 182 Clinton Street, Brooklyn." It records Oxford Group ideas that attracted Lois and may well have been heard by her at houseparties. It lists Oxford Group houseparties she and Bill attended. It mentions a number of well-known Oxford Group leaders that she and Bill heard, or met, or both, with notations as to their backgrounds.

Lois made the following notations about her Oxford Group thoughts:

1. "A supernatural network over live wires. Why not the voice of God in every parliament, every business? Every last man in every last place. Definite adequate, accurate information from God" (p. 3).[1]

2. "Repentance is sorry enough to quit" (p. 4).

3. "Sat. A.M. Chas. Haines—Bible . . . Home Quiet Time" (p. 7).

4. "I realized that I had not really put my reliance in God but have been trying under guidance as I thought to do it all myself" (p. 8).

---

[1] See this expression, frequently used by Dr. Frank Buchman, in Frank N. D. Buchman, *Remaking The World*. New and Rev. ed. (London: Blandford Press, 1961), p. 72: "Direct messages come from the Mind of God to the mind of man—definite, direct, decisive. God speaks." Buchman often spoke of the Voice of God, saying, for example: "The Voice of God must become the voice of the people." See Buchman, *Remaking The World*, p. 91.

5. "Read July 22—*Utmost For My Highest*—I really saw myself" (p. 9).[2]

6. "List of sins: Feeling of being special, self conscious, feeling of inferiority, self indulgence in small things, dependency on human law" (p. 10).

7. "Sin blinds, binds, multiplies, deadens" (p. 11).[3]

8. "True democracy is Tom, Dick & Harry under God Control" (p. 12).[4]

9. "Oxford Group is spiritual revolution whose concern is vital Christianity under dictatorship of spirit of God" (p. 12).[5]

10. "Sunday—AM. Leader Shep [Cornell]. Making for better human relationship for unselfish cooperation, for cleaner business, cleaner politics, elimination of political, industrial, & racial antagonisms. A new spirit is abroad in the world, a new illumination can bring men & women of every social situation back to the basic principles of the Christian faith" (pp. 13-14).

11. "Speak from experience. Guidance no substitute for hard thinking. The beauty of country & the inspiration of so many people working toward such a purpose & the fellowship meant the most to me at House Party" (p. 15).

12. "Help Margaret to get back to God. Let go of my possessiveness of Bill" (p. 17).

---

[2] Bill Pittman learned from Lois in an interview with her that "she and Bill frequently read *My Utmost for His Highest* by Oswald Chambers." See Bill Pittman, *AA The Way It Began* (Seattle: Glen Abbey Books, 1988), p. 183. From his own research, the author learned that Chambers was not connected with the Oxford Group at all, but that Oxford Group people, as well as Dr. Bob, Anne Smith, and Henrietta Seiberling, used Chambers' Bible devotional a great deal. It was also used in Akron meetings of the "alcoholic squad of the Oxford Group."

[3] This is an expression that Dr. Frank Buchman used quite often. It is covered at length in an important Oxford Group book that was widely read in early Akron A.A. and recommended by Dr. Bob and Anne. See A. J. Russell, *For Sinners Only* (London: Hodder & Stoughton, 1932), pp. 318-19.

[4] This expression, "God Control" can be found throughout Dr. Frank Buchman's speeches and writings. See, for example, Buchman, *Remaking The World*, pp. 3, 18, 24, 25, 28-30, 35-36, 39, 42, etc.

[5] In a manifesto in *Rising Tide*, in November of 1937, Buchman repeated this expression of his and said, "This is the dictatorship of the living Spirit of God, which gives every man the inner discipline he needs, and the inner liberty he desires." See Buchman, *Remaking The World*, p. 42.

13. "There ain't no white lies. All sins have blue eyes & dimples when they are young" (p. 25).

14. "Helen Shoemaker—Surrender to God" (p. 26).

15. "Fear of giving up that little special private citadel—oneself" (p. 28).[6]

16. "Fears of all kinds will disappear if self is forgotten" (p. 29).

17. "What do we say when someone asks us whether we think OG [Oxford Group] is the only way to God, that they have their own God perfectly satisfying?" "What do we say to agnostics?" (p. 35).

A number of Lois Wilson's notes related to two houseparties she and Bill attended. Noting the "Pocono House Party Dec 4-6," Lois mentioned Garrett Stearly, Garth Lean, Ted Watt, Alex Smith [Shoemaker's father-in-law], and Jim Newton-Florida. At pages 19 through 23, Lois listed a large number of well-known Oxford Group people, including: (1) James Newton-Florida; (2) Howard Davison-businessman; (3) Garth Lean; (4) Irving Harris; (5) Ray and Elsa Purdy; (6) Vic Kitchen-advertising; (7) Philip Marshall Brown-Princeton; (8) James Watt-Scotland; (9) Cleveland Hicks. The reader may recall the context in which we have discussed these names—Newton, Lean, Harris, Purdy, Kitchen, Philip Marshall Brown, and Hicks.

Speaking of the "Houseparty at West Point-Jan 10/37," Lois mentioned: (1) Loudon Hamilton-Oxford; (2) Sam [Shoemaker]; (3) Frank [Buchman]; (4) James Newton-Firestone; (5) Eleanor Forde. We consider all these entries significant because they specifically name the following important Oxford Group people whom Bill and Lois either heard or met, or both, and whose lives are discussed in our book:

1. Jim Newton—who was so very much involved in Akron A.A.'s beginnings.[7]

2. Eleanor Forde, Jim Newton's wife-to-be, whose writings were much discussed in Anne Smith's workbook.[8]

3. Garth Lean—Frank Buchman's close associate and biographer.[9]

---

[6] Overcoming fear by abandoning self to God-control was a major Buchman theme. In *Remaking The World*, Buchman said: "What is the disease? Isn't it fear, dishonesty, resentment, selfishness? We talk about freedom and liberty, but we are slaves to ourselves" (p. 38).

[7] And see James D. Newton, *Uncommon Friends* (New York: Harcourt Brace, 1987).

[8] And see Eleanor Napier Forde, *The Guidance of God* (The Oxford Group, 1930).

[9] And see Garth Lean, *On The Tail of a Comet* (Colorado Springs, Helmers & Howard, 1988).

4. Irving Harris—Sam Shoemaker's assistant minister, who became a close friend of Bill Wilson's.[10]

5. Ray and Elsa Purdy—important Oxford Group leaders, Ray being a member of the clergy, a long-time associate of Shoemaker's, and an early member of Shoemaker's Calvary Church staff. Ray Purdy was an early friend of Sam Shoemaker's at Princeton.

6. Victor Kitchen—member of the Oxford Group business team and author of the Oxford Group book, *I Was A Pagan*—which tells of recovery from alcoholism through the Oxford Group.[11]

7. Professor Philip Marshall Brown, who met with the Oxford Group businessmen's team and with Rowland Hazard, and who wrote the important Oxford Group book, *The Venture of Belief*.[12] Shoemaker wrote the introduction to this book; and an entry in his journal indicates he may have sent a copy to Bill Wilson.

8. Reverend Cleveland Hicks, who conducted many of the Oxford Group houseparty Bible sessions, according to Julia Harris.

9. A. S. Loudon Hamilton, the omnipresent Oxford Group business team member, who warmed the group up on Friday nights with "Scotch" stories.

10. Charles Haines, an early Oxford Group activist, closely associated with both Frank Buchman and Sam Shoemaker.

11. Reverend Sam Shoemaker, who became Bill Wilson's close friend, and to whom Bill W. attributed much material for the Steps.

12. Dr. Frank Buchman, founder of the Oxford Group.[13]

Brief though they are, we believe these "Oxford Group Notes" of Lois Wilson's provide much additional evidence of the nature and extent of Bill Wilson's exposure to Oxford Group principles and practices, to the Bible, and to some of the most important Oxford Group personages and writers of the 1935-1936 period of which Lois wrote.

---

[10] And see Irving Harris, *The Breeze of the Spirit* (New York: The Seabury Press, 1978).

[11] And see V. C. Kitchen, *I Was A Pagan* (New York: Harper & Brothers, 1934).

[12] And see Philip Marshall Brown, *The Venture of Belief* (New York: Fleming H. Revell, 1935).

[13] And see Frank N. D. Buchman, *Remaking The World* (London: Blandford Press, 1961).

Entries in Lois Wilson's diary for 1937, which is also located at Stepping Stones and which the author inspected, indicated she frequently talked of Guidance, "being convicted," God's plan, and quiet times—all major Oxford Group ideas as to which Bill Wilson was also, presumably, informed and familiar.

Appendix 8

Two Important Wilson Letters

Bill's Letter of April 23, 1963, to Sam *

You must remember, Sam, that you were the personification here in New York of all the best that went on in Calvary and in the O.G. of A.A.'s early days. Your impact on me, and upon some of our other people, was simply immense. So whether the transmission of Grace occurred by night or day is quite beside the point. It is also entirely true that the substance of A.A.'s Twelve Steps was derived from the O.G.'s emphasis on the essentials and your unforgettable presentation of this material time after time.

After the alcoholics parted company with the O.G. here in New York, we developed a word-of-mouth program of six steps which was simply a paraphrase of what we had heard and felt at your meetings. The Twelve Steps of A.A. simply represented an attempt to state in more detail, breadth and depth, what we had been taught - primarily by you. Without this, there could have been nothing - nothing at all.

Certainly there were other indispensable contributions without which we should have probably got no place. But none of these were so large or so critical as your own. Though I wish the "co-founder" tag had never been hitched to any of us, I have no hesitancy in adding your name to the list!

[* NOTE: The text of the letter quoted above was given to the author by Nickie Shoemaker Haggart in September of 1993.]

Bill Wilson's April, 1953, Memo as to "Original AA Steps" *

1. Admitted hopeless	[The Need—Step One]
2. Got honest with self	[Inventory—Step Four]
3. Got honest with another	[Confession—Step Five]
4. Made amends	[Restitution—Steps 8 & 9]
5. Helped others without demand	[Witness—Step Twelve]
6. Prayed to God as you understand Him	[Prayer, Surrender, Conversion, Guidance—Steps 2, 3, 6, 7, 10, & 11]

[* NOTE: The memorandum quoted above was written in Bill Wilson's own hand, and was "For Ed," signed "Ever Bill W.," dated "Apr/1953," and titled "Original AA Steps." A photocopy of the memorandum was supplied to the author by Lee S. of the Washington, D.C., Area Intergroup Association. (The comments in brackets are those of the present author.)]

Appendix 9

The Twelve Steps of Alcoholics Anonymous *

1. We admitted we were powerless over alcohol—that our lives had become unmanageable.

2. Came to believe that a Power greater than ourselves could restore us to sanity.

3. Made a decision to turn our will and our lives over to the care of God *as we understood Him.*

4. Made a searching and fearless moral inventory of ourselves.

5. Admitted to God, to ourselves, and to another human being the exact nature of our wrongs.

6. Were entirely ready to have God remove all these defects of character.

7. Humbly asked Him to remove our shortcomings.

8. Made a list of all persons we had harmed, and became willing to make amends to them all.

9. Made direct amends to such persons wherever possible, except when to do so would injure them or others.

10. Continued to take personal inventory and when we were wrong promptly admitted it.

11. Sought through prayer and meditation to improve our conscious contact with God *as we understood Him*, praying only for knowledge of His will for us and the power to carry that out.

12. Having had a spiritual awakening as the result of these Steps, we tried to carry this message to alcoholics, and to practice these principles in all our affairs.

[* *The Twelve Steps of Alcoholics Anonymous* is reprinted with permission of Alcoholics Anonymous World Services, Inc.]

Appendix 10

Excerpts from *The Calvary Evangel* and *Calvary Church Yearbook*

Preliminary Comments by the Author

As this book was going to press, the author was able to review key issues of *The Calvary Evangel* and the *Calvary Church Yearbook* at the Calvary Church archives during his most recent trip to New York City. These source materials contained information that not only confirmed many of the points made in our book, but also revealed some important new bits of history about Bill Wilson, Sam Shoemaker, and the people from Calvary Church who were in their company. The evidence at the Calvary Church archives shows that:

1. The names of the members of the Oxford Group businessmen's team—names such as Rowland Hazard, Shepard Cornell, Hanford Twitchell, and Victor Kitchen—are often seen in company with each other in the church publications and records.

2. Rowland Hazard, Shepard Cornell, Hanford Twitchell, and Victor Kitchen were very much involved in the lay leadership at Calvary Church in the 1930's and also in the Oxford Group work of the church.

3. There are possible confirmations of Bill Wilson's statement that Shoemaker inspired Dr. Bob as well as Bill. Thus there is substantial writing in *The Calvary Evangel* about Oxford Group team excursions to Akron, Ohio, *after* the 1933 Firestone events; and there is a strong suggestion that Sam Shoemaker also was in Akron with the teams in 1934. These writings show either a direct or at least an indirect influence of Shoemaker himself in Akron and very possibly the influence of his Calvary Church circle on Dr. Bob, Anne Smith, Henrietta Seiberling, and T. Henry and Clarace Williams who were all attending Oxford Group meetings in Akron at that time. The articles may explain why Anne Smith refers in her spiritual workbook to Shoemaker and Oxford Group members James Watts and Eleanor Forde, as well as to books that appear in the Calvary Church Oxford Group Literature List for that period. For Oxford Group books were usually available at Oxford Group functions, including, presumably, those in Akron.

4. There is definite confirmation of the close association of Sam Shoemaker with Bill Wilson in the 1935-1936 period. Thus the parish register and *The Calvary Evangel* issues reviewed by the author show that Bill Wilson was present in March, 1935, when Frederick E. Breithut (the man Shoemaker mentioned in his letter to Wilson in January of 1935) was baptized. Bill was present in the church at the ceremony and served as Breithut's godparent. Entries for this period show that Bill's Oxford Group friend (and sponsor) Ebby Thatcher was becoming a communicant at Calvary at the same ceremony as Breithut with Shep Cornell as Ebby's godparent. Ebby's other godparent was Tex Francisco, the superintendent at Calvary Rescue Mission, where both Ebby and Bill made decisions for Christ. Both Bill and Shoemaker were present at the confirmation ceremony.

5. Oxford Group writers, Philip Marshall Brown and Victor Kitchen, as well as Shep Cornell, were very much involved with each other at the time Kitchen and Cornell were involved with Bill Wilson in the 1935 time period.

6. There is a strong possibility that Bill might have heard, or read, or been exposed to Shoemaker's "God as you understand Him" sermon in 1935, either directly from Shoemaker, or from Shoemaker's associates. This was long before Bill was working with Hank P. and Jim B. (the atheists) were supposed to have had a part in suggesting the "God as you understand Him" idea to A.A. in 1938. Shoemaker's "The Way to Find God" sermon, referred to below, seems to provide some additional evidence for our belief that Shoemaker had directly conveyed to Bill and to others in the Oxford Group his "God as you understand Him" ideas as part of his suggested experiment of faith, and that these Shoemaker ideas were adopted both by Anne Smith and Bill Wilson during the 1935 time frame.

Specific Evidence Found at the Calvary Church Archives

1. The October, 1928, issue of *The Calvary Evangel* contains a photograph of Sam Shoemaker and his staff in full vestment, preceded by a member of the church who is carrying a Cross. The caption states, *"On Our Way To Rejoicing" to Madison Square*. One church member in the 1928 photo was carrying a sign which stated, "Jesus Christ Changes Lives." Other signs urged onlookers to "Come With Us To Calvary Church." Parks Shipley, an Oxford Group member interviewed by the author, recalls marching to such events in the 1930's where the march would be followed by public witnessing at a park from a "soap box." Shipley believes Bill Wilson was among the "rejoicers" at one or more of these events during Wilson's involvement with the Oxford Group.

2. The February, 1933, issue of *The Calvary Evangel* contains a "Book List." The list is accompanied by the statement that the following books and pamphlets dealing with "A First Century Christian Fellowship" (the Oxford Group) could

be obtained from the Calvary Church Book Stall, 61 Gramercy Park, New York City. (The Book Stall was later operated by Mrs. W. Irving Harris at the 61 Gramercy Park Calvary House headquarters.) The books were Shoemaker's *The Conversion of the Church*, *Children of the Second Birth*, *Twice-Born Ministers*, *Confident Faith*, and *Realizing Religion*; Begbie's *Life Changers*; Russell's *For Sinners Only*; Allen's *He That Cometh*; Reynold's *New Lives for Old*; Forde's *The Guidance of God*; Duesbury's *Sharing*; Day's *Principles of the Group*; and Carruthers' *How to Find Reality in Your Morning Devotions*. Most of these books were recommended for reading by Anne Smith in her spiritual workbook and thus, as we explain in *Dr. Bob's Library*, were read by Dr. Bob.

3. *The Calvary Evangel* "Oxford Group Literature List" for the 1934 issues added Kitchen's *I Was A Pagan*; Winslow's *Why I Believe in the Oxford Group*; Grensted's *The Person of Christ*; Olive Jones's *Inspired Children*; *What is the Oxford Group?*; Cuyler's *Calvary Church in Action*; Smith's *The Meaning of Conversion*; MacMillan's *Seeking and Finding*; and Shoemaker's *Christ's Words from the Cross*, *Religion That Works*, *If I Be Lifted Up*, and *The Gospel According to You*.

4. The February and May, 1934, issues of *The Calvary Evangel* contained articles by Oxford Group member Victor C. Kitchen. Kitchen's February, 1934, article, "Points West," stated that between January 19th and February 10th of 1934, Reverend Sam Shoemaker, Reverend Jack Smith, Reverend John Cuyler, Olive Jones, and others from Calvary Church, including Kitchen, took their Oxford Group "traveling team" to Syracuse, New York; Columbus, Ohio; Cincinnati, Ohio; and Louisville, Kentucky. Kitchen stated that some of the team "went on to Akron." He mentioned the Oxford Group team visit to Akron in 1933 (when the famous Firestone events occurred). Kitchen stated the 1933 Akron team had "sewn generously of the first four of the 5 C's." "There had not," he said, "been much of the 5th 'C' or continuance work in Akron [in 1933] and this seemed to be our guided task. While the opportunity for changing lives was never overlooked, we were led to concentrate particularly on the deepening of lives already changed. With but a single open meeting and comparatively few church engagements, our work [in Akron] centered about personal interviews with members and leaders of local groups and on a school of life which featured further reaches of sharing and surrender, group formation, loyalty, identification and leadership. While we were quartered throughout this period at the Mayflower Hotel, we found an ever-ready welcome at the home of Mrs. F. A. Seiberling. Some of us could always be found dining under Mrs. Seiberling's gracious hospitality. A buffet supper, held there the last night of our stay, gave us the opportunity to meet many of Akron's leading citizens while a session of the School of Life in the Seiberling's music room preceded by the playing of their organ, marked perhaps the spiritual high spot of our entire trip. It was here that the team split up—a handful going on to California, another handful remaining behind to gather up loose ends in Akron and other Ohio cities, while the rest of us occupied all but two berths in a Pullman car and headed for New York."

5. In a 1934 issue of *The Calvary Evangel*, Shoemaker's assistant minister, John Potter Cuyler, referred to a huge [Oxford Group] team that went to the West and included Victor C. Kitchen, Rowland Hazard, Reverend Ray Purdy, Charles Haines, John and Alexander Beck, Hanford Twitchell, Parks Shipley, Mrs. F. A. Seiberling, Carl Vrooman, Cuyler himself, and Reverend Norman Schwab.

6. The "Oxford Group Literature" list contained in the February, 1935, issue of *The Calvary Evangel* added Walter's *Soul Surgery* to the recommended list.

7. A 1935 issue of *The Calvary Evangel* announced that Frederick E. Breithut was confirmed on March 24, 1935, as a member of Calvary Episcopal Church, having previously been sponsored at a baptism on March 14, 1935, by William G. Wilson [Bill W.] as his godfather, with Reverend Samuel Shoemaker performing the baptism. The issue also announced that on the same date [March 24, 1935] Edwin Throckmorton Thatcher ["Ebby," Bill Wilson's sponsor and close friend] was confirmed as a communicant at Calvary, having on December 9, 1934, been baptized under the sponsorship of F. Shepard Cornell and Taylor L. [Tex] Francisco [the superintendent at Calvary Rescue Mission] as Ebby's godparents.

8. In August of 1935, Shoemaker's sermon of June 30, 1935, was printed in full in *The Calvary Evangel.* The title was, "The Way to Find God." Shoemaker preached on his theme that "Give in-Admit that I am God" is the Bible's injunction for self-surrender to God. Shoemaker also covered the topic of "God as you understand Him." Shoemaker said, "Because He is, and because He loves us, He begins with us where we are. We need know little about His nature, or the completeness of His self-revelation in Christ, to make the initial step towards Him. Understanding will come later; what is wanted first is relationship. That begins, as thousands will tell you from experience, at the point where we 'give in' to God. . . . Begin with the premise of God as a postulate."

9. The 1935 *Calvary Evangel* table of contents contained the following list of Shoemaker's reprinted sermons for that year:

   The Prophet, the Vision and God, January
   Marks of a Converted Life, February
   You Can Be in Touch with God, March
   Calvary Church and God's Plan for the World, April
   God's Will and Immortality, May
   The Price of Spiritual Leadership Today, July
   The Way to Find God, August
   "*There is a River*", September
   Creating Peace in the World, December

10. The August, 1935, issue reported that Shoemaker had taken abroad with him Victor C. Kitchen, Professor Philip Marshall Brown, and Parks Shipley.

11. *The Year Book of Calvary Church for 1938* lists the following as the staff of Calvary Church's "corporation":

    Hanford Twitchell, Junior Warden
    F. Shepard Cornell, Clerk of the Vestry
    Rowland Hazard, Member of the Vestry as of March 27, 1938 (and continuing in later issues through 1940)

12. *The Year Book* for earlier years listed as members of the church corporation Reverend Ray Foote Purdy (Assistant Treasurer of the Church) and Reverend Garrett R. Stearly.

Bibliography

Publications by or about Samuel Moor Shoemaker, Jr.

Shoemaker, Samuel Moor, Jr. "Act As If." *Christian Herald*. October, 1954.
———. "And So From My Heart I Say . . ." *The A.A. Grapevine*. New York: The A.A. Grapevine, Inc., September, 1948.
———. . . . *And Thy Neighbor*. Waco, Texas: Word Books, 1967.
———. *A Young Man's View of the Ministry*. New York: Association Press, 1923.
———. *Beginning Your Ministry*. New York: Harper & Row Publishers, 1963.
———. *By the Power of God*. New York: Harper & Brothers, 1954.
———. *Calvary Church Yesterday and Today*. New York: Fleming H. Revell, 1936.
———. *Children of the Second Birth*. New York: Fleming H. Revell, 1927.
———. *Christ and This Crisis*. New York: Fleming H. Revell, 1943.
———. *Christ's Words from the Cross*. New York: Fleming H. Revell, 1933.
———. *Confident Faith*. New York: Fleming H. Revell, 1932.
———. *Extraordinary Living for Ordinary Men*. Michigan: Zondervan, 1965.
———. *Faith at Work*. A symposium edited by Samuel Moor Shoemaker. Hawthorne Books, 1958.
———. *Freedom and Faith*. New York: Fleming H. Revell, 1949.
———. *God and America*. New York: Book Stall, 61 Gramercy Park North, New York, n.d.
———. *God's Control*. New York: Fleming H. Revell, 1939.
———. *How To Become A Christian*. New York: Harper & Brothers, 1953.
———. *How To Find God*. Reprint From Faith At Work Magazine, n.d.
———. *How to Help People*. Cincinnati: Forward Movement Publications, 1976.
———. *How You Can Find Happiness*. New York: E. P. Dutton & Co., 1947.
———. *How You Can Help Other People*. New York: E. P. Dutton & Co., 1946.
———. *If I Be Lifted Up*. New York: Fleming H. Revell, 1931.
———. *In Memoriam: The Service of Remembrance*. Princeton: The Graduate Council, Princeton University, June 10, 1956.
———. *Living Your Life Today*. New York: Fleming H. Revell, 1947.
———. *Morning Radio Talk No. 1, by Reverend Samuel M. Shoemaker*, American Broadcasting Co., 1 page transcript of program for October 4, 1945.
———. *National Awakening*. New York: Harper & Brothers, 1936.
———. *One Boy's Influence*. New York: Association Press, 1925.
———. *Realizing Religion*. New York: Association Press, 1923.

———. *Religion That Works*. New York: Fleming H. Revell, 1928.
———. *Revive Thy Church*. New York: Harper & Brothers, 1948.
———. *Sam Shoemaker at His Best*. New York: Faith At Work, 1964.
———. *So I Stand by the Door and Other Verses*. Pittsburgh: Calvary Rectory, 1958.
———. *The Breadth and Narrowness of the Gospel*. New York: Fleming H. Revell, 1929.
———. *The Calvary Evangel, monthly articles in*. New York. Calvary Episcopal Church.
———. *The Church Alive*. New York: E. P. Dutton & Co., Inc., 1951.
———. *The Church Can Save The World*. New York: Harper & Brothers, 1938.
———. *The Conversion of the Church*. New York: Fleming H. Revell, 1932.
———. "The Crisis of Self-Surrender." *Guideposts*. November, 1955.
———. *The Experiment of Faith*. New York: Harper & Brothers. 1957.
———. *The Gospel According To You*. New York: Fleming H. Revell, 1934.
———. *The James Houston Eccleston Day-Book: Containing a Short Account of His Life and Readings for Every Day in the Year Chosen from His Sermons*. Compiled by Samuel M. Shoemaker, Jr. New York: Longmans, Green & Co., 1915.
———. "The Spiritual Angle." *The A.A. Grapevine*. New York: The A.A. Grapevine, Inc., October, 1955.
———. *They're on the Way*. New York: E. P. Dutton, 1951.
———. "Those Twelve Steps As I Understand Them." *Best of the Grapevine: Volume II*. New York: The A.A. Grapevine, Inc., 1986.
———. *Twice-Born Ministers*. New York: Fleming H. Revell, 1929.
———. *Under New Management*. Grand Rapids: Zondervan Publishing House., 1966.
———. *What The Church Has to Learn from Alcoholics Anonymous*. Reprint of 1956 sermon. Available at A.A. Archives, New York.
———. *With The Holy Spirit and With Fire*. New York: Harper & Brothers, 1960.

"Buchman Religion Explained to 1,000." *New York Times*. May 27, 1931, p. 19.
"Campus Calls by Dr. Shoemaker Foster Chain of Religious Cells." *New York Tribune*. February 25, 1951.
Centennial History: Calvary Episcopal Church, 1855-1955. Pittsburgh: Calvary Episcopal Church, 1955, pp. 81-85.
"Church Ejects Buchman Group." *New York Times*. November 8, 1941, p. 21.
"Crusaders of Reform." *Princeton Alumni Weekly*. June 2, 1993.
Cuyler, John Potter, Jr. *Calvary Church In Action*. New York: Fleming H. Revell, 1934.
Day, Sherwood S. "ALWAYS READY: S.M.S. as a Friend." *The Evangel* (New York: Calvary Church, July-August, 1950), pp. 246-247.
Harris, Irving. *The Breeze of the Spirit*. New York: The Seabury Press, 1978.
———. "S.M.S.—Man of God for Our Time." *Faith At Work* (January-February, 1964), pp. 19-24.
"Houseparties Across the Continent." *The Christian Century*. August 23, 1933, p. 1058.
Knippel, Charles Taylor. *Samuel M. Shoemaker's Theological Influence on William G. Wilson's Twelve Step Spiritual Program of Recovery (Alcoholics Anonymous)*. Dissertation. St. Louis University, 1987.
"Listening to God Held Daily Need." *New York Times*. December 4, 1939, p. 20.
Norton-Taylor. "Businessmen on Their Knees." *Fortune*. October, 1953.

Olsson, Karl A. "The History of Faith at Work" (five parts). *Faith At Work News*. 1982-1983.

Peale, Norman Vincent. "The Unforgettable Sam Shoemaker." *Faith At Work*. January, 1964, pp. 16-18.

———. "THE HUMAN TOUCH: The Estimate of a Fellow Clergyman and Personal Friend." *The Evangel* (New York: Calvary Church, July-August, 1950), pp. 245-246.

Pitt, Louis W. "NEW LIFE, NEW REALITY: A Brief Picture of S.M.S.'s Influence in the Diocese of New York." *Faith At Work*, July-August, 1950, p. 248.

"Pittsburgh Man of the Year." *Pittsburgh Post Gazette*. January 12, 1956.

Sack, David Edward. *Sam Shoemaker and the "Happy Ethical Pagans*." Princeton, New Jersey: paper prepared in the Department of Religion, Princeton University, June, 1993.

"Sam Shoemaker and Faith At Work." Pamphlet on file at Faith At Work, Inc., 150 S. Washington St., Suite 204, Falls Church, VA 22046.

Schwartz, Robert. "Laymen and Clergy to Join Salute to Dr. S. M. Shoemaker." *Pittsburgh Press*. December 10, 1961.

Shoemaker, Helen Smith. *I Stand By The Door*. New York: Harper & Row, 1967.

"Sees Great Revival Near." *New York Times*. September 8, 1930, p. 19.

"Soul Clinic Depicted By Pastor in Book." *New York Times*. August 5, 1927, p. 18.

"Ten of the Greatest American Preachers." *Newsweek*. March 28, 1955.

"Urges Church Aid Oxford Group." *New York Times*. January 2, 1933, p. 26.

Wilson, Bill. "I Stand By The Door." *The A.A. Grapevine*. New York: The A.A. Grapevine, Inc., February, 1967.

Woolverton, John F. "Evangelical Protestantism and Alcoholism 1933-1962: Episcopalian Samuel Shoemaker, The Oxford Group and Alcoholics Anonymous." *Historical Magazine of the Protestant Episcopal Church* 52 (March, 1983), pp. 53-65.

[The reader may find additional material by or about Samuel Shoemaker, Jr., at: (1) the Maryland Historical Society, Manuscripts Division, under "Shoemaker Papers;" (2) the Princeton University Archives at Princeton University, Olden Lane, Princeton, New Jersey, in the Samuel Shoemaker alumnus file; (3) the Episcopal Archives in Austin, Texas; (4) the Library of Congress, in the Ray Foote Purdy files of the Moral Re-Armament (and Oxford Group) Archives; (5) the Maryland Diocese of the Protestant Episcopal Church; (6) the Stepping Stones Archives, Bedford Hills, New York, the Shoemaker-Wilson letters; (7) the Hartford Theological Seminary Archives, Hartford, Connecticut; and (8) the parish offices of Calvary/St. George's in New York City. In addition, articles by or about Shoemaker were written in *The Calvary Evangel*, published by Calvary Episcopal Church in New York; and in the *Faith at Work* magazine, 150 South Washington Street, Suite 204, Falls Church, Virginia.]

Publications by or about the Oxford Group & Oxford Group People

A Day in Pennsylvania Honoring Frank Nathan Daniel Buchman in Pennsburg and Allentown. Oregon: Grosvenor Books, 1992.
Allen, Geoffrey Francis. *He That Cometh*. New York: The Macmillan Company, 1933.
Almond, Harry J. *Foundations For Faith*. 2d ed. London: Grosvenor Books, 1980.
Austin, H. W. "Bunny". *Frank Buchman As I Knew Him*. London: Grosvenor Books, 1975.
———. *Moral Re-Armament: The Battle for Peace*. London: William Heineman, 1938.
Begbie, Harold. *Life Changers*. New York: G. P. Putnam's Sons, 1927.
———. *Souls In Action*. New York: Hodder & Stoughton, 1911.
———. *Twice-Born Men*. New York: Fleming H. Revell, 1909.
Belden, David C. *The Origins And Development Of The Oxford Group (Moral Re-Armament)*. D. Phil. Dissertation, Oxford University, 1976.
Belden, Kenneth D. *Is God Speaking-Are We Listening?* London: Grosvenor Books, 1987.
———. *Meeting Moral Re-Armament*. London: Grosvenor Books, 1979.
———. *Reflections on Moral Re-Armament*. London: Grosvenor Books, 1983.
———. *The Hour of The Helicopter*. Somerset, England: Linden Hall, 1992.
Bennett, John C. *Social Salvation*. New York: Charles Scribner's Sons, 1935, pp. 53-60.
Benson, Clarence Irving. *The Eight Points of the Oxford Group*. London: Humphrey Milford, Oxford University Press, 1936.
Blair, David. *For Tomorrow-Yes!* Compiled and edited from David Blair's Notebook by Jane Mullen Blair & Friends. New York: Exposition Press, 1981.
Braden, Charles Samuel. *These Also Believe*. New York: The Macmillan Company, 1949.
Brown, Philip M. *The Venture of Belief*. New York: Fleming H. Revell, 1935.
Buchman, Frank N. D. *Remaking The World*. London: Blandford Press, 1961.
Frank Buchman-80. Compiled by His Friends. London: Blandford Press, 1958.
Cantrill, Hadley. *The Psychology of Social Movements*. New York: John Wiley & Sons, Inc., 1941.
Clapp, Charles Jr. *The Big Bender*. New York: Harper & Row, 1938.
Clark, Walter Houston. *The Oxford Group: Its History and Significance*. New York: Bookman Associates, 1951.
Crothers, Susan. *Susan and God*. New York: Harper & Brothers, 1939.
Day, Sherwood Sunderland. *The Principles of the Group*. Oxford: University Press, n.d.
"Discord in Oxford Group: Buchmanites Ousted by Disciple From N.Y. Parish House." *Newsweek*. November 24, 1941, p. 65.
Driberg, Tom. *The Mystery of Moral Re-Armament: A Study of Frank Buchman and His Movement*. New York: Alfred A. Knopf, 1965.
Eister, Allan W. *Drawing Room Conversion*. Durham: Duke University Press, 1950.
Ferguson, Charles W. *The Confusion of Tongues*. Garden City: Doubleday, Doran Company, Inc., 1940.
Foot, Stephen. *Life Began Yesterday*. New York: Harper & Brothers, 1935.
Forde, Eleanor Napier. *The Guidance of God*. Oxford: Printed at the University Press, 1930.

Grensted, L. W. *The Person of Christ*. New York: Harper & Brothers, 1933.
Grogan, William. *John Riffe of the Steelworkers*. New York: Coward—McCann, 1959.
Hamilton, Loudon. *MRA: How It All Began*. London: Moral Re-Armament, 1968.
Harris, Irving. *An Outline of the Life of Christ*. New York: The Oxford Group, 1935.
Harrison, Marjorie. *Saints Run Mad*. London: John Lane, Ltd., 1934.
Henson, Herbert Hensley. *The Group Movement*. London: Oxford University Press, 1933.
Hicks, Roger. *How To Study The Bible*. (Oxford Group, copy not yet located).
Hofmeyr, Bremer. *How to Change*. New York: Moral Re-Armament, n.d.
———. *How to Listen*. New York: Moral Re-Armament, n.d.
Holmes-Walker, Wilfrid. *New Enlistment* (no data available).
Howard, Peter. *Frank Buchman's Secret*. Garden City: New York: Doubleday & Company, Inc., 1961.
———. *That Man Frank Buchman*. London: Blandford Press, 1946.
———. *The World Rebuilt*. New York. Duell, Sloan & Pearce, 1951.
Hunter, T. Willard. *Press Release*. Buchman Events/Pennsylvania, October 19, 1991.
———. *The Spirit of Charles Lindbergh*. Madison Books, 1993.
———. *Uncommon Friends' Uncommon Friend*. A tribute to James Draper Newton, on the occasion of his eighty-fifth birthday. (Pamphlet, March 30, 1990).
———. *World Changing Through Life Changing*. Thesis, Newton Center, Mass: Andover-Newton Theological School, 1977.
Jones, Olive M. *Inspired Children*. New York: Harper & Brothers, 1933.
———. *Inspired Youth*. New York: Harper & Brothers, 1938.
Kitchen, V. C. *I Was A Pagan*. New York: Harper & Brothers, 1934.
Lean, Garth. *Cast Out Your Nets*. London: Grosvenor, 1990.
———. *Good God, It Works*. London: Blandford Press, 1974.
———. and Martin, Morris. *New Leadership*. London: William Heinemann, Ltd., 1936.
———. *On The Tail of a Comet: The Life of Frank Buchman*. Colorado Springs: Helmers & Howard, 1988.
Leon, Philip. *The Philosophy of Courage or The Oxford Group Way*. New York: Oxford University Press, 1939.
"Less Buchmanism." *Time*, November 24, 1941, p. 59.
Macintosh, Douglas C. *Personal Religion*. New York: Charles Scribner's Sons, 1942.
Macmillan, Ebenezer. *Seeking And Finding*. New York: Harper & Brothers, 1933.
Moyes, John S. *American Journey*. Sydney: Clarendon Publishing Co., n. d.
Murray, Robert H. *Group Movements Throughout The Ages*. New York: Harper & Brothers. 1935.
Newton, James. *Uncommon Friends*. New York: Harcourt Brace, 1987.
Nichols, Beverley. *The Fool Hath Said*. Garden City: Doubleday, Doran & Company, 1936.
Petrocokino, Paul. *The New Man for the New World*. Cheshire: Paul Petrocokino, n.d.
Phillimore, Miles. *Just For Today*. (Oxford Group, copy not yet located).
Raynor, Frank D. and Leslie D. Weatherhead. *The Finger of God*. London: Group Publications, Ltd., 1934.
Reynolds, Amelia S. *New Lives For Old*. New York. Fleming H. Revell, 1929.
Roots, John McCook. *An Apostle To Youth*. Oxford, The Oxford Group, 1928.

Rose, Cecil. *When Man Listens*. New York: Oxford University Press, 1937.
Rose, Howard J. *The Quiet Time*. New York: Oxford Group at 61 Gramercy Park, North, 1937.
Russell, Arthur J. *For Sinners Only*. London: Hodder & Stoughton, 1932.
———. *One Thing I Know*. New York: Harper & Brothers, 1933.
Sangster, W. E. *God Does Guide Us*. New York: The Abingdon Press, 1934.
Selbie, W. B. *Oxford And The Groups*. Oxford: Basie Blackwell, 1934.
Sherry, Frank H. and Mahlon H. Hellerich. *The Formative Years of Frank N. D. Buchman*. (Reprint of article at Frank Buchman home in Allentown, Pennsylvania).
Spencer, F. A. M., *The Meaning of the Groups*. London: Metheun & Co., Ltd., 1934.
Spoerri, Theophil. *Dynamic Out of Silence: Frank Buchman's Relevance Today*. Translated by John Morrison. London: Grosvenor Books, 1976.
Streeter, Burnett Hillman. *The God Who Speaks*. London: Macmillan & Co., Ltd., 1943.
The Bishop of Leicester, Chancellor R. J. Campbell and the Editor of the "Church of England Newspaper." *Stories of our Oxford House Party*., July 17, 1931.
The Layman with a Notebook. *What Is The Oxford Group?* London: Oxford University Press, 1933.
Thornton-Duesbury, J. P. *Sharing*. The Oxford Group. n.d.
"Calvary's Eviction of Buchman." *Time Magazine*, November 24, 1941.
Twitchell, Kenaston. *Do You Have to Be Selfish*. New York: Moral Re-Armament, n.d.
———. *How Do You Make Up Your Mind*. New York: Moral Re-Armament, n.d.
———. *Regeneration in the Ruhr*. Princeton: Princeton University Press, 1981.
———. *Supposing Your Were Absolutely Honest*. New York: Moral Re-Armament, n.d.
———. *The Strength of a Nation: Absolute Purity*. New York: Moral Re-Armament, n.d.
Van Dusen, Henry P. "Apostle to the Twentieth Century: Frank N. D. Buchman." *Atlantic Monthly* 154 (July 1934): 1-16.
———. "The Oxford Group Movement." *Atlantic Monthly*. 154 (August 1934): 240-52.
Viney, Hallen. *How Do I Begin?* The Oxford Group, 61 Gramercy Park, New York., 1937.
Vrooman, Lee. *The Faith that Built America*. New York: Arrowhead Books, Inc., 1955.
Walter, Howard A. *Soul-Surgery: Some Thoughts On Incisive Personal Work*. 6th. ed. Oxford: at the University Press by John Johnson, 1940.
Weatherhead, Leslie D. *Discipleship*. London: Student Christian Movement Press, 1934.
———. *How Can I Find God?* London: Fleming H. Revell, 1934.
———. *Psychology And Life*. New York: Abingdon Press, 1935.
Williamson, Geoffrey. *Inside Buchmanism*. New York: Philosophical Library, Inc., 1955.
Winslow, Jack C. *Church in Action* (no data available to author).
———. *Vital Touch With God: How to Carry on Adequate Devotional Life*. The Evangel, 6 East 40th St., New York, n.d.
———. *When I Awake*. London: Hodder & Stoughton, 1938.
———. *Why I Believe In The Oxford Group*. London: Hodder & Stoughton, 1934.

Books by or about Oxford Group Mentors

Bushnell, Horace. *The New Life*. London: Strahan & Co., 1868.
Chapman, J. Wilbur. *Life and Work of Dwight L. Moody*. Philadelphia, 1900.
Cheney, Mary B. *Life and Letters of Horace Bushnell*. New York: Harper & Brothers, 1890.
Drummond, Henry. *Essays and Addresses*. New York: James Potts & Company, 1904.
———. *Natural Law in the Spiritual World*. Potts Edition.
———. *The Changed Life*. New York: James Potts & Company, 1891.
———. *The Greatest Thing in the World and other addresses*. London: Collins, 1953.
———. *The Ideal Life*. New York: Hodder & Stoughton, 1897.
———. *The New Evangelism*. New York: Hodder & Stoughton, 1899.
Edwards, Robert L. *Of Singular Genius Of Singular Grace: A Biography of Horace Bushnell*. Cleveland: The Pilgrim Press, 1992.
Findlay, James F., Jr. *Dwight L. Moody American Evangelist*. Chicago, University of Chicago Press, 1969.
Fitt, Emma Moody, *Day By Day With D. L. Moody*. Chicago: Moody Press, n.d.
Goodspeed, Edgar J. *The Wonderful Career of Moody and Sankey in Great Britain and America*. New York: Henry S. Goodspeed & Co., 1876.
Guldseth, Mark O. *Streams*. Alaska: Fritz Creek Studios, 1982.
Hopkins, C. Howard. *John R. Mott, A Biography*. Grand Rapids: William B. Erdmans Publishing Company, 1979.
James, William. *The Varieties of Religious Experience*. New York: First Vintage Books/The Library of America, 1990.
Meyer, F. B. *The Secret of Guidance*. New York: Fleming H. Revell, 1896.
Moody, Paul D. *My Father: An Intimate Portrait of Dwight Moody*. Boston: Little Brown, 1938.
Moody, William R. *The Life of D. L. Moody*. New York: Fleming H. Revell, 1900.
Pollock, J. C. *Moody: A Biographical Portrait of the Pacesetter in Modern Mass Evangelism*. New York: Macmillan, 1963.
Smith, George Adam. *The Life of Henry Drummond*. New York: McClure, Phillips & Co., 1901.
Speer, Robert E. *The Marks of a Man*. New York: Hodder & Stoughton, 1907.
———. *The Principles of Jesus*. New York: Fleming H. Revell Company, 1902.
Stewart, George, Jr. *Life of Henry B. Wright*. New York: Association Press, 1925.
Wright, Henry B. *The Will of God And a Man's Lifework*. New York: The Young Men's Christian Association Press, 1909.

Alcoholics Anonymous

Publications About

A Guide to the Twelve Steps of Alcoholics Anonymous. Akron: A.A. of Akron, n.d.
Alcoholics Anonymous. (multilith volume). New Jersey: Works Publishing Co., 1939.

Alcoholics Anonymous: An Interpretation of Our Twelve Steps. Washington, D.C.: "The Paragon" Creative Printers, 1944.

A Manual for Alcoholics Anonymous. Akron: A.A. of Akron, n.d.

B., Dick. *Anne Smith's Spiritual Workbook: An A.A.—Good Book Connection*. Corte Madera, CA: Good Book Publishing Company, 1992.

———. *Dr. Bob's Library: An A.A.—Good Book Connection*. Wheeling, WV: The Bishop of Books, 1992.

———. *The Akron Genesis of Alcoholics Anonymous: An A.A.-Good Book Connection*. Seattle: Glen Abbey Books, 1993.

———. *The Books Early AAs Read For Spiritual Growth: An A.A.-Good Book Connection*. Seattle: Glen Abbey Books, 1993.

———. *The Oxford Group & Alcoholics Anonymous: An A.A.—Good Book Connection*. Seattle: Glen Abbey Books, 1992.

B., Jim. *Evolution of Alcoholics Anonymous*. New York: A.A. Archives.

B., Mel. *New Wine: The Spiritual Roots of the Twelve Step Miracle*. Minnesota: Hazelden, 1991.

Bishop, Charles, Jr. *The Washingtonians & Alcoholics Anonymous*. WV: The Bishop of Books, 1992.

———. and Pittman, Bill. *The Annotated Bibliography of Alcoholics Anonymous 1939-1989*. Wheeling W. Va.: The Bishop of Books, 1989.

Blumberg, Leonard, and William L. Pittman. *Beware The First Drink: The Washington Temperance Movement and Alcoholics Anonymous*. Seattle: Glen Abbey Books, 1991.

Bufe, Charles. *Alcoholics Anonymous: Cult or Cure*. San Francisco: Sharp Press, 1991.

C., Chuck. *A New Pair of Glasses*. Irvine, CA: New Leaf Publishing, 1984.

C., Stewart. *A Reference Guide To The Big Book of Alcoholics Anonymous*. Seattle: Recovery Press, 1986.

Central Bulletin, Volumes I-II. Cleveland: Central Committee, Oct. 1942-Sept. 1944.

Clapp, Charles, Jr. *Drinking's Not the Problem*. New York: Thomas Y. Crowell, 1949.

Cutten, C. B. *The Psychology of Alcoholism*. New York: Scribner's & Sons, 1907.

Conrad, Barnaby. *Time Is All We Have*. New York: Dell Publishing, 1986.

Darrah, Mary C. *Sister Ignatia: Angel of Alcoholics Anonymous*. Chicago: Loyola University Press, 1992.

E., Bob. *Handwritten note to Lois Wilson on pamphlet entitled "Four Absolutes."* (copy made available to the author at Founders Day Archives Room in Akron, Ohio, in June, 1991).

———. Letter from Bob E. to Nell Wing. Stepping Stones Archives.

First Steps: *Al-Anon . . . 35 Years of Beginnings*. New York: Al-Anon Family Group Headquarters, 1986.

Ford, John C. *Depth Psychology, Morality and Alcoholism*. Mass: Weston College, 1951.

Hunter, Willard, with assistance from M. D. B. *A.A.'s Roots in the Oxford Group*. New York: A.A. Archives, 1988.

Kessel, Joseph. *The Road Back: A Report on Alcoholics Anonymous*. New York: Alfred A. Knopf, 1962.

Knippel, Charles T. *Samuel M. Shoemaker's Theological Influence on William G. Wilson's Twelve Step Spiritual Program of Recovery*. Ph. D. diss. St Louis University, 1987.

Kurtz, Ernest. *AA The Story: A Revised Edition of "Not God: A History of Alcoholics Anonymous"*. San Francisco: Harper/Hazelden, 1988.

———. *Not-God: A History of Alcoholics Anonymous*. Expanded Edition. Minnesota: Hazelden, 1991.

———. *Shame and Guilt: Characteristics of the Dependency Cycle*. Minnesota: Hazelden, 1981.

———. and Ketcham, Katherine. *The Spirituality of Imperfection*. New York: Bantam Books, 1992.

McQ., Joe. *The Steps We Took*. Arkansas: August House Publishing, 1990.

Morreim, Dennis C. *Changed Lives: The Story of Alcoholics Anonymous*. Minneapolis: Augsburg Fortress, 1991.

Morse, Robert M., M.D. and Daniel K. Flavin, M.D. "The Definition of Alcoholism." *The Journal of the American Medical Association*. August 26, 1992, pp. 1012-14.

Peale, Norman Vincent. *The Power of Positive Thinking*. New York: Prentice-Hall, 1952.

Pittman, Bill. *AA The Way It Began*. Seattle: Glen Abbey Books, 1988.

Poe, Stephen E. and Frances E. *A Concordance to Alcoholics Anonymous*. Nevada: Purple Salamander Press, 1990.

Playfair, William L., M.D. *The Useful Lie*. Illinois: Crossway Books, 1991.

Robertson, Nan. *Getting Better Inside Alcoholics Anonymous*. New York: William Morrow & Co., 1988.

Second Reader for Alcoholics Anonymous. Akron: A.A. of Akron, n.d.

Seiberling, John F. *Origins of Alcoholics Anonymous*. (A transcript of remarks by Henrietta B. Seiberling: transcript prepared by Congressman John F. Seiberling of a telephone conversation with his mother, Henrietta in the spring of 1971): Employee Assistance Quarterly. 1985; (1); pp. 8-12.

Sikorsky, Igor I., Jr. *AA's Godparents*. Minnesota: CompCare Publishers, 1990.

Smith, Bob and Sue Smith Windows. *Children of the Healer*. Illinois: Parkside Publishing Corporation, 1992.

Spiritual Milestones in Alcoholics Anonymous. Akron: A.A. of Akron, n.d.

Stafford, Tim. *The Hidden Gospel of the 12 Steps*. Christianity Today, July 22, 1991.

The Four Absolutes. Cleveland: Cleveland Central Committee of A.A., n. d.

Thomsen, Robert. *Bill W.* New York: Harper & Row, 1975.

Walker, Richmond. *For Drunks Only*. Minnesota: Hazelden, n.d.

———. *The 7 Points of Alcoholics Anonymous*. Seattle: Glen Abbey Books, 1989.

Wilson, Bill. *How The Big Book Was Put Together*. New York: A.A. Archives, Transcript of Bill Wilson Speech delivered in Fort Worth, Texas, 1954.

———. *Bill Wilson's Original Story*. Bedford Hills, New York: Stepping Stones Archives, n.d., a manuscript whose individual lines are numbered 1 to 1180.

———. *W. G. Wilson Recollections*. Bedford Hills, New York: Stepping Stones Archives, September 1, 1954 transcript of Bill's dictations to Ed B.

Wilson, Jan R., and Judith A. Wilson. *Addictionary: A Primer of Recovery Terms and Concepts from Abstinence to Withdrawal*. New York: Simon & Schuster, 1992.

Wilson, Lois. *Lois Remembers*. New York: Al-Anon Family Group Headquarters, 1987.

Windows, Sue Smith. (daughter of AA's Co-Founder, Dr. Bob). Typewritten Memorandum entitled, *Henrietta and early Oxford Group Friends, by Sue Smith Windows*. Delivered to the author of this book by Sue Smith Windows at Akron, June, 1991.

Wing, Nell. *Grateful To Have Been There: My 42 Years with Bill and Lois, and the Evolution of Alcoholics Anonymous*. Illinois: Parkside Publishing Corporation, 1992.

Publications Approved by Alcoholics Anonymous

Alcoholics Anonymous. 1st Edition. New Jersey: Works Publishing, 1939.

Alcoholics Anonymous. 3rd Edition. New York: Alcoholics Anonymous World Services, Inc., 1976.

Alcoholics Anonymous Comes of Age. New York: Alcoholics Anonymous World Services, Inc., 1979,

As Bill Sees It: The A.A. Way of Life . . . selected writings of A.A.'s Co-Founder. New York: Alcoholics Anonymous World Services, Inc., 1967.

Best of the Grapevine. New York: The A.A. Grapevine, Inc., 1985.

Best of the Grapevine, Volume II. New York: The A.A. Grapevine, Inc., 1986.

"Bill W." *The A.A. Grapevine*. [An issue dedicated to the memory of the Co-Founder of Alcoholics Anonymous, Bill W.] New York: A.A. Grapevine, Inc., 1971.

Came To Believe. New York: Alcoholics Anonymous World Services, Inc., 1973.

Daily Reflections. New York: Alcoholics Anonymous World Services, Inc., 1991.

DR. BOB and the Good Oldtimers. New York: Alcoholics Anonymous World Services, Inc., 1980.

Members of the ***Clergy*** *ask about Alcoholics Anonymous*. New York: Alcoholics Anonymous World Services, 1961, 1979—Revised 1992, according to 1989 Conference Advisory Action.

Pass It On. New York: Alcoholics Anonymous World Services, Inc., 1984.

"RHS". *The A.A. Grapevine*. [An issue dedicated to the memory of the Co-Founder of Alcoholics Anonymous, Dr. Bob.] New York: A.A. Grapevine, Inc., 1951.

The A.A. Service Manual. New York: Alcoholics Anonymous World Services, Inc., 1992-1993.

The Co-Founders of Alcoholics Anonymous: Biographical sketches; Their last major talks. New York: Alcoholics Anonymous World Services, Inc., 1972.

The Language of the Heart. Bill W.'s Grapevine Writings. New York: The A.A. Grapevine, Inc., 1988.

Twelve Steps And Twelve Traditions. New York: Alcoholics Anonymous World Services, Inc., 1953.

The Bible—Versions of and Books About

Authorized King James Version. New York: Thomas Nelson, 1984.
Bullinger, Ethelbert W. *A Critical Lexicon and Concordance to the English and Greek New Testament*. Michigan: Zondervan, 1981.
Burns, Kenneth Charles. *The Rhetoric of Christology: A Content Analysis of Texts Which Discuss Titus 2:13*. San Francisco: San Francisco State University, May, 1991. An unpublished thesis for Master of Arts.
Harnack, Adolph. *The Expansion of Christianity in the First Three Centuries*. New York: G. P. Putnam's Sons, Volume I, 1904; Volume II, 1905.
Jukes, Andrew. *The Names of GOD in Holy Scripture*. Michigan: Kregel Publications, 1967.
Moffatt, James. *A New Translation of the Bible*. New York: Harper & Brothers, 1954.
New Bible Dictionary. 2nd Edition. Wheaton, Illinois: Tyndale House Publishers, 1987.
Revised Standard Version. New York: Thomas Nelson, 1952.
Strong, James. *The Exhaustive Concordance of The Bible*. Iowa: Riverside Book and Bible House, n.d.
The Abingdon Bible Commentary. New York: Abingdon Press, 1929.
The Companion Bible. Michigan: Zondervan Bible Publishers, 1964.
The Revised English Bible. Oxford: Oxford University Press, 1989.
Vine, W. E. *Vine's Expository Dictionary of Old and New Testament Words*. New York: Fleming H. Revell, 1981.
Young's Analytical Concordance To The Bible. New York: Thomas Nelson, 1982.
Zodhiates, Spiros. *The Hebrew-Greek Key Study Bible*. 6th ed. AMG Publishers, 1991.

Spiritual Literature: Non-Oxford Group

Allen, James. *As A Man Thinketh*. New York: Peter Pauper Press, n.d.
Barton, George A. *Jesus of Nazareth*. New York: The Macmillan Company, 1922.
Brother Lawrence. *The Practice of the Presence of God*. Pennsylvania: Whitaker House, 1982.
Carruthers, Donald W. *How to Find Reality in Your Morning Devotions*. Pennsylvania: State College, n.d.
Chambers, Oswald. *Studies in the Sermon on the Mount*. London: Simpkin, Marshall, Ltd., n.d.
Clark, Glenn. *Fishers of Men*. Boston: Little, Brown, 1928.
———. *I Will Lift Up Mine Eyes*. New York: Harper & Brothers, 1937.
———. *The Lord's Prayer and Other Talks on Prayer from The Camps Farthest Out*. Minnesota: Macalester Publishing Co., 1932.
———. *The Man Who Talks with Flowers*. Minnesota: Macalester Park Publishing, 1939.
———. *The Soul's Sincere Desire*. Boston: Little, Brown, 1925.
———. *Touchdowns for the Lord. The Story of "Dad" A. J. Elliott*. Minnesota: Macalester Park Publishing Co., 1947.

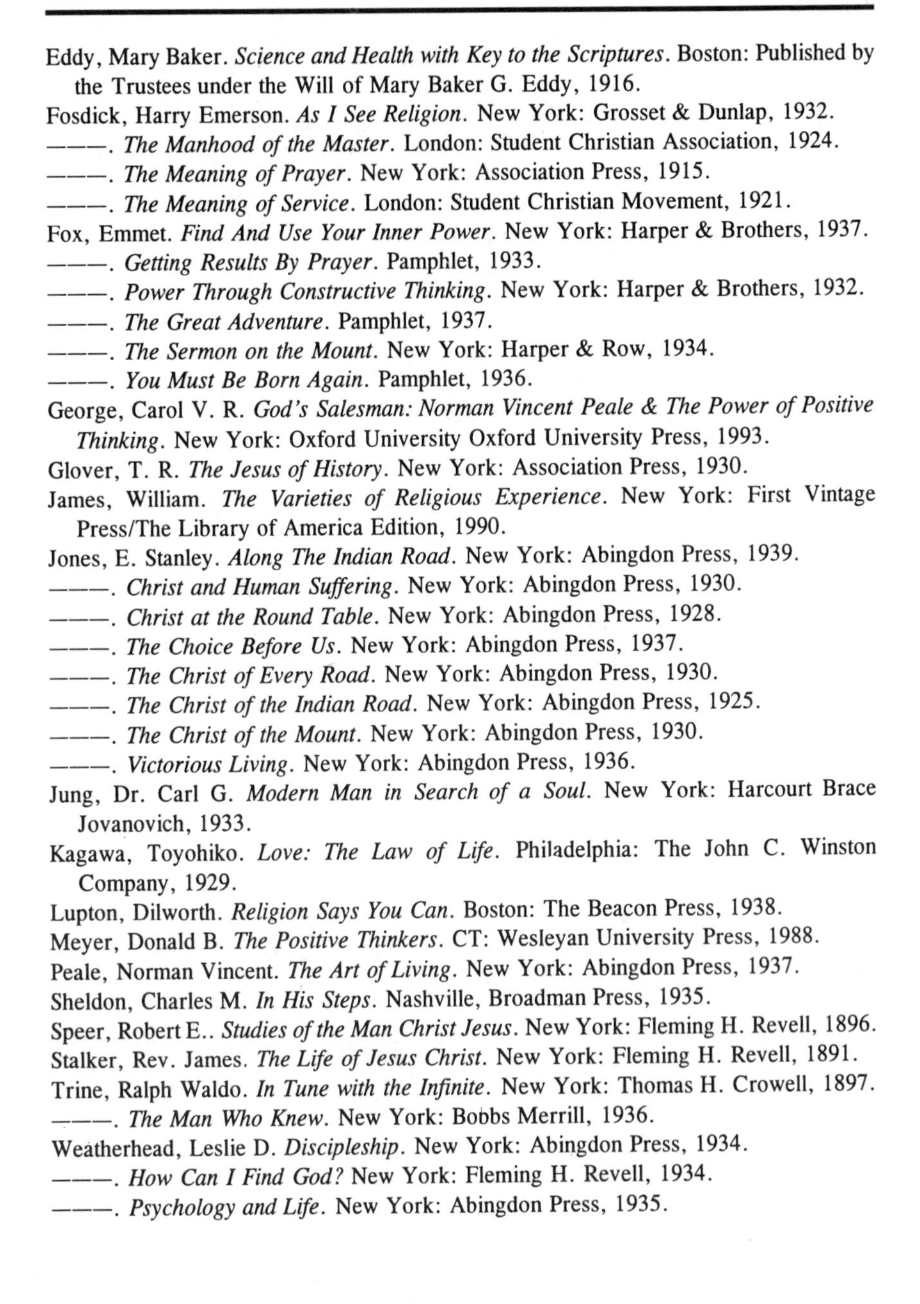

Eddy, Mary Baker. *Science and Health with Key to the Scriptures*. Boston: Published by the Trustees under the Will of Mary Baker G. Eddy, 1916.

Fosdick, Harry Emerson. *As I See Religion*. New York: Grosset & Dunlap, 1932.

———. *The Manhood of the Master*. London: Student Christian Association, 1924.

———. *The Meaning of Prayer*. New York: Association Press, 1915.

———. *The Meaning of Service*. London: Student Christian Movement, 1921.

Fox, Emmet. *Find And Use Your Inner Power*. New York: Harper & Brothers, 1937.

———. *Getting Results By Prayer*. Pamphlet, 1933.

———. *Power Through Constructive Thinking*. New York: Harper & Brothers, 1932.

———. *The Great Adventure*. Pamphlet, 1937.

———. *The Sermon on the Mount*. New York: Harper & Row, 1934.

———. *You Must Be Born Again*. Pamphlet, 1936.

George, Carol V. R. *God's Salesman: Norman Vincent Peale & The Power of Positive Thinking*. New York: Oxford University Oxford University Press, 1993.

Glover, T. R. *The Jesus of History*. New York: Association Press, 1930.

James, William. *The Varieties of Religious Experience*. New York: First Vintage Press/The Library of America Edition, 1990.

Jones, E. Stanley. *Along The Indian Road*. New York: Abingdon Press, 1939.

———. *Christ and Human Suffering*. New York: Abingdon Press, 1930.

———. *Christ at the Round Table*. New York: Abingdon Press, 1928.

———. *The Choice Before Us*. New York: Abingdon Press, 1937.

———. *The Christ of Every Road*. New York: Abingdon Press, 1930.

———. *The Christ of the Indian Road*. New York: Abingdon Press, 1925.

———. *The Christ of the Mount*. New York: Abingdon Press, 1930.

———. *Victorious Living*. New York: Abingdon Press, 1936.

Jung, Dr. Carl G. *Modern Man in Search of a Soul*. New York: Harcourt Brace Jovanovich, 1933.

Kagawa, Toyohiko. *Love: The Law of Life*. Philadelphia: The John C. Winston Company, 1929.

Lupton, Dilworth. *Religion Says You Can*. Boston: The Beacon Press, 1938.

Meyer, Donald B. *The Positive Thinkers*. CT: Wesleyan University Press, 1988.

Peale, Norman Vincent. *The Art of Living*. New York: Abingdon Press, 1937.

Sheldon, Charles M. *In His Steps*. Nashville, Broadman Press, 1935.

Speer, Robert E.. *Studies of the Man Christ Jesus*. New York: Fleming H. Revell, 1896.

Stalker, Rev. James. *The Life of Jesus Christ*. New York: Fleming H. Revell, 1891.

Trine, Ralph Waldo. *In Tune with the Infinite*. New York: Thomas H. Crowell, 1897.

———. *The Man Who Knew*. New York: Bobbs Merrill, 1936.

Weatherhead, Leslie D. *Discipleship*. New York: Abingdon Press, 1934.

———. *How Can I Find God?* New York: Fleming H. Revell, 1934.

———. *Psychology and Life*. New York: Abingdon Press, 1935.

Bible Devotionals

Chambers, Oswald. *My Utmost For His Highest*. London: Simpkin Marshall, Ltd., 1927.

Clark, Glenn, *I Will Lift Up Mine Eyes*. New York: Harper & Brothers, 1937.

Holm, Nora Smith. *The Runner's Bible*. New York: Houghton Mifflin Company, 1915.

Jones, E. Stanley. *Abundant Living*. New York: Abingdon-Cokesbury Press, 1942.

———. *Victorious Living*. New York: Abingdon Press, 1936.

The Upper Room: Daily Devotions for Family and Individual Use. Quarterly. 1st issue: April, May, June, 1935. Edited by Grover Carlton Emmons. Nashville: General Committee on Evangelism through the Department of Home Missions, Evangelism, Hospitals, Board of Missions, Methodist Episcopal Church, South.

Tileston, Mary W. *Daily Strength For Daily Needs*. Boston: Roberts Brothers, 1893.

Index

A

B

C

D

E

G

H

I

J

K

L

M

N

O

P

Q

R

S

T

U

Y

ABOUT THE AUTHOR

Dick B. writes books on the spiritual roots of Alcoholics Anonymous. And they show how the basic and highly successful Biblical ideas used by early A.A. can help reverse a plummeting success rate in today's A.A. His research can also help the religious community work more effectively with alcoholics and Twelve Step programs.

The author is an active, recovered member of Alcoholics Anonymous; a retired attorney; and a Bible student. He has sponsored more than fifty-five men in their recovery from alcoholism. Consistent with A.A.'s tradition of anonymity, he uses the pseudonym "Dick B."

He has had six titles published: *New Light on Alcoholism: The A.A. Legacy from Sam Shoemaker*; *The Books Early AAs Read for Spiritual Growth*; *The Akron Genesis of Alcoholics Anonymous*; *The Oxford Group & Alcoholics Anonymous*; *Anne Smith's Spiritual Workbook*; and *Dr. Bob's Library*. The books have been the subject of newspaper articles and author interviews. They have been reviewed in *Library Journal*, *Bookstore Journal*, *For A Change*, and *Sober Times*.

Dick is the father of two married sons (Ken and Don), and a grandfather. As a young man, he did a stint as a newspaper reporter. He attended the University of California, Berkeley, where he received his A.A. degree, majored in economics, and was elected to Phi Beta Kappa in his Junior year. In the United States Army, he was an Information-Education Specialist. He received his A.B. and J.D. degrees from Stanford University, and was Case Editor of the Stanford Law Review. Dick became interested in Bible study in his childhood Sunday School and was much inspired by his mother's almost daily study of Scripture. He joined, and later became president of, a Community Church affiliated with the United Church of Christ. By 1972, he was studying the origins of the Bible and began traveling abroad in pursuit of that subject. In 1979, he became much involved in a Biblical research, teaching, and fellowship ministry. In his community life, he was president of a merchants' council, Chamber of Commerce, church retirement center, and homeowners' association. He served on a public district board and was active in a service club.

In 1986, he was felled by alcoholism, gave up his law practice, and began recovery as a member of the Fellowship of Alcoholics Anonymous. In 1990, his interest in A.A.'s Biblical/Christian roots was sparked by his attendance at A.A.'s International Convention in Seattle. He began traveling widely; researching at archives, and at public and seminary libraries; interviewing scholars, historians, clergy, A.A. "old-timers" and survivors; and participating in programs on A.A.'s roots.

The author is the owner of Good Book Publishing Company, writes a newsletter, and has several works in progress. Much of his research and writing is done in collaboration with his older son, Ken, who holds B.A., B.Th., and M.A. degrees. Ken has been a lecturer in New Testament Greek at a Bible college and a lecturer in Fundamentals of Oral Communication at San Francisco State University. Ken is a computer specialist.

Dick is a member of The American Historical Association, Maui Writers Guild, American Society of Journalists and Authors, and The Authors' Guild. He is available for conferences, panels, seminars, and interviews.